Shanghai Splendor

A

Philip E. Lilienthal (signature)

■   ■   ■

B O O K

The Philip E. Lilienthal imprint
honors special books
in commemoration of a man whose work
at University of California Press from 1954 to 1979
was marked by dedication to young authors
and to high standards in the field of Asian Studies.
Friends, family, authors, and foundations have together
endowed the Lilienthal Fund, which enables the Press
to publish under this imprint selected books
in a way that reflects the taste and judgment
of a great and beloved editor.

Shanghai Splendor

Economic Sentiments and the
Making of Modern China, 1843–1949

Wen-hsin Yeh

UNIVERSITY OF CALIFORNIA PRESS
Berkeley · Los Angeles · London

University of California Press, one of the most
distinguished university presses in the United
States, enriches lives around the world by
advancing scholarship in the humanities, social
sciences, and natural sciences. Its activities are
supported by the UC Press Foundation and
by philanthropic contributions from individuals
and institutions. For more information, visit
www.ucpress.edu.

University of California Press
Berkeley and Los Angeles, California

University of California Press, Ltd.
London, England

Library of Congress Cataloging-in-Publication Data

Yeh, Wen-hsin.
    Shanghai splendor : economic sentiments and the
making of modern China, 1843–1949 / Wen-hsin Yeh.
        p.   cm. — (Philip E. Lilienthal book in Asian
studies)
    Includes bibliographical references and index.
    ISBN 978-0-520-24971-4 (cloth : alk. paper)
        1. Merchants—China—Shanghai—History.
2. China—Economic conditions—1912–1949.
3. China—Politics and government—1912–1949.
I. Title.

HE3836.Y44   2007
330.951'13204—dc22   2007014871

Manufactured in the United States of America

16   15   14   13   12   11   10   09   08   07
10   9   8   7   6   5   4   3   2   1

This book is printed on New Leaf EcoBook 50,
a 100% recycled fiber of which 50% is de-inked
post-consumer waste, processed chlorine-free.
EcoBook 50 is acid-free and meets the minimum
requirements of ANSI/ASTM D5634-01 (*Permanence
of Paper*).

For Irvin & Jim

Contents

Illustrations

Acknowledgments

This study has been long in the making. From a simple curiosity about the Shanghai urbanites in their myriad walks of life, this research has evolved into a focused study of the aspirations and frustrations of the literate workers at their desks, and the convergence of circumstances that brought them out of the buildings and into the streets. With the recent emergence of Shanghai as a global destination, the voices of these urbanites have further inspired reflection on the relevance of history in the transformation of space.

Numerous individuals and organizations have contributed to the making of this project. A judicious acknowledgment would have amounted to a massive listing of much of the academia. I wish to acknowledge nonetheless the generous support of the Committee on Scholarly Communications with China, the Luce Foundation, the Hoover Institution, the Chiang Ching-kuo Foundation for International Scholarly Exchanges, the President's Office of the University of California, and, on the Berkeley campus, the Chancellor's Office, the Townsend Center for the Humanities, the Center for Chinese Studies, the France-Berkeley Fund, and the Committee on Research for fellowships and awards.

Earlier versions of aspects of this project have been presented at scores of workshops, seminars, and conferences. I wish to acknowledge in particular the stimulation and exchanges with colleagues and students who took part in the Shanghai Studies projects funded by the Luce Foundation at the University of California at Berkeley, Cornell University, University of Maryland at College Park, and the Shanghai Academy of Social Sciences, especially Frederic Wakeman, Elizabeth Perry, Sherman Cochran, Jason Kuo, Julia Andrews, Jonathan Hay, Zhang Zhongli, Xiong Yuezhi, Luo Suwen and Zhang Jishun; the participants of the multiple-year project on the Internationalization of China jointly organized by Harvard University, Berlin Free University, Peking University, and the University of California at Berkeley, especially William Kirby, Mechthild Leutner, Klaus Muelhahn, and Niu Dayong; the participants of the multiple-year Wartime Shanghai project jointly organized by Université Lyon II and the University of California at Berkeley, especially Christian Henriot; and members of the Institute of Modern History, Academia Sinica, especially Chang Yu-fa, Chen Yung-fa, Chen San-ching, Li Hsiao-ti, and Lu Fang-shang, who endured several talks over an extended period of time.

I acknowledge with gratitude the comments and conversations with colleagues in the field, including Marie-Claire Bergère, Prasenjit Duara, Susan Glosser, Bryna Goodman, Philip Kuhn, Jean Oi, Ramon Myers, Susan Naquin, Paul Pickowicz, Don Price, Brett Sheehan, David Strand, Robert Weller, and Timothy Weston. At Berkeley colleagues have been exemplary with their interest, encouragement, astute questions, and inexhaustible good will. In particular, Margaret Anderson, Andrew Barshay, John Connelly, Paula Fass, Gerry Feldman, Thomas Laqueur, Lawrence Levine, Martin Malia, Robert Middlekauff, Irwin Scheiner, Yuri Slezkine, Leslie Peirce, and William Taylor have been most supportive with their readings and conversations. I could not have wished for a more congenial set of colleagues.

I owe a great debt to the librarians and archivists at the Shanghai Academy of Social Sciences, the Shanghai Municipal Archives, the Shanghai Municipal Library, the Number Two State Archives, the Academia Historica, the Academia Sinica, the Harvard-Yenching Library, the Hoover East Asian Collections, the East Asiatic Library, and the Center for Chinese Studies Library at the University of California at Berkeley. My special thanks to Annie Chang, Jing Han, Han Weizhi, Li Xueyun, Shi Meiding, Wang Shiwei, Zhao Nianguo, and Yeh Fei-hung for facilitating access and guidance to invaluable materials.

Last but not least, my students at Berkeley have offered not only valuable research assistance, but also energetic intellectual engagement. Charlotte Ono took time from her own research to assist with the preparation of the final manuscript. I could not have asked for more punctual and meticulous assistance than she has offered. Elinor Levine coordinated the entire publication process with her usual composure. Above all, Reed Malcolm at the University of California Press has become a friend.

If this book succeeds in making interesting points in any way, it is to my colleagues and students that the credit is due. The faults and flaws are mine alone, and I thank those around me for bearing with them so long and so well.

After my son went to college I began hearing resonances of his voice and that of his friends in my classroom. I like to think that such awareness and this insight into campus life outside the class has made me a better teacher. I have learned a great deal from my interactions with Berkeley undergraduates. I also came to recognize how it can be a mixed blessing for a kid to have a professor as a parent. It is to Irvin that this work is dedicated.

Introduction

In the century after the Opium War (1839–42), against the backdrop of deeply seated anti-mercantile ambivalence, a middle class emerged and gained social legitimacy in Shanghai. It embraced the pursuit of industrial wealth on the grounds that it would bring material benefits to the nation. It succeeded in framing the discourse of wealth in terms of science while forging an alliance with the modernizing Chinese state. The new wealth was presented, in the first half of the twentieth century, as patriotic, scientific, and democratic. Even though much of the new money was held in the foreign concessions and by networks of mercantile elite with bureaucratic ties, it was argued that private capitalist enterprises contributed to the wealth of the Chinese nation.

This new doctrine of commercial wealth inspired a generation of aspiring youths to prepare themselves in particular skills and to pursue careers in the new economy. The rewards would include a "good life" that brought modern material comforts to the individual and the family. In the first decades of the twentieth century, Shanghai's image industry and corporate culture worked in tandem to construct the idea of a nuclear family as the locus of emotional bonds and unit of consumption. As for the nation, it was a tacit understanding that what would enrich the nation would also benefit the family, and vice versa.

In the 1930s recession intervened, and the newly fashioned middle-class cultural construct, with its norms of self and work, family and nation, was subjected to severe strain. Virtue and skill at work guaranteed

neither comfort nor security for the family. Deprived of the material basis
of a salaried income, the nuclear family was doomed to lose its viability.
Workplace relationships that had been compared to familial bonds were
exposed to be no more than ties subjected to market transactions. Social
crisis in the second quarter of the twentieth century bred angry cynicism
in the lower middle class. This anger supplied the main force for an ideological shift in urban popular climate to the left. In a popular critique
of the middle-class quest for respectability, foreign invasion and colonial
exploitation were blamed for domestic distress. The critique, fused with
underground Chinese Communist Party doctrines, generated strong demands for a radical reorganization of the Chinese state so that an invigorated Party-state would embrace and care for social justice and material
well-being on behalf of the entire people.

The above, in a nutshell, is the main story contained in this book,
which is organized around the lives of Shanghai's middle-class office
workers in the decades of private enterprises and the free labor market.
Several points deserve further elaboration in the interest of clarification.

Historical scholarship concerning Shanghai or China in the late nineteenth and early twentieth centuries has devoted much attention to the
study of new economic activities in banking, manufacturing, mining, shipping, merchandizing, and so forth in the course of Sino-Western interactions. Not much attention has been paid, however, to the shifts in the
discursive arena that accompanied the development of such activities. It
is worthwhile pointing out that to sustain such foreign-inspired enterprises like cotton mills or steamship companies, the business elite in
Shanghai did not simply build factories or set up companies. They also
advanced the prestige and respectability of their pursuits, and it was imperative that they persuaded the powerful and resourceful of the social
legitimacy of the changes that were coming in the wake of the new economy. This quest for legitimacy and respectability involved subtle negotiations in arenas that impinged upon cultural norms and economic sentiments, and political power and institutional arrangements. At the time
such negotiations were particularly complex and challenging, given that
new capitalist enterprises of mechanized production were in fact spear-
heading a new economic culture in the context of China's encounter with
European colonial expansion.

In the first two chapters of this book we ask the following questions:
How did China's emerging economic elite manage to construct that respectability? What resources did they mobilize and what arrangements
were they able to make, especially with regard to the Chinese state, in

order to achieve a reallocation of existing political and cultural capital that worked to their advantage? What were the circumstances that made it possible for such arrangements to be made? And under what terms might that respectability be lost? Answers to these questions lie within an understanding of the constructed nature of middle-class respectability in twentieth-century China. The latter, as the chapters show, was both contingent upon changing circumstances and containing internal points of contradiction.

By the 1940s, under the stress of war and military occupation, bourgeois respectability was substantially eroded. Corporate employees formed their own associations, which challenged the patriarchal authority of the executives. There were subtle but important differences, to be sure, between losing respect and losing respectability. There was a time when Shanghai's business elite would command respect even if they had disappointed a large number of their employees. Yet by the 1940s, even the most beloved among the executives—those who had done well by the rituals of wisdom and benevolence—had been diminished simply by dint of occupying the organizational positions they did. All managers, *as individuals,* risked losing, at all times, the respect of their subordinates with their individual failures and incompetence. But it was when the very construct of middle-class respectability was eroded by wartime politics that the managerial elite *as a class* lost the support of their employees. By the end of the Chinese War of Resistance against Japan (1937–45) the former corporate patriarchs were commonly denounced as capitalists. A discursive shift had taken place, and workplace relationships entered a new era.

On the question of space, many studies have invoked "Shanghai" as a place where events occurred. Lately, a growing amount of information has become available concerning the infrastructural changes that transformed the physical city, such as the addition of tramways, street lights, electricity, paved roads, and so forth. Yet when historicizing Shanghai, scholars have yet to take into full account the spatial ramifications of such material specifics, especially the social significance in terms of the interactive dynamics between space and people.

The use of the clock, as we know, was prominent in Shanghai. The largest clock in East Asia at the time adorned the face of the Maritime Customs House (see chapter 4). Corporate discipline ran on the clock, as did the transportation systems and all other urban establishments. For the multitude of desk workers employed in white-collar positions, going to work and getting around both concerned adhering to a new sense of time.

To cover the space, meanwhile, Shanghai's vocational youth in the 1930s measured urban distance both in terms of the commute ("three hours") and the transportation costs ("on foot at no cost"). Neither the masters of their own time nor the owners of private vehicles, these workers made up the faces of the crowds walking the streets, peering into shop windows, and moving around the city. Their everyday sense of time and distance, which was mechanically measured, financially calculated, bound by routine, and demarcated by obligation, nonetheless coexisted with an emerging style of sociability made possible by the opportunities offered in the city.

It was within the "timed sectors" of the city where the vocational youth spent their after-work leisure hours. Of the divided municipalities of 1920s Shanghai, Nanshi (the old Chinese City) and the townships under its jurisdiction, awaiting transformation by electric lighting and public transportation, grew dark and quiet once night fell. The foreign concessions, in contrast, were able to extend their days with the addition of electricity throughout their neighborhoods. Vocational educators and civic organizers took advantage of the illuminated spaces in schools, offices, and club buildings to hold events and give classes in the evenings. It was of comparable significance that tramways in the concessions ran on schedule; a working youth could thus dependably budget his nights out in terms of commuting time.

As the influence of the state was weak in the first decades of the twentieth century, networking in Shanghai was active and important. Prominent individuals built influence by becoming nodal points of communications across different sectors of urban society; the spatially confined and temporally bound lower middle class, meanwhile, networked through institutionalized channels. The latter attended evening programs both to acquire useful skills and to meet others who might share comparable life and career experiences. In addition, literate though rarely credentialed beyond secondary school, these vocational youth were avid readers of newspapers and magazines that were passed around from hand to hand. Their reading of these publications amounted to virtual participation in discussions that otherwise would be taking place in disparate social spaces such as teahouses.

With time on their hands and worry on their minds, young urbanites sought out social contacts and were the most likely participants in rallies and campaigns at moments of mobilization.[1] Liu Liangmo, the music director at the YMCA, found himself conducting Sunday chorus joined by thousands in an athletic field in the 1930s. Of the roughly three hundred thousand shop clerks and desk workers in Shanghai, the "vocational youth" constituted a subset which was both a product of vocational education programs and individual drive and personal aspiration. By taking into account the economic culture and the spatial dynamics in Shanghai, we may argue that the crisis of the lower middle class was a crisis of those who had taken part to the fullest extent in the promises of modernity, while attempting to sustain the mercantile elite's claims to respectability.

Past scholarship has often debated whether Shanghai was more Chinese or more Western. From the perspectives of those who lived there, Shanghai seemed above all a place of tension and contradictions. It was hardly a Westernized or Westernizing enclave existing against a passive backdrop of continental China. From the waves of migrant workers to the throngs of Nanjing Road shoppers, from occupying Nationalist soldiers to underground Communist cadres, the country seeped through the city in myriad ways. The foreign concessions, despite (or because) of their constantly expanding boundaries, were never capable of keeping "China" out of Shanghai, nor the Chinese out of concession affairs. Shanghai was characterized by the ceaseless contentions between opposing forces that sought to shape the city according to their diverging projects.

The reach of Shanghai, meanwhile, was not solely confined to the collection of buildings and roads rising at the confluence of its two rivers.[2] Images and "influence" crossed the ill-defined and endlessly contested borders. Shanghai was not just a place of local happenings—it was the center of an image industry that disseminated powerful ideas about being modern and urban. The modern Chinese understanding of the "city," whether in terms of consumer culture, municipal administration, lifestyles, career opportunities, or political participation, was largely fashioned in Shanghai. Over the course of the twentieth century, the city has been alternately branded as China's pride and shame, a place of infinite glamour and unequalled squalor. These contrasting constructions said less about the conditions in the city than Shanghai's primary strategic significance in the never-ending contest between the countryside and the city.[3]

In closing, two other points merit brief coverage.

Maritime trade in China did not begin with the opening of Shanghai as one of the five treaty ports. The history of seafaring economic activities along the Chinese coast is traceable back to the ninth or tenth centuries A.D. (if not the Bronze Age). Quanzhou in the eleventh century contained a bustling community of Arab merchants, as did Ningbo, with its Nagasaki sojourners. The Jesuit Matteo Ricci sailed on a merchant ship and reached Nanjing in the sixteenth century. Through silk and silver, scholars have connected late Ming China to the global "seventeenth-century crisis."[4] The three-way connections between England, India, and China with the trade of opium, silver, and tea not only fueled British expansion in the Indian Ocean, but also led to court debates in Beijing over deflation and drug addiction in the decade leading up to the Opium War.[5] A long history of maritime trade, in short, predated 1843, and a rich historical scholarship has been produced to explore the multiple dimensions of China's global connections via the maritime routes.

The arrival of the English in Shanghai nonetheless marked an important departure, for what used to be *maritime* activities had now been transformed into *international* trade. Along with trade at the port came international treaties, consular officers, nationality certifications, property rights legislations, and, increasingly, European notions about state-to-state relationships. Recent scholarship has continued the debate over whether the Opium War was fought over the British import of opium or Chinese protocols under the tribute system.[6] The debate, however, does not change the outcome of the mid-century wars, which ended China's tributary protocols in its conduct of trade and diplomacy with Western nations. The formal treaties, with their legal ramifications in the international context, not only brought the Chinese state into the conduct of Chinese business (which was not unprecedented in China's variegated past) but necessitated the Chinese state's considerations of the laws and the institutions of other states while doing so.

The internationalization of the maritime trade made it necessary, in other words, that the Chinese state look beyond its own system and answer to *other states* in its dealings with its own merchants. Chinese merchants learned, for their part, to conceive of the reach of commercial activities in international terms, and to consider the pragmatic benefits as well as compelling necessities to position themselves strategically (or opportunistically) among the contending states. Such strategies ranged from the choice of passports and laws for corporate registrations to the declaration of primary citizenships and the cultivation of official favors.[7] These imperatives, needless to say, carried profound ramifications that transformed relationships between the state and the economy in China's modern times.

Merchants and officials had mixed, similarly, well before the internationalization of the maritime trade.[8] The modern fusion between the merchants and the state nonetheless marked a meaningful departure from the developments that had been gathering momentum for centuries. The fusion in modern times was characterized, first, by a restructuring of the *state* to suit the needs of mercantile enterprises, instead of the adjustment of the *merchants* to conform to bureaucratic norms. It was inspired, secondly, by an agenda that demanded the reform of *both* the merchants and the state.[9] The new measures ranged from new ministries in the government to new merchant associations throughout the country, as well as the addition of new laws and school subjects. It elevated the development of the economy to the top of state agenda and promoted the financiers, manufacturers, entrepreneurs, engineers, scientists, and technocrats to the top stratum of urban society. It demanded, in short, that both the state and the merchants conducted their old business in new ways.

Shanghai emerged as a new Chinese city on the conjoined forces of international trade and state-sponsored enterprises. The confluence of the "maritime" and the "continental," and "foreign" and "Chinese," gave rise to a new order that, albeit poised in competitive tension, functioned in practice in collaboration. Translators, brokers, fixers, and mixers were heroes in the city's stories of marvel and imagination.[10] Beyond the surface glamour, the emerging order provided an environment that hosted the remapping of fields of knowledge (the rise of "commerce" and "business" as fields of study in colleges and universities, for example), the coexistence of dual temporalities in urban lives (the observance of the lunar calendar at home and the solar calendar at work), the articulation of a "public" arena, whether in person or print, materially or discursively, through the mediation of associations and procedures, and a keen awareness of an international system beyond the shores that impinged upon everyday happiness within the Chinese nation.[11]

It is a long-standing Confucian tenet that the people look towards their rulers for edification and sustenance. It was also well established in late imperial institutional practice to leave matters of education and economy to societal initiatives and local official oversight. In contrast, the modern quest for national wealth elevated issues of economy to the top of state agenda. It not only redefined the role of the central state in the national economy, but also allowed the rise of an entire economic bureaucracy. Meanwhile the claims of science and technology as the basis for the creation of new wealth, buttressed by schools of commerce and disciplines in economics, contributed to the rise of a new political regime of numbers and regulations in addition to words and virtues. The reconstitution of an economic discourse in Shanghai in the century after the Opium War thus was not just a local matter, but carried ramifications for the remaking of the modern Chinese state.

The chapters that follow are arranged roughly in chronological order. Some sectors of the new urban economy—the department stores, the publishing industry, banking, and accounting—have been singled out for closer examination than others. Regardless of the choice of domain for empirical grounding, the chapters draw attention to the socio-cultural dynamics that fashioned the people and their politics in the city. Through shopping, working, reading, and forming connections, Shanghai urbanites forged the extending networks and fashioned the expanding opportunities that were transforming the city. The lure of modernity was the lure of a good life of moral as well as material respectability. When the mercantile elite, riding on the opportunities brought by a forceful new wave of global connection at the end of the nineteenth century, emerged to become organizational patriarchs and civic patriots, they inspired, in the early Republican years, an entire generation to follow their lead. As later developments would suggest, this generation's simple quest for a wholesome familial life, which fulfilled their sense of ethical and emotional responsibilities on the strength of individual intellect and integrity, became one of the most potent forces driving the development of Chinese politics in and beyond the city.

CHAPTER I

The Material Turn

Despite the modern origin of social science theories about capitalism, it remains controversial whether "capitalism" is uniquely modern. By comparison, it is a point of much less ambiguity, even if only for its general inclusiveness, that "economism," characterized by a decisive materialistic turn in culture and society, is of recent origin. "Economism," as Leah Greenfeld identifies it, is a state of mind and a view of life in which issues of economy occupy a place of centrality. In social and political thought it emerges in the assumption that continuous economic growth is considered not only a possibility but also an imperative, a natural condition as well as a positive virtue. In everyday expectations it finds expression in the belief that in modernity there is continuous improvement in comfort and conveniences. Economism sums up a sweeping set of changes that reassigns social value and redistributes political advantages. It is a force, like capitalism, with transformative capacity. It distances the mind from the reverence of immanence and turns it towards the secular reasoning of calculation and transaction.

It is in this sense that, from Europe to East Asia, it is only in the recent past that societies turned "economistic" and rearranged their ethics and rationality in accordance with the production of wealth. This modern shift, Greenfeld suggests, often draws its energy from the rise of modern nationalism.[1]

In China, an important publishing event took place in 1901 with the translation of Adam Smith's *The Wealth of Nations*. The translator, Yan

Fu, was known not only for his earlier rendition of Thomas Huxley's *Evolution and Ethics,* but also for a series of essays on the wealth and power of the Chinese nation.[2] Smith's publication in 1776 was a summary statement regarding the "modern" state of economy in England. In China, Yan's translation acquired urgency in the aftermath of the Boxer debacle, when the Qing court, defeated and humiliated, agreed to indemnities payments totaling over 400 million taels *(liang).*[3] Yan produced a text that combined literal translation with his own paraphrases. In total, *Guofu lun* (Disquisition on the Wealth of Nations) included nearly a thousand annotated commentaries, in which Yan outlined European economic thinking in the century since the original publication of *The Wealth of Nations.* On one level, *Guofu lun* covered a wide range of topics, from government debts to societal wealth. It succeeded in rephrasing the terms of court debates on fiscal policies that, less than a quarter of a century earlier, had been conducted largely in a traditional language of morality versus instrumentality, or "talent and integrity" versus "tools and skills."[4] On another level, Yan's text provided a comprehensive set of categories and vocabulary that made it possible to think, in Chinese, "economistically." Ethical and material orders were no longer viewed as necessarily in opposition to each other. In the process and rationality of the material world's production and regeneration there are higher principles of an ethical nature that dissolve the opposition.

In hindsight, it seems obvious that a salient feature of China's twentieth-century concerns was the rise of economism and the challenge it presented to morality. Under Chinese Communism, economic issues not only defined the Party line and dominated the state agenda, but also functioned as the most important set of constitutive factors in the determination of individual social identity. In the early twentieth century, economism as an emerging way of thinking contributed to the pursuit of capitalist enterprises, which in turn contributed to a redistribution of social power and prestige legitimized by these new concepts.[5]

Yan Fu's commentaries, in short, did not take place in a historical vacuum. In this chapter we begin with an examination of the maritime merchants who appeared along the China coast in the decades after the Opium War (1839–42). These merchants, many of them comprador agents for foreign firms in Shanghai, evolved from the culturally compromised to the officially honored by the late nineteenth century.

This is not to say that there was no honor attached to China's old merchant class. Nor that other types of long-distance transactions, involving goods such as tea, silk, and rice, were unknown before the maritime trade. Besides merchandise procurement at the source of production and wholesale transactions, there was shipping, docking, storing, renting, leasing, warehousing, pawning, currency exchanges, and lending.[6] Late imperial China had developed one of the world's most sophisticated mercantile economies, in which commercial wealth and official honor coexisted. Nonetheless, there were significant differences between the old and new merchants of China, both in the area of business organizations and the strategies for success.

THE VIRTUOUS MERCHANTS OF OLD CHINA

In spite of Confucian denigration, Chinese merchants in the late imperial days saw a steady rise in their social standing from the fifteenth century onward. Merchants and traders continued to contend, to be sure, with long-standing norms and conventions that placed them on the bottom rungs of social respectability. But by the fifteenth century in the silk-producing Jiangnan region (the delta area south of the lower Yangzi) where silver was abundant and monetary transactions were complex, circumstances had changed so much that a growing number of merchants hailed from gentry-scholar-official households—a recognition that mercantile pursuits were no longer beneath contempt. Social critics were quick to charge, in fact, that only scions of mercantile wealth were privileged enough to afford a private classical Confucian education, which opened the door to government service.[7] Throughout the empire, the rich and the learned became entangled in kinship networks and material connections. This development elevated the social standing of the merchants and broke down the age-old divisions between the *shi* (scholar-officials) and the *shang* (merchants).

It was in this environment that leading intellectuals offered a new assessment on the moral worth of profit-seeking activities. When composing the tombstone inscription of a wealthy merchant who had once been a scholar, Wang Yangming, a Neo-Confucian thinker, took the opportunity to state that a merchant in his proper pursuits actually embodied a scholar's vision of the rightful way of the world. Wang invoked the "ways of the ancients" to advance the idea that all "four classes of people"—scholars, farmers, artisans, and merchants—"adhere to the same *dao* (way)" despite their divergent pursuits in life *(yi ye er tong dao)*.[8] Wang's followers further affirmed that gentry-scholar-officials and merchants were united on matters of value *(shi shang yi shu er tong zhi)*.[9] The fall of the Ming saw many former Neo-Confucian gentry-scholar-officials turning to trade both for support and as an escape from political service. By the nineteenth century it no longer remained an issue whether merchants deserved equal standing with the other classes of society. So many gentry-scholar-officials originally hailed from merchant families that "they had become obsessed with the minute and preoccupied themselves with penny-pinching," whereas the true merchants of the day had acquired "the magnificence of the ancients" that had been lost among the scholars.[10] In the eyes of some, it was the merchants rather than the gentry-scholar-officials who now embodied not only wealth but also virtue.

A successful merchant was a man of Confucian virtue. But in addition to a general understanding of the sagely way, these men were also exemplary practitioners of specific economic virtues. The Anhui merchants of Xindu were among the wealthiest people in late imperial Chinese society, and were renowned for both their hard work and frugality.[11] According to the observations of the seventeenth-century scholar Gu Yanwu, these men would make the entire journey to Beijing on foot. They wore garments that barely reached the mid-calf and straw sandals with no socks. They traveled with homemade food and carried only an umbrella to protect themselves from the elements. Despite owning assets that valued in the tens of thousands, these men simply would not indulge in the luxury of the horse and carriage.[12] Whether motivated by thrift or modesty, proper merchants who knew their place traveled in a style that was distinctively different from the pomp and circumstance of imperial officials. A virtuous merchant remained socially unobtrusive and invisible, regardless of his accumulated wealth.

This thriftiness was accompanied, meanwhile, by a reverence for "rightful" ownership, or a carefully maintained sense of boundaries regarding proprietorship. One popular cliché that appears in many vernacular tales tells how an honest merchant would endure hardship in order to return a significant sum of silver or gold to the rightful owner.[13] Such deeds occurred, furthermore, not to satisfy the latter, who were unaware of their loss, but to gratify the "gods and ghosts" *(guishen)* watching in silence.[14] In these tales, virtue and vice were balanced in much the same way as assets and debits. Virtuous acts produced material rewards, because heaven rarely failed to reward honesty and punish the dishonest. Whether out of reverence or righteousness, ethical standards were attached to the pursuit of wealth in both practice and belief.[15] Those who pursued the "end" *(mo)* of profits were not without their principles or pride.

Recent scholarship has gone a long way to document the steady rise of the merchant class's standing from the late Ming through the Qing. The indigenous ethical system functioned more than adequately to sustain the pursuit of monetary wealth. Additionally, there was plenty of evidence of an "inner worldly asceticism" that was buttressed by a deep reverence for a certain spiritual value. But unlike the Osaka rice merchants of Tokugawa Japan, Chinese merchants, despite the vastness of their capital accumulation, shied away from a vision of virtue that was their own. There was no institutional or intellectual equivalent to the Kaitokudo enterprise either among the salt merchants of Yangzhou, the hong merchants of Guangzhou (Canton), or the tea exporters of Taiwan.[16] To follow their "way," late imperial Chinese merchants produced manuals and handbooks that were long on the pragmatics but short on principles, and detailed on local specifics but negligible with regard to a broader vision of the world. An exemplary merchant conducted himself with a scholar's sense of ethics and honor. A merchant of virtue was virtuous because he *acted* like a scholar. A man as such had much to learn from the non-mercantile; yet he had little to offer in return. Ultimately, Confucianism, like Protestantism, was compatible with the pursuit of mercantile wealth.[17] Mercantile wealth was made acceptable, meanwhile, only to the extent that it could be seen as conforming to the norms of scholarly respectability—gaining acceptance, so to speak, at the cost of its own visibility.

THE NEW MERCHANTS OF SHANGHAI

In the second half of the nineteenth century a new mercantile culture emerged in the treaty ports on the Chinese coast. A new breed of merchants appeared in order to serve as the brokers and translators that bridged the gap between China and the West. Known as the comprador, these "bicultural middlemen" worked on commissions or fixed salaries, and served as house stewards, business assistants, upcountry purchasers, "ship compradors" (independent purchasers), or independent merchants.[18] Whether of humble origins or from a merchant family, many compradors—from Guangzhou, Ningbo, Suzhou, or elsewhere—amassed a significant amount of wealth within a short period of time. Jardine, Matheson and Co.'s Shanghai comprador, Yang Fang (Takee), accumulated several million taels in the 1850s, as did Chen Zhuping (Choping), Russell and Co.'s Shanghai comprador in the 1860s and '70s. The "scholarly comprador," Zheng Guanying, who worked for Butterfield and Swire from 1873 to 1881, was wealthy enough to invest four hundred thousand taels in China's modern enterprises in the 1880s and '90s. Similarly, Tang Jingxing (Tong King-sing), who worked for Jardine's from 1873 to 1881, invested some three hundred thousand taels in the Kaiping coal mines. Xu Run, Dent's Shanghai's comprador from 1861 to 1868, invested a total of 1,275,000 taels in various state-initiated modern enterprises. The garden villa Xu Run built in Shanghai was so vast that visitors sometimes risked getting lost. It was so immaculately maintained by scores of servants that the "floors and desks were as shining as glass."[19] One estimate suggests that between 1842 and 1894 the total amount of private assets accumulated by the several tens of thousands of compradors was approximately 530 million taels.[20] This wealth did not overshadow the property assets of the tens of millions of gentry elite who drew as a group an estimated annual income of 645 million taels from landholdings and commercial enterprises.[21] Nonetheless it represented a new source of wealth that came from the compradors' unique capacity to occupy the middle ground—to "squeeze" both the Europeans and the Chinese alike. It was also a new source of income that brought fabulous wealth to a small number of individuals in a short period of time.

In lifestyle and business practice, the comprador merchants set themselves apart from both the old merchants and the gentry. They wore "the long gown of blue silk and the closely fitting black cap on the shaven head," but were equally at ease in a tuxedo. They built English-style manor houses filled with imported pieces of Venetian furniture, decorated the rooms with Jingdezhen porcelain, and landscaped the surrounding grounds with Suzhou-style gardens. A majority spoke a sort of pidgin English that followed Chinese word order but deployed a smattering of words of Anglo-Indian and Portuguese origins. They were Buddhists yet they took Christian names. They observed lunar festivals but scheduled their work and leisure according to the Western calendar. They joined the YMCA and, in 1865, presented the "Compradors' Cup" to the Hankou spring race meeting. They also bought government-official titles (daotai) and donned the mandarin's garb so as to avoid presenting themselves as mere commoners to the gentry and the imperial officials.[22] In appearance as well as in practice, the comprador merchants drew upon elements of East and West and forged a style that mixed the exotic and the conventional in unprecedented ways.

Some of the comprador merchants (Zheng Guanying, for example) received an early education in Confucian classics. Yet even for those without such an upbringing, it was scarcely an issue whether they would reject the ethical norms that had governed the Confucian merchants of late imperial days. The same virtues of trust, honesty, reliability, and integrity continued to be desired between the comprador and the foreigners. Foreign employment did not cost the compradors their economic virtue; such virtue was in great demand from foreign buyers and employers.[23] What set the compradors apart from their late imperial predecessors was not what they might have lost, but what had become necessary for them to learn. This included both foreign language skills and knowledge of the world that lay beyond China.

Foreign language ability was the first criterion that distinguished the new merchants from the old ones. English in particular was the key to the middleman's successful fulfillment of his duties.[24] In the decade following the Opium War, Shanghai families were already paying tuition to send their children to English classes.[25] Foreign missionaries contributed to the availability of such instructions. The Church Missionary Society established the Anglo-Chinese School (Yinghua shuyuan) in Shanghai in 1865, and engaged John Fryer, formerly of St. Paul's College in Hong Kong, to be its headmaster. The enterprise enjoyed the support of foreign merchants (William Keswick, Jardine's Shanghai partner) and compradors (Chen Zhuping of Russell and Co.) alike. It taught English "carefully" and attracted a student body of "sons of mercantile families." Among its graduates were some of the most successful compradors of the late nineteenth century.[26]

English-Chinese wordbooks and dictionaries began to appear. Tang Tingshu (Tong King-sing; 1832–1892), who at age ten attended one of the earliest missionary teaching institutions in East Asia, the Robert Morrison School in Hong Kong, was the compiler of *The Chinese and English Instructor,* which was published in 1862. An able linguist who spoke English "nearly like a Briton," Tang began his career working as a translator for the courts of the Hong Kong colonial administration when he was barely twenty. After serving briefly as a secretary and interpreter at the Maritime Customs House in Shanghai, Tang joined Jardine, Matheson and Co., traveling in between Hankou, Shanghai, Fuzhou, and Hong Kong on behalf of the firm; by 1863 had risen to become Jardine's chief comprador in Shanghai. He compiled this six-volume set in response to the frequently asked questions that arose as he dispatched his multifarious responsibilities in Jardine's various offices.[27] This compilation included lists of English and Chinese words arranged by different categories of transaction (including metal, trade rules, tobacco, silk, tea, weights, measurements, accounts, lawsuits, personnel, fabric, shipping, hiring, currency, warehouse, and deliveries). It also contains situational dialogues useful in negotiations over hiring, chartering, renting, inventory checking, and so forth. The "model conversation" between the comprador and his foreign employer, stripped down to the bare minimum of the functionally adequate in both languages, skipped all niceties in favor of matters such as "how much," "when," "how," "which currency," and "whose account." The expressions varied from being awkwardly stiff and unembellished to being peremptory or threatening. Chinese translations of English words were given with the Cantonese pronunciation. It was a text compiled with the tangible presence and pragmatic needs of a specific constituency in mind, especially the people who spoke "in the Canton dialect . . . the Canton people who have transactions or are connected with foreigners."[28] And it was among the first of many others that were to appear in print in the next half century.

A new breed of Chinese merchants appeared who sought the pragmatic value of the "learning of commerce." The Society for East Asian Business Studies (Yadong shangxue she) was a club formed by a dozen young men in their twenties, working as accountants, bookkeepers, warehouse custodians, and managerial assistants in Hong Kong's various merchant houses. As practitioners of trade they sought to organize their experience into a systematic body of knowledge. Travel, conversations, newspapers, and foreign language proficiency featured largely in their work and life, as did writing and publishing. These friends put out a journal, *Shangwu kaocha bao*, in 1907. Their venture received support from thirty-some Chinese businesses in Hong Kong, including over a dozen *Jinshan zhuang*—firms that specialized in trade with California.[29] The journal set as its goal "the study of everything" that had something to do with the conduct of "commerce," which ranged from finance, trade, shipping, insurance, commercial geography, market condition, commercial regulations, tariffs, and trade agreements to local history and current events. Additional subjects for study included partnerships, contracts, government registration, debt services, agents, brokers, mining, manufacturing, railroad management, colonial administrations, and, with Southeast Asian economies in mind, plantations.[30] The colleagues used photographs and drawings to teach each other about the wide variety of coins and currencies in use in the Southeast Asia maritime trade. Much of their writings concerned details and the materially tangible—to the trained eye, the journals depict a maritime environment fragmented by myriad differences, large and small, that ranged from matters of money, language, diet, and measurement to the rules of law and the power of local authorities.

It is arguable whether these new merchants and their hybrid cultural styles won acceptance or respectability, even in the first decades of the twentieth century. Yet the maritime trade and the wealth they represented did not escape attention. Over the course of the second half of the nineteenth century, trade expanded steadily on the Chinese coast in the context of repeated armed conflicts; it came to be thought of as war. Economic affairs, as international dealings, were no longer private businesses outside the purviews of the state.

TRADE AS WAR

The earliest usage of the term *shangzhan* (war of commerce) is sometimes attributed to Governor-general Zeng Guofan and his reflections on the state of the world in the late nineteenth century—especially in comparison with the Warring States period in the third century B.C.[31] History taught that Lord Shang of the state of Qin had devised a strategy of *gengzhan* (war of the tillers) that used agricultural surplus to fill the state's coffers.[32] Thus enriched, he assembled a powerful army that, under Qin Shihuang, unified China's separate kingdoms for the first time in history. What the Europeans introduced in the decades after the Opium War, Zeng observed, was a war in which traders were like soldiers and commerce played a pivotal role in determining the outcome of rivalries among the nations.

Deeply impressed with the "unprecedented" nature of British commercial wealth and military might, one school of thought in mid-nineteenth-century China explained Western power by focusing on commerce and industry, especially on state action that encouraged and supported such activities.[33] In an 1878 memorial to the throne, the censor Li Pan explained:

> Western nations regard the rise and fall of commerce as a matter of consequence for the fortunes of the state. Rulers and subjects join their hearts in this belief. Commerce is where everyone's interest lies; all give their best efforts in this regard. . . . To invade a rival state in ancient times, rulers dissipated their wealth in order to expand their territories. To invade a country in today's world, Western nations expand territories and gain wealth at the same time. . . . Grand Councilor Zeng once remarked, "Shang Yang fought wars of tillers and Western nations are fighting wars of traders." How true this statement is![34]

Arguments like these ultimately confirmed the harmony of interest between the state and the "merchants" *(shang)*, or more precisely, the mar-

itime traders who dealt with foreigners.[35] It was in the self-interest of the
state to extend to the new merchants necessary protection *(bao)* and to
aid their competition against foreign merchants for profits. But what *bao
shang* actually meant in practical measures was open to interpretation.
It went beyond the issue of how the merchants and bureaucrats cooper-
ated, and encompassed broader questions of the role of the state in facilitating the rise of a modern economy. This became further entangled
in the court politics of the late Qing.

It is noteworthy that Li Pan's memorial appeared in 1878, a critical
juncture in the development of state-sponsored Chinese mercantilism. Li
continues: "Earlier, under the rallying cry for 'self-strengthening' in the
aftermath of the Taiping Uprising (1850–1862), provincial governors had
launched several projects to build arsenals and shipyards in the hope of
modernizing China's military industry. But court conservatives greeted
these initiatives with skepticism. They argued that the strength of the nation stemmed from the moral quality and not the technological know-
how of the Chinese people."[36]

Conservative officials had criticized the Fuzhou Arsenal and Shipyard,
citing its large expenses as evidence of wastefulness, and sought to shut
it down.[37] In 1872, in a famous response that defended the military industrialization projects, Li Hongzhang, governor-general of Zhili Province (present day Hebei and Henan), presented a memorial that proposed
the shipyard expand its operations and build merchant vessels. These
ships would then service a mercantile operation, the China Merchants
Steamship Navigation Company. To organize the company, Governor-
general Li formulated the slogan *guandu shangban* or "official supervision, merchant management." The steamship company was to come under the direction of an official who was appointed by a regional governor
and managed by merchant executives with treaty port experience. To at-
tract merchant capital and to ensure the new company's profit, Li further proposed that it be granted the exclusive right to carry the state's
tribute rice from south China to Tianjin.[38] In advancing the proposal, Li
envisioned Chinese ships carrying cargo and passengers and competing
successfully with foreign ships—"taking back" *(wanhui)* from foreign
companies profits and interest *(liquan)* that should rightfully be Chinese,
"so that every penny we earn will be a penny less to profit a foreign enterprise."[39] In other words, state concern with Sino-foreign rivalry was
not to be restricted to armed struggles on the battlefields, but was also
to take into account national contests in the acquisition of wealth. It was
well within the scope of the self-strengthening endeavors of the Chinese

state to sponsor commercial enterprises. It was in this context that officials and merchants were to collaborate on mercantile projects.

Li Hongzhang's memorial led to the organization of the China Merchant Steamship Navigation Company, which was used as a template for the organization of other "official supervision, merchant management" enterprises that included mining, telegraph bureaus, railroads, machine-powered weaving, cotton spinning, and banking.[40] Invoking self-important arguments about their contribution to national interest, Li and other regional officials were able to obtain court concessions such as tariff reductions and tax exemptions for the business enterprises that they had sponsored. In addition, they placed public funds in these enterprises as a source of credit. They expected, in return, profits from these operations to help pay for new expenses such as the purchase of military uniforms and ammunition.

Bao shang in the context of "self-strengthening" proponents justified bureaucratic sponsorship of mercantile projects. It also gave official blessing to commercial profits in the name of statist goals. Late Qing mercantile enterprises functioned as the economic arm of regionally centered "bureaucratic machines" that potentially challenged the power of the imperial court. Regional officials in coastal provinces—Li Hongzhang, Zhang Zhidong, and, later, Yuan Shikai—were among the first to grasp the economic significance of Western-style industrial and mercantile enterprises.[41] These officials pursued *guandu shangban* projects that tapped treaty-port comprador wealth as a new source of investment capital.[42] Their notion of *shang* or "commerce" went beyond what a subsistence economy might sustain to encompass goals of entrepreneurial growth and development.

To the extent that imperial officials turned to sponsor large-scale modern enterprises, a new arena of interaction emerged between officialdom and the new merchants. Few comprador merchants, for example, attained civil service examination degrees through scholarly merit. Instead, the merchant elite found opportunities to purchase such degrees, and also held expectant titles for government offices. Tang Tingshu, Xu Run, and Zheng Guanying, the principal merchant managers of the China Merchant Steamship Navigation Company, were all commoners from Guangdong who made their fortunes as Chinese compradors for foreign firms. They also all purchased civil service degrees and held bureaucratic titles as expectant *daotai*.[43] Within the framework of "official supervision, merchant management," these men not only invested their private wealth, but also contributed their experience as managers of Western firms. Their service in government-sponsored projects, meanwhile, served to induct them into a bureaucratic culture of status and hierarchy.

Guandu shangban enterprises provided the opportunity, in addition, for the rise of a new breed of officials who wielded enormous influence as business directors of expanding modern enterprises. Sheng Xuanhuai (1844–1916), who held the lowest examination degree *(xiucai)*, began his career in 1870 as a staff assistant who oversaw the supply of the Huai Army, which was under the command of Li Hongzhang. Shrewd and capable, Sheng Xuanhuai served, from the 1870s onward, as the top official manager of the China Merchant Steamship Navigation Company. The success of the steamship company, in turn, led to Sheng's directorships in other *guandu shangban* enterprises that ranged from telegraph bureaus and railroad lines to coal mines. Sheng's predominant position in these enterprises made him a pillar of Governor-general Li Hongzhang's bureaucratic enterprise. His ability to hold on to managerial positions had less to do with the profit performance of the companies, however, than the power of his political backing. It was his bureaucratic connections rather than his capitalist acumen that accounted for Sheng's towering stature as China's leading bureaucratic capitalist in the late nineteenth century.[44]

Merchants and officials joined efforts, in short, as managers and investors in state-sponsored modern enterprises. But this proximity guaranteed neither consensus nor harmony. In the case of the China Merchant Steamship Navigation Company, Sheng Xuanhuai's major nemesis was none other than the fabulously rich Xu Run. Xu, who sent his children and grandchildren to Oxford and the United States, was the leader of a group of comprador investors from Guangdong, some of whom had learned English in Hong Kong. In comparison, Sheng, who was more persuasive among shareholders from northern China, was the son of a provincial degree-holder and a retired official who had spent years working on the compilation of a statecraft compendium for fellow Confucian bureaucrats.[45] For years the two men fought for each other's dismissal from the company, a contest that was settled only after the death of Li Hongzhang, Sheng's powerful patron.

Comprador merchants and Confucian bureaucrats were not meant to commingle seamlessly. But the most striking aspect of the *guandu shangban* enterprises was not that merchant shareholders and government directors clashed, but how the new lines of wealth and old lines of prestige mixed. The new enterprises represented a veritable "amalgam" of merchants and officials, with men of merchant backgrounds bearing official titles and interacting with "regular" authorities at all levels. The titles carried prestige. They were, furthermore, essential for carrying out the company's business, because contact with officialdom—whether through tribute rice, tariffs, inland duties, official freight, or passengers—was facilitated when company managers could interact as equals, or near equals, with incumbent officials.[46] In this process merchant enterprises under official supervision became "bureaucratized"—mindful of status and attentive to protocol. The ritualized practices and conventionalized etiquette of the imperial bureaucracy were superimposed upon an emerging culture of semi-official industry and business.

Likewise, merchant impact on the officialdom was just as significant. Sheng Xuanhuai amassed, towards the end of his life, a personal fortune consisting of dozens of pawnshops and multiple pieces of Shanghai real estate valued between 20 and 40 million silver taels. He lived on Bubbling Well Road in the International Settlement, the same street as his comprador rival, Xu Run, and hosted hundreds of guests in just as grand a style.

The two men came from divergent places and backgrounds and followed different career paths. But a mere thirty years after the founding of the steamship company, and within both men's lifetimes, the official had spoken of himself as a private merchant (*shang*) while the comprador came to be greeted as an expectant official. Within the framework of *guandu shangban,* the new middleman had found his bureaucratic niche. At the same time the officialdom had devised a means both to tap the comprador wealth and harness their knowledge of the world beyond China.

MERCHANT BUREAUCRATS

In 1895, after the signing of the Treaty of Shimonoseki, foreign industries obtained the right to own and operate manufacturing facilities in Chinese treaty ports. Economic rivalries between Chinese and foreign merchants extended from commerce to production, and from finished goods to capital investment. In response to a perceived intensification of foreign economic exploitation, court policy shifted once again. It went from statements of encouragement to active government promotion of private mercantile enterprises. The state not only sanctioned official and gentry investment in commerce and industry, but also promoted private merchant investment in industry.

Private Chinese merchants responded accordingly. Between 1895 and

1911 privately owned merchant enterprises *(shang ban)*, numbering in the thousands, appeared all over China, the majority of which were valued at no more than fifty thousand taels in initial capital investment. Many engaged in food processing, producing flour, oil, egg powder, tea, sugar, salt, wine, canned food, and so forth for consumption. Others made soap, cosmetics, light bulbs, porcelain, rubber, tiles, glass, cement, matches, paper, candles, dye, chemicals, and the like, supplying households and businesses alike.[47] Individuals with strong bureaucratic connections—Sheng Xuanhuai (1844–1916), Zhang Jian (1853–1926), and Zhou Xuexi (1866–1947), for example—also participated with their own funds as private merchants *(shang)*.[48] The steady diminution of the role of officials in the operation of industries was matched by a corresponding rise of privately operated enterprises.[49] As a growing number of private individuals turned to new-style mercantile enterprises in response to state encouragement, the notion of *bao shang* took on new meaning. It went beyond state patronage of industrial projects to encompass the creation of conditions that facilitated mercantile undertaking. In order to promote commerce and industry for the benefit of the Chinese nation, the time had come for a broad reevaluation of the status of the merchant in Chinese society.

Merchants complained that they had been hampered, on one hand, by an abundance of restrictive rules at home, and were thus unable to exercise their entrepreneurial initiatives; on the other hand, they felt the state was not adequately involved in their protection in the courts. To extend its benevolence *(bao)* to the merchants *(shang)*, the state had to reform its laws and reorganize its institutions. The merchants also wanted more effective representation of Chinese mercantile interest against that of the foreigners.[50]

In the general political climate fashioned by reformers and revolutionaries such as Liang Qichao and Sun Yatsen, young educated merchants were particularly vocal on behalf of their newly acquired knowledge about the outside world. Chinese poverty and military defeat, they argued, were the results of a general Chinese ignorance of the ways of "civilized nations," especially of the "self-governing" *(zizhi)* societies of the West. Successful conduct of commerce required knowledge. Methodical study of commerce as a new branch of "learning" *(shangxue)* was necessary, because the Chinese had to change the way they conducted business. [51]

In the mid-1890s, Zheng Guanying emerged as the most important voice regarding *shangzhan.* A former comprador, an official-in-waiting, and the author of several editions of collected essays entitled *Sheng shi wei yan,* Zheng gained a national audience in the aftermath of China's defeat in the first Sino-Japanese War. Zheng affirmed the concept of *shangzhan,* but attacked the bureaucratic presence in the mercantile domain: "Western nations send their merchants to engage in wars of trade. To oppose them, our merchants meet their Western counterparts. But how difficult things are on our side that we remain habituated in old ways and mired in the norms of the past; that we insist that all decisions rest with civil service degree-holders who are [not merchants] but scions of gentry official families!"[52]

The issue of the moment, in other words, was not whether the merchants deserved the support or protection of the state, but whether the old-line bureaucrats were competent enough to perform their duties with regard to commerce. From the perspective of many treaty port intellectuals and comprador merchants, their differences with the Confucian officialdom were better off being emphasized instead of concealed: it was these differences that enabled the merchants to claim a greater capacity to handle China's commerce in the interests of the Chinese nation and state.

It became a prevalent view, by the end of the decade, that the practice of new-style commerce required training and preparation in a new body of knowledge, and that business schools *(shangwu xuetang)* should be established to fulfill this function. In addition, as part of this new knowledge consisted of up-to-date market information and familiarity with local practices across vast regions, the creation of business gazettes *(shangbao)* as well as merchant associations *(shanghui)* was proposed, in order to facilitate the accumulation and circulation of such intelligence. The new merchants, in other words, rose to success on the basis of a new discipline of knowledge and information that required training, and thus new institutions.[53]

A classical Confucian education, clearly, was no longer an adequate preparation for merchants. The imperial bureaucracy, staffed by individuals trained in the classics, therefore had to be reformed in order to accommodate the needs of mercantile activities. It should come as no surprise that Zheng Guanying was among the first to propose the creation of a new Ministry of Commerce to address the issues at hand. Merchant demands—or rather, mercantile arguments—began to yield results around the turn of the century. Sheng Xuanhuai, the leading bureaucratic entrepreneur, memorialized the throne in 1899 for the creation of an office *(yamen)* of commercial affairs, as well as a separate minister of commercial treaties *(shangyue dachen):*

All nations have government offices that deal with commercial affairs. These offices complement the boards of revenue and are separate and distinct from ministries of foreign affairs. . . . All treaty nations, whenever negotiations turn to commerce, would refer such matters to the *yamen* of commercial affairs. . . . On matters such as the produce and productions of various places, the management, transportation, distribution, and sale of all merchandise, the *yamen* may obtain information from merchant associations in various places. Chinese and foreign merchants should be permitted to present matters in writing to the *yamen* about commercial affairs at any time. Merchants should also be permitted to meet with commerce officials without putting on official robes. Such interactions will assure that information and viewpoints on the ground reach the higher circles of authority.[54]

Until the creation of these new offices, Sheng Xuanhuai went on, Chinese mercantile interest would continue to be hindered by old bureaucratic practices. The Zongli *yamen,* which since its establishment in the 1860s had been negotiating commercial treaties, had neither the resolve nor the skills to defend Chinese merchant interest when confronted with foreign demands. Instead of being placed at the mercy of the bureaucracy, Sheng suggested, Chinese merchants should be allowed and encouraged to organize themselves so as to look after China's commerce. There should be chambers of commerce in all towns, so merchants could gather to study conditions that affected their affairs. Sheng Xuanhuai not only subscribed to the view that merchants, rather than bureaucrats, should serve as the custodian of China's mercantile interests, but also outlined a comprehensive readjustment of interactions between the two.[55]

Riding on the momentum of such viewpoints and taking advantage of the pro-reform climate in the aftermath of the Boxer Uprising in 1900, bureaucratic reformers and mercantile interest groups were able to push through a range of institutional innovations in the 1900s. In 1899 the court established the minister of commercial treaties position *(shangyue dachen)* and appointed Sheng Xuanhuai. It was in this capacity that Sheng negotiated international contracts, entered agreements, revised terms, and directed all semi-state modern enterprises (coal mining, railroads, telegraph bureaus, steamships, and banking) that involved foreign investments. In 1903 a new Ministry of Commerce was set up, initially as part of the Ministry of Agriculture, Industry, and Commerce, and later as an independent entity, to coordinate commercial affairs and to assure the dissemination of information and expertise. In the same year the Imperial Law Drafting Commission, led by a team of three that included Wu Tingfang, a former comprador from Hong Kong and a Qing emissary to the United States, announced a range of new laws including commercial laws. The new laws encouraged (or ordered) Chinese merchants in all major towns, both in China and overseas, to form chambers of commerce. These associations *(shanghui)* with elected leaderships helped not only to implement the state's new laws, but also to gather and submit local information by means of bureaucratic channels. The newly established Ministry of Commerce, meanwhile, worked to facilitate the creation of schools of commerce and the advancement of "business learning" *(shang-xue)* at administrative and commercial centers on all levels. The ministry collected trade information, published the *Shangwu guanbao* (Government Gazette on Commercial Affairs), and supervised the formation of local chambers of commerce. In addition, it also encouraged the formation of local societies for the study of business knowledge *(shangxue hui)*. By the first decades of the twentieth century, the new-style merchants had succeeded not only in attaining social respectability, but also in establishing a significant foothold in the imperial bureaucracy.

Two pieces of commercial legislation were announced in 1903: the "merchant code" *(shangren tongli)* and the "corporation code" *(gongsi lü)*.[56] Under the former, the state enumerated and recognized as commerce activities of twenty-some categories. These included purchasing, sales, letting, renting, manufacturing, reprocessing, public utilities (electricity, gas, and water), publishing, printing, banking, money exchange, lending, advancement of credit or credit-related services, operation of public gathering places, warehousing, insurance, delivery, delivery-related services, brokerage services, middleman services, or agency services. Old-fashioned street peddling and "handicrafts," or anything else that failed to incorporate the use of machinery or necessitate a permanent business premise or address, were explicitly excluded from the coverage of the new laws. To obtain legal recognition, all eligible merchants, as defined and qualified by law, had to register with local government authorities. To be qualified for registration, they were required, in trade practices, to observe new laws concerning the use of trademarks. And in areas not yet covered by law, merchants were required to follow the rules and principles of bookkeeping, accounting, record keeping, account balancing, and so forth as spelled out in the various textbooks of *shangxue*.[57]

But while drafting laws, setting up offices, and taking up responsibilities in ways that seemingly responded to mercantile demands, the state also turned the argument against the merchants. According to the imperial law commissioners, the backwardness of Chinese commerce was not a result of traditional state prejudices, but rather had its roots in the general ignorance of the vast majority of the mercantile population. The latter had been held back in their pursuit of wealth because China had never had a tradition of "teach[ing] the merchants what they need to know in a school of business." Chinese merchants learned their trade informally, "either from their fathers or from their master-employers," which contributed to the fragmentation of practice and undercut the state's ability to provide aid. In essence, the government believed Chinese merchants needed to reform their ways in order to benefit from official assistance.

In the 1900s the imperial government ordered the organization of numerous local chambers of commerce. A principal duty of the chambers was the distribution of standardized record-keeping forms to registered members; these included daily record books, monthly balance sheets, and annual total balance sheets by revenue and assets. Merchant conformity to the use of these new forms was a precondition for successful applications for business registration. Proper registration with local authorities, meanwhile, was not only a precondition for a merchant's legal capacity to act, but also for the legal recognition and representation of the business in court.

From the perspective of the state, then, business education, which taught standardized rules of record keeping and accounting, was worthwhile as it provided a foundation for the implementation and enforcement of commercial law. The idea of commerce as learning received prominent endorsement when the ministry used its official gazette to list the names of leading foreign business schools in Germany and the United States. It also outlined a business curriculum, using the undergraduate curriculum from the College of Commerce at the University of California as an example. University-level knowledge was linked, in turn, to a whole new field of professions, including accounting, banking, and brokerage services.[58] As a model and a vision, foreign examples and state endorsement combined to legitimize business schools and to lend prestige to the pursuit of commerce. Meanwhile, the legal framework laid down by the imperial government was reaffirmed in 1913, and again in 1928. Despite regime shifts, the state-merchant relationship continued to evolve within these terms for the next half century.

Whether as bureaucratic capitalists, merchant-officials, or official-merchants, the very appearance of such mixed functions and crossed identities suggested a new pattern of relationships between the merchant and the state. Mercantile perspectives gained legitimacy, and merchants gained respectability either as businessmen or officials. There were two sets of agents of modernization: the state and the merchants. Under their partnership commerce and industry became the concerns of the nation and the state. The first undertakings of the newly constituted provincial chambers of commerce included the promotion of "national goods" manufactured in China, and the occasional boycotting of foreign imports.[59] Chamber projects were guided by regular customs reports of trade figures, which were read as vital statistics of the economic health of the nation and the state. By all indications, "economism"—as a new way to think of the role of merchants and economy in the Chinese state and society— had taken hold by the first decade of the twentieth century.

VOICES OF THE MARKETPLACE

In the 1908 novel *Shisheng* (Market Sounds; 1908), we come upon the first literary statements regarding the new merchants and their place in society. Li Bozheng is an affluent entrepreneur and a salt merchant who enters the silk business at a time when Chinese silk production is feeding the French looms in Lyon. Li Bozheng "deliberately buys cocoons at a price much higher than that offered by foreigners." His explanation: "I am not afraid of losing money. I may lose it to a Chinese, but I am not letting foreigners make money out of us."[60] Author Ji Wen lavishes praise on Li because he behaves "less like a merchant than a philanthropist motivated by the Confucian virtues of benevolence and righteousness."[61] Ji's characterization of the merchant offers yet another case of an operative "axiological system" in literary representations at the turn of the last century. It is the merchants rather than the scholars who exhibit Confucian virtues and shoulder the educated man's public responsibility.[62]

Yet there is a twist in this early twentieth-century version of the transposition of virtue from the scholars to the merchants. Unlike earlier vernacular stories, Merchant Li does not forego his profits because he is afraid of the supernatural. He does so, instead, out of concern over the rivalry between "the Chinese" and "the foreigners" in the silk market. To protect Chinese interests, Li acts out of a self-ascribed public spirit and sacrifices his own self-interests for the good of his fellow compatriots. Even if he is ridiculed as a pompous fool, merchant Li sets himself apart from the ordinary profit-seekers who clutch the abacus and follow the dictates of the numbered beads.[63]

Fan Muli, another main character in the story, is a "gentleman-merchant" who engages in a variety of unconventional activities despite his old-fashioned admiration for Fan Li, a model of business virtue in the second century B.C. Fan Muli spearheads a number of early twenti-eth-century innovations. He launches a co-op to organize rural artisans. He sponsors a homemade harvesting machine, the invention of an in-genious villager, for use in the rice field. He establishes a training school to turn ordinary peasants into inventors. He opens an exhibition hall to showcase new products. He buys up large chunks of land to build schools and service centers. He believes in the pragmatic efficacy of machines, mathematics, science, and accounting. But above all, he has faith in the innate intelligence of the Chinese people, especially those who work with their hands and are close to the soil. Fan's grand solution that defeats foreign competition, it turns out, is simply the education of China's peas-ants and artisans—the nurturing and disciplining of the innate intelli-gence and capacity of the Chinese masses. Fan Muli opens a school, hires teachers who have studied in Japan, offers a curriculum that consists of literacy, foreign languages, mathematics, and technology, inspires young peasants to attend classes, and turns their inventions into business en-terprises and industrial products.[64] While Pan Mingduo, a nineteenth-century merchant, "wouldn't open a volume unless it teaches the way of the sagely *dao*,"[65] Fan Muli is only interested in new knowledge. Unlike Pan, whose private virtue ultimately brings him material rewards, Fan sees public deeds as a means to societal wealth.[66] Like his friend Li Bozheng, Fan sees himself as serving the collective cause of the "Chinese." It is the new task of the merchants to share with their fellow citizens a world of new knowledge. Hard work and integrity continue to matter. Yet what distinguishes the new merchants from the old ones—what al-lows them to look down upon the old-style bureaucrats locked in their backward-looking norms—is their knowledge of the world beyond China and its established ways.

By the early twentieth century the new merchants, confident and ea-ger, were ready to advance their claim to patriotic citizenship. From their perspective, the virtuous Xindu merchants—thrifty, diligent, honest, self-effacing, and praised by late Ming Neo-Confucian thinkers—no longer served as adequate paragons for the new merchant heroes of Shanghai. Fan Muli moves about the city riding in a horse-drawn carriage. He puffs Havana cigars held in between fingers glittering with diamonds. His filter holder is encircled in translucent green emerald. He wears silk, satin, and matching jackets and gowns trimmed with fox, lined with sable, woven in patterns, and embroidered in gold.[67] Merchant Li, who entertains with grandeur in his mansion, receives compliments for the magnitude of his wealth and aspires to world-class monopolies and trusts.[68] In Shanghai a whole new style of life evolved, based upon the wealth and spending of the new merchants. In contrast, the Xindu merchant of disciplined frugality and social anonymity—traveling by foot, carrying his own umbrella, wearing straw sandals, and clad in simple cloth—had become the very image of backwardness and conservatism.

CHAPTER 2

The State in Commerce

In the 1920s a new elite emerged in Shanghai. Some, educated overseas and recipients of advanced degrees, presided as bankers, industrialists, entrepreneurs, lawyers, accountants, deans, and so forth. Others, seasoned with long years of experience in the city, served as managers, shareholders, traders, distributors, advertisers, agents, and brokers. They formed companies, launched firms, established schools, ran businesses, hired trainees, signed contracts, dealt with foreign partners, formed civic associations, and engaged in an expanding range of social, political, and charitable activities. They cut across conventional lines of social divisions, built a dense network of relationships, and interacted with each other in multiple capacities. These interactions included joint investment projects, overlapping board memberships, duplicated club associations, and strategic marriage alliances, in addition to school bonds, provincial ties, and even political party affiliations. The YMCA was one such networking "hub" for the Westernized and the affluent. So was the Chinese Society for Vocational Education, which enabled networking for the lower middle class while facilitating elite social enterprises. Networking activities filled the after-work hours of a large number of the "gowned" (desk workers) and opened up a sense of the city beyond the shop floors and office desks. For the elite such networks made it possible to mobilize significant amounts of resources on the basis of shared information and ideas. With the weakening of the state during the Republican era, the expanding networks enabled both the middle class and the petty urbanites to run the city and look after their needs.

Yet no relationship, in the end, was of greater consequence for the new economic class than that with the state, which was prominent both structurally and discursively, in law, education, and in the civic arena. For those aspiring to join the ranks of the elite, a whole generation of white-collar workers learned, sometimes the hard way, that in order to practice accounting or legal consulting, one had to be certified by the state. A great number of companies understood that if government representation in international disputes was to work in their favor, they needed to fully comply with state regulations. Liberal educators and new entrepreneurs, who had allied with each other to train middle-level managers and to satisfy the job aspirations of junior employees, came to learn that they only had access to the public arena via the state. The state, for its part, recognized the mobilization capacity of these civic networks and was quick to be suspicious of their intent.

China's Republican governments, especially the Nationalists in the 1920s and '30s, functioned to regulate, represent, reform, and repress. The imperial court drew up the first set of nationality laws in 1909 and established the rules defining property rights. It represented "Chinese" interest in international commercial treaties and was instrumental, along with the new entrepreneurs, in facilitating the standardization of business practices all across China. It lent its support, following the campaigns mounted by merchant associations, to the promotion of Chinese "national" products that were defined against foreign imports. As the twentieth century progressed, economic affairs gained growing prominence in the state's agenda. The state, for its part, assumed new functions, expanded its power, and established an increasing presence in the everyday lives of the people.

COMMERCE AS LEARNING

In the 1900s *shang* (commerce) and *xue* (study) became linked thanks to the joint sponsorship of the imperial government and the new merchants; the resulting concept of *shangxue* or "commercial learning" came to be recognized as a new category of knowledge. It no longer seemed unthinkable that superior knowledge, as opposed to greed or dishonesty, should be the primary factor of a merchant's wealth and success. Knowledge became a critical element in the success or failure of commercial enterprises, thereby transforming career preparation for commerce at the same time. To make a living in the city, one needed to obtain a job. And to get a job one had to go to school—and not any school, but the right kind of school.

Just what exactly was "commercial learning" in the 1920s? The Shanghai General Chamber of Commerce, which poured resources into its library, monthly journal publications, sponsorships of book translations and compilations, and the distribution of manuals, textbooks, newsletters, and other useful information, was an authoritative voice on the entire scope of professional expertise.

Following trends in the United States, chamber publications identified two major breakthroughs in industry and commerce in the nineteenth century: an industrial revolution centered upon technological innovations, and a managerial revolution that evolved around the organization of corporate structures. What Chinese businesses needed to acquire, in addition to technological expertise, were the managerial insights and techniques of this second revolution, which in turn was built, ultimately, upon mathematical knowledge and an improvement in the methods of counting.[1]

Modern firms consisted of multiple shareholders and a complex array of business involvement. They relied upon accounting to offer an accurate and scheduled description of the status of operations.[2] "Scientific management," wrote the Chicago-trained Min Zhishi, required a survey of empirical data, consultation of statistics, budget planning, inventory checks, projections of sales volumes, reports on market size, and so forth. There existed a world of material reality and scientific methods, so to speak, and business decisions could never be made on the basis of individual impulse. Nor should matters of marketing, finance, sales, and accounting be left in the hands of non-experts.[3] All business failures were traceable to a lack of knowledge or an insufficient application of the important principles of "commercial learning."[4] The rewards of scientific management were as great as the failures were severe.

No fewer than a dozen journals and periodicals were in regular circulation in Shanghai in the mid-1920s, promoting the "science" of commercial learning.[5] These journals were sponsored by elite banking associations in various major cities, money guilds, economics studies associations, university economics and business departments, and provincial bureaus of business affairs, and supported an editorial staff and a pool of contributors. These specialists often lectured either full- or part-time in colleges of commerce, or worked in government departments of finance, auditing, accounting, or statistics. They were also generally active or prominent on the boards of various "study associations" on branches of commercial knowledge. It is important to remind ourselves that most of these institutions—colleges, universities, banks, journals, accounting firms, and so forth—were new or newly reconstituted based upon Western models in China in the early twentieth century. The writers did not always author. It was not uncommon for books and articles to be the results of compilations, translations, or adaptations of English texts, carried out by a team of contributors.[6] Nonetheless, by the mid-1930s a number of individuals were established as "grand masters" of *shangxue,* and titles carrying their names were deemed as particularly authoritative in specific areas. "Business learning," much like the study of the Confucian classics or dynastic histories, had established its canonical core and found its great teachers.[7]

One of these "masters" was Pan Xulun, Shanghai's leading accountant in the Republican era. Pan received his MA from Harvard and PhD in commercial economics from Columbia. He chaired the department of accounting at Shanghai Commercial College and the department of commerce at Ji'nan University. He also held positions in the ministries of finance, agriculture, and commerce, as well as with the Maritime Customs Service. The founder and director of the Lixin Accounting Firm, the most prominent firm in Shanghai, Pan was additionally the copyrighted author of a large number of textbooks. So many of China's practicing accountants in the 1930s and '40s had either had their initial training with Pan or had read his books that it assured Pan his seat on the executive board of the Chinese Accounting Society for decades.

The career pattern of such individuals gave evidence that, in Shanghai, advanced degrees from top-notch foreign universities could open closed doors. Pan Xulun's reputation soared when his firm, established in 1924, was engaged to serve as an external auditor for the Shanghai Municipal Council. Certified accounting and economic expertise moved in a close-knit circle, in which client lists and personal references weighed as much as credentials. Pan's other auditing and accounting clients eventually included the Ministry of Finance, the Ministry of Industrial Affairs, and the Maritime Customs Service. In the 1940s Pan himself became a deputy minister of economics.

In teaching, Pan endeavored both to demystify and popularize his subject. As the principal of the most notable accounting school in Shanghai, Pan taught that accounting was a discipline that designs, records, organizes, estimates, analyzes, and audits changes in wealth and assets under any social circumstances and in anyone's life. The discipline is as relevant to household finance as it is to factory management, and as critical to personal planning as it is to corporate budgets or municipal spending. It is, furthermore, a skill and understanding that can be acquired by anyone, and not just the purview of professional accountants, auditors, bookkeepers, finance administrators, and lawyers.

Pan's firm published textbooks that were targeted at students of all levels. The subjects he covered included advanced commercial bookkeeping, various kinds of accounting (corporate, cost, government, and bank), corporate finance, trademark, and corporate registrations. The profits from textbook sales brought in as much revenue as the school's tuition fees. An active public speaker, Pan sometimes delivered his lectures in English, explaining that only by using the original terms was he able to avoid the confusion caused by multiple translations. His Lixin Accounting School (an offshoot of the firm) enrolled female and male students, both for vocational training and household bookkeeping. It offered courses for some of Shanghai's most exclusive missionary schools for women, enriching, with the addition of household finance, a curriculum also distinguished by courses in nutrition and hygiene. Lixin ran a correspondence program and operated its own radio programs. Both forms of "distance learning" carried Pan's voice far and wide, from the inner recess of shops and homes in back alleys to the upper reaches of the Yangzi River.[8] Pan Xulun, in short, was not only the most visible accountant in public view in the 1930s, but also a billboard "model of success" *(chenggong de bangyang)* in the pages of the *Shenghuo Weekly,* thus worthy of the emulation of aspiring urbanites (see chapter 5). By the time the school marked its tenth anniversary, no fewer than eighty thousand individuals had sought to elevate themselves with some measure of accounting.[9]

With the ascendancy of *shangxue* and the intellectualization of business, there was, correspondingly, a commercialization of culture in Republican Shanghai that induced the urban mind to make its material turn. A whole host of business schools and colleges appeared, conferring the much coveted diplomas and degrees. A fast-growing educational movement gathered momentum, retailing pragmatic skills to urban youths who paid to learn. A specialized business language evolved, adding no fewer than ten thousand new terms into the Chinese language in the century after the Opium War. And an encyclopedic compilation designed for shopkeepers went through multiple printings within a matter of eighteen months. The sales figures were particularly impressive as they coincided with massive Japanese military assaults on the city.

BUSINESS SCHOOLS

The teaching of business began in Shanghai in 1904 under a technical management program at the semi-public Nanyang College. In the next thirty years, scores of self-styled "colleges" and "universities" came into being, including eighty-nine that folded after a negligible duration. Of these, at least seventeen were "fly-by-night" operations that offered courses in commerce.[10] By the 1930s, under the tightened rules of the Nationalist Ministry of Education, only six colleges of commerce remained. These were Ji'nan, Fudan, Shanghai Baptist, Datong, Daxia, and Guanghua, each attached to a university and containing multiple departments of study. In addition, there were two public institutions: the Shanghai College of Commerce, funded by the Ministry of Economics, and the Institute of Tax Revenue, funded by the Ministry of Finance, both training students to take on specialized and technical assignments in government offices.[11]

Despite the somewhat uneven quality of some of these programs, the surviving institutions of the 1930s represented an elite sector of business education. Only a small number of students were able to afford the tuition, and no more than several hundred new degrees were conferred each year in commerce. Some went on to attain significant achievements: Xu Guanqun, a graduate of the Shanghai College of Commerce, launched his own enterprise and assumed leadership in the "national products movement."[12]

Colleges of commerce, to be sure, were not among the priorities of the Ministry of Education. The ministry suspected, perhaps not without reason, that business colleges were not as academically serious as schools of science or engineering. They did not teach laboratory skills, their intellectual pedigree was low, their canonical texts unproven, and they tolerated low standards and lax student conduct. They were also likely to operate as business enterprises that sold degrees on payment. In the mid-1930s, a combination of hard times and market saturation forced a growing number of business graduates into unemployment. This gave ammunition to the additional charge that business schools relied so heavily upon English language textbooks and translated materials that they failed to prepare their graduates for the reality of business practices in China.

Still, even if it possessed only tenuous relevance to jobs or applicable skills, a bachelor's degree in commerce conferred status. The degree hardly lost value simply because, as the ministry charged, it confirmed the amount of wealth already acquired instead of value that the graduate was thereafter prepared to create.

VOCATIONAL EDUCATION

Western-style colleges and universities in early twentieth-century China could not meet the needs of the younger generation; a large number of them were barred from entering the system. A rough estimation showed that in the 1920s, less than 10 percent of Jiangsu's secondary school students entered college upon graduation.[13] In Shanghai there was, alongside the professional elite, a growing sector of lower middle-class youth, from both rural and urban backgrounds, who were envious of middle-class life yet frustrated about their prospects. The idea of vocational education gained support in this environment. It preached the idea of social advancement through hard work and persistent discipline, and encouraged young people to focus their energy on pragmatic knowledge. Capitalist enterprises would, according to this representation, reward merit and virtue as in the old imperial bureaucracy, albeit in a different way.

The principal promoter of the idea of vocational education was Huang Yanpei, a former minister of the Jiangsu Provincial Bureau of Education and the head of the Jiangsu Provincial Educational Association. Huang was a fervent advocate of "vocational education," a position he had adopted among a wide spectrum of contending pedagogical notions that ultimately linked education to national salvation.[14] Huang envisioned a curricular program featuring business English, mathematics, accounting, and bookkeeping. Traditional literary education had "trained China's youths to play with words but not to respect productive work," Huang lamented. Much of the modern economy of the new century, meanwhile, required that talented youth prepare themselves with pragmatic skills.[15]

Huang Yanpei, a native of Chuansha County, was the son of a merchant. He received a classical education and earned the *juren* degree in 1904. He also worked for several summers in family shops as a clerk. His career in the bureaucratic system was thwarted in 1905, when the imperial court abolished the civil service examinations. Huang then went to Shanghai, where he attended Nanyang College. Nanyang was Sheng Xuanhuai's strategic project (see chapter 1) for training technical and managerial executives for the state-owned railroad lines, steamship companies, telegraph bureaus, mines, and shipyards. Nanyang offered a curriculum with an emphasis on science and engineering, ranging from mathematics and machinery to industrial management. A lot of teaching was carried out in English and Japanese because there were no suitable texts in Chinese; Huang thus learned Japanese along with sciences. He also made the acquaintance of Cai Yuanpei, a teacher at Nanyang and member of Sun Yatsen's secret Revolutionary Alliance.

Huang Yanpei's point of entry into Shanghai's elite circle contrasted in interesting ways with that of Pan Xulun. Pan, the American-educated accountant, achieved wealth and prestige in a new profession, working in Shanghai's English-speaking International Settlement. Huang, a former *juren*, rose through social networking and enterprises that leveraged public causes and political connections. Upon the creation of the Republican government in Nanjing, Cai Yuanpei, a veteran revolutionary, was named the minister of education. The following year, Huang Yanpei was named the minister of education of Jiangsu Province. Huang went to work as an architect of the provincial educational system. He drafted a five-year plan that included eleven provincial secondary schools, seven county schools of agriculture, a school of commerce in Shanghai, and a higher normal school in Nanjing that eventually became, with the full support of the Jiangsu Provincial Educational Association, Dongnan University.[16] He served on the executive board of the association and turned it into a critical organ for his educational vision.

Huang's vision of "vocational education" was fashioned as he traveled inland and struck up conversations with tea growers, pottery makers, herbal doctors, silk merchants, and the like—the literate and pragmatic of the old school. He knew from first-hand experience, of course, the usefulness of skills such as letter-writing, use of the abacus, and bookkeeping in a provincial setting.[17] By contrast, he was skeptical of foreign degrees, fancy advertising campaigns, mail catalogues, and spotless display windows in shops.

In his lecture, "Learning and Career," he affirmed the principle: "All business pursuits need to be based upon science; all learning must derive from facts. . . . In today's world we must work with knowledge. Whether the pursuit is political studies, commerce, engineering, or something else, none should be done without knowledge and learning."[18] Yet he turned the idea of "knowledge" into an empirical grasp of the ongoing business practices in China. Huang declared that the goal of education was neither to turn schools into businesses nor to confer degrees for decorative purposes, but to close the gap between school curriculums and business practices and to elevate the scientific basis of vocational pursuits.

Unlike the business elite in the foreign concessions, Huang Yanpei's educated man of pragmatic knowledge neither dressed in Western suits nor gave cocktail parties in garden mansions. Instead, he shaved his head and wore straw sandals. He would, like the Xindu merchants of old, find frugality and self-effacement appropriate virtues for success. He would immerse himself in business practices on the ground floor, instead of talking up theories and global trends suitable for glossy prints. Huang's formulation of knowledge and virtue apparently appealed to large sectors of Shanghai society, especially those concerned with secondary school students and middle-tier employees—provincial youth with literary aspirations who had no financial resources. The result was the founding of the Chinese Society for Vocational Education (Zhonghua zhiye jiaoyu she; hereafter CSVE) in May 1917.

Huang Yanpei was the principal force in the creation of the society, and was joined by forty-seven others who signed the founding charter. The founding roster was a list of luminaries of national stature, who also had strong connections in Shanghai. At the head of the list was Cai Yuanpei, the former minister of education who was then president of the prestigious Peking University. After Cai were Fan Yuanlian, another former minister of education who had strong ties to the business elite in Tianjin, and Jiang Menglin, a future president of Peking University and minister of education. Other signatories included Ma Xiangbo, the founder of the Catholic Aurora University, Yu Rizhang, the Chinese general secretary of the YMCA, Shi Liangcai, the publisher of *Shenbao,* Zhang Yuanji, a Hanlin scholar and the publisher of the Commercial Press, Guo Bingwen, president of the government-funded Shanghai College of Commerce, Qian Xinzhi, chairman of the state-held Bank of Communications and president of the Shanghai General Chamber of Commerce, Song Hanzhang, a veteran of the money guild and the general manager of the Shanghai branch of the Bank of China, Mu Ouchu, the founder of a leading textile firm, Nie Yuntai, a liberal entrepreneur who was also a member of Governor-general Zeng Guofan's family, and scores of other deans and administrators of Chinese-funded universities.[19] Cursory background research would suggest that this handful of individuals represented a sizable sector of China's progressive-looking and interconnected coastal elite who held strategic positions in finance, manufacturing, publishing, education, and the news media in the early twentieth century.

The CSVE's first order of business was the establishment of a secondary school, the Chinese School of Vocational Education (Zhonghua zhiye jiaoyu xuexiao), that taught basic sciences, Chinese and foreign languages, business skills, and the making of machine-manufactured products. The first class of July 1918 enrolled eighty students, all recent graduates of Shanghai's primary and junior high schools. The school's first major undertaking was to buy several acres of land beyond the old southwestern gate of the Nanshi district and construct several buildings with a total of fifty-some rooms. Life was similar to other schools: students attended classes, went to the libraries, carried out laboratory experiments, took up residence in the dormitories, and staged dining hall protests against the kitchen staff over the quality of their meals.[20] In addition, they took up various assignments in school factories for hands-on training. These factories manufactured machine tools, furniture, buttons, and enamel. Machine and furniture workshops were opened, because school surveys showed that these skills had strong presence in Nanshi. Buttons and enamel were selected, because there were no such Chinese products with significant market position. Twenty years later, the school proudly announced that it had successfully driven foreign buttons and enamel products out of the Chinese market.[21] The school's career guidance department eventually expanded to serve the entire city. In the mid-1930s, the Chinese School of Vocational Education placed over three-quarters of its graduates in an array of jobs.[22]

To provide opportunities for vocational training in a white-collar setting, Huang Yanpei entered into a three-way agreement with the banker Qian Xinzhi and the American-trained educator Guo Bingwen in August 1921. Both men were heads of state-funded modern enterprises that reported respectively to the Ministry of Communications and the Ministry of Economics. The collaboration produced the Shanghai Society for Supplementary Education in Commerce, which gave vocational school students access to college-level courses along with internships at member businesses in the Shanghai General Chamber of Commerce.[23] From his study report we learn that a Shanghai teenager of modest means, Sun Jianqiu, interned at the Tongchang Bicycle Shop in the summer of 1936. He studied the shop's business (importing and servicing bicycles and parts from the United States) and management (bookkeeping, accounting, accounts receivable, credit, wholesale, retail, mail catalogues, and so on) and published a report in the school journal.[24] Other students of the vocational school interned at the Xinhua Savings Bank, the Commercial Press, and the Shanghai Ferry administration and similarly produced reports about their findings. These reports are among the earliest ones that we have from institutionalized arrangements that encouraged Chinese students to conduct "field visits" as part of their school work.[25]

A third CSVE operation was the creation of evening schools and continuing education programs, launched in collaboration with the Federation of Nanjing Road Merchants, a store owners' association. The store owners paid five *yuan* for each of their workers, who went to the CSVE to take courses on abacus use, English, and math. Other after-work programs were created for the clerks of the Maritime Customs Service, the National Goods Department Store, and the Guanshengyuan Food Company. These programs brought young employees into contact with their peers and freed them, no matter how fleetingly, from personal dependency on their masters, as in the old apprenticeship system.[26]

The CSVE reached out far and wide to form networks, leverage resources, borrow ideas, and promote its programs. It printed several journals including *Jiaoyu yu zhiye* (Education and Career) that specialized in pedagogical theories about vocational education. It published monthly reports, weekly newsletters, and series of books. It ran public lectures in multiple cities. It collaborated with several colleges of commerce to organize lectures on commercial law, government bonds, investing, banking, money shops, statistics, pricing, advertising, international trade, financial institutions, and so forth.[27] It dispatched study missions to the United States, Japan, and provincial China. Huang Yanpei toured Manchuria and Southeast Asia, inspecting trade and industrial schools run by the Japanese, the British, the French, and the Dutch.[28] Much like a state planner of a later day, Huang Yanpei thought "big" on behalf of his mission. He was, however, operating in a private context and had to respond to the manifested needs of his organization.

Huang Yanpei led the CSVE with vigor and resourcefulness. He had the support of the new business elite, and the programs grew as demand increased.[29] The CSVE occupied a critical niche between the business schools and the new firms, teaching pragmatic skills and business knowledge that ranged from the general to the technical.

When the society celebrated its thirtieth anniversary in 1947, it was able to publish an alumni roster with no fewer than ten thousand names. Amidst all its accomplishments, there was but one problem. The skills that the CSVE taught led to jobs but not status—a much less tractable thing that sometimes came only with properly conferred academic degrees. The CSVE's very effort to place the "vocational youth" in a school-like environment and to erase the boundaries between work and study, it turned out, often worked paradoxically to increase rather than reduce lower middle-class ambivalence towards those who owned status without ever having had to work for it.

A NEW VOCABULARY

The massive compilation *Shangye shiyong cidian,* which appeared in 1935, testified to the richness of *shangxue* and the liveliness of imagination supporting its growth. It listed more than ten thousand entries and contained over 1.4 million characters in explanatory texts. The compiler, Chen Jiaxuan, was a senior editor with the Shanghai Commercial Press. Chen enlisted the help of two colleagues at the press, and the three set to work on the project in 1930. The team worked steadily over the next five years. They produced a dictionary that they hoped would capture the transformation of the Chinese commercial idiom in the full context of the relevant legal, political, economic, and commercial institutions since the end of the Opium War.[30]

The compilers consulted comparable dictionaries in English and Japanese extensively. This was necessary because so many terms had been borrowed from these languages. The editors then culled a large number of government gazettes and, in the spirit of *diaocha* (investigation), sent out letters to various chambers of commerce and local merchant groups to inquire about customary practices throughout the country.

Several factors combined to contribute to the multiplication of Chinese business terms. Modern renditions of commercial terms, the editors noted, had varied from place to place and translator to translator. Each time a new law was drafted or a new economic theory was introduced, a large number of new terms were introduced into the language. The creation of new departments in the government and new merchant organizations, similarly, led to the coinage of new expressions. Given the regional diversity of China, the challenge to map overlapping meanings was enormous. Thousands of terms had circulated without commonly recognized meanings—the result of different Chinese dialects, divisions in the field of economic theories, the ongoing revisions of old laws and the drafting of new ones, and the steady departure from traditional practices in society. It thus became necessary to collect, record, and explain these terms as comprehensively as possible in the hope that a standardized usage would emerge.

The editors arranged their work in a number of categories.[31] Some terms in the dictionary were direct borrowings and phonetic renditions of foreign words: *kateer* for cartel, *qiaokeli* for chocolate, and *beni huaituo* for the English penny weight. Others, such as *can guohuo* (products funded or manufactured in China or under Chinese ownership, but involving imported materials or foreign investment), reflected the preoccupation in the 1930s with the exact "national content" of the *guo-huo* (national products).

The longest listings in the dictionary came under terms that began with the character *shang* (commerce). There were 105 such entries, many with long explanatory texts, which filled nearly twenty pages. A small number of terms (for example, *shangren* for merchants, *shanglü* for traveling merchants, *shangye* for business, *shangbu* for commercial town, *shanggang* for trading ports, *shangdian* for shop) would have been known to merchants and literate men of an earlier generation. But these "natural" descriptive terms of an earlier time had since been defined in twentieth-century law and had acquired changed meanings.

The codification of commercial laws introduced a significant number of new terms.[32] Merchant activities similarly gave rise to another cluster of new usages.[33] Both the state and the merchant created new organs and offices for various tasks.[34] New objects, concepts, methods, and processes appeared in business. Political commentators, social critics, and economic theorists thought of wealth and money in new ways and began pronouncing on social problems in economic terms.[35] A multitude of new schools appeared so that people could learn about the history of business *(shangye shi)* or geography for commerce *(shangye dili).*[36] As seen throughout the pages of a single dictionary, the rise of new commerce in early twentieth-century China was accompanied by major shifts in both culture and language.

"WHAT IS A SHOP?"

Unlike Chen's dictionary, Zhang Shijie's encyclopedic 1936 compilation, *Shangren baojian* (Precious Mirror for the Merchant), is framed as a manual for the shopkeeper. After some disquisition about the differences between wholesale, retail, and brokerage, the manual delves into the subject of "commercial management" and proceeds to offer instructions about important do's and don'ts. Do make sure that your clerks are clean-shaven, courteous, healthy, and alert. Do make them wash and change as often as possible, show their interest, and hide boredom. Keep the shop free of all mud, dirt, garbage, bugs, and cobwebs. No food odors or noise of children running or yelling. Do not haggle with your customers over prices. Do not underestimate the less well-dressed. Do be sure to pay your clerks well so that they will not wear a sour expression.

Keeping the shop spotlessly clean is fundamental, but what really matters is how you decorate it. Basic matters consist of lighting (ample), windows (large), display (focused), and space (plenty). The point is to maximize the visibility of goods and to minimize the crowding of people. A well-decorated shop presents a theme and creates ambiance. It impresses, entertains, entices, and pleases, all at once. It ultimately directs the customers' gaze to quality items of the highest price range.

A well-decorated shop realizes its value only when customers walk through its doors. No expense must be spared, therefore, when it comes to the dressing of the shop fronts and the windows. In addition, advertising is important, whether it appear in print, on billboards, buses, cigarette packages, the radio, or via any other medium. As the shop can only be at one place and prospective customers are everywhere, advertising must do an effective job to project the store's presence and draw customers in. Along with good hygiene, an impeccable reputation, and aesthetically pleasing décor, advertising as a science of customer psychology will multiply the value of the merchandise and transform the nature of shopkeeping.[37]

Other sections in Zhang's manual take up other subjects. A modern shop makes use of all sorts of new equipment. These include the telephone, the cash register, the pictograph, the "Lamson carriers," the typewriter, the stenographic machine, the "checking signature machine," the "telegraphone," the letter opener, the postage stamp affixer, the address machine, the blackboard, the bookkeeping machine, the time recorder, the time stamp, the "comptu-card," the loose leaf inserter, the flexible steel ruler, the carbon paper, the copying press, the copy printer, the revolving duplicator, the mimeograph, the pencil sharpener, and the paper fastening machine.[38] A modern shop manager must possess knowledge about all sorts of things: commercial law, customary law, bookkeeping, business correspondence, business memos, means and weights, currency exchange rates, banking, transportation, customs, tariffs, and tax regulations. The *Shangren baojian* compiled the law codes based on government bulletins. It also filled its pages with articles reprinted from newspapers, journals, vocational school textbooks, and public lectures. The final section listed schedules, fares, routes, and regulations for shipping and traveling by trains, ships, and airplanes.

The manual went into its fourth printing even as war broke out in Shanghai and bombs blew a twenty-foot crater in the middle of the city's fanciest shopping district. It was unclear whether Shanghai's shop owners—the majority ran their businesses by pinching, scrimping, crowding, and short-changing—were reviewing the instructions. The *Baojian* suggested not only that commerce is science, but also that shopping is pleasure; a modern merchant is a sophisticated person, and a properly managed shop is a work of art and science. The shop, in short, is a microcosm of the best that the material world, in an advanced state, has to offer. A good merchant, who answers to the state as well as to the public, is its maker and owner. Customers are to be manipulated for their own pleasure. With advertising and décor, the merchant uses images and ambiance to transform his shop floor. The ultimate measures of his success or failure, of course, are the sales figures. For the wheel of commerce to keep on spinning, customers must be made to pay so that the world of pleasure and sophistication can carry on.

NATIONALIST "PARTIFICATION" AND THE LEGAL SPACE

In 1927 the Nationalist Party took power in Nanjing. The new regime mounted a campaign to "Partify" *(danghua)* colleges and universities through its declared political doctrine, the *Three Principles of the People.* It also organized Party cells and opened up departments of political education on college campuses. Through the Ministry of Education, the state handed down rules and devised means to assert direct control over key aspects of academic operation. The ministry assumed the function of accreditation, and instituted review and reporting requirements that went beyond the initial evaluations of funding and curriculums. Colleges and universities, whether private or public, were required to submit detailed financial and personnel reports on an annual basis. Eventually, the ministry wielded enough power to grant or withhold the final approval on a vast array of matters, ranging from the hiring of individual faculty members to the conferral of academic degrees, and the selection of required texts in certain disciplines (such as history) to the appointment of university presidents. The punishment for institutional noncompliance was either the suspension of permission to recruit new students or government non-recognition of graduate degrees. Few universities could afford to defy and still survive. St. John's University in Shanghai was perhaps the most notable exception.

In business operations in the modern sector of the economy, the new regime also adopted measures to enhance the presence of the state. The Ministry of Economics conducted itself both as a regulatory and a planning entity. Business enterprises had to present papers to the ministry in order to receive recognition as a corporation. They also had to submit quarterly reports on finance, shareholding, board meetings, and executive appointments. In addition, they filed applications for permits or permissions on matters that pertained to quotas, shipments, import of machinery, methods of payment, content of goods, and so forth. The state, in short, demanded a wealth of information and routinely required the submission of detailed minutes and explanations of resolutions adopted in executive sessions or board of director meetings.

State initiatives like these, to the extent that they certified quality and enhanced trust in the public domain, were no doubt legitimate in a modern society. What seemed dubious about Nationalist practice in the 1930s, however, was the close connection that the regime forged between the accreditation of schools and the incorporation of companies, which in turn was linked to the certification of professionals such as accountants, auditors, tax planners, and legal advisors. Those who held academic degrees from schools without Nationalist accreditation, for example, were not eligible for positions in state-managed enterprises or government offices that required such credentials. Those who prepared financial statements yet had not received Nationalist certification as accountants risked compromising the companies they worked for. The Nationalist government required that a duly incorporated business employ only certified professionals. To receive such certification, it was not enough that a professional possess training and work experience; it was imperative that the individual received such training from a state-accredited school or had previous experience with a state-managed or incorporated enterprise. Rules and laws of accreditation, incorporation, and certification, through a variety of means, triangulated to reinforce each other in practice. The result was that the state became a significant presence in the distribution of employment opportunities and the operations of businesses.

STATE CERTIFICATION: A TALE OF ACCOUNTING

In June 1935, Tang Yi'e, a thirty-eight-year-old man from Changsha, applied to the Nationalist government for a certificate to practice as an accountant. Tang had earned a bachelor's degree in political and economic studies from the Henan Public Institute of Law and Political Studies. He had also worked, for over two years, in the accounting department of the Jiangxi provincial government's bureau of finance. Tang thus was among a select group of educated men who had earned a college-level academic degree with an economic focus. He had also met the requirement of a minimum of two years' accounting experience in a government office or with a registered corporation. In other words, he met the "academic qualifications" and "work experience" criteria as spelled out in

Article 3 of the 1931 *Kuaijishi tiaoli,* "statutes and guidelines regarding the certification of the accountant." Like scores of others each year, Tang composed a petition, filled out the forms, drew up his curriculum vitae, had two photographs taken, purchased a money order for fifty-one *yuan* from the Bank of China, assembled as many official documents as seemed relevant, and submitted his application to the Ministry of Economics in Nanjing.

There was only one flaw to this otherwise perfect application. The ministry required the original official documents. For his initial application to the Jiangxi provincial government, Tang had submitted his diploma, which was then destroyed when the government building caught fire. There was a full-page report in the local *Nanchang xinwen ribao* (Nanchang Daily News) about the fire, and Tang attached the clipping. Since he had no copy of his diploma, Tang submitted a variety of documentation to prove his credentials.

First, there was a statement of proof prepared by the Jiangxi provincial government, which gave a full list of all materials lost in the fire and included Tang's diploma. This statement came as a formal resolution adopted by the provincial government in its two-hundred-and-fortieth executive meeting and had been submitted to the Ministry of Interior.

Second, there was a catalog prepared by the Jiangxi Provincial Review Board, which listed the names and academic backgrounds of the provincial personnel. Tang's name and credentials were listed here.

Sometime after the fire, the Jiangxi government organized a civil service examination to recruit prospective district magistrates for the province, and Tang had signed up for the exams. In lieu of the destroyed diploma, he submitted a letter signed by Hu Dingyi, the former president of Tang's alma mater. Hu's personal knowledge of the former undergraduate made it possible for him to certify that Tang had indeed graduated from the college with a degree in economics. The Jiangxi Examination Board printed a yearbook on this occasion and listed Tang's name and degree, along with those of all the other applicants. This yearbook was included in Tang's submission to the Ministry of Economics.

Tang was apparently successful in the provincial exams, and began working for the Jiangxi government thereafter. In September 1930, the secretariat of Jiangxi published its first edition of the *Provincial Government Directory,* listing the names of all officials and their degrees. Tang took his place along with his colleagues.

There was little question that Tang had worked as an official for the Jiangxi provincial government since 1931. But as the formal diploma was missing, the Ministry of Economics referred the application to the Ministry of Education.

In 1928, the Ministry of Education had ordered that all colleges and universities register for accreditation. To be eligible for registration, an institution had to comply with certain guidelines, including, most famously, the requirement that all college presidents be Chinese nationals. A properly registered institution would thereafter make annual submissions of specified information, including lists of students and diplomas awarded. The ministry would thus maintain a "master file" of all properly conferred degrees.

When Tang's case came before the ministry, the latter was unable to respond. The founding and registration of the Henan Public Institute of Legal and Political Studies had taken place prior to 1927—before the founding of the Nanjing government itself. The Ministry of Education therefore forwarded Hu Dingyi's letter to the Henan provincial government, which in turn forwarded it to the provincial bureau of education.

The initial response from the bureau was disappointing. Their files were in such a state of disarray that officials were unable to look up any information that dated more than a few years back—and Tang's degree had been issued almost eighteen years prior, in 1917. The review board at the Ministry of Economics held its fourth meeting over Tang's application and made little progress.

And then word came from Henan—perhaps someone had gone to visit the institute. The province reported that the school had had no economics major in 1917. Moreover, the former president, Hu Dingyi, whose signature appeared on the letter of proof on Tang's behalf in November 1929, had died in 1919.

On receiving this information, the Ministry of Economics not only denied Tang Yi'e's application to be an accountant; it declared him a fraud. It rejected his application and returned an assembled total of eleven documents. It sent a request to the Henan provincial government that Tang's letter of proof, which bore the seal of inspection from the Jiangxi District Magistrate Examination Board, be nullified at once. It also notified the Jiangxi provincial government and requested that Tang be duly discredited, expunged from the government registry, and have his qualifications reevaluated.

Tang's story was not the only horror story in the ministry archives. There were many other accounts of unsuccessful applications on a variety of grounds. Some of these had to do with matters of substance: insufficient length of time working as an accountant, not enough responsibility as an accountant in previous positions, and so forth. Other rejections concerned technicalities: current or past employers had not properly registered with the ministry under the corporation code (*gongsi lü*), degrees were issued from institutions not recognized by the Ministry of Education, or applicants had graduated without sufficient credits in accounting or economics. It was often hard to distinguish between the matters of substance and the technicalities. An application's "technical" failings, moreover, were often beyond an applicant's power to correct. From time to time, an applicant was not only rejected, but also found himself having to prove to the state that he actually was who he said he was. It should come as no surprise, then, that of the eighty-some cases of applications in 1935, only a handful received certification as accountants.

THE ASSOCIATION AND THE STATE

When the Nationalists took power in 1927, civic organizations that were active prior to that date suffered serious disruptions. The Jiangsu Provincial Educational Association was ordered to dissolve. Dongnan University, the association's principal project, was taken over by the Nationalists and reorganized under the Ministry of Education to become Central University.

The CSVE, as discussed earlier in this chapter, drew on the resources of the Shanghai General Chamber of Commerce and the Jiangsu Provincial Educational Association and was one of the strongest expressions of societal associative capacity. Organizationally, the CSVE consisted of an executive secretariat staffed by full-time employees and a board of directors elected by the fee-paying members. In 1917 there were nearly eight hundred individual members. Twenty years later this number grew to exceed twenty-three thousand.[39]

From the very beginning, membership dues hardly met the Society's needs for various sorts of expenditure. During the first decade of the CSVE's existence, Huang Yanpei, who had twice declined to serve as the minister of education, persuaded the government in Beijing to subsidize about half of the society's annual budget. Another source of support came from the Chinese Cultural and Educational Foundation (Zhonghua wenhua jiaoyu jijin hui) that was under the Ministry of Foreign Affairs.[40]

The CSVE weathered the transition to the Nationalist government and reemerged after a hiatus. It was allowed to remain in operation and even continued to receive state subsidies. In exchange, the CSVE agreed to comply with Nationalist registration requirements as specified by the

Ministry of Education. It revised its charter and agreed to locate its head office *(zonghui)* in the Nationalist government's capital city, wherever that was to be. It also agreed that no individual who had previously opposed the *Three Principles of the People,* the founding doctrines of the Nationalist Party as explicated by Sun Yatsen, was ever to be eligible for CSVE membership.[41]

Later developments would show that the energy and dynamics nurtured by the CSVE under its various programs often lay beyond the control of both the administrators and the regulators. CSVE students, for instance, read *Shenghuo Weekly,* the society's organ, which became, in the aftermath of the Manchurian Incident in September 1931, one of the most stridently patriotic voices demanding an immediate armed resistance against the Japanese (see chapter 5). In the 1930s CSVE students organized their own military training exercises and volunteered for war efforts. In 1935, at the height of the urban mass mobilization for national salvation, the "vocational youth" joined college students, university professors, urban professionals, and "women" in publishing their own bulletins and electing association officers.[42]

The Nationalist government responded in various ways either to co-opt or to suppress the pro-war demonstrations unleashed by the National Salvation Movement. The Chinese Communist Party, meanwhile, seized the opportunity to recruit anti-government activists and enlarge its membership. During the war in the 1940s, many former CSVE students crossed behind Japanese lines to join the Nationalist or Communist troops in southern Anhui and northern Jiangsu. Just as many remained in Shanghai or took up positions as accountants, bookkeepers, printers, or mechanics in other parts of China.

Nationalist government intervention with the CSVE produced inconclusive results. What seems clear, however, was that when proper means and strategies became available, neither the Nationalists nor the Communists would pass up the opportunity to build their influence among the CSVE following.

THE STATE IN ECONOMY

Economic historians of late imperial China have argued that under the Qing there was considerable freedom in the conduct of economic affairs. The imperial governments of the Ming and the Qing had done little to interfere with market freedom. There was plenty of movement of labor and goods in response to market information. Few legal restrictions existed, furthermore, to either constrain the transactions of property or the choice of a profession. The Chinese people, in short, had long been permitted by the state to pursue profit-seeking activities as opportunities arose.

Legal scholars have noted, meanwhile, that in the area of law, traditional Chinese governments had been equally hands-off toward the conduct of commerce and the affairs of the marketplace. Prior to the promulgation of the 1903 *shangfa*, mercantile affairs hardly appeared in the law books except in the context of a criminal offense. Merchants everywhere went about their business following the customary practices established by the guilds and the associations. These rules of "customary law" did not become formalized until the twentieth century, when the new Republican authorities, continuing a trend started by the New Policies reformers, sought to encode the rules and to reorganize the institutions of governance.

It was thus a recent development and a rather dramatic departure from China's long historical culture that, by the second half of the twentieth century, Chinese economy had become one of the most heavily regulated and tightly planned in the world. Despite the ideological split that separated the Nationalists from the Communists, the new concepts of *shangxue* and *shangfa* that arose under the former contributed, wittingly or not, to the rise of standardized economic regulations and centralized enforcement mechanisms under both Party-states. State control of professional education, vocational training, corporate licensing, business registration, and so forth, all central to the development of a modern economy, straddled the regime shift in 1949. What had begun in the early twentieth century, with the support of merchant associations and civic initiatives, as the pursuit of new knowledge and self-definition on the part of the merchants, was ultimately to set in motion the rise of an economistic state of centralized planning.

CHAPTER 3

Visual Politics
and Shanghai Glamour

Hu Xueyan passed a clothier's shop one day and caught sight of an attractive young woman leaning by the entrance. He stopped to look at her; she turned away and shut the door. Displeased, Hu Xueyan sent a go-between to the clothier. Hu offered seven thousand *yuan*. The clothier gave in and Hu took the woman as his concubine.

On the wedding day Hu Xueyan threw an extravagant banquet and entertained a large number of guests. At the end of the evening he went into the bridal chamber. He broke open a new jug of wine and sipped alone. After he had had enough to drink he ordered the bride to take off her clothes and lie naked in bed. Hu ordered a male servant to follow him, holding high a tall candle thicker than the arm that gave out brilliant light. Hu moved about and encircled the bed multiple times, viewing and gazing from all angles. After a long while he stroked his beard and gave out a gratified laugh. He said to the woman: "You spurned my gaze the other day. How did you like it at this moment?" With that, he hastened out of the chamber and spent the remainder of the night in the quarters of another concubine.

At dawn Hu sent a maid to the bride with a message. "Take anything you'd wish from this chamber. Leave and marry someone else. There is no room in my house for you."

The bride did what she was told and hauled away objects that were worth over twenty thousand pieces in gold. She returned to her father and the clothier became a very wealthy man.

—*Li Boyuan, "Hu Xueyan," Nanting biji (1906)*

In the year 1853 the Taiping rebels burst through the mountain passes of southwestern China and poured down the Xiang River valley. They sacked Wuhan, the imperial stronghold in the upper Yangzi, and emptied out the governor-general's office, which contained over two million taels of silver. Thus fortified, rebel forces charged eastward to take town after town, the ranks of their followers swelling into the tens of thousands. They captured Nanjing, declared it the capital of the "Heavenly Kingdom of Great Peace," and went on to take Suzhou, the seat of the governor-general of the lower Yangzi. The Suzhou elite, famed for their poetry, refinement, titles, and wealth consisting of silk, rice, silver, and copper coins, fled before the charging rebels. Many sought refuge in

Shanghai, doubling the city's population and necessitating the creation of new offices that regulated hygiene, housing, public works, and relief in the concessions.

On a fine spring day in 1856, Ge Yuanxu, one such Suzhou aristocrat who had fled his hometown, strolled through a seasonal market near Nanshi. He found himself gazing through the bars of wooden cages and reinforced crates at parrots, cranes, mandarin ducks, peacocks, deer, and leopards. The produce stalls offered a splendid display of harvest colors: grapes, lychees, honey tangerines, almonds, cashews, dates, prunes, chestnuts, and pomegranates. There were also imported plants, trees, fish, birds, fruits, and nuts, often with perplexing foreign names containing multiple syllables.[1] The market seemed to have everything: ginseng and chocolate, clocks and seal stones, glass balls and sutra beads, and anatomical drawings and acupuncture charts. The goods enriched restaurant menus and cuisine selections, added interest to homes and gardens, introduced new prescriptions for medical cures and happiness, and, by and large, enhanced the imagination for consumption.[2]

The emporium, a place of abundance, incongruity, variety, and exoticism, consisted of hundreds of stalls and booths and was the setting of proud discoveries, intricate bargaining, triumphant conclusions, and, in some cases, recurrent patronage and long-standing relationships.

In emulation of life, art albums appeared. They contained disparate assemblages of pictures that displayed a wide range of styles and techniques—a visual mélange of shapes, lines, forms, and colors. There were pictures that depicted plants, flowers, birds, and animals rarely seen before, possibly inspired by illustrations used in merchandise catalogues in the Guangzhou trade. There were those that juxtaposed depictions of real objects with images of demons, spirits, fairies, and ghosts. Some drawings showed blue-eyed figures capped, collared, cuffed, decorated, buckled, caped, and booted. Other drawings offered introspective portraits of dark-haired subjects with shaven foreheads and long queues, returning a viewer's gaze like the image in a mirror.[3] Many drawings told historical stories and reported news. They depicted the fury of modern firearms, the rowdiness of marketplaces, the outlandishness of foreign things, the grandeur of public ceremonies, and so forth. The best-known painter of this genre was probably Wu Youru, whose three-volume set depicted the city's "hundred trades," "hundred sights," and "hundred beauties," in addition to various events.[4] These volumes, lithographed and published, distributed images of Shanghai far and wide.

The local people, meanwhile, behaved in ways that raised eyebrows.

Shanghai's "good-for-nothing" ruffians sold beef and "blatantly" displayed cut-up oxen parts despite long-held Buddhist sensitivities. Their customers used knives and forks and ate steak medium rare. Contemporary reactions to elaborate meals of steak and wine seemed evenly divided between labored admiration for the etiquette and involuntary horror at the cuisine.

The city's mercantile rich, in blatant disregard for sumptuary laws and modesty, donned silk, fur, jewels, and jade, and had horse-drawn carriages attended to by private entourages.[5] They frequented the pleasure quarters, gave lavish banquets of shark-fin soup and lamb chops, and struck deals in the company of women. Their "retained" ladies wore diamonds and jeweled wristwatches, and rode with men in open coaches through the busiest sections in town. These women put such exquisite care into their appearance that they began new fashion trends, from makeup and hairstyles to jewelry, watches, shoes, and clothing.[6]

At the turn of the last century, cross-dressing and costume plays came into vogue.[7] With the establishment of the first women's schools in Shanghai, even daughters from gentry families began unbinding their feet, attending social events, and conversing with men.[8] Diplomats and Westernizers approved of such trends. Sheng Xuanhuai's numerous daughters, who added prestige to the exclusive McTyeire School, were among the first to convert to the Protestant faith, to insist on monogamy, and, eventually, to sue their brothers for an equitable share of their father's vast estate.

Women featured largely in the gossip columns and exposé fiction produced by a new breed of professional voyeurs who wrote for the city's emerging publishing industry.[9] Guidebooks contained detailed reviews of what to see, where to dine, what to order, and where to stay—essentially advising how to hold on to one's purse strings and not act like a country bumpkin. In the late 1890s local gazettes periodically sponsored beauty contests and ranked the women in the pleasure quarters according to—as we would say today—"customer satisfaction."[10] By the 1920s leading magazines such as *Liangyou* devoted full sections to the photo portraits of "college queens." In the eyes of many, Shanghai's grandest "spectacle" was the figurative consumption of women and the commodification of their public image.

But the "spectacular" nature of Shanghai derived ultimately from the presence of the Europeans, who built the city and created the space in which these women found their new place. The authorities of the International Settlement, through the adoption of municipal codes, did much to regulate civilian conduct on the street and at public places. The municipal law required, for example, that all carriages slow down when crossing a narrow bridge. No one was allowed to stop a cab or cart in the middle of a road, to dig a ditch, or pave over a road without first notifying the police. All vehicles were required to light lamps after sunset. No one was to dump garbage or urinate on the street. Venders and peddlers could not shout their way across town or park their stands at the doorways of trading firms. It was against the municipal code to sell unlicensed alcohol, spoiled fish or meat, or wild animals either on the street or in teahouses. No fireworks, gambling, brawling, fighting, or noisy arguing was permitted, either on the street or in teahouses. It was against the law to hold live poultry by the feet when transporting them. It was also against the law to break off the branches of trees or plants growing on public property.[11]

The Europeans, in short, had built a place of a different order. Apart from all the imported items—birds, animals, prints, pictures, cameras, telescopes, printing presses, anatomical knives, light bulbs, detergents, gramophones, and moving pictures—Shanghai was a spatially re-imagined place of clock towers, church steeples, park greens, paved roads, street lights, tramways, domed tops, vaulted ceilings, stepped entrances, colonnaded fronts, and steel and cement structures that housed images of the Madonna and child. Functionally and organizationally, in addition to the trading houses, banking offices, docks, warehouses, clubs, hostels, and waterfront bars, there were fire stations, schools, newspapers, printing houses, churches, police stations, court houses, consular offices, and a municipal council. Eventually, in the shade of mature trees, there were also cemeteries containing the remains of the inhabitants from previous generations.

SHANGHAI FROM AFAR

At the turn of the last century, educated young men contemplated the lure of Shanghai from behind the high walls of their upper-class compounds in Suzhou. Suzhou's kerosene lamps were ten times brighter than the oil lamps used elsewhere in China's interior. Yet the electric street lights in Shanghai's concessions were ten times brighter still. In Suzhou, the well-informed learned about the world by reading newspapers printed elsewhere, which took up to a week just to reach the county seat. In Shanghai, every person on the street could hear breaking news the same day.

One fictional account tells of Master Yao, a respectable provincial degree-holder *(juren)* from Suzhou, who takes his son and three disciples,
all of old-stock gentry, to Shanghai on a study tour.[12] Upon their arrival
in the International Settlement, the group has breakfast in a teahouse,
during which Master Yao announces his planned curriculum. They are
to meet with fellow scholars and students, browse in bookstores and publishing houses, tour new-style schools, listen to a presentation of "Suzhou
storytelling" in tea gardens, and attend theater performances. After the
evening play they will have supper, which is also to be an educational
experience as they plan to sample different cuisines, especially "Western
food." The weekends are for sightseeing in and around Shanghai. They
will ride in horse-drawn carriages and explore every inch of the city, from
the avenues to the back alleyways. They are also to go to the Zhang Garden (Zhang Yuan) to hear public speeches and to join the gentry rally.[13]

Someone comes by to sell the daily *Shenbao, Xinwenbao,* and *Hubao*
newspapers as the group finishes breakfast. Just as they begin reading, a
quarrel breaks out at the next table. A young woman, casually dressed
and wearing cheap jewelry, sits in the company of three men. She has
been sharing the same pot of tea with them. She begins to speak excitedly in a raised voice.[14] Once a student, she is now the mistress of the
man sitting opposite her at the table, who works as a clerk in a European trading firm. Their companions are a coach driver, who had introduced the couple for a fee, and a runner on the detective squad of the
Shanghai Municipal Police. The young woman pounds on the table to
underscore her argument, the many gold bangles on her wrist jangling
together. Soon after, she jumps to her feet, grabs her estranged lover by
his vest, and the two begin struggling with one another. The detective
tries to separate them, but has no success. With the help of the coach
driver he drags both of them down to the street, where two waiting policemen, "one Chinese and the other a foreigner with red turban and dark
face,"[15] promptly step forward. The episode ends with the couple being
taken to appear before the foreign magistrate of the concession court.

Master Yao tries to rush his students away from this scandalous scene
in the teahouse. But before that happens, a tall man walks up the stairs
and steps inside. All eyes turn to this man, who appears to be Western.
He has a sunburned face, carries a walking stick, and wears a suit and
brown leather shoes. A man by the name of Huang Guomin (literally
"yellow countryman") hails from a corner table; this man is wearing a
cotton gown with patched holes. The suited man joins the gowned one,
removing his straw hat to reveal a "full head of hair tied into a bun, rather

different from the short hair of the foreigners." Instead of a Westerner, the newcomer is but "a transformed Chinese."[16]

The Westernized person speaks of his transformation. "Ever since my adoption of Western-style clothing, I have changed all my habits of eating, drinking, sleeping, and walking."[17] He eats two meals a day and refrains from having snacks in between. He tried taking a cold shower one time and nearly died of it. He tries to take a bath everyday, but has not been altogether successful. He is not sure whether to keep his hair long or cut it short, and he is confused about which the foreigners believe is more hygienic.

The two episodes in the teahouse share a refrain about the strangeness of Shanghai seen through provincial eyes: women in public, foreigners in the city, and a new breed of Chinese that have adopted Western ways. The state and elite promoted new schools and a new curriculum, the *shangxue* and its declared value of science and patriotism. The teahouse audience nonetheless saw immodesty and transgression, absurdity and humiliation. What to make of the foreign in their midst remained an issue of mixed feelings and uncertainty.

Much of Shanghai's urban history in modern times concerns the efforts made by a Westernizing economic elite, in collaboration with the state, to bring about the indigenization of the foreign and the domestication of novelty. Imported gadgets, so long as they remained "foreign" and "exotic," were occupying only a marginal place in Chinese lives. Goods that had emerged to play a large role in a changed way of life, on the other hand, were those that had necessarily become domesticated in that very process. In the first decades of the twentieth century, with the rise of light industry based in Shanghai, the city's new enterprises invested considerable effort to promote the novel and to tame the strange, to produce the lure of the modern and to soothe unease over the uncomfortable. By the 1920s there were Chinese owners making and selling Western-style hats, walking sticks, leather shoes, handkerchiefs, and suits, along with a multitude of other articles. Meanwhile, a new culture of image-making developed, producing popular advertising campaigns and transforming the visual dynamics of the urban space.

ADVERTISING AND THE MAKING OF NANJING ROAD

In the 1920s, Nanjing Road (then known as Nanking Road), the main thoroughfare in the International Settlement, became a leading shopping street and the home of a new commercial culture.[18] Four major department stores (Sincere, Wing On, the Sun, and Sun Sun) were located on Nanjing Road, in addition to a whole host of makers and retailers of fine jewelry, watches, shoes, hats, satin, fabrics, dresses, suits, children's clothing, eyeglasses, cosmetics, and so forth.[19] Local historians refer to a "Nanjing Road Phenomenon" that combined new designs for shop fronts, new patterns of merchandise displays, new standards of quality assurance, and new attitudes in customer service.[20] These changes reinvented the "shop" much as the manuals advised (see chapter 2) and turned shopping into entertainment. A stroll down Nanjing Road, as the Suzhou gentleman's stroll through the Nanshi market had been a half century earlier, was a pleasure and an experience. Yet the two strolls underscored not only the differences between the seasonal markets of old and the newer fancy shops on municipal blocks, but also that between a predominantly male versus female shopping crowd. The new shops were often housed inside steel and cement buildings with large glass panes. Window shopping became more in fashion, as customers were able to look in from the anonymity of the street without being accosted by the clerks. A whole range of restaurants, bakeries, food companies, theaters, movie houses, and amusement halls established their presence along the way. Shopping acquired certain glamour. It had also shed its dimly unsavory taint so as to permit women from middle-class households to indulge in this pleasure in the company of their "sisterhood."[21]

The leading store that glamorized the shopping experience was no doubt the Wing On Department Store. Wing On was a subsidiary of the Hong Kong Wing On Company that was launched by a group of Cantonese investors who had learned their craft from British department store operators in Sydney. But Wing On was not Shanghai's first retailer offering a diversified line of imports—that distinction belonged to the equally glamorous Sincere Company, which opened in 1916 as an offshoot of two Western-owned shops of limited scale, in operation since the turn of the century.[22] Nor did Wing On spearhead the practice of selling a diversified inventory of household goods. Retailers featuring an assortment of Chinese and Western goods (*hua yang zahuo* or "Chinese-Western miscellany") had already appeared in Shanghai in the mid-nineteenth century. These shops had derived their practice, in turn, from retailers merchandizing an assortment of goods transported across long distance from north and south China—the *Jing Guang zahuo* or "Beijing-Guangzhou miscellany."

Yet when the Shanghai Wing On Company opened its doors for business on September 5, 1918, it surpassed all other retailers in a variety of ways. It occupied a prime location in the International Settlement. It had taken out a thirty-year lease, at fifty thousand *yuan* a year, from Silas Hardoon, a Sephardic Jew who had become Shanghai's leading real estate magnate. And its opening was the culmination of two years of careful planning that included the construction of a four-story building with a basement. It was capitalized at two million Hong Kong dollars, a record figure for a retailer. It featured forty departments with goods that included light industrial products (towels, linen, bath robes, undergarments, soap, toothpaste, electric fans, heaters, kitchen appliances, utensils, dinnerware), clothing and accessories for women, men, and children (fabric, silk, ready-to-wear, scarves, sweaters, hats, shoes, walking sticks), luxury items (jewelry, watches, pens, musical instruments, clocks, radios, cameras, vases, antiques), specialties (ginseng, herbs, Western medicine, tea, alcohol), home furnishing (furniture, rugs, lamps, luggage), and Chinese and Western candy, canned foods, dry goods, and delicacies. The management put much thought into both the organization of the goods into sales departments and to their strategic placement within the store's vertically-differentiated space. There were spatial designs and suggestions, based on the "science" of customer psychology, that were to suggest a purposeful flow instead of the aimless wandering of shoppers.[23]

Wing On's announced distinction, meanwhile, lay not in the diversity of goods that it carried, but in its stocking of *all* valuable brands. While the seasonal markets of the 1860s displayed whatever happened to come their way, Wing On proudly presented itself as the "universal provider." It provided the "hundred goods [*baihuo*] from all around the globe [*huanqiu*]" by casting its shopping net far and wide with the help of its Hong Kong parent company, Shanghai's foreign firms, traveling factory agents, and company buyers in Japan and America. In the past Shanghai retailers had procured their goods from all corners of China. Wing On broke new ground as an active procurer methodically importing from Western Europe, North America, and Japan.

The forty sales and service departments at Wing On were a synergized result that had been studiously managed and astutely commercialized for the realization of the greatest profit potential. In its management, accounting, financing, merchandizing, pricing, advertising, organization, customer service, backend integration, brand name promotion, and the diversification of its operations into real estate, credit service, entertainment, hotels, and restaurants, the company drew on accumulated experiences, customary practices, and European and American models. The "modernity" at Wing On rested on its resolve to be "scientific" in its pursuit of reliable performance and high return. Other department stores on Nanjing Road—Sincere, the Sun, and Sun Sun in particular—followed suit.

These stores of the Republican era were, in that sense, significantly different from the decentralized assemblage of the seasonal markets of Nanshi in the mid-nineteenth century. The earlier emporium, with its random assemblage of live tropical birds and gruesome bear paws, had stimulated the city's visual imagination with its mindless transgression. The makeshift stalls of the late Qing, with minimal overhead costs, opened or folded as circumstances might dictate. The incorporated Wing On, with its neon lights and cluster of buildings in multiple stories, functioned as a tightly managed corporation and became a Shanghai landmark that was there to stay.

In the 1920s foreign imports made up of about three quarters of Wing On's merchandise. Of the imports, the ratio between European and American goods (Palmolive soap, Quaker oats, Kronin powdered milk, Siemens electronics, Parker pens, Philips radios, Context cameras, typewriters, eyeglasses, refrigerators, space heaters, butter, biscuits, canned foods, brandy) versus Japanese products was about four to one. Machine-manufactured goods made in China rarely appeared on the floors of Wing On, where the "Chineseness" in its global construction consisted almost exclusively of handicrafts and local specialties: Suzhou embroidery, Jiangxi porcelain, Fuzhou lacquer, Jinhua ham—an "Orientalized" conception, one might say, of Chinese goods from a Westernized perspective.[24]

Wing On operated Chinese and Western restaurants in its luxury hotel, with bars and amusement halls that featured a variety of shows. Much like le Bon Marché in Paris, Wing On endeavored to create a new kind of environment in which the pleasure of modern shopping was fused with that of dining, drinking, and entertaining. It filled over sixty-four thousand square feet of space with products and consumers, deployed an inventory valued at over five hundred thousand Hong Kong dollars, and engaged the service of four hundred men and women, all with a secondary education.[25] Sales staff spoke multiple Chinese dialects—Cantonese, Wu, and Mandarin—in addition to English and a smattering of Japanese. "The customer," a large neon sign in the store announced in English, "is always right." Wing On abolished the practice of bargaining, permitted the return of purchased items, collected payments upon delivery, extended credit to prized Chinese and foreign patrons, stood behind the quality of its goods, and provided the services of a host of master craftsmen who had been engaged in special house contracts. For those who could afford

Wing On's prices, shopping was transformed into an experience of luxury and entertainment.

To meet the needs of the multilingual commercial environment, Wing On assembled an educated work force that was versed in languages and numbers. It housed them in dormitories, provided them with meals in company dining halls, dressed them in uniforms, set their daily schedules, regulated their conduct, warned them against gambling and unruly behavior, and handed out rewards and punishments in accordance with sales performance evaluations and revenue results. The Kwoks, who controlled Wing On's management, like the Mas, who ran the Sincere Company, were devout Christians educated in English missionary schools. Until the end of the 1920s, they required that employees attend sermons on Sundays when the stores were closed to observe the Sabbath.[26] Wing On was among the first, in 1930, to place women on its sales staff in select departments. The pretty ones created a sensation and acquired nicknames such as "Xishi," the Chinese equivalent of Helen of Troy, or "queen" as was the fashion in missionary colleges. The stationary department had a "queen" selling fountain pens to college dandies. The sweater department, which priced its articles at eighty to ninety *yuan* a piece (at the time a family of four was able to manage on a monthly income of eighteen *yuan*), had a Xishi to model the latest styles. To protect the company's image and reputation, the management nonetheless set stern rules about female respectability. Pregnancy was a condition that often jeopardized career prospects.

The rise of Wing On represented the construction in Shanghai, with professional expertise and institutionalized support, of an incorporated environment that was dedicated to sensory stimulation and material consumption. The company, to be sure, functioned with the able management of a disciplined work force. Yet it prospered not just from the allure of its products, but also from the excitement of shopping that its advertising campaigns and promotional techniques worked to produce. The inauguration of Wing On in September 1917, for instance, began with a grand party. Hundreds of notables and dignitaries were issued invitations to attend a gala reception held on its floors. The party, in turn, was preceded by an intensive newspaper campaign that went on for two weeks, which did much to arouse the public's interest and curiosity, not only about its goods and displays, but also about its bargains. Just as in Émile Zola's novel *The Ladies' Paradise,* where Octave Mouret "revolutionized" nineteenth-century Parisian retail by underselling the smaller, surrounding shop owners—thereby attracting society ladies whose carriages jammed his entrance—Wing On drew a multitude of housewives who came for the cut-rate Jinhua ham: a dried, cured, and flavored delicacy made from the choicest cuts of pork raised on family farms in the central hills of Zhejiang.[27]

Business historians who examined the rise of le Bon Marché have argued that the department store—a "drapery shop" that departed from medieval French guild conventions and carried a diverse range of merchandise—was an expression of emerging machine-manufacturing capacity in the mid-nineteenth century. In an expanding economy of size and scale, le Bon Marché "democratized luxury" by passing on to urban customers the savings that resulted from more efficient manufacturing and distribution techniques.[28]

By contrast, the rise of Wing On—and Sincere—had less to do with the store's connection with domestic Chinese manufacturers than its access to liquid capital and overseas suppliers. In its first two decades of operation, Wing On gave less than 15 percent of its shelf space to Chinese products, which were stocked to address the low end of the pricing structure. A frequent target of public criticism during the anti-foreign boycotts in the 1920s and '30s, Wing On achieved success not by improving the efficiency in the distribution of manufactured products in increased quantity to a larger market; it excelled, instead, both in the packaging of luxury that targeted an exclusive clientele and in the reorganization of sales and advertising that glamorized shopping.

Business historians have argued that the rise of enterprises such as le Bon Marché and Macy's meant a simultaneous decline of old-style retailers, who lost out under heavy competitive pressure. Unable to compete in price, quality, and selection, master-proprietors in Paris and New York, who practiced their craft in family settings with the help of a handful of clerks and apprentices, were left behind in their dark and cheerless workrooms.

In contrast, the rise of Sincere and Wing On appeared to have the opposite effect on small retailers. Instead of pushing them out of business, the department stores inspired entire districts of old shops to modernize their practices and keep up with new trends. Shanghai's master hatters, shoemakers, cosmetic dealers, leather goods manufacturers, silk merchants, fur dealers, tailors, jewelers, umbrella makers, scissors makers, and so forth were spared the fate of Zola's Uncle Baudu or neighbor Bourras. Profiting from the new shopping fad generated by the department stores, old-line retailers transformed their business operations and offered new products. Some made use of imports, while others thrived on their mastery of new Western-inspired techniques such as the tailoring of coats, *qipao*, or suits. They offered services and products at prices that suited the needs of different sectors of the urban population. They also filled the niches—early morning, late evening, Sundays and Western holidays—left open by department stores. The largest single-product retailers on Nanjing Road were the fabric stores Baodaxiang, Xiedaxiang, and Xindaxiang, which each employed about one hundred employees.[29] They addressed the needs of an urban constituency that desired quality and convenience yet were reluctant to pay the price. These shops prospered with the development of niche sales channels. The "backend integration" often went no further than workshops in the back, and stores up front. Yet some cosmetic outlets on Nanjing Road, for example, thrived nonetheless on becoming wholesale suppliers to the provincial hinterland.

Shops on Nanjing Road occupied the top notch in Shanghai's pyramid of consumer culture. Contemporaries observed that by the 1920s, this part of Shanghai gave evidence that it was quite in tune with the latest fashion trends in the world. With the conclusion of the First World War, Chinese students and workers went to Europe and America in growing numbers. [30] They returned home to function as conduits for the dissemination of what they had learned abroad, teaching at fine arts institutes and publishing journals, catalogues, newsletters, or collections with a hefty inclusion of translated articles.[31] Their work brought new resources to an emerging image industry on its way to professionalizing the practice of advertising, painting, photographing, decorating, building, and so forth.

Art Deco images and motifs, for example, traveled from European cities to Shanghai via students, tourists, designers, and patrons. By the 1930s, Art Deco was the style of choice for a multitude of Shanghai's palatial dance halls, theaters, and hotels in the foreign concessions. The Park Hotel, commissioned by a consortium of Chinese bankers (Jinchen, Dalu, Yanye, and Shanghai), was a monumental structure that aimed to make a strong statement. Designed by the Hungarian-born Jewish architect, Ladislaus Hudec, it stood, upon its completion in 1934, as the tallest building in Shanghai, and remained so until the 1980s. Its staff was trained by the Shanghai Baptist College's business school and the CSVE (see chapter 2). As soon as it opened, the cruise industry listed the Park as one of the grand hotels in Asia.[32]

The bustling quality of the shopping district on Nanjing Road—the shops and restaurants vying for customers, the assortment of banners and signs announcing slashed prices and new stock, the eager clerks, paid by commission only, competing for customers—set the scene for numerous photographs. The "Nanjing Road Phenomenon," embedded as it was in the midst of an ever-changing cityscape, was no mere intensification of traditional forms of commercial activities. The printing press, the publishing industry, the use of photographs and the commercialization of art allowed Shanghai merchants to advertise in new ways. They sponsored posters, calendars, billboards, cigarette cards, and advertisements in newspapers and periodicals.[33] Their use of radio programs, model sites, display shows, and neon signs that lit the night sky also transformed the city's popular culture. The "Nanjing Road Phenomenon" was not just about the promotion of goods, but also about the production and consumption of images—a collage of images that was more than the aggregate total of the shops and stores. It was the image industry that transformed Nanjing Road into the locus of a commercial phenomenon—a celebration of sponsored pictures that enabled a mobile and "disembedded" consumption of the glamour and abundance of modernity.[34]

THE IMAGE INDUSTRY

As participants in a business that sought both to entice and to persuade, Shanghai advertisers in the early twentieth century explored multiple strategies. One strategy involved the mobilization of established genres of communication to produce new meanings. Another involved the use of new media to circulate age-old ideas. In both cases the means employed were undeniably "modern," yet the cultural components that supplied the content were of mixed temporal and spatial origins. Technologically and organizationally "modernized," "modern" advertising did not prevent advertisers from circulating clichéd notions. On the contrary, as is the case in most other places in the world, the most effective way to promote novel images was to infuse them with old ideas.

In the second half of the nineteenth century, photography, lithography, and the publication of newspapers combined to alter the way pictures were made, reproduced, and circulated in China.[35] New technology was initially used to make familiar images. Eventually, it broke with the convention of pictorial composition and enabled composition in new visual forms. Pictures and texts were equally important components of a complex tool used to describe and represent the world. They fascinated a wide range of audiences and proved to be particularly effective as a medium of communication with a popular audience.

Photographic portraitures, for instance, initially borrowed the established conventions of ancestral portraits that had long been a feature in
affluent households. Studio portraitures, meanwhile, made use of props
and developed their own conventions of staging.[36] These formulaic
arrangements made their way into advertising posters featuring young
women. Artistically, a compositional "genealogy" thus linked the painted
portraits of ancestors, commonly used on ritual occasions in late imperial times, to the poster images of young women, colorfully represented
for visible display in the Republican era. As common people sought out
the colorful prints to adorn their walls, the stern stares of the ancestors
eventually gave way to the coquettish smiles of young women. The cam-
era was especially instrumental in replacing the stare with the smile in
picture-taking.[37]

The rise of the textile industry in the early twentieth century played
a significant part in the production of images for machine manufacturing. Graphic designs for fabrics, handkerchiefs, pillows, sheets, and quilts
used to be the work of young women embroidering at home. By the 1920s
such designs became part of a larger industrial manufacturing process.[38]
Similarly, the printing industry embraced book covers featuring designs
of photographed or hand-drawn illustrations.[39] They borrowed freely
from European and Japanese image-making techniques to produce works
of mixed genres, producing pictures that mixed figures, landscape, birds,
flora, and calligraphy.

In funding the rise of the image industry, cigarette makers and pharmaceutical companies, with their in-house advertising departments, led
the way. The British American Tobacco Company set up an in-house unit
for advertising production in 1902; their rivals Nanyang and Huacheng
followed suit.

The publishing industry was not far behind. The Shanghai Commercial Press, which dominated the publishing industry with its state-of-the-
art printing machines and sales revenue, engaged Chinese, German, and
Japanese artists to instruct its trainees on the design of book covers and
illustrations. Zhonghua and Kaiming, the former the Commercial Press's
long-standing rival and the latter its emerging one, did the same.[40] Pictorial illustrations gained particular prominence for Kaiming as it developed the niche market of secondary school textbooks and children's
literature. The British American Tobacco Company and the Commercial
Press were the most important enterprises fostering the growth of commercial art in Shanghai. They led in the investment of resources and nurtured a network of image designers who professionalized the practice.

Chemical companies that produced household consumer goods came slightly later, in the late 1920s. The China Chemistry Company advertised heavily in newspapers and magazines. In Tokyo, the same decade witnessed the launching of the cosmetics company Shiseido and the intensive use of colorful pictorial images in the promotion of factory-manufactured beauty products.[41] In Shanghai, the China Chemistry Company used drawings accompanied by texts to promote its brands of mosquito repellent, facial cream, toothpaste, and body lotion. Local businesses in the manufacturing and promotion of fashion products and cosmetics appeared to have barely moved into the machine age. There were no glossy catalogues, as Chinese chemical companies placed their advertisements in newspapers and magazines. As a result, it was the chemical companies, more than the cigarette distributors and the publishing companies, that fostered the careers of cartoonists who excelled in drawings and captions.[42]

By the 1920s independent studios came into existence. They provided designs for shop signs, advertising banners, trademarks, packaging materials, and, in some cases, fabric patterns, filling out company orders and servicing independent merchants.[43] In 1926 Shanghai's first major pictorial magazine, *Liangyou,* was inaugurated. *Liangyou*'s success attested to the viability of a commercial formula that combined photographs and images of young women with a modern outlook of life. In the early 1930s two advertising firms, Huashang and Lianhe, came into being. The firms were partnerships of seasoned commercial artists who preferred autonomy to corporate directives.[44] They accepted contractual engagements from a wide range of business and sought efficiency in artistic production through a methodical system of the division of creative labor.

The most significant visual product, which spearheaded the expansion of cigarettes and soap beyond the Chinese coast, was the calendar poster.[45] Distributed *en masse* as bonus gifts to customers of various products, successful poster designs reached a circulation of tens of millions per image. In the 1930s Shanghai designs penetrated Chinese-speaking markets not only in the Chinese interior, but also in Hong Kong, Singapore, and throughout Southeast Asia.[46]

Of the first generation of Shanghai's commercial designers, both Zhou Bosheng (1887–1955) and Zhou Muqiao (?–1923) trained with Wu Youru at Taohuawu in Suzhou to design traditional woodblock prints.[47] In 1917 Zhou Bosheng moved to Shanghai, where he took a job with the Chinese-owned Nanyang Tobacco Company. Zhou's calendar posters featured female figures in historical costumes, adorned with traditional symbols of felicity and accompanied by clichéd aphorisms of morality. Zhou Muqiao joined Wu Youru's studio after working in Nanshi in southern Shanghai, where he painted shop signs, cigarette cards, and old-fashioned posters for woodblock prints. He too took his images from historical stories, producing series of characters based on dramatized episodes in historical romance. His drawings of opera scenes, often based on *Journey to the West* or *Romance of Three Kingdoms,* featured large casts of characters enacting familiar events.[48] His myriad characters were clearly outlined in bright colors, and were almost always set in busy scenes that overwhelmed viewers with their complexity of composition.

Zheng Mantuo (1885–1959), who was an apprentice at a photo studio (Eryouxuan) in Hangzhou, arrived in Shanghai in 1914. He had learned the technique of etching, with both pencil and charcoal, to sharpen the contours of enlarged or blurred prints of photo portraits through the manipulation of light and texture. In Shanghai, Zheng Mantuo combined this technique with the use of watercolors, producing subtly layered images of modern women dressed in contemporary fashions. Rather than placing these women in busy settings, he situated them inside the tranquility of private gardens or comfortably furnished rooms, Western-style.[49]

Zheng Mantuo acquired watercolor techniques through his partnership with Xu Yongqing (1880–1953). Xu had been raised in Shanghai's French Jesuit orphanage at Tushanwan, in Xujiahui.[50] There he learned painting as an apprentice in the production of church iconographic portraits.[51] As partners, Zheng and Xu collaborated on the production of poster images, each complementing the other's talents. Zheng painted the *meiren* (beautiful women) with photo realism, while Xu added Westernized landscapes imbued in a halo of serenity. The partnership produced some of the most popular calendar posters of the 1920s—they vastly eclipsed the popularity of the historical Suzhou folk style (Zhou Muqiao died an impoverished man). They also received the aesthetic endorsement of the brothers Gao Jianfu and Gao Qifeng, leading painters of Lingnan style (Guangzhou) and publishers of the elite Shenmei shuguan (Art Critics Books).[52]

By the 1920s a second generation of commercial artists came to the fore, who had either apprenticed with the pioneering commercial artists, worked with elite painters of the old school, or graduated from new-style institutes of fine arts. Xie Zhiguang (1900–1976) studied with Wu Youru and Zhou Muqiao, as well as Zhang Yuguang. The latter taught Western-style stage setting at the new Shanghai Institute of Fine Arts. Xie was credited with the design of thousands of calendar posters in his long career, first as the director of the advertising department for the Huacheng Tobacco Company, and then as a principal with an advertising firm. Liang Dingming (1895–1959), famed in the 1930s for his government-commissioned wall-sized paintings of the Nationalist Revolutionary Army's Northern Expedition campaigns, worked briefly with the British American Tobacco Company in the 1920s. He blended oil-painting techniques into his poster designs and presented images in exceptionally brilliant colors—a feathery shawl in peacock blue atop a flowing dress of silk and satin; the dress, with embroidered borders in cream and burgundy, is tied around the waist with strands of pearls clasped in knots of rubies.[53] Liang's sister, Xueqing, also a painter and commercial artist, pioneered the design of fashion.[54] Hang Zhiying (1900–1947), who entered the Shanghai Commercial Press as a trainee in 1913, took lessons from Xu Yongqing and Zheng Mantuo and claimed inspiration from Disney animation.[55] Hang's studio, a partnership with Jin Xuechen (1904–1996) and Li Mubai (1913–1991), grew into the best-known and most sought-after design studio in the 1920s. The partners collaborated on the composition of the pictures, each concentrating on aspects of the figure, landscape, advertised objects, and calligraphy.[56] At the peak of the studio's fame in the 1930s it produced an average of eighty poster designs each month.[57]

The first lithographed poster-calendars, from the late 1890s, were distributed free of charge to patrons of the Shanghai racecourse. The calendars displayed twelve photographs (one for each month) of famous Shanghai landmarks: the Jing'an Temple, the Yu Gardens, the old police station clock, and so forth, plus drawings of a cheering crowd celebrating the winning tickets at the racecourse. The calendars were framed with elaborate border designs accompanied by advertising messages.[58]

Classical beauties, fictional or historical, retained their popularity with painters and audiences throughout the Republican era.[59] The new sensitivities acquired from photography and human anatomy inspired artists to concentrate on skin tone and texture, to present facial close-ups, and to place the female body under close scrutiny. One Hang Zhiying poster, for example, portrayed a cheerfully smiling young woman with long legs and high heels standing astride a bicycle, her triangular sleeveless top barely covering her full bosom.[60] Other images from the 1930s depicted women with extended arms and exposed thighs, dressed in gauzy fabrics and situated in an intimate interior space.

The sensual and alluring qualities of these images encouraged desire and possession. But the female figures, despite the center-stage positioning, were but pretexts for the display of an array of goods that included fur-trimmed jackets, high-heeled shoes, electric fans, cigarettes, cushioned love seats, bicycles, cotton thread, and copper thimbles. The faces, eternally youthful and freshly made-up, were virtually identical from poster to poster. But the clothing, jewelry, fashion, furniture, house, and garden displayed an infinite variance in detail. Not even the woman, handsomely adorned and lavishly accommodated, embodied the full picture of Shanghai materialism and consumerism. It was the woman in the midst of an abundance of products that ultimately made up the Shanghai vision of commercial modernity.

Thanks to the persuasiveness of such advertising, smoking became fashionable among affluent Chinese women in the early twentieth century. Women of status sported gold filters and matching cigarette cases—smoking had become the new standard of ultimate sophistication.

STORYTELLING FOR ADVERTISING

In addition to pictures, Shanghai advertisers made use of songs and stories, often via emerging forms of communication such as radio and film, to project ideas and images beyond their immediate sites of production. In the case of Laojiuhe, one of Shanghai's premium retailers of silk and fur, the advertiser's use of popular storytelling *(tanci)* transformed traditional folk performances into a commercialized radio program produced by professionals.[61]

Laojiuhe's use of a certain Mr. Ni's storytelling talent, for instance, aired almost as soon as commercial radio became available in Shanghai, which was in the late 1920s. The advertisers selected storytelling because it was a well established form of popular entertainment that had been an integral part of city life for decades. Performed in teahouses from Nanshi to the International Settlement, storytelling consisted of itinerant performers, generally female, who presented their songs and stories to a predominantly male neighborhood audience in an interactive setting. The migration of the art to the radio changed its nature. Listeners from all walks of life could now hear the stories, aided by printed songbooks. The performance was a shared experience that followed a common script rather than a community.

Storytelling on the radio, furthermore, contributed to the rise to stardom for male performers who, as disembodied voices on the airwaves, reached thousands of middle-class female listeners in the privacy of their homes. These women, previously isolated in the insularity of their sheltered lives, became members of a "listening public" *(tingzhong)* of intimate anonymity via the radio.

Although Laojiuhe, a well-established store that initially operated out of Nanshi, was selling familiar lines of products, the advertisements that it sponsored nonetheless promoted their silk gowns and fur coats as an indispensable part of modernity. The store used images of fashionable young women walking down Shanghai streets lined with multistoried buildings. With bobbed haircuts, silk and fur garments, and high heels, these women seemed weighed down by new purchases in their moments of celebrated gratification. The store's radio ads sang the delight of sisterhood when modern women went shopping together at Laojiuhe. In this newly fashioned culture of consumption, shopping was not only safe and proper, but also the very embodiment of feminine well-being.

While some advertising campaigns drew attention to the merchandise, others promoted their goods by investing new significance into the act of buying. When selling new or unfamiliar foreign products to prospective customers, for example, consumption went beyond pleasure to become an act informed by an understanding of material progress and advancement, or an enlightened and scientific appreciation of well-being. Such advertising strategies appeared to be particularly relevant when selling utterly unfamiliar products such as milk, or promoting new behaviors such as taking baths.

SELLING SOMETHING NEW

Susan Glosser's research on You Huaigao's attempts to sell dairy products, especially milk, is a case in point.[62] You, the son of Jiangsu gentry, returned to Shanghai in the mid-1930s, after studying agriculture at Cornell, to open a dairy farm in the suburbs. Milk, however, was neither tea nor ice cream, and You had a hard time finding it acceptance as either a regular drink or a special treat. To promote his product, You became the author, editor, and publisher of a weekly pamphlet, which he distributed free of charge to his prospective and established customers. In this pamphlet, *Jiating xingqi* (Family weekly), You idealized the image of happy, prosperous urban nuclear families *(xiao jiating)*, managed by women no less fashionably dressed than the customers of Laojiuhe. These women, however, now appeared not as carefree shoppers, but as wives and mothers shouldering familial responsibilities—the drawings placed them in the interior of their homes rather than in city streets. Regular consumption of milk, You wrote, was healthy not only for babies, but for all members of the family. Yet drinking milk was a habit still to be acquired by most Chinese. A decision to include milk as part of the dietary routine of the family required knowledge and creative innovation on the part of mothers. Only a modern woman, You suggested, would be sufficiently enlightened and thoughtful to see in this unfamiliar product a major opportunity to benefit her family.

As might be expected, images of chubby babies and overflowing bottles of milk adorned the pages of You's journal. In addition, his weekly gave advice to housewives on matters such as how to open a family savings account along with other suggestions related to "scientific" child care and home economics.[63] You's messages resonated with the latest instructions dispensed in the classrooms of American missionary schools for girls. They were also endorsed in the pages of publications that amounted to Chinese versions of the *Lady's Home Journal*. Those who bought You's bottles of pasteurized milk were delivered a whole package of pragmatic suggestions about what to do with the rest of their lives. You's advice was presumably intended for the all-around health, physical as well as financial, of every member of the family.

While the owners of Laojiuhe fashioned traditional luxury items, such as silk and fur, into images of modernity, You Huaigao promoted milk by prescribing an entirely new system of home management—to the extent that it became virtually impossible to tell whether You was primarily a family reformer or a dairy farmer. Those who sold known products and those who promoted new items, then, faced different kinds of advertising challenges. If an entrepreneur happened to be dealing with something new, he not only had to buy and sell; he was obliged, in addition, to explain the product's use and justify its proper place in a desired way of life.

PRODUCING THE "NATIONAL"

Goods in themselves, of course, did not drive cultural change. They changed the way people led their lives only to the extent that uses were found for them. Foreign goods engendered changes built around their uses in the process of indigenization. That process was often characterized by a push and pull between the foreign attributes of the thing in itself and the domesticating practices that had been taken up to acclima-

tize them. This tension between the foreign and the domestic was prominent in the material transformation of Chinese lives in Shanghai during
the Republican era. A closer examination of the city's recurrent advertising campaigns to promote "national goods," much lauded by contemporaries as spontaneous urban expressions of anti-foreign sentiment,
helps to further illuminate this critical paradox.

The "national goods" *(guohuo)* campaigns of the 1920s and '30s had
their origin in the popular boycotts against foreign goods.[64] The most
notable of these included, for example, the late nineteenth-century anti-
American boycotts organized in Guangdong in protest of American ex-
clusionary acts against Chinese, the nationwide anti-Japanese boycotts
in the aftermath of the May Fourth Movement in 1919, and the massive
anti-British boycotts of 1925 as a popular reaction against the killing of
Chinese workers by the Shanghai Municipal Council police force during the May Thirtieth Incident. The national goods campaign, which gathered momentum in the years after 1925, turned a negative campaign to
boycott the foreign into a positive campaign to promote Chinese products.[65] Riding the wave of popular anger against the British, for instance,
the Nanyang Tobacco Company sought to undercut the business of its
arch rival, the British American Tobacco Company, by running ads that
appealed to the patriotic sentiments of fellow Chinese. These ads urged
Chinese consumers to support fellow Chinese manufacturers and to buy
"national goods." This choice and consciousness on the part of the consumers were lauded as patriotic deeds.[66]

The national goods movement, as the case of the Nanyang Tobacco
Company suggests, was launched by Shanghai's new-style manufacturers and supported by the city's leading financiers. It used the language
of nationalism to promote Chinese manufactured goods, and was prop-
agated, among other media, in the pages of Chinese-owned newspapers
that sought to fuse mass anti-foreign campaigns with a buy-Chinese merchandising push. Whatever the effects of such efforts, their high visibility and multiple recurrences drew attention to the critical role played by
Shanghai's modern business interests in the construction of a nationalist discourse.

But the nationalist language and avowed patriotism of the commercial campaigns were quite misleading at times. In a global capitalist economic system, it was difficult to determine the exact "national" content
of any manufacturing process or product.[67] The owners of the Nanyang
Tobacco Company, the Jian brothers, actually held Japanese passports

and had developed very close business connections with Japanese suppliers in their Southeast Asian operations. The company's use of patriotism in its advertising campaigns, furthermore, produced at best mixed results in various sectors of the domestic market. This was because as normative categories, the "nation" and the shared sentiments of "citizenship" were largely urban constructions that had yet to take hold in the country as a whole. Provincial consumers did not always make the connection between their choice of cigarettes and their allegiance to the country. Nationalism, like modernity, was itself a new idea born in the city.

The patriotism of the national goods movement was misleading in yet another sense. There were, generally speaking, at least four sets of dichotomies commonly used by contemporaries as they tried to determine the national content of any given set of goods. A product could be either "domestic" or "imported," and "native" or "foreign," when classified spatially with regard to its place of origin. A product could also be either "Chinese" or "Western," and "traditional" or "modern," when classified temporally with an eye on the differences between China's past and present. Thus oriented, "national goods" such as tobacco, matches, and bedroom linen were "national" only in the sense that they were domestically produced and not imports. To the conservatives, they could readily represent a foreign rather than a native line of products in the not-so-distant past. In other words, though safely "Chinese" as a result of associations with their Chinese owners and promoters, these goods were nonetheless "modern" as opposed to "traditional" in Chinese terms—they challenged rather than maintained established ways. Each one of the national goods, insofar as it entailed a crisscrossing of attributes along these spatial and temporal divisions, had to become the result of an active process of indigenization. The indigenization of these goods was vigorously pursued by a new generation of Chinese entrepreneurs who did not mind mixing the foreign and modern with the Chinese and domestic. In this process, they succeeded in constructing a new material culture which they labeled as "national."

Because national goods were not traditional, Chinese manufacturers of Western-style products thus became active promoters of a new style of life that often combined both Chinese and Western elements. To sell bathrobes and cotton facial towels, for example, the Sanyou Company ran ads that essentially beautified a new rhythm of everyday life. If you rise early, says the ad, you will hear birds singing and find dewy blossoms greeting you under a rosy-hued sky. Be sure to exercise and shower, and then put on the recommended brand of bathrobe so you can enjoy

the morning without exposing yourself to its chill.[68] Chinese manufacturers of bathrobes and facial towels, in other words, ended up selling
recommendations of frequent baths and exercise in which their products
were embedded.

Similarly, to sell bedroom linen, mosquito nets, pillow cases, window
curtains, and other items of interior decoration, the Sanyou company created a display room on Nanjing Road. Furnished as a home and named
the "Peach Blossom Spring" after a fifth-century literary construction of
a timeless utopia, the manufacturer used it both to showcase home furnishing products and to suggest new ways to arrange the interior. Apart
from its many rooms, each with a specific function, the "Peach Blossom
Spring" presumably also comfortably housed a nuclear family. Dolls were
tucked into bed like children, wearing pajamas that bore the company's
brandname.[69] Urban familial happiness was tangibly producible, the
showroom suggested, so long as the proper material conditions had been
arranged with the help of the right products.

The model home, with its living room, dining room, study, master bedroom, children's bedroom, and kitchen, corresponded in spatial design
to the floor plans of housing units known as *shikumen*: the two-to-three-
storied townhouses of stone façades that formed a residential block featuring its own archways and interior courtyards.[70] Urban housing in this
style emerged after the turn of the century and proliferated during the
first decades of the twentieth century. The design assumed the needs of
the *xiao jiating*, or a nuclear family supported by the income of the head
of the household.[71] The *shikumen*, with their enclosed and self-contained
design, followed a pattern of spatial arrangement that was distinctively
different from traditional-style Chinese gentry compounds. In its attempts
to sell a full line of Western-inspired products that were promoted as "national goods," the Sanyou company ended up merchandising a non-tra-
ditional style of life that supported the modern sector of the economy.

One could not, in short, promote new products without also selling
new practices in which the products were embedded. Nor would it produce satisfactory results to simply advertise certain goods without arguing for their desirability in a broader sense. Bedroom linens thus led
to steel-framed beds, bedrooms in which the beds were placed, floor plans
that included bedrooms, and so forth. From bathrobes and bedroom
linens it was but a short leap to the promotion of nuclear families,
women's education, savings plans, child welfare, dental hygiene, Western medicine, and more, though the logic was far from binding. Nonetheless, wittingly or not, the manufacturers of China's "national goods"

turned themselves into the most interested and determined promoters of a transformed way of everyday life in China.

Thanks largely to "national goods" advertising campaigns, a visual culture emerged, in which symbols from China, the West, past, and present were taken out of context, broken apart, and then fused back together to produce new images that gained a growing familiarity in the eyes of urban consumers of the 1930s. Golden Arrow Cigarettes, for instance, offered its customers free gifts that included silver-plated cigarette cases, leather briefcases, wristwatches, and raincoats. To receive the gifts, however, customers had to first collect a complete set of cigarette cards depicting all seventy-two of Confucius's disciples.[72] A dye factory presented Snow White and the Seven Dwarves as a new set of "Eight Immortals" belonging to the Daoist pantheon. The new immortals, however, did not ride ocean waves or fly across the sky on the backs of crimson clouds as their Chinese counterparts were known to do—they played innocently in front of a Disney-style castle.[73] In another ad, a handful of doves peck away on a lawn while a Chinese woman and her two small children watch with interest. The family and birds share a landscape composed of a pond, sprinkling fountain, winding path, and patches of lawn bordered by hedged green. This tranquil scene was constructed to promote the Shandong Tobacco Company's cigarettes.[74]

Finally, consider a Coca-Cola poster designed by a famous commercial artist, in which a young woman raises a glass to propose a toast. The smiling girl is portrayed in the color of a Western bride: she has white teeth, pearl earrings, and ivory-colored high heels that perfectly match a sheer *qipao* of shimmering white. She sits alone in a room that emanates the radiant red of a Chinese bridal chamber. On the wall behind her is a Coke logo in red and white. The woman dressed in white and sitting in a red chamber, in other words, is none other than the stimulating drink she is offering.[75]

The national goods movement was thus instrumental not only in the indigenization of a foreign line of goods, but also in the production of consumer images that brought together modern and Chinese. The "Coke girl," who so alluringly embodied the suggestive sweetness of an American drink, was, in a way, emblematic of the culmination of a quarter century of Shanghai marketing, where the forces of commerce were working both to indigenize the foreign and to commodify images of women. The image places a Western object inside a private chamber, thus revealing the inner chamber to the public. Thanks to the mechanisms of commerce and the mediation of imaging technology, the imported foreign had been brought *in* just as the Chinese feminine had been brought *out*. In the case of Coke, consumption became linked to that of the Chinese girl; the image filled an interior space that was framed for public gaze. The concept of the "transformed Chinese," who in the eyes of the turn-of-the-century teahouse observers seemed so awkwardly absurd with his plans for daily showers and Western-style clothing, had thus already become naturalized by the early 1930s as an ordinary urban consumer of casual sophistication and national respectability.

After the founding of the Manchukuo, Shanghai's department stores called for an all-out boycott of Japanese imports. In November 1932, under the initiatives of Chinese machine-manufacturers, the National Goods Department Store (Guohuo baihuo gongsi) was launched to serve as an outlet for their products.[76] The Bank of China played a crucial role in facilitating direct connections between the manufacturers and retailers, extending credit where it was needed and reducing risks when its assurance made a difference. Wing On, the "universal provider," dropped Japanese goods and replaced them with Chinese products. Over seventy Chinese manufacturers signed on with Wing On to become suppliers of flannel and straw hats, parasols, thermos bottles, mosquito repellent, blankets, and a variety of pills for the presumed enhancement of health or alleviation of minor ailments. Over a thousand Chinese manufacturers submitted their samples in the hope of benefiting from Wing On's marketing prowess. Wing On placed orders, meanwhile, on terms that helped its financial management. This became crucial especially after the Silver Purchase Act of 1934.[77] Wing On's turn to "national products" in the mid-1930s was not only a gesture of patriotism, but also a matter of calculated self-interest.[78]

The increased use of cameras, lithography, printing presses, animation films, and oil painting in the 1920s and '30s had significantly enlarged the repertoire of commercial artists. The rise of a modern sector of economy in Shanghai had contributed, furthermore, to the subversion of pictorial conventions. But the users of these new techniques, who produced images of modernity, were not necessarily bent upon a critique of clichés and conventions. They placed roses on the lapels of a smiling woman who was defined against a spring sky filled with plum blossoms. They put peonies in between her fingers to twirl, and enrobed her brightly made-up face in a collar of fur. Xu Yongqing, the orphan artist raised by Jesuit teachers to paint the Madonna and Child, was the artist of two famous paintings, *Huqiu* (Tiger Hill) and *Jingyin huiye tu* (Dharma Vision). He placed a Buddhist pagoda atop the well-known hill in the backdrop. He also placed diminutive human figures, either seeking entrance through a gate or contemplating on a rock, under the protective arms of a tall standing tree whose outline is reminiscent of the cross.[79] The hybrid defies clear-cut interpretive readings of China versus the West, or old versus new. As modernizers, Shanghai's visual artists, who performed by the rules of the marketplace, had taken incremental steps. The visual culture of their making offered ample evidence of innovation and vitality. At the same time, it almost never gave evidence of a self-conscious effort to confront convention or break with the past.

THE POLITICS OF VIEWING

How a "spectacle" came to be perceived as such depended on factors that went beyond the merely intrinsic. It mattered how the practice of viewing took place in context. To promote goods and to show progress, new-style entrepreneurs, in collaboration with the state, organized exhibitions of "national products" and took part in world exhibitions—such as the one in San Francisco at the turn of the century—to present "Chinese goods." Commodities in arranged settings became proper objects of viewing not as goods, but as objects with civilizational attributes, that is, as "Chinese," "modern," and so forth. Technology and the organizational forces of commerce and state thus joined efforts to place before the consumers, as patriotic citizens, spectacles of the machine and the material.

Along with spectacles came display. The Xindu merchants of old had believed in the virtue of self-effacing modesty. Hawking was hardship and peddling produced little dignity. Shanghai advertising, however, trumpeted display and visibility. So much of the Nanjing Road phenomenon was built upon appearance that outfits, accessories, and trappings supplanted genealogy as the source of urban identity.

What then were the sensitivities that informed the production of images from Shanghai? Whose sensitivities were these and what sorts of viewpoints did they promote? How was the Shanghai gaze disciplined to revere or to dismiss, to engage or to avert, to support or to subvert the systems of interest and power at work? What sorts of mechanisms were at work to train Shanghai's viewing eye and to set its visual expectations about the "natural"?

In the lithographed drawings that circulated with newspapers in the

1880s, women saw new things thanks to new patterns of connections with machine-made tools and imported gadgets. In the inner recess of the home, by the bamboo-screened window, a woman sat in front of a sewing machine, her eyes following the movement of the needle on the fabric.[80] From the top of a balcony, a gathering of young women passed around a telescope to look at distant views for their amusement.[81] A party of well-dressed women, jade bracelets on their wrists, stood around a pool table in a chandeliered room. All eyes were on the one who held her breath and was poised to push the cue, her body delicately arched and her eyes intently focused.[82] Aided by machines and tools, these women, from multiple angles in their everyday activities, enacted new patterns in the distribution of viewing advantages. By doing so they also turned themselves, through print and drawing, into objects worthy of viewing.

Hu Xueyan, the merchant official of fabulous wealth, was said to pay extraordinary attention to eye care. As part of his morning routine, he would have set before him a plate of colored gemstones. He would devote fifteen minutes to following the rolling stones with his eyes so as to "nourish" his sight. An essential aspect of being privileged in modern times had to do with an ability to see the unseen or unseeable.

With wealth at their disposal, Shanghai's mercantile rich acquired viewing advantages that challenged the patterns of distribution and threatened the constraining norms within the accepted cultural vista. Yet—to return to the story told at the beginning of this chapter—did wealth justify visual violence? Did Hu's money make things proper for the clothier's daughter, who was stripped for his gaze? In bringing her to his house, Hu Xueyan had paid handsomely, in seeming observance of ritual propriety. In sending her away, he had scorned the intent of the ceremonies and rejected the bonds that the performed rituals were to seal. With wealth at his disposal, he emptied the rites of trust and sincerity, turning a solemn act for long-term commitment into a device used for a short-term transaction.

The tale, which begins with the spurned gaze, is thus a story about tension and contestation. It explores the power of money and the bounds of sight vis-à-vis the imperatives of rites. It captures a pivotal moment when market wealth was perceived to threaten the sanctity of established systems of ethics and understanding. It was poised to accept the proposition that money makes right. Yet the tale was not without ambivalence.

Consider the issue of "economism" as Leah Greenfeld has defined it: How far did the material turn succeed in reorganizing ethnical norms in social practice in Shanghai in the first half of the twentieth century? To what extent did the mercantile logic of transaction gain its legitimacy in the ethical realm, dominated historically by an ethical denigration of the material? Answers to these questions, as the rest of the book will show, provide powerful insights into China's history in the twentieth century.

CHAPTER 4

The Clock and the Compound

A major landmark on the Shanghai waterfront was the giant clock above the Maritime Customs House. Made in England and an exact copy of Westminster's Big Ben, it sat at a height of ten stories atop the customs building, its four faces visible to all who approached the Bund. The largest clock in Asia at the time, it chimed the quarters and hours just like its London counterpart. More than the jazz concerts in the riverside park, the fog horns on the water, or the clamor rising from the streets, it was the chimes sounding from the Customs House that set the tone for Shanghai in the first half of the twentieth century.[1]

The clock was prominent in Shanghai, where, more than anywhere else in China, large timepieces could be seen atop buildings at schools, banks, factories, hospitals, department stores, train stations, and so forth. And with the clock came timetables and schedules. On Nanjing Road clock makers and watch dealers occupied a prized place in the midst of jewelers, tailors, opticians, hatters, and fabric dealers. To belong to the modern crowd of mechanized and powered mobility, it was necessary to accept punctuality as a virtue. To take part in the modern sector of the economy, time had to be experienced as standardized measurements that synchronized and structured the rhythm of life.

The clock was less audible, to be sure, where Shanghai's urban boundaries dissolved into rural hinterland, and in the places where tramways, buses, trains, steamships, and telegrams did not reach. This does not mean that without the clock communities would not have formed certain com-

mon expectations that became the basis of communal time.[2] It means
that when aided by the mechanical ticking of the clock, Shanghai businesses were empowered to use its synchronizing capacity to set the pace
of their corporate community. For desk workers living in the city, mechanical clocks structured the temporal frame within which their everyday life was to unfold. And, like today, the clock failed to distinguish the
boundaries between work and home, and private and public life.

Clocks, to be sure, were by no means new objects in Shanghai in the
nineteenth century. European clocks and watches had been in China since
the sixteenth century. From Jesuit missionaries to English trade missions,
Europeans had used clocks as gifts to open doors to the higher circles of
power and society in Beijing. The palaces of the Qianlong Emperor contained clocks, watches, carillons, repeaters, organs, spheres, and astro-
nomical clocks—in total, "more than four thousand pieces from the best
masters of Paris and London."[3] But Qing aristocrats and imperial
officials regarded the clock as "a toy and only as a toy."[4] They passed
them around as gifts of "curious oddities." Chinese commoners bought
and sold inexpensive, mass-produced English and Swiss timepieces—a
kind of chronometric currency.[5] Despite the ready availability of such
mechanical instruments of temporal precision, in vast regions of China,
time continued to be counted "in days and months, not in minutes or
hours," up to the turn of the twentieth century.[6]

Clocks do not govern their own usage or usher in a new technological culture. For the clock to become part of everyday life, it had to acquire a "practical meaning" in a sociocultural environment as "an expression of man's response to the problems set by his environment and
by his fellow men."[7] To the extent that the "ordinary Chinese did not
need to know the hour in order to do what had to be done,"[8] no number of watches or clocks could, simply by being available, change the
temporal structure of everyday life in late imperial Chinese society.

For clocks to become important, significant shifts in the underlying
structure of everyday life needed to take place. Jacques le Goff has suggested that in Europe, the rise of the mechanical clock and an accom-
panying sense of public time in stringent units of measurement could be
traced to a specific set of historical circumstances in the fourteenth century. It was a time when crises in the textile industry in Italian mill towns
permitted owners to elevate the importance of clocks and impose tight
organizational discipline on their laborers. The church bells that rang terce
and nones gave way to the strident "work clocks" of mill owners and
cloth merchants. These ticking machines thereafter wove "a sort of

chronological net in which urban life was caught."[9] The use of the mechanical clock and the emphasis on a precise measurement of time was thus an integral part of an emerging socioeconomic order dominated by urban-based merchants, manufacturers, and their fellow members of the bourgeoisie.

Despite momentum for change outside Shanghai's foreign concessions, late imperial Chinese society by and large honored culture and learning in connection with office-holding and landed wealth. During the Ming and the Qing dynasties, it was not as if there was a shortage of skilled craftsmen capable of dealing with clockmaking.[10] Rather, precision in timekeeping was simply not a concern of sufficient priority to turn the clock into an organizing instrument of centrality.

Yet at the turn of the last century, the clock emerged to set the pace of urban life in Shanghai.[11] Chinese manufacturers of "national goods" found this "modern" device to be such an integral part of their management of the production process that the clock went beyond being "foreign." The import had simply served to differentiate a new style of life from the old without diminishing the "Chineseness" of the Chinese enterprises.

But the clock, though "modern" and "Chinese," was nonetheless problematic as it was also "urban." Office workers were not masters of their own time; they were timed and measured by a schedule set by the corporate clock. The *social* relationships between the superiors and the subordinates within a company, which evolved around the control and allocation of time, was mapped out onto a *spatial* contrast between the countryside and the city. Because the use of the clock was urban and modern, resistance to its discipline took the form of an idealization of the rural and pre-modern. Vertical tension within Shanghai's corporate structure found expression, as it turned out, not in a critique of the hierarchy but instead in a dialogue between the countryside and the city.

This chapter offers an examination of the everyday life of the employees of Shanghai's Bank of China in the 1920s and '30s.[12] Banking as a profession enjoyed high prestige in the 1920s. Bank workers were among the highest paid and most securely employed in Shanghai middle-class society. During the boom that followed the end of the First World War, scores of banks, drawing on Chinese merchant capital, were launched in Shanghai and Tianjin.[13] In Guangzhou, the Nationalist Party under Sun Yatsen formed the Zhongyang (Central) Bank in 1923.[14] Still, the Bank of China, with its nationwide presence, sizable capital, semi-official status, and government connections with origins dating back to the Qing, was the largest and most prestigious among Chinese banks.[15]

As individuals, few of the bank's middle-level employees made much of a name for themselves. Collectively, however, they were among the best educated, licensed, or trained career workers climbing the ladder in large organizations. Visible in daily life as tram passengers, shoppers, movie-goers, newspaper readers, postal customers, restaurant patrons, and so forth, they occupied the middle space that separated the city's small financial elite from its multitude of migrant laborers from the countryside.

These men shuttled between home and work day after day. Embedded materially as well as socially in the city, they fashioned the kind of life that articulated and embodied the urban ideas sustained by the modern economy. Their aspirations and frustrations also suggested both the limits and the possibilities of the sponsored campaigns of modernity.

RECONSTITUTING THE BANK OF CHINA

The Bank of China traces its origins to an imperial decree in 1897. Named initially as the Board of Revenue Bank and renamed the Qing Imperial Bank after the reorganization of the Qing ministries in 1903, it was China's very first Western-style bank with central government backing.[16] Headquartered in Beijing, the bank processed tax funds, paid official salaries, transported legal specie, issued paper currency, and functioned as the modernizing arm of the state treasury. It was staffed with former tax collectors and boards of revenue clerks, renowned for their "copper-coin eyes" and "cold face[s]," who were adept in old-fashioned dealings with major interest groups, such as the salt merchants, money guilds, and regional warlords.[17] After the 1911 revolution, the bank was reconstituted, after much negotiation, to become the Bank of China. In 1911 China was still a quarter century away from the circulation of a national currency issued by a central government. The bank's regional offices in Tianjin, Shanghai, and Wuhan continued to issue paper notes circulating in three different regions of China. Each division maintained its relative fiscal autonomy; bank notes were not exchangeable beyond its jurisdictional boundaries. The first years of the new republic witnessed major state expenditures (Yuan Shikai's inauguration as emperor), military expenses (China declaring war on Germany), foreign debt service, and payments on indemnities funds. In addition, bank officials operated in the midst of factional strife caused by civil warfare and local banditry.[18]

The bank experienced substantial growth nonetheless, especially in the 1930s. As a state-sponsored enterprise created by imperial decree, the Bank of China was nationwide in its scope of operation virtually from the moment of its inception.[19] Unlike private American financial institutions, its subsequent growth had less to do with geographical expansion than with the density of local presence and the size of its workforce. Nor was "market share" much of an issue, thanks to its state-issued charter with specific mandate.[20] It worked instead to improve the professional training of its employees and the overall capacity of the organization, especially after 1928 when the Bank moved its headquarters from Beijing to Shanghai[21] and moved in the direction of "marketization" of its business.[22]

The relocation to Shanghai (where in a small district like the Eight Immortals Bridge there were dozens of private banks and scores of *qianzhuang* [traditional money shops] competing for accounts) necessitated the development of a new corporate culture and complemented a strategic repositioning of the bank.[23] While the bank's northern offices operated as if they were branches of government fiscal bureaucracy, the newly reconstituted Shanghai headquarters and branch offices now pioneered a market-oriented business culture that aimed to win accounts, increase revenue, and generate profits. The bank hired young graduates with degrees in business, economics, English, and law from Shanghai's Western-style colleges and universities. It placed emphasis on discipline, efficiency, responsiveness to customer needs, and adaptability to market signals. It sought to build an organization in which mercantile-driven aspirations would take precedence over state-assigned functions. In short, the early Nanjing Decade (1928–1937) witnessed the remaking of the Bank of China from state bureaucracy to vibrant business, as the bank distanced itself from the Nationalist government and gained stature in Shanghai's multinational banking community.

The man who presided over the Bank of China's transformation was Zhang Gongquan (1889–1979), who began in 1917 as a vice-president (at the age of twenty-eight), and was elected, in 1928, to serve as the bank's top officer, bearing the title of General Manager of the Head Office. A native of Shanghai, Zhang came from an eminent gentry-official family of progressive leaning. He received his early training in classics and Neo-Confucian moral philosophy from leading contemporary thinkers such as Tang Wenzhi and Yuan Guanlan, who taught the Mencian moral philosophy of "sincerity," "integrity," and "generosity."[24] Zhang then went to Tokyo (1906–1909), where at Keio University he studied monetary theory and banking "with a preference for theories of liberal political economy over those of state capitalism."[25] Zhang was a student when Sheng Xuanhuai made his visit, inspecting Japanese banks and admiring state capitalism.[26] Zhang used his spare time to master the formal practices of Japanese banking institutions in Tokyo. Through the introduction of his brother, Zhang Jiasen, a finance expert and political philosopher, he also became a member of the well-connected gentry-reformer group of Constitutionalists in early Republican parliamentary politics that was led by Liang Qichao.[27] Zhang, in short, was neither a mere "merchant" nor a scholar in the old sense, but a new-style fusion of the two and a degree-holding product of the new educational system and the new *shangxue* (see chapter 2) at its most advanced level.

The Bank of China of the late 1920s, reconstituted under Zhang's tutelage, was remarkably successful in its market reorientation. The early 1930s was generally regarded as a golden era in the bank's history. It fashioned a conservative image of low risk and high security. It grew, by 1933, to a national workforce of two thousand employees in over one hundred and forty branches. It was more than competitive against the *qianzhuang*, beating the latter in its core business with substantial reductions in the costs and risks of long-distance remittance. [28] It took the advice of consultants and partners from the Midland and Darmstadt banks and reorganized its accounting system. It improved its intra-branch account keeping and communications, opened up new offices in London, New York, and Osaka, and created new departments to focus respectively on foreign exchange, trust, and deposits. It created a research unit to advance the study of banking and collect economic data, and invited specialists to publish journals on finance and the national economy.[29] It aimed, in short, to catch up with the global community on the products and concepts of banking and financing, and built a complex organization to complement that goal. In Shanghai, the Bank of China replaced the Hongkong and Shanghai Banking Corporation as the central clearing house to which all financial institutions brought their bills of exchange at the end of the business day.[30] It assumed the leading position in Shanghai's Chinese banking association. In addition, the Bank of China mobilized its considerable connections and visibility to engage in charitable enterprises, and acquired a solid reputation for its civic responsibility and public-mindedness.

Despite its manifested emphasis on *shangxue* and modern expert knowledge, however, a profound Confucian moralism informed the bank's managerial philosophy in practice. Bank superiors required, for instance, that their subordinates show dedication and integrity. The "personnel handbook" *(hangyuan shouce)*, a copy of which every employee was required to carry, contained detailed instructions on the "proper spirit and attitudes" that a good company man was expected to show. A well-managed institution required, according to the manual, that each employee show his superiors absolute allegiance and obedience, the way "one would obey a parent." It also required that each employee devote his spare time to "self-improvement" through participation in activities such as evening classes, lectures, reading clubs, and study societies. This was because white-collar workers of Republican Shanghai lived in an age of "relentlessly forward-pressing trends," bank executives explained. To avoid becoming obsolete on the job, one must "seize every moment to gain broad exposure" to various branches of new knowledge and "adapt to the trends of the changing time[s]."[31]

This twin emphasis on knowledge and virtue led to the construction of a corporate belief that top corporate leaders were not just executives holding power, but also morally exemplary individuals and teachers of new knowledge who set standards for every individual in the company. Not unlike the corporate culture that later emerged in the Pacific Rim in the second half of the twentieth century, junior employees rarely challenged the judgment and integrity of a superior. This restraint was deeply ingrained in a culture in which it was believed that an individual's very superiority in the corporate hierarchy was sufficient proof and certification of his superior vision and morality.[32]

Seen from another perspective, for a young man seeking to earn his promotion in the bank, it was not enough to concentrate only on assigned responsibilities and to report "getting his job done"; it was crucial that he paid attention to his over-all self-cultivation. Employment security, to be sure, was hardly ever an issue. If a junior person "failed" to perform, so to speak, his mentor-superior was equally, if not even more, at fault. To earn promotion in addition to such security however, a young man had to demonstrate that he was not only functionally competent, but also morally worthy.

Part of an individual's job entailed constant involvement in learning and teaching, either in the role of the less informed subordinate learning from his manager-superior, or as the better educated and morally exemplary teacher instructing one's subordinates. There was no dignity in *shang* if it was carried out without the intellectual discipline and moral constraints of *xue*. Conversely, *xue* was a mere ivory-tower operation with little benefits to the nation or the people if it was separated from the utilities of *shang*. Consequently, designated mentors were appointed to train entry-level recruits, the majority of whom secondary school graduates. Evening classes were held for middle-level clerks in accounting, economics, English, and Japanese. There was also the practice of corporate rituals and the inculcation of value. No gathering or occasion was ever without didactic implication. There was no escape from such corporate discipline, unless one wished to place oneself beyond the pales of the civilizing community of modernity.

TRAINING

At the end of the business day on September 6, 1933, over one hundred employees from the Shanghai branch of the Bank of China gathered in the fifth-floor dining room to hear a lecture on "Important Dates in the History of the Bank of China." The talk was part of a series to inform the staff about the institution. Senior managers gave the lectures and junior employees made up the audience. The latter were required to take notes and submit them, within three days, to the associate managers for review. The associate managers, in turn, would grade the notes and select the best ones for circulation among the staff.

On this particular September evening the speaker, a senior accountant, explained the rise of the bank and attributed it to the decisive leadership of the general manager, Zhang Gongquan, during Zhang's earlier associate directorship of the Shanghai branch. In 1916, in an infamous episode of major state interference with banking operations, the government in Beijing ordered the two semi-state banks, the Bank of China and the Bank of Communications, to hand over their silver reserves and to stop payment upon the presentation of bank-issued notes. The Bank of Communications complied with the order as did the head office of the Bank of China in Beijing. The Tianjin branch of the Bank of China gave in after offering some resistance.[33] The Shanghai branch, which was under the management of Zhang Gongquan, defied the order and refused to surrender its silver reserve. Word got around and the news led to several panic-stricken days. Zhang Gongquan called upon the entire financial community in Shanghai—private Chinese banks, foreign banks, and the money guild—for support and placed his career on line. In the end, the Bank of China in Shanghai managed to honor all requests for payment against its notes and quelled the public's fear of default.[34] The branch weathered the confidence crisis and emerged with far greater autonomy than before versus both the government authorities and the corporate headquarters in Beijing.

On that September evening more than a decade after the event, the speaker related for the benefit of the young clerks the financial storm that the bank had weathered under the stewardship of Zhang Gongquan. The crisis had tested its leadership, whose response subsequently defined the institution. As branch manager in 1916, Zhang had shown courage and judgment protecting the bank's credibility, the most important asset for a financial institution in the public arena. It was Zhang's grasp of the value of this intangible asset and his decisive action on its behalf that showed his readiness to lead the bank as its general manager.[35]

On other evenings the staff learned about different episodes in the bank's history. The narratives invariably looped back to underscore the judgment and courage of the senior leadership as the most critical factors that defined the institution at critical junctures. Because the Shanghai leadership had successfully met an unprecedented test, the bank had not only retained but had also strengthened the confidence of its shareholders, customers, and employees. Integrity at the highest executive level, it was believed, was the most important factor for a bank to earn the trust of the public. Integrity at all levels, however, was crucial to the successful operation of the bank on a daily basis. Those who chose banking for their career must thus learn from these moral examples. To be a banker, one must espouse the bank as one's own home *(yi hang wei jia)* and lead a life of selfless dedication to it.

Much like at school, junior employees at the Bank of China became members of a "class" according to the year of their entrance. Members of the same class trained together, each under the designated mentorship of a manager. Twice a year the "students" would ritually present themselves to the mentor in a formal ceremony, in practices patterned on the rites traditionally observed between masters and apprentices.[36]

With managers doubling as teachers, the mentors were expected to show a firm hand in the guidance and instruction of their subordinates or students.[37] The relationship, in its ideal form, was like that of "a company of soldiers of sons and younger brothers to their commanding fathers and uncles." Both would "feel for each other as members of the same family." They would see themselves as sharing common goals and broader interest. Eventually junior employees would develop such a profound attachment to the corporate home that they "would be reluctant ever to leave."[38]

Thus a trainee's day was often fully scheduled for him from dawn until dusk. He was to rise at a certain hour, take classes in abacus and calculator use and English, and to practice composition and calligraphy in Chinese. He was to read the right kinds of journals, books, and newspapers "that bring benefits" to his mind. As was common in Confucian academies in the olden days, as well as in contemporary Japanese banks, he was also to keep a diary.[39] Diary entries would record daily activities, personal conduct, and individual reflections. This record was to be submitted daily to the manager-mentor for review. On the basis of such diary entries the manager-mentor would perform his annual evaluation of the trainee. Trainees were evaluated in a range of categories, including "competence," "diligence," "responsiveness," "willingness to cooperate," and so forth. The mentor would "raise questions and make comments" on the basis of his reading of the diary so as to "offer guidance on personal conduct." It was his charge to prevent a student from "going astray."[40] Manager-mentors rated and ranked their class of trainees by moral categories so as to distribute awards and punishments publicly. A young worker would thus find his place in the corporate hierarchy on the basis of this ranked moralistic order.

While the initial molding of a trainee took place in the insularity of the office, the further conditioning of average employees, married and with children, required the construction of a larger and more encompassing corporate environment. In the late 1920s the bank, like many other Chinese-owned modern enterprises at the time, began building housing compounds for its employees in numerous cities. These projects initially did not elicit much enthusiasm from the staff, who would have to give up their various living arrangements upon moving in. There were concerns about neighbors peering over each other's shoulders. Nor did it escape notice that the spatial configuration of the residential units bespoke a certain corporate imposition of value. When the time came, a good number of families nonetheless overcame their skepticism and moved into the new corporate compound.[41]

LIVING

The Bank believed that there were many advantages to having their employees living close to each other, specifically "order," "managerial convenience," "friendship," "unity as a group," and "uniformity in thinking." The Republican decades witnessed numerous occurrences of civil warfare, local armed conflicts, military coups, and bandit raids. Bank offices were often prime targets at moments of armed violence and social disturbance. The bank had learned from experience that placing all its employees inside walled compounds would make a difference during such emergencies.[42] In practice the residential compounds worked to achieve additional goals. In the end the most important use of the compounds was the imposition of corporate discipline onto all aspects of daily life.

The compound for the Bank of China in Tianjin in the 1920s was a fully fenced enclosure with metal gates. Above the main entrance facing the street were the name and the logo of the bank; above the main entrance on the interior was a large clock. Those who entered under the ticking clock first passed between hedges following a path that led to a landscaped compound. Then, coming into view at the end of the path, was the official residence of the branch manager, a stately two-story building with an elaborate entrance. The layout on the compound was such that four houses stood behind the mansion. These smaller houses, also two stories, were the designated homes of the associate managers. Then came two rows of eight three-story buildings, each containing six apartments. Each apartment featured its own bathroom, kitchen, and private entrance, which made it a comfortable structure by the standards of its time.[43] All units included a living room, dining room, study, and bedrooms that were designed to meet the needs of a young couple with small children. There were quarters for maids, but no rooms for in-laws. The bank's housing compound for its employees did not extend company hospitality to the workers' extended families.[44]

While the parents, grandparents, uncles, aunts, cousins, in-laws, and so forth received no accommodation, the bank endeavored to turn the enclosed space into a world unto itself for an extended corporate community.[45] Shaded footpaths crisscrossed the compound, connecting gardens, pavilions, athletic fields, tennis courts, basketball courts, an auditorium, and classrooms. The last two provided space both for an elementary and secondary school. In the early 1930s, the school enrolled over thirty students and maintained a regular staff of three professional teachers. There were also plenty of mothers available to volunteer as the teachers' aides. In the evenings the same classrooms provided space for classes on English, economics, accounting, and the local dialect. The auditorium, meanwhile, was the setting for numerous celebrations on multiple occasions: the birth of a new child, the marriage of a young clerk, the promotion of a junior employee, or the appointment anniversary of a manager. Three times a week a bank-contracted physician would see patients and go to appointments in the compound. Early risers played tennis or practiced *taiji* with coaches and *gongfu* masters on the athletic field. Children played in the gardens while their mothers socialized in the pavilions. The bulk of the household chores were done by maids and servants. With the exception of shopping, the genteel wives of the bank's employees appeared to have little need to venture beyond the gates of the company compound.[46]

Similar conditions prevailed in other cities. The residential compound of the Shanghai branch, at the western end of the International Settlement, was located across town from its offices on the Bund. The Shanghai staff thus shared the additional routines of the company bus in the morning, dining hall meals at noon, and an after-work bus ride back home.

Shortly after the bank moved its head office to Shanghai in 1928, it purchased a spacious English-style country estate at 94 Jessfield Road. A carefully landscaped estate with gardens, lawns, tennis courts, fish ponds, and multiple guest suites, the building was intended to serve as the official residence of the general manager. Zhang chose, however, to occupy only a part of the house. He turned the rest of the mansion into conference rooms and guest quarters for visiting branch managers. In the 1930s, Zhang instituted a tradition of informal Friday dinner meetings at the mansion for about sixty bank employees. Zhang set a chatty and confiding tone at such gatherings, encouraging the guests to speak. Colleagues traded information, learned about developments outside their own departments, and read the collective company mood. Business initiatives often emerged as a result, and Zhang's dining room became an off-site center for the bank. [47]

As in Tianjin, sports and exercises featured largely at the corporate compound. At Shanghai, Sunday was tennis. At Harbin, it was ice hockey. At Yichang, there was enough space along the Yangzi River to make horseback riding popular. These outdoor activities entailed the investment of economic capital.[48] The return was an accumulation in cultural capital, as banking came to be thought of as a high-class vocation of youthful energy and progressive dynamism.

Team and spectator sports, meanwhile, provided opportunities for institutional networking. By the early 1930s the bank boasted both a soccer team and a basketball team, and regularly competed in the annual college and amateur matches organized by the YMCA.[49] The bank playing at such matches indicated the ascendance of a new corporate culture of English-speaking graduates trained at business schools, which contrasted with the habits that had prevailed in the money guild.

By 1933, certain activities became bank routines. Senior experts lectured at classes to an audience of junior subordinates. All listened to dinner talks and joined club meetings. Besides sports, there was a whole range of other activities that included painting, drama, chess, choir, charity, reading, social service, hiking, and domestic and foreign travel. Bank employees watched movies, read newspapers and periodicals, studied photography, took bicycle trips, and cheered at spectator sports. A full schedule and an all-encompassing community enveloped an employee's life both at work and at home—and it was all paced by the ticking of the clock.

PATERNALISM

In the 1930s the Bank of China rebuilt its corporate culture on the ideological assumptions of enlightened paternalism. As noted earlier, the Bank lost much of its treasury connections after 1928 and became "commercialized" under the Nationalist government. Bank leaders nonetheless sought to differentiate the institution from the scores of ordinary banks that chased after profits. It claimed a higher purpose as the moving force behind China's modernization projects. It also presented itself as a champion of public good.

In order to do this, the bank's senior executives sought to project an image of themselves that integrated modern financiers with old-style gentry statesmen. They fostered an environment in which "time" was not only mechanically marked, but infused with moral significance. They built a corporate culture that derived its sense of discipline from the constant experience of the ticking clock and its forward-moving thrust. At the same time, they insisted that such discipline was to serve and complement the attainment of a higher sense of timeless goal. The result was a paternalism that stressed both the utility of modern professional expertise and the validity of timeless Confucian norms.[50]

This enlightened paternalism was not without its contradictions. In its guise as a modernizer, the bank espoused progress and pursued innovation.[51] In its self-image as a civic force for public well-being, the bank embraced Neo-Confucian norms framed in timeless terms. In truth, the latter often outweighed the former. The latest in economic theories and banking knowledge was of less importance than the constant presence of a dedicated group of men of integrity. While soccer teams playing under the bank's logo boldly asserted a new style in the urban money business, for a financial institution what mattered in the end was its permanence and stability. Such stability could only come from the moral steadiness of the senior executives at the helms of the institution. It was the upper management, with charismatic leaders such as General Manager Zhang, that had to lay down the timeless ethical guidelines for all to follow.

The story of the bank, told didactically to edify its employees, was therefore often told in a way that failed to reflect the daily experience of the work force. So much of the moral authority of the bank was vested in its upper echelons that many workers found their place within the corporate entity drained of significance. No matter how hard a young clerk might have worked to improve upon his professional expertise and broaden his intellectual and social horizons, the unchanging daily grind placed him in a situation of constricted existence and prescribed passivity—a life that bordered upon tedious boredom, in which one searched in vain for meaning.

BOREDOM

Boredom often lurked just beneath the surface of the strict routines that constituted a bank worker's life. At the Bank of China it was not uncommon for individuals to come forward with such complaints. A code clerk, after ten years of dealing with telegrams, announced that his work was mechanical and his life was boring. Worse yet, he saw little prospects for promotion or transfer. He felt trapped.[52]

Speaking on behalf of the general manager's office, the editor of *Zhonghang shenghuo,* the in-house newsletter, responded to the complaint with a long commentary. "General Manager Zhang has often remarked," the commentary began, "that it takes talent, gift, superior intelligence, energy, moral integrity, efforts of self-cultivation, and right opportunities for a man to rise and become a top banker." Everyone aspired to become a top banker. But most people were just ordinary ones without exceptional virtue. These ordinary individuals were thus advised to be "anonymous heroes," each doing their duty and being content with their due.[53] The corporation, the editor went on, was not exactly a large family; it was more like a huge machine of interconnected spokes and gears. All parts must function for the machine to work properly. The code clerk thus should be content about spending his life as "a cog in this complex machine." If he was beset by boredom then *he* must change. He should "nurture his spirit in order to change his attitude and learn to be content with his due."[54]

But the telegram room was not the only site of tedium in the bank. As the institution became progressively modern in its division of labor, employees found their assignments becoming progressively narrowed to assure efficiency and quality. Decision-making power was concentrated in the hands of a minority at the top. The majority performed specific tasks that were mind-numbingly repetitive. On the ladder of corporate hierarchy, all reports went upward while all directives came downward. Promotion was slow, and business contacts were confined to a small part of the operation. There was plenty of vertical supervision, but little horizontal liaison. The newsletters were filled with complaints about dull jobs and strict discipline, about how there hardly seemed to be an opportunity even to look out the window.[55]

Yet banking as a leading profession in China's newly emergent maritime economy had fashioned for itself a dynamic and progressive image. In the early decades of the twentieth century it meant glitter and glamour to work for a Shanghai bank. The bankers association had, by the late 1920s, displaced the money guild to become the most powerful leader of Shanghai's business community. Bank clerks, with their high pay and job security, were highly valued in the marriage market. Local slang referred to a bank position as a "golden rice bowl" that compared favorably with the "silver" bowl (jobs at the Maritime Customs Service), and the "iron" bowl (held by Railroad Bureau engineers in the Ministry of Communications). Even an "iron rice bowl" commanded considerable value in an economic environment of much volatility. Few clerks with the Bank of China were thus prepared to quit their jobs, despite their complaints. Yet the constrictiveness of the office and the relentlessness of the boredom seemed to contrast sharply with the popular images of dynamism and cosmopolitanism.

In the end, the bank's management conceded the point and concurred with this assessment about working conditions. It entered "boredom" into the official training handbook and addressed it as a widespread personnel problem. Boredom posed disciplinary problems and deflated workplace morale. When boredom set in, it increased the risk of turning young men toward hedonistic pleasures such as gambling, smoking, drinking, and womanizing. A taste for urban consumption enhanced the desire for expendable income, thereby lending motivation for embezzlement, corruption, risky speculative investments, and other white-collar crimes that could arise in the handling of bank account.[56] Seen in this light, the Bank of China's strong emphasis on after-work "beneficial activities," such as reading and exercising, were intended in part to combat the temptations of urban vice and the doldrums of boredom.

As a group of forward-looking young men newly graduated from high school and college, many Bank of China employees had shown a willingness to organize their lives around books and sports.[57] But their feelings of boredom were symptomatic of a deeper malaise concerning the loss of control at work and the diminishing relevance of individuals in the complex corporate machine.[58] Against this sense of anomie, reading and exercise brought but paltry relief. In the early 1930s young clerks wanted "honest examinations of their situation" and "concrete measures" of structural change.[59] But the corporate leadership, instead of making responsive changes, dwelt instead on rhetoric about how things *ought* to be, especially on how young employees ought to reform themselves in order to contribute to the corporate community.

Somewhere on the corporate ladder a gap appeared that separated those at the top from those at the bottom. Corporate time, as constructed by the former, was continuous and suffused in meaning. Time, as experienced by the latter, however, was truncated and drained of significance. While the former saw themselves as personifying the institution, the latter found themselves depersonalized by corporate conditioning. General Manager Zhang's stature grew in tandem with the continuous expansion of the bank. Within the corporate space so profoundly structured by the bank, however, the average employee found his individual space steadily compressed as he became increasingly aware of his status as a mere mechanism that was imprisoned in an all-encompassing schedule timed to the corporate clock.

In Zhang Gongquan's vision of the bank, the key to the institution's improved efficiency and invigorated growth was the creation of a corporate culture of enlightened paternalism. While the leadership envisioned an urban oasis of perfect contentment, there lurked beneath the surface a crippling sense of boredom. Because ethical and intellectual authority had been distributed in a way that underpinned the corporate hierarchy, the bank's paternalistic order, despite its benevolent intent, was an authoritarian structure in which all forms of power were amassed at the top. A growing restlessness stirred beneath the calm surface of employee life, even as the leadership worked to achieve the stability of a perfect structure. This restlessness strained relationships between leaders and followers, threatening at times to undermine the very claim to a higher meaning upon which the bank was built.

A NEW COURSE OF ACTION

In the early 1930s, under the leadership of Zhang Gongquan, the Bank of China gradually turned its attention away from the city to address the economic problems in the Chinese countryside. The bank was neither the first nor the only one among Shanghai's major businesses to redirect its business attention thus; the reorientation took place amidst a growing concern with the domestic and international agenda of the Nationalist government. A whole sector of Shanghai's upper-middle class society turned to China's agrarian problems with a new sense of urgency. These individuals ranged from old-fashioned Neo-Confucian social reformers to new-style educators, publishers, journalists, industrialists, and financiers, many with advanced overseas education. They devised remedies that sometimes carried a socialist resonance. It was against this backdrop that bank officials looked to the countryside and launched new programs. The move was greeted with interest by employees, who saw the countryside as a way to escape the boredom of their urban life.

Zhang Gongquan's sense of crisis and critical attitude towards the Nationalist government became manifest in March 1932, in the Bank of China's annual report to its shareholders. Zhang reviewed the regional wars that had plagued the country the previous year, the unavailing military campaigns against the Communists, the devastating summer floods in the Yangzi valley, the Mukden Incident in September that cast the shadow of Japanese military occupation on the gates of Beiping (Beijing), and the severe economic recession that gripped the country toward the fourth quarter of the year. Zhang stated that the banking industry needed "political stability and general economic prosperity" in order to function. Yet ever since the Nationalists took power there had not been a single year of peace. Nor had the state made any effort to save the country from the brink of bankruptcy.[60]

Things only went downhill from there. Global depression, which began with the crash of the American stock market, reached Shanghai in the early 1930s. Export trade was severely curtailed. With the drop in the price of cocoons and raw silk, shock waves ran through Shanghai's financial system. In Zhang Gongquan's next report in April 1933, he declared that 1932 was "a year of unprecedented national calamities."[61] The rural economy was severely depressed. There was a frantic transfer of capital from the countryside into large cities, resulting in an urban cash glut.[62] The peasants' ability to repay debts on loans diminished sharply during the same period. Many cotton mills, flour mills, and silk factories, meanwhile, faced cutbacks and teetered on the edge of bankruptcy. For modern banks these developments were particularly distressing, because it meant that they were in a cash glut with no safe outlets for investment.[63]

The influx of capital into Shanghai, meanwhile, touched off a frenzy of speculation in the high-risk bond market. The market fluctuated wildly after the Manchurian Incident of 1931, when huge chunks of salt and customs income, which the government had previously pledged to secure the bonds, fell into Japanese hands. There were ominous signs that the Green Gang, Shanghai's largest drug and gambling syndicate, was operating in the bond market.[64] Chaos descended in mid-January 1932, when the Ministry of Finance announced without warning that the government was to delay and reduce its payment on principal and interest. Bond trading at the Shanghai Security Exchange ground to a halt. Two weeks later, Japanese troops attacked Nationalist army positions in the Chinese part of Shanghai. This episode later came to be known as the "Shanghai Incident." At that point a large number of Shanghai banks simply suspended their operations entirely.[65]

Zhang Gongquan, projecting the image of a statesman-financier, made public speeches to defend his bank's actions as being in the best interest of the country and the people.[66] He saw the unmitigated crises of the early 1930s as posing a major threat to the future prospect of the bank, and he felt compelled to embark upon a new course of action. Because Shanghai was home to fierce competition, Zhang sought to develop new business opportunities by redirecting the bank to China's interior. Financial service in connection with the import-export trade was fully in the hands of Shanghai's foreign banks. But large parts of rural China remained untouched by modern banking. Zhang envisioned a future for the bank in the "backward" areas unaffected by modernity, as well as in regions peripheral to the coastal population centers.[67]

With this understanding, the Bank of China introduced new lending programs and sought to develop a market of direct lending to provincial manufacturers and producers of "national goods" (see chapter 3). The bank helped with the organization of co-ops that promoted the distribution of Chinese-manufactured goods. It also extended low-interest loans to handicraft industries. It set up county liaison offices with storage facilities to which peasants could bring their goods in kind as collaterals for loans. Where no collateral was involved, the bank made loans to rural cooperative organizations such as the experimental stations at Dingxian in Hebei and Zouping in Shandong .[68] Above all, it began in 1933 to set up offices in large market towns in rural areas, making direct loans of up to fifty *yuan* (roughly the equivalent of three months' wages for a Shanghai laborer) per peasant household. The size of individual loans was sometimes as small as 1.50 *yuan* (approximately $0.50 at late 1933 exchange rates).[69] By December 1934, over nineteen thousand peasant households owed the bank a total of 1.12 million *yuan*.[70]

While the bank's leadership turned towards the countryside for pragmatic reasons, bank employees who were trapped in their urban offices saw this move as a solution to their existential malaise.[71] Young clerks in particular romanticized an image of bank employees working under village trees instead of on the top floor of some tall building. Modern banking could thereby be brought into the once hard-pressed and exploited villages. The Bank of China, with a humane face and benevolent intentions, was to transform the poverty-stricken interior into patches of rural gardens. The bank, meanwhile, would set up a network of rural operations staffed by a handful of people. Each would both serve and enlighten the community that revolved around it. Urban professionals and village customers together would construct a new financial order in which the corporate space was dissolved into the natural community.

Writing in late 1933, a member of the bank imagined himself taking a walk through the southern Jiangsu countryside in two years' time. "One day I took a walk, wasn't mindful of where I was going, and came upon village S. It was a small place teeming with houses and busy with the coming and going of people. The fields were lined with hemp and mulberry trees as far as the eye could see. Roosters crowed and dogs barked. Neighbors came and went as they pleased."[72]

This passage invoked, almost verbatim, the time-honored Daoist ideal of a peaceful village of utter self-sufficiency, immortalized by the poet Tao Yuanming in the fifth-century classic, "Peach Blossom Spring."

The 1933 essay continued: "At the bottom of the village was its trading sector. There were about a dozen stores clustered in some simple buildings. . . . I walked into this picture of simple needs and contentment, and there, at the very end of it, stood the sign 'Bank of China' in the midst of the country's greenery and tranquillity."[73]

The banker in the office was an amicable young man in his early thirties. He had an honest and sincere face. He wore the traditional scholar's garb of dark blue cotton instead of the urban clerk's Western-style uniform. The dark blue cotton, nicknamed "national products cloth" (guo-huobu), was the trademark item of machine-manufactured Chinese fabric of the 1930s. This rural banker's office was neat and clean, without any of the elaborate furnishings of a city office.[74] Just a year earlier, the village had been a financial backwater with merchants hauling their cash around and landlords hiding the silver under their floorboards. After the arrival of the bank, things changed for the better. Villagers now earned interest on their deposits, mortgaged their harvest to the bank at a fair interest rate, and sold their grain when the market returned. The village was no longer struggling below the margin of subsistence.[75]

For the two men who worked in the village bank, life had also improved considerably compared to the boring, grueling life that they had left behind in the city office. Clocks no longer mattered. The progression of the day was measured by the movement of the sun; the change of the seasons followed the crops in the field. The two bankers spent the mornings in their office and closed the shop in the afternoon, when everyone was working in the fields. In late afternoon the bankers assembled their villagers under the cucumber trellis and explained modern banking, so as to elucidate on the differences between rural creditors of the old and new sorts. In addition, the bankers taught children in the village school and organized reading classes for the illiterate.[76] They had stepped into the role of the village schoolmaster in his scholarly gown. With thousands of these "naturalized" operations dotting the rural landscape, the romanticized bank of the future would win the love and loyalty of an army of peasant followers who were assisted in their labor to cultivate the land.[77]

This vision of rural banking was, of course, no more than a dream. The Bank of China's rural initiatives were much disrupted by the endless social unrest. In addition, the Nationalist government was suspicious of the seemingly left-leaning sympathies of the initiative and refused to offer its cooperation. In March 1935, even as Zhang Gongquan pondered ways to win the Nationalist government over to the Bank's plans for rural reconstruction, the Ministry of Finance struck. Taking advantage of a sharp reduction in China's silver supply as a result of the American Silver Purchase Act and the subsequent turmoil in the financial market, the government seized majority control of the bank's board of directors, and, on March 28, forced Zhang Gongquan to submit his resignation.[78] Zhang's departure ended the bank's relative autonomy vis-à-vis the Nationalist authorities. Thereafter the bank was once again reorganized into a government institution in which the state held a predominant stake. It was thrust into the next round of financial crises over the underwriting of government bonds. The rural projects that might have redefined the bank, along with the idealized dreams of bucolic life that lured the young clerks, were thus forcibly put to an end.

THE CLOCK, THE COMPOUND, AND DISCIPLINE

In hindsight, the self-contained residential compounds of the Bank of China bore a striking resemblance to the walled *danwei* (work units) of the post-1949 Communist regime. Many social scientists have argued that the *danwei* system was unique to socialism, because it met the twin demands of control and the distribution of social welfare in an economy of material paucity. The history of the Bank of China suggests, however, that comparable communal organizations were at the structural core of Shanghai's middle-class existence, and *danwei*-style work and home had been well in evidence in the city before the coming of the peasant soldiers. The point here is not to debate whether urban corporate communities were in fact the immediate or principal institutional precursors of the socialist *danwei* in Communist cities. It is to note, instead, that by the time the Communists moved into the city with their system of collective residential and work arrangements, a significant portion of Shanghai's middle-class urbanites had already been socialized in a comparable communal experience. For the salaried employees in the city, the 1949 transition to Communist rule hardly represented a stark contrast between bourgeois individualism and peasant socialism.[79] Rather, the very corporate capitalism that the Communists proceeded to reconstitute had prepared the urbanites for their transition to socialism.

Corporate discipline in the style of the Bank of China bore relevance to China's twentieth century in more than one way. Although the mechanical clock was first introduced into bank compounds by China's economic modernizers, this did not prevent the new socialist state from appropriating the timepiece for its own purpose in the second half of the century. In pre-Communist Shanghai, the city remained a place of multiple times dominated by a small financial elite. After coming under the discipline of a unifying Party-state, Shanghai became part of the standardized national time—a single time zone that stretched from the Yangzi Delta in the east to the snowy peaks of the Pamir Mountains in western Xinjiang. Shanghai in the Republican era witnessed the introduction of economic discipline through the regimentation of corporate time. Communist Shanghai, meanwhile, witnessed the imposition of political discipline over the ubiquitous *danwei* in a multitude of urban entities. The work unit, once a spatially discrete entity borne on a self-imposed corporate temporal scheme, had now become a spatially generalized metaphor for an entire society ruled by the clock.

Under the corporate capitalism of Zhang Gongquan, furthermore, the clock and the didactic lectures combined to discipline and legitimize. When junior employees practiced their timeless moral lessons in the Confucian style, their practice became of value only when performed in the context and on a schedule set by the corporate clock. Quite apart from rhetorical moralism, "integrity" and "knowledge" mattered less for their timelessness than for their timeliness: timely attainments that must respond to the forward-pressing imperatives as set by the corporation. The most intriguing consequence of the emerging on-time capitalist corporate moralism, in other words, was a systematic production and reproduction of the economic value of virtue: an institutionalized push towards an economistic turn of ethics and knowledge that was to characterize much of China's twentieth century.

1. Nanjing Road, Shanghai, in the 1920s. From *Zhuiyi—Jindai Shanghai tu shi* (Recollections—A Pictorial History of Modern Shanghai), p. 193.

2. "Dynasty and early Republican era, portraits of
two generations of Hong Huaigong" illustrating
both new and traditional modes of dress. In *Ming
qing guanxiang shu tulu* (The Great Exhibition of
Portraits of Ming and Qing Officials), p. 77.

3. Women playing billiards, illustrated by Wu Youru during the late Qing period. In *Wu Youru Huabao* (Treasury of Wu Youru's Illustrations).

4. Women eating with Western utensils in a modern dining room; illustrated by Wu Youru during the late Qing period. In *Wu Youru Huabao* (Treasury of Wu Youru's Illustrations).

5. Portrait of Zhang Gongquan (Zhang Jia'ao), president of the Bank of China. In *Zhongguo shi yinhang jia* (Ten Chinese Bankers), pages prior to text.

6. Portrait of members of the Wing On Company. From *Zhuiyi—Jindai Shanghai tushi* (Recollections—A Pictorial History of Modern Shanghai), p. 186.

7. Wing On Department Store (date unknown). From *Lao Shanghai* (Old Shanghai) p. 188. (Image from the "Virtual Shanghai" website, image ID: 1485.)

8. Bird's-eye view of Nanjing Road, Shanghai, 1936. From bottom right going back are the following buildings: Sincere Department Store, Sun Sun Department Store (spire), The Sun Department Store, China United Apartments, YMCA, Park Hotel, and the Grand Theater. (Quoted from "Virtual Shanghai" website, image ID 1632.) Image originally appears in *Survey of Shanghai 1840–1940*, p. 67.

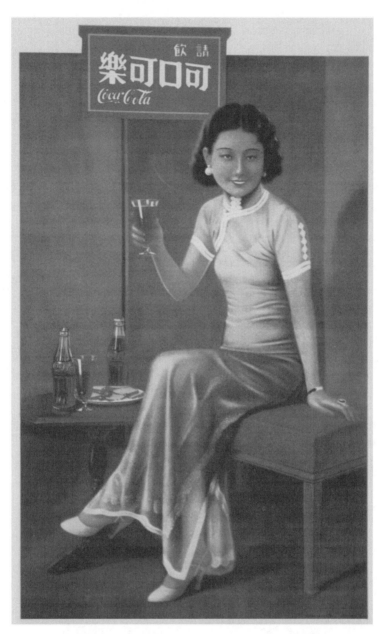

9. "Coca-Cola girl," undated, in *Lao Shanghai guanggao* (Old Shanghai Advertisements), p. 72.

10. Cigarette advertisement depicting a happy family in the 1930s, by Jin Meisheng for the Shandong Cigarette Company, in *Lao yuefen pai* (Old Calendar Pictures), p. 37.

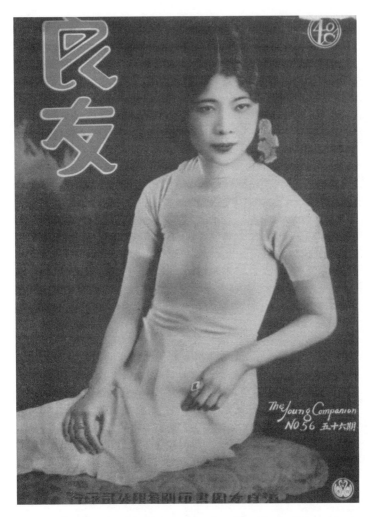

11. "Modern" cover girl, *Liangyou huabao* (The Young Companion), no. 56, 1931.

12. Winter fashions in *Liangyou huabao* (The Young Companion), no. 53, 1931, p. 23. (The Young Companion), no. 101, January 1935, p. 40.

小家庭學

第一課

三　插花

揭除被完了。今天天氣多麼晴朗。燦和的日光直射進我們的臥室裏。把這可愛的花插在花瓶裏。白的缸的，多鮮艷。一個放在書桌，一個放在這美麗。

今天早晨鶸芬嫂改着：「這是姊姊頂喜歡的花吧……」而特地買給我的。她真可愛。

Preliminary Lessons for the House-keeping Bride

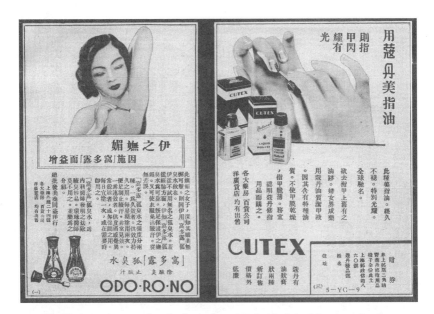

13. "Preliminary lessons for the housekeeping bride," in *Liangyou huabao* (The Young Companion), no. 101, January 1935.

14. Advertisements for women's beauty products in *Liangyou huabao* (The Young Companion), no. 109, September 1935, p. 9.

15. "Employed in a shop" in "A Common Story" by Hu Qizao, from *Lu Xun cang Zhongguo xiandai muke quanji* (Lu Xun's Collection of Modern Chinese Woodcuts), vol. 2. This story was first published in November 1935; the collection was reprinted in 1991, p. 337.

16. "Mother and child pacing on the wharf in Shanghai" in "A Common
Story" by Hu Qizao, from *Lu Xun cang Zhongguo xiandai muke quanji*
(Lu Xun's Collection of Modern Chinese Woodcuts), vol. 2. This story was
first published in November 1935; the collection was reprinted in 1991, p.
350.

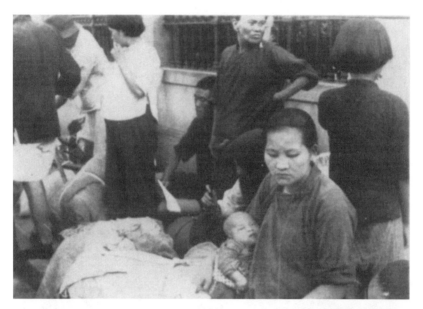

17. Refugees at a street corner, August 1937. Photo held at the Institut d'Asie Orientale. (Image from the "Virtual Shanghai" website, ID 2227.)

18. Identifying the bodies after the August 14 bombing, 1937. Photo held at the Institut d'Asie Orientale. (Image from the "Virtual Shanghai" website, ID 2409)

19. Shanghai skyline (seen from Pudong) at night, 2002. In *Ye Shanghai 20 jing* (20 Views of Shanghai at Night), plate 4.

20. Shanghai skyline (facing Pudong), 2006. In *Pudong kaifa zazhi* (Pudong Development Magazine), p. 22.

Enlightened Paternalism

"Modernity" in Shanghai, with its indigenization of foreign products and its promotion of machine-related science, mobilized the capacities of the printing press to undertake a campaign of negotiation and persuasion. Entrepreneurs, officials, and educators all took part, in different capacities, in this process. The result was the emergence of a new belief that with science as its foundation, modern enterprises would facilitate economic progress and bring material benefits, and that this combination of science and prosperity would serve to enrich the nation and enlighten the people. There were books that explained the connections between science and wealth, and schools that taught aspiring job-seekers the necessary skills. Financiers and industrialists funded business and vocational schools, financed journals and publications, gave lectures, formed civic associations, and took part in discussions on economic and labor legislations. They earned prestige and built networks, promoted a heightened sensitivity of fashions and trends, and succeeded in packaging their new culture of money in terms of modernity and patriotism. Not only was it possible to be simultaneously "modern" and "Chinese," it was virtually imperative for a patriotic Chinese to be modern.

Modernity, to be sure, was not only about a good life in the material sense, but also about a just one in ethical terms. Associations such as the Chinese Society of Vocational Education (CSVE; see chapter 2) were built on the idea that the new economy was an open system that operated on principles of individual merit. Access to the many opportunities in the new economy was open and equitable, and young aspirants who wished to take part in its benefits simply needed to be initiated in the rules.

To propagate its message, in 1925 the CSVE began publishing its organ, the *Shenghuo zhoukan* (Shenghuo Weekly). The journal targeted the "vocational youth" *(zhiye qingnian)* of Shanghai's workplaces. Under the editorship of Zou Taofen (1895–1944), *Shenghuo* emerged to become the most influential journal among Shanghai's "petty urbanites."

THE AUDIENCE

An estimated total of three hundred thousand individuals worked in Shanghai's businesses and enterprises in the 1920s. A majority of these individuals worked for family-owned shops employing fewer than a dozen workers. There were hundreds of different trades, though there were not as many guild associations in various parts of the city. For junior workers, work conditions ranged from old-fashioned apprenticeship to modern-style corporate training. As a social "class" these urban workers, literate and employed, represented a highly diverse work force.[1] There were few common factors uniting them all, except the shared attribute of literacy.[2] This literacy was acquired, furthermore, under a diverse set of circumstances that ranged from elementary lessons with private tutors to formal instructions in secondary schools.[3]

Among these clerks and apprentices were the "vocational youth," former students who now occupied junior positions in various trades. These young men worked while their erstwhile classmates continued their education in high schools and universities. Eventually they joined the ranks of the "petty urbanites" *(xiao shimin)*: the tenants of Shanghai's *shikumen,* who constituted the audience and consumers of the city's images and products of modernity.

The "petty urbanites," like the "vocational youth," were products of contemporary sociopolitical constructions and literary representations. They held desk jobs and received a salaried income. They were the faces in the crowds at amusement halls, teahouses, pleasure quarters, and on streets lined with shops. For diversion they read newspapers and listened to radio programs. Their taste sustained the circulation of trashy novels and comic strips supplied by backstreet sidewalk vendors. The bachelors among them were likely to enjoy a little drinking and gambling, whiling away their spare time in the company of neighbors and coworkers. Those who were married might smoke and partake in domestic conversations about living expenses. Their days were filled with the demands, rituals, expenses, gossip, and politics of the shops, neighborhood, and family. They might complain about entrapment in lesser circumstances, yet they seemed incapable of larger ambition. From the perspective of the educators and reformers, these men lived at a time of major change but were mired in the petty concerns of old-fashioned ways.

"Vocational youth," by contrast, were dissatisfied young men. They had been disadvantaged because they lacked the necessary credentials required for the top positions in the new economy. They were exploited at entry-level jobs and exposed to the harshness of the marketplace. They had been apprenticed or trained to become tradesmen and office workers, and were thus among the "gowned": those who sat behind desks and worked with acquired skills. Yet they had been asked to perform menial tasks that barely offered enough dignity to separate them from the "garbed"—those who tucked in their shirttails to toil under the sun. Daily calculations were a mixture of both anxiety about falling off the social ladder, and a determination to advance in a hierarchical environment of superiors and subordinates.[4] "Vocational youth" as a class were uniquely plagued by an acute sense of status anxiety.

Shenghuo's mission was to explain the circumstances and to offer hope and guidance to those who harbored discontent over the injustice of the new system. For those who seemed content with their petty vices and innocuous pleasures, *Shenghuo* endeavored to shake them out of complacency and convert them to the logic of the new economy. The modern era had brought unlimited progress and invaluable new wealth, it was said. The new order promised a good life that was attainable to all. It was the proper task for educators and publishers to give the *right* kinds of advice to a large number of young people.

THE *SHENGHUO ZHOUKAN* (1925–33)

In October 1926, Zou Taofen (1895–1944) accepted the CSVE's invitation to assume the editorship of the lackluster *Shenghuo zhoukan*.[5] At the time, Zou had served as the editor of the CSVE's monthly publication, *Jiaoyu yu zhiye* (Education and vocation), and its book series since 1922.[6] There were fewer than five hundred students in the CSVE's instructional programs.[7] *Shenghuo*'s mission was to convert young urbanites, unhappy or otherwise, to the unique relevance of vocational education in connection with current concerns and future prospects.

For many years Zou Taofen served as the sole editor, contributor, proofreader, and manager of the entire enterprise. He assumed a multitude of pen names for his essays. His work consisted of scores of compositions each week, including summary translations based on articles in American sports and travel magazines. The majority of *Shenghuo*'s commentaries were concise and to the point. Studiously contained within a limit of fifteen hundred characters, each essay efficiently conveyed graphic images and quotable phrases to grab the attention of those on the run. As a publisher and essayist, Zou Taofen had taken into account the reading practices of his intended audience and perfected a style for the masses. He understood well the limited range of vocabulary and the truncated moments of leisure available to working urbanites. His essays promised to gratify his readers even if they could spare no more than a quick read.

As a mass communicator, Zou Taofen pioneered the use of the autobiographical voice and the device of first-person narratives to discuss social and economic issues. Without talking down to his readers, he projected himself as a man of worth based on the merit of hard work. Additionally, he presented the life stories of a whole cast of economic elite: the accountant Pan Xulun, the banker Wang Zhixin, the manufacturer Xiang Kangyuan, the attorney Xu Yongzuo, and so on. The difference in status and accomplishment between the featured elite and the anonymous readership was not so much an issue of luck or inheritance as of age and aspiration. Through its description of the career paths of Shanghai's new economic elite, *Shenghuo* demystified their fame and wealth and encouraged the struggling youth to follow in those footsteps.

The editor set the tone by unveiling the secrets of success in Shanghai. Zou's readers learned that he was a graduate from the Episcopalian St. John's University, the most exclusive missionary college in Shanghai. Yet unlike a majority of St. John's students, Zou came from a family that could ill afford to pay his tuition fees. The oldest son of an expectant *(houbu)* official from Fujian who commanded status but not income, Zou wrote with deep feeling about the hardships that the family endured when its fortunes declined. The senior Zou appeared to have left his wife and children to their own devices. The younger Zou subsequently grew up with fond memories of his mother, who came from an eminent Zhejiang scholarly family and died at the age of twenty-nine, when her oldest child was barely twelve.

Zou wrote movingly about his mother, describing her as "the most beautiful woman I have ever known." She would send her maid to the temple for charity rice. She herself, with a small child in her arms, would stay behind and pace the room. Zou Taofen told his readers: "I would sit on a small stool in a corner of the room and follow her movement with my eyes. I would wonder why her face was so pale and her thoughts so deep. I did not realize that it was the portrait of poverty."[8]

Money was an issue when Zou Taofen entered St. John's. He solved it by working in the library and offering tutoring services. He did well enough to support not only himself, but also to pay for a younger brother's college tuition. He received royalties by sending articles to local magazines, taking ideas from American science journals and sports reports.[9] Like many of his young readers, he came from a genteel family in decline. He showed them, however, that the new economy offered rewards and opportunities for those who were willing to work according to the venerable rules of intellect and diligence.[10]

Work ethics and personal qualities were thus the most important factors in an individual's struggle for advancement. Such qualities were attainable, of course, through moral cultivation *(xiuyang)* in the Neo-Confucian sense.[11] The path to middle-class success in modern Shanghai began with Confucian practices of self-reflection. To offer assistance in print and in public, Zou Taofen acted as a moderator and a respondent and turned the "Readers' Mailbox" *(Duzhe xinxiang)*, a special column that printed *Shenghuo* readers' "letters to the editor," into a lively forum that explored social issues in first-person voices from multiple perspectives. Scores of letters arrived each day, and a handful were selected for printing in each issue. Additional ones were compiled and published into volumes later on. All addressed the concerns and hardships of working youth who sought a better future and desired guidance about the "correct" way of leading their lives.

EMBRACING HARDSHIP

Hardship was a fact of life for young workers; it was a condition from which there was no escape. To be young and underpaid was a sure way to know the taste of *ku* (bitterness). In old-style apprenticeships the masters would repeat the age-old motto: "Young people *ought* to learn diligence and experience hardship."[12] The work hours were long and the living conditions spartan. Opportunities for pleasure were limited, and disposable cash was close to nil. The superiors were likely to be demanding while the peers envious. Gossip was vicious and politicking was in the very air that one breathed. It might have been a natural school for jungle-style political survival, but it was hardly a nourishing environment for individual development. All of these set limits on the exercise of personal freedom and choices, and led to questions about fairness and opportunities.

"The life of an apprentice is full of hardship," wrote the twentieth-century poet Liu Bannong. "A young man apprentices himself to learn the skills of a trade; yet the master teaches neither reading nor arithmetic!"[13]

> The master lectured the apprentice on "diligence":
> At dawn he is to unlock the shop and sweep the floor.
> At nightfall he is to sleep on the floor and watch the door.
> He is the cook when not manning the store.
> He grows vegetables by the garden door.
> The mistress has a small child. She orders:
> "You! Lad! Hold the baby!"
> The baby lets out a wail.
> The mistress erupts in rage.
> She leaps out of her chair to pound on the table.
> Her verbal abuse insults the apprentice's parents!
>
> Endlessly from morning till afternoon,
> The apprentice runs east to fetch liquor and juice,
> West to buy vegetables and bean curd;
> He waits at the table three meals a day.
> He serves the tea when visitors come.
> He rolls the tobacco when the master takes a break.
> By the front door he responds to the summons of the customers.
> By the back door he washes the pots and urns.
> Without a moment's rest he is hurried around from sunrise to sunset.[14]

Liu depicts the teenage apprentice as living in a constant fear of the master and the mistress. No matter how hard he works or how pleasant he forces himself to be, "still, the master's blows fall on his head like rain pellets in a storm."

Meanwhile, the young man's hardships bring the mistress no end of joy:

> His shoes are worn and he mends the holes in the middle of the night with
>   tears in his eyes.
> The mistress minds the oil that is being burned in the lamp.
> Repeatedly she says her curses!
> His meals are leftovers that do not satisfy his hunger.
> In the summer he is given no shirts to wear. In the winter he shivers
>   in rags.[15]

Likewise, the teenager's sickness from malnutrition was viewed as an excuse for laziness:

> In December the master eats cakes and the apprentice works on the stone
>   and the mortar.

In the summer the master eats melons and cools off in the shade while
   the apprentice tends to the fire and boils the water.
The apprentice is ill. The master shouts:
"How dare you, lazy bone, pretend to be ill!"[16]

Yet the young man's capacity for reflection is innate and irrepressible,
regardless of how harsh the circumstances may be:

The apprentice rinses rice by the river as ordered by the mistress:
The flowing water is as clear as a mirror . . .
The apprentice sees his own face in that mirror.
He says to himself: "I, too, have been born to parents who give life
   and love!"[17]

Liu's poem movingly injected new sensibilities into the hardships that
had been routinely endured throughout the ages. The list did not go beyond a clichéd litany of the abuses under petty authoritarianism. The poet
nonetheless ended the poem on a note about the irrepressible human capacity to reflect. In reflection there was redemption. No misfortune
seemed greater, in that regard, than the denial of an opportunity for
education—the *shixue* (deprived of schooling) that robbed young minds
of their opportunities for challenges and development.

One of the major disappointments in the lives of the vocational youth
was *shixue*, the very condition that took them out of schools and placed
them at the workplace in the first place. There were several dimensions
to this issue, and *Shenghuo* explored them all together with its readers.

In a letter to the editor, reader Hong Gengyang listed the flaws of the
educational system of his day. The schools collected tuitions and fees,
which in turn denied access to those without financial means. The subjects in the curriculum were far removed from any pragmatic knowledge,
which diminished the "return" on anyone's educational "investment."
Nor did the campus culture instill any respect for self-reliance or honest
work as compared with inherited wealth. Old preferences survived in new
lines of work and became the basis of new prejudices. Young people of
comfortable backgrounds were proud of being spared the necessity to
work.

None of this seemed just, Hong went on, because the pampered children of the wealthy contributed little to the overall creation of national
wealth. "How can the nation escape impoverishment," Hong asked, "if
so many people give themselves to consumption rather than production?"
Productive members of the new economy—hard-working vocational
youths like Hong—deserved their opportunities with vocational edu-

cation. In America, "Abraham Lincoln had been able to rise from modest circumstances to the presidency of the United States."[18] China's vocational youth deserved an opportunity to be able to accomplish the same.

Shenghuo lashed out against the conservative attitude of old-fashioned employers. Yet it went no further than urging the masters to reform their behavior. Instead of calling for a structural overhaul of the system, *Shenghuo* placed the burden of personal advancement upon the individuals. A young man's career hinged, in the end, on his attitude toward work and his ability to take initiatives. The basic message that came through biographical sketches was straightforward: wealth and comfort were the rewards of diligence and integrity. The new economy offered opportunities that were fair and accessible. It was up to the aspiring youths to perfect their personal qualities and enhance their prospects.

Experiencing hardship in one's youth was in fact a great preparation for later success, since personal qualities held the key to economic success. Classical philosophers—Wang Yangming in the fifteenth century, Sun Xiafeng in the seventeenth century, Zeng Guofan in the nineteenth century—had embraced hardship as conducive to goodness. Wang Yangming, the Neo-Confucian thinker of the "school of the mind," had, according to *Shenghuo,* recommended the "exhaustion of feelings and emotion" so as to allow good deeds to influence the gentle power of persuasion over the brute force of coercion. "The best way to bring someone to your viewpoint is to speak to him with sincerity. Offer ample guidance. . . . Exhaust your sincerity and feeling, and exhaust, too, your sense of delicacy and thoughtfulness. . . . Be sure to touch his feelings and move him. If you berate, denounce, or give no quarter, you are surely provoking him to violent reactions."[19]

Sun Xiafeng, the Qing scholar, taught that moral learning advanced "precisely at junctures of poverty, illness, setbacks, and disappointments."[20] Zeng Guofan, the nineteenth-century statesman, urged patience and taught that one must embrace hardship, postpone gratification, be attentive to details, and practice "reverence" *(jing)* and "persistence" *(heng)*.[21] The entire classical canon, in short, provided useful guidance that was of vital importance to business success in the modern world.

It was true, according to *Shenghuo,* that heaven had endowed human beings differentially when it came to innate ability and individual talent. Only a handful of individuals had been born with exceptional talents, yet everyone could attain virtue through cultivation. Virtue was indispensable not only for the achievement of worldly success, but also for a state of spiritual composure. "Those who are pure in virtue enjoy the pleasure of innocence. They will not lose this innocence when circumstances change."[22]

Shenghuo's message to the "vocational youth," in short, consistently emphasized Neo-Confucian *xiuyang,* or moral self-cultivation. If things did not quite turn out the way one had planned, a working person must examine the self for explanations of failure. The best way to improve one's odds was to follow the moral teachings of the Neo-Confucian thinkers. A young man must make the best of his circumstances, exercise self-control, and cultivate spiritual composure. This was because financial success was not innate, but always the result of discipline and resolve; poverty posed no obstacle to a young man's eventual advancement. Anyone could climb to the top of Shanghai's commercial and industrial world, so long as the heart and mind had been oriented in the right direction.

Contemporary sources agreed, meanwhile, that to get a job in Shanghai, kinship ties and personal connections mattered. At its middle level the city contained numerous pockets of dense networks, in which employers and master tradesmen were interconnected through regional associations, master-disciple relationships, matrimonial affiliations, and other ties.

Shenghuo was not oblivious to such connections. It stressed nonetheless that kinship and personal ties *alone* were insufficient to guarantee business results. Competence and accomplishments were gaining in importance in a modernizing economy. Hard work and self-improvement mattered, especially when multiple candidates with comparable personal claims presented themselves for the same job. Additionally, it worked toward the advantage of the family units as a whole if a young person knew his calling and was capable of real contributions.[23]

Xiuyang thus held the key both to getting a job and keeping it. It deserved to be practiced not only during work hours, but also in moments of leisure. If a young man was to succumb to the temptations of gambling and prostitution after work, he stood little chance of escaping debt and crime, and, with that, the corrupting influences of urban vice.[24]

Conversely, it was the employer's paternalistic responsibility to see to it that young employees spend their leisure moments wisely and productively.[25] Enlightened paternalism in the multiple trades and industries in Shanghai in the 1920s required, much as in the case of the Bank of China, that junior employees be provided with opportunities for self-improvement. To that end, the Shanghai General Chamber of Commerce lent its support to the creation of the CSVE. Under paternalism, the line between "advice" and "demand" was nonetheless blurred. There were times when the employers' paternalistic concerns, combined with their control over resources and opportunities, became prescriptive. Junior workers thus found themselves required, rather than invited, to embark upon a specific course of action designed for their own good.

THE ENIGMA OF SUCCESS

In a time-honored fashion, hard-working young men aspired to become their own masters. They wanted to own their own enterprises. They wanted to be the masters of their own trade. There should be others who looked up to them for guidance and support. They would take on responsibilities for their wives, children, underlings, and elders and thereby attain the full stature of manhood, which entailed a capacity to fulfill all responsibilities as the head of the household.

But the modernizing economy of the city, with its complex organizations, appeared to deny clerks and accountants the prospect of such self-ownership. Long years of service guaranteed neither advancement nor autonomy. Nor did long hours of toil promise recognition.

There was a proofreader, Zou Taofen reported, who once worked for a Shanghai newspaper:

Fifty-five years old, he has worked in this position for some twenty or thirty years. His monthly salary was ten-odd *kuai* [*yuan*] at the beginning. He now makes fifty *kuai* a month.

This man's family lives in an industrial town on the Shanghai-Nanjing Railway line. He goes home once each year, always during the Spring Festival [Chinese New Year]. He spends the rest of his time in Shanghai in the newspaper office and rarely sets foot anywhere.

He allows himself three *kuai* a year for pocket money. He has no bank account and deposits his salary with the paper's cashier. He has little faith in the solvency of the banking institutions. He won't pay for the charges of remittance, so he sends money home with the help of friends. He refuses to pay for the expenses of the tramway, so for his annual home visit he walks from the newspaper's office on Wangping Street to the train station, then takes the train and rides in the fourth-class with the poorest. It takes three hours either direction.

His wife back home makes his shoes and socks. She also does his laundry. He puts on his fur gown on the first day of the twelfth month, his summer garments on the first of the sixth month. He changes his clothing once a month. He never varies this routine regardless of the actual weather.

It costs about a *mao* for a haircut in the barber shop. This man shaves his head like a monk, and gets it done at the open-air haircut stand by the

English cemetery. The shave costs eighteen copper coins. He never goes to the bathhouse. Nor does he ever use the post office. He enjoys proofreading and never bothers to learn about the content.

He gets bored after spending seven days at home. He hands all his money to his wife. He has already accumulated several thousand ounces of gold. His sons are all grown, and the sons have children of their own. This proofreader plans to retire at the age of sixty. After retirement he plans to go back to the countryside.[26]

A proofreader who does not read—a wordsmith who has no interest in the meaning of words—was a new kind of social being and a metaphor for larger forms of social disengagement. The man's disengagement from the meaning of the words that he was proofreading was matched neatly by his disengagement from the urban surrounding in which he worked. Adhering rigidly to the temporal discipline implicit at his workplace, the proofreader maintained a style at a level of spending that was appropriate in the countryside, despite his urban placement. His consumption of clothing, housing, hygiene, transportation, and financial services were dictated not only by preoccupations with expense, but also by a lack of trust in urban value and institutions. His many years of hard work led to riches in savings. Yet his savings maintained for him a style of life that was principally characterized by paucity. Unlike the Bank of China clerks who imagined themselves in the countryside and dreamt up an idyllic existence (see chapter 4), this Shanghai proofreader was a man from the countryside entrapped in urban employment. In Shanghai he raised a family without the comforts of home, and established a foothold without ever leading an urban style of life. He was the very embodiment of the simple virtues that Shanghai's aspiring young men had been urged to acquire: he was the dependable "screw" in a complex machine that was the newspaper enterprise. Not unlike the telegram clerk with the Bank of China, after decades of work the newspaper proofreader would retire. He could go home to enjoy the countryside and his familial home. Yet it seemed a foregone conclusion that he would never climb his way up the organizational hierarchy in town.

FAMILY

The family that emerged from the pages of *Shenghuo* stemmed from the ideal of the *xiao jiating* (small household): the nuclear family consisting of a married couple and their unmarried children.[27] The "small household" was defined in opposition to the *da jiazu* (big family; clan): the traditional extended family that continued to be the norm in vast areas of Republican China. While the *da jiazu,* sanctified by Confucian ethical norms of filial piety and female docility, had functioned for centuries as the foundation of lineage power in the provinces, the *xiao jiating,* Western in inspiration and urban in its constituency, was to present a direct challenge to old authority. A unit of consumption instead of production, the *xiao jiating* drew its strength from emotional bonds and promised new kinds of happiness to the hard-working individuals in the new economy.

A nuclear family, according to *Shenghuo,* must be the result, first of all, of open social interactions between men and women, who came together as the result of their own free choice rather than paternal arrangements. Such unions were predicated on mutual commitments, and invariably led to the establishment of separate residences from the parents. Under the new civil codes promulgated by the Nationalist government these conjugal units were recognized, furthermore, as legal entities with full property rights.

Earlier in the century, a cultural revolution had taken place in Chinese intellectual circles that challenged ethical norms such as filial piety and female chastity.[28] In contrast with the radical intellectuals, Zou Taofen avoided categorical denunciations and normative assaults. He focused, instead, on the concrete and pragmatic happenings in everyday arrangements. He championed a kind of linguistic shift in the construction of intimate and familial relationships. He made, for example, terms such as "the sweetness of love" and "the quest for happiness" part of the everyday speech of the petty urbanites.[29] He praised couples, including Chiang Kaishek and Song Meiling, who referred to each other as "my love."[30] In contrast there were many parts of China where a girl was referred to as a piece of "money-losing merchandise" *(peiqian huo)* and a daughter's marriage was a "sale" *(mai)* of the bride.[31] Gentility in speech, in Zou's view, marked the advancement in state of mind.

Shenghuo's readers responded with *cris du coeur* that reflected their own clash with traditional attitudes about love and marriage.

> My family is old-fashioned and conservative. . . . My elders have arranged a marriage contract for me. They evaluated the groom's family status and assets but paid no attention to his character. . . . My father plans to get me married to the debauched son of a corrupt official. . . . Lately I have grown very close to someone. . . . Our love has led to physical intimacy . . . and I am carrying the fruit of our love! . . . My father threatens to put me to death.[32]

A characteristic letter to the Readers' Mailbox read in part:

Dear Editor:

> Your journal has done so much to change social customs. . . . Your
> stance on *xiao jiating* speaks to the hearts of us unmarried youths . . . I am
> nineteen, with an elementary school education, and have been employed in
> business for three years. My income is just enough for my personal expendi-
> ture. My parents, however, are putting pressure on me to get married . . .
> I have learned from reading your journal that financial independence is cri-
> tical . . . I have also learned about the evils of arranged marriages. . . . But
> how am I ever to find opportunities for interaction with women? There are
> few opportunities for such encounters in Shanghai. Nor can I afford the
> huge expenses of social occasions in Shanghai. I am unwilling to go along
> with my parents' arrangements. On the other hand, I am fearful of their
> displeasure. . . . What am I to do?[33]

Many letters to the editor conveyed a sense of urgency: a wedding to
take place within a week, a deadline imposed by the family, a threat to
cut off financial support, a declaration of intent to pursue legal action
unless immediately satisfied, and so forth. *Shenghuo* regularly reported
the suicides committed by young men and women caught in their various personal dilemmas. Youthful rebellion against paternal authority was
not without tears and risks. Zou Taofen usually spoke firmly but pru-
dently when confronting such domestic crises. The editor's opinions at
such critical junctures were treated by the panicked or confused correspondents as no mere editorial commentary but as guidance for action.
Meanwhile, the publication of their correspondence gave *Shenghuo*'s
other readers, witnesses to the unfolding drama, a chance to reflect and
to voice their thoughts. Readers writing for help and advice were assured
of the moral support of a chorus of voices as they embarked upon their
quest for an unconventional solution.

The recommended solutions could certainly turn out to be unconventional. Take, for example, *Shenghuo*'s coverage of a "celebrity scandal"—
the affair between Huang Huiru, a young woman from an elite family,
and Lu Genrong, a servant in her brother's household. Miss Huang had
been engaged to marry a certain Mr. Bei, scion of a leading Suzhou merchant family that held a seat on the Shanghai Municipal Council. For
some reason the engagement was broken, and Huang Huiru began an
affair with her brother's servant. The secret came to light when Miss
Huang became pregnant and the brother sued the servant in the municipal court. Shanghai's "mosquito press" went wild with titillating head-
lines and salacious details.

Shenghuo followed the story closely. But it set itself apart from the mosquito press by focusing on the brother rather than the couple. There would have been no case, Zou suggested, had the brother been a little less old-fashioned with his sense of status and propriety, or been a bit more respectful of his sister's feelings. Miss Huang's disgrace was her brother's doing.[34]

Zou was equally critical of the servant Mr. Lu, whose behavior suggested that he was taking advantage of his mistress in her moment of distress.[35] Miss Huang emerged in *Shenghuo*'s pages as a victim of feuding self-centered men, rather than a fallen woman caught in a scandalous case of illicit sex. "In our view Miss Huang is a decent woman," Zou wrote, "whose misfortune was entirely the result of familial and social circumstances."[36] Huang Huiru, to be sure, was not a heroine to be emulated. But her disgrace underscored the inadequacy of existing norms for male conduct. *Shenghuo* believed that she deserved sympathy and support rather than shame and condemnation. Any man who would step forward at this time to save her with true love deserved to be admired as a hero.[37] Zou was so effective in introducing a different perspective to general gossip that *Shenghuo* received numerous letters from young women who showed sympathy for the disgraced Miss Huang. [38]

It was commonplace in those days for a young man working far from home to learn, with surprise, that he was engaged to be married. The news would be broken to him in a letter from his family. On his next visit back home during the Spring Festival, he might find himself a groom, his bride a total stranger to him but nonetheless his parents' choice. After the consummation of the marriage, the groom would have used up his vacation. He would leave for Shanghai by himself, either too financially insecure or too unhappy with her to take his new wife along, or too conventional to contest the parental expectation that the bride would stay behind to wait on them.

Excerpts from the following letter identify a pattern of common problems:

> I come from an old-fashioned family. My marriage was arranged for me . . . . I was fourteen when engaged. I tried to get to know her but had no success. . . . A mere hint of the desire to break up the engagement provoked such sharp responses from both sets of parents; a divorce will be utterly scandalous. . . . She is completely uneducated and very stubborn. I was so completely put off by her that I left home three days after the wedding. . . . I have been reading about the new-style marriage. It is absolutely beyond my power to remake this woman into a lovable wife. . . .

I believe it is necessary for my happiness as well as for hers that we get a divorce. Are there legal entanglements? May I fall in love with someone else before I get the divorce?[39]

While sexual impetuosity and the freedom to love served as powerful solvents in attacks against the *da jiazu,* the *xiao jiating* that was subsequently brought forth was hardly the height of romantic passion. Once married, the ideal couple began the construction of a new domestic order. The heart of this order was the nuclear home: a neat and immaculate place managed by a full-time housewife.[40] The home provided material comfort and emotional solace to its members. Children were born, nurtured, and educated to health and happiness. Dinner was prepared and served upon the return of the head of the household from work. Visitors presumably would be greeted by the gentle voice of the mistress, the laughter of the children, and singing voices accompanied by piano or violin music, instead of the harsh sounds of invectives accompanied by sobbing.[41]

Not every woman was naturally competent or suited for a life like that. Young wives in old-style households had been socialized to preoccupy themselves with other women—mothers, grandmothers, sisters-in-law, aunts, cousins, nieces, maids, female visitors, and so forth—instead of with their husbands. An assemblage of women usually meant chatting and gossip, and needless attention to details and trivialities. Illiterate women, in particular, tended to excite each other's conservative instincts and superstitious beliefs. They could become alternately quarrelsome, hysterical, vicious, or simply shrill. Such women made sorely deficient mothers, if the primary function of mothering was not simply to raise children, but also to edify the young. Such women also made undesirable wives, since they deprived their unfortunate spouses of much needed peace and tranquility at home after a long day of hard work in the office.

As homemakers, young wives of extended families made poor managers, because the household economy was usually controlled by the mother-in-law. Few in an extended family had much sense of personal financial accountability, because assets and liabilities were communally owned and managed. Individuals maintained styles of lives that matched their social standing rather than their levels of financial means. In houses of high status men and women were kept away from productive labor, regardless of whether this practice was financially sensible.[42] Hu Shi, a leader of the New Culture movement, complained that time seemed to have no value for many of his countrymen, who whiled away entire days in teahouses over idle chatter. Women of affluent households often knew little better than to kill time with frivolous pursuits, such as gambling, smoking, and going to the theater.[43]

For there to be young women suitably fit to perform their modern wifely and motherly roles in the *xiao jiating*, women must be permitted to acquire an education in new-style schools. "Women are often enslaved by men, exploited, manipulated, and pushed around, without means to independence," lamented Wang Xiaozhong in a letter to the Readers' Mailbox, making an observation that had become commonplace in Republican urban circles.[44] Women's standing had to be improved. The benefits of literacy and common sense alone were enough to justify education for women, not to mention the advantages of additional training in home economics, child rearing, domestic hygiene, beautification, and the social skills of a middle-class hostess.

Already in Republican cities a new breed of cultured women was being brought forth through the new schools. Compared with old-fashioned ladies, these capable wives saw the virtue of refined manners, educated language, smart household management, and sound judgment. Missionary schools for women taught, in addition, a whole range of subjects that ranged from an appreciation for Western arts and music to nursing, interior decorating, household finance, and accounting.[45]

Shenghuo's ideal middle-class housewife was a hard-headed home economist, a dedicated domestic manager, an effective disciplinarian for her children, and a good citizen in the neighborhood—all the while projecting an acceptable feminine persona.[46] The venerable Confucian notion of an "able wife and good mother" *(xian qi liang mu)* still applied. These women, in short, were to attain happiness by adhering to the same sort of eclectic work ethic that contributed to the success of an urban career. While the men worked hard in the office, their wives would work just as hard at home. A mother was to take up jobs outside the home only when the children were fully grown. Reputable choices for female employment, as elsewhere in the world, were by and large confined to caring, nurturing, and assisting, such as in schools, banks, and hospitals.

Despite the indispensable role of the woman in the *xiao jiating*, the mainstay of this happy new order was still to be the hard-working husband. It was the function of the husband to provide and to protect, and it was the earning capacity of the husband that would make the *xiao jiating* materially viable. "A young man's financial independence is the precondition for his marriage," advised Zhuang Zexuan, a U.S.-trained educator and author of counseling manuals for youth.[47] Zou Taofen agreed, advising young people to put off marriage until they could safely do so without incurring debts from relatives.[48] To gain a voice among the elders in his extended lineage, a young husband must first acquire a capacity to support his own family. Financial independence was critical to a couple's plan to "extricate" *(tuoli)* themselves from the *da jiazu*. This extrication was the first step towards breaking away from the web of entangled relationships that characterized the extended family.[49]

In contrast to the emphasis placed on personal improvement and moral cultivation in discussions of career advancement, *Shenghuo* adopted a materialistic perspective with regard to the viability of the nuclear family. Solid finance laid the foundation of autonomy and security, without which there could have been no happiness. Those who found themselves in unhappy marital arrangements, furthermore, learned that they were not the ones to bear the guilt and the blame. It was the dated customs, reactionary practices, and the besotted authorities who were at fault. Instead of provoking lectures on how they might improve their own conduct, young readers who wrote in to the Mailbox about personal problems received unconventional advice and encouragement. In addition, just as many letters that purportedly came from women had in fact came from men. Little wonder, then, that the "family" discussions, more than the "job" ones, contributed enormously to the popularity of the journal. From time to time, the Readers' Mailbox also responded to inquiries about venereal diseases and sexual health. For its audience of the 1930s, *Shenghuo* was the journal that provided its readers with information about everything they ever wanted to know, but were afraid to ask.

MIXED MARRIAGES: TWO TALES

If the journal ever attempted a systematic critique of traditional familial relationships, it was in Zou Taofen's freestyle rendition of two American novellas that featured a Western woman marrying a Chinese man. The translations, accompanied by extensive editorial commentaries, left out elements of racial inequality prominent in the English original, and concentrated instead on providing point-by-point comparisons between the Chinese and the Western practices of courtship, marriage, and family life as seen through the eyes of Sino-Western couples supposedly at ease in both cultures.[50]

In two separate series of presentations, Zou told the story of two couples meeting and getting married in the West, overcoming the barriers and prejudices that might have prevented their union. Once married, the

Chinese husbands took their English or American bride back home to meet the extended network of relatives. In each case, despite the family's large fortune, the reserve of good will, and the new couple's high standing among their kinsfolk, the return to the husband's birthplace nearly destroyed the romantic bond between the husband and wife. The wife found that the proper assumption of the privileges of the genteel forced her to become idle, with no responsibilities even for the couple's affairs. Men and women socialized separately. At the same time women attended to endless rounds of scripted and ritualized occasions, especially those centering upon the matriarch of the house, the mother-in-law.

Zou Taofen refrained from sweeping denunciations of traditional rituals and expectations. The message was nonetheless loud and clear: in extended Chinese families the norms of respectability and propriety prohibited emotional expression, stifled individual initiatives, and forced the healthy and robust into a ritually correct life of boredom and lethargy. In the end, the husbands in both tales died of inexplicable illnesses, and their foreign wives and Eurasian children chose to return to the West.

Because every *xiao jiating* in Shanghai during the 1920s represented a purposeful choice to go against the prevailing norm of the *da jiazu,* one of the critical functions for the head of a nuclear household was to act as a negotiator on behalf of the integrity of the conjugal unit vis-à-vis their own extended lineage. The burden fell exclusively upon the husbands, for women were bound by norms that prohibited them from vocalizing their wishes. Unless a husband actively fought for the assertion of conjugal integrity, there could be no operative nuclear family. Sun Li of the Dalong Iron Works on Shanghai's Gordon Road, for instance, had taken a wife but did not build a nuclear family. Sun married so he could send a woman back to his home village, about three hundred *li* (one hundred miles) from Shanghai, to wait upon his elderly parents.[51] Alternatively, those who wanted a nuclear unit might find themselves caught in an unenviable situation mediating between parents and wife.[52]

The large number of letters printed in the Readers' Mailbox tackled the issue of urban families from two different ends. There were letters that extolled the ideal *xiao jiating:* an urban-based nuclear family predicated upon the financial independence of the vocational youth and the aspirations of new-style educated women. There were also letters that denounced the existing extended families as "rural," "traditional," "oppressive," "unhealthy," "unproductive," and "immoral." The *xiao jiating* and the *da jiazu* were spatially dichotomized, so to speak, into the "urban" versus the "rural." In the countryside, the *da jiazu,* with all its attendant personal and property relationships, not only stifled the genuine expression of human feelings, but also encouraged unworthy individuals to abandon their basic social responsibilities. In the city, the formation of the *xiao jiating* was not only the urban vocational youths' chance to domestic bliss, but also a civil endeavor on their part to contain the pernicious influence of the hinterland. Without such an endeavor, the backwardness of the provinces would surely spoil everyone in a morass of evil customs, closed minds, poverty, ignorance, superstition, inefficiency, and irresponsibility.[53] It was the civic duty of the urbanites, in other words, to promote the value of the *xiao jiating* with vigor and determination.

Middle class in constituency and conservative in moral outlook, the arguments in favor of the *xiao jiating* were nonetheless "progressive" in early Republican social thinking, because they represented a direct challenge to an old system that had privileged not only the male, but also the elderly. In the context of the 1920s and '30s, this brand of bourgeois family ideals combined a popularized Confucian ethic of personal accountability and instrumental morality. According to *Shenghuo*, there was not much that could be done to change the economic order. But for those who managed to gain a foothold in the new economy, there was certainly a great deal that could be done in terms of building a new kind of ideal family.

As urban middle-class employees surveyed the landscape, they saw—as *Shenghuo* had shown in commentaries and reports—China's vast rural interior in the grip of famine, flooding, banditry, warring generals, marauding soldiers, rioting peasants, opium addicts, and gamblers.[54] The city, by contrast, was not only a place of jobs and opportunity, but also a carefully constructed space with tree-lined boulevards, public parks, private gardens, neon lights, glittering shop fronts, bustling entertainment quarters, towering office buildings, and so forth. Urban inhabitants had access to various forms of modern culture: theaters, cinemas, concerts, sports, bookstores, publishing houses, newspapers, schools, and so on. It was also a more secure life because of the availability of doctors, hospitals, policemen, fire fighters, welfare agencies, and benevolent societies.[55] Was the city not the country's best defense against the hopelessness in the countryside? An urban middle-class life of hard work, self-sufficiency, domestic felicity, and personal accountability was surely the best course of action. By presenting this argument, *Shenghuo* showed that middle-class ideas of home and work, with its emphasis on the *xiao jiating* and its ethic of moral improvement and self-sufficiency, was a valuable enterprise not only for individual happiness, but also "for the creation of a healthy society" and "the happiness of the people."[56]

LOVE AND THE LAW

In his comments on observed circumstances, Zou Taofen often spoke in a voice of concern and emotion. He would thunder his outrage at family elders who insisted on traditional norms with oppressive rigidity. Or he might furiously denounce some perfectly arranged marriage that failed to consult the wishes of the prospective partners.[57] He made his points straightforwardly. Yet when offering direct responses to letters sent to the Readers' Mailbox, Zou's voice was characteristically reasonable and restrained. In these exchanges it was not uncommon for the young correspondents to gripe, page after page, about their grievances. And it was the editor's usual practice to offer no more than a handful of practical guidelines.

Zou Taofen's understanding of love was straightforward enough: true love entails a serious moral commitment; it must never be confused with either sexual licentiousness or emotional blackmail. In practice, this basic insight translated into several axioms. Do not seek happiness at the expense of others. Do not send false signals during courtship. Always take full responsibility for what you have done. In the case of disputes, always try gentle persuasion before confrontation. Never give in to coercion or manipulation. A man should always recognize his responsibility to his dependents and never speak lightly of divorce. A woman, on the other hand, must always recognize her rights to a decent existence whether she chooses to divorce or not. Women should never allow themselves to be driven to suicide out of despair, according to Zou. "Always remember that you are, first of all, human, whether you are a wife or not."[58]

There was an obvious effort to seek simple solutions to complex problems, and Zou's advice to the young was nearly always measured and realistic. "You should again plead with your mother and hope that she may change her mind," he often advised. "Perhaps your uncle may put in a few good words on your behalf to your father. You must be patient and not despair." "Do you have a close friend or relative to whom you may turn for a few days till your father's rage subsides?" "You must remember that it's easier to insist on a cancellation of the marriage contract before the wedding has taken place than [to] ask for a divorce afterwards. Insist!" Patience and persistence combined were clearly seen as the most effective means of persuasion in the long run.

After 1928 the Nationalist government put new laws into effect. These laws substantially altered, at least on paper, the conditions governing marriage and divorce. Anyone over twenty was entitled to sign his or her own marriage contract without parental consent. Only natural parents—not grandparents, uncles, aunts, brothers, in-laws, or any other family members—had the right to arrange the marriages of their dependent minors. For women, divorce, at least in law, had become an option that was more accessible than ever before.[59]

Zou cited the new laws whenever applicable, consulting attorneys on his readers' behalf and providing information on court procedures and expenses. "The law says that when a marriage contract is signed without the consent of the principals who are minors, he or she may disavow the contract when reaching adulthood at the age of twenty. Who does your grandmother think she is to defy the law of the land?" "The Ministry of Education has banned the practice of secondary school students getting married while a student. Your future in-laws are violating the ministry's rules when they demand that your sixteen-year-old daughter be married at this time. If the groom's family is so thick-headed, it certainly portends serious problems after marriage. You are better off canceling the marriage now and saving your daughter from further misery."[60] The law, however, was far from adequate in offering protection to the domestically abused, and, in reality, divorce was difficult to obtain. Zou would sigh with resignation: "Perhaps your sister may seek the help of the local women's association, though I doubt that they are effectual. I am truly sorry to say that there seems to be no better way other than urging her not to give up hope."[61]

When the law failed to help, the publisher and his readers would offer moral support:

> I am sorry to hear that your fiancé turned out to have another lover. Fortunately you are not yet married, and you have a lover of your own. The law says that once engaged to marry, a person may not have an affair with a third person outside the engagement. An illegitimate affair constitutes sufficient ground for the dissolution of the marriage contract. Since you are over twenty years old and have received a secondary education, you may consider leaving home and supporting yourself by getting a job; this may be your last resort to escape the wedding. Your father need not worry about being legally liable to your fiancé's family because you are no longer a minor. You must, of course, plan carefully for your travel in order to assure a safe journey.[62]

Over time the cases in the journal became precedents in themselves and formed a framework of reference. "What you may try under the circumstances is to flee from home, as Miss Shen had done in a similar situation," wrote Zou. With an expanding repertoire of viable action, an audience that was called into existence by its shared interest in reading constituted itself as a community of action informed by its own memory, vocabulary, value, and aspirations.

THE STATE

As *Shenghuo* invoked the law in defense of the young, it also accepted the new Nationalist government as a partner in the articulation of a new way of life. It pinned its hopes on the capacity of the modernizing state, through its enlightened cadres, to loosen the grip of the "evil gentry and local bullies" on provincial affairs, thereby weakening the power base of the conservatives and the reactionaries. The revolutionary party founded by Sun Yatsen, Zou hoped, would bring order and integrity to the emerging new society.

Shenghuo devoted little space to the Nationalists before 1927. But once the Nationalist government was announced in Nanjing, the journal welcomed the development with considerable enthusiasm. On December 29, 1927, the day General Zhang Xueliang, the governor and supreme commander of the three northeastern provinces, pledged his allegiance to Nanjing, *Shenghuo* commented excitedly: "One flag over all of China!"[63] The Nationalist Party gave Sun Yatsen a state funeral. It brought his remains down from Beiping, and buried him in a hillside mausoleum overlooking the new national capital. In Shanghai, tens of thousands saw the newsreel in movie theaters. The audience, Zou reported, broke into a thunderous applause when Sun's portrait came onto the screen. They were then moved to tears, watching in solemn reverence as uniformed guards brought the founding father's coffin down the tomb steps.[64]

The Nationalist Party declared its allegiance to Sun Yatsen's "Three Principles of the People" *(Sanmin zhuyi)*. In the "Principle of People's Livelihood" *(Minsheng zhuyi)*, Sun called for the state to own and manage the major enterprises concerning public utilities, heavy industry, and economic infrastructure. Other sectors of the economy were to be left to private ownership and initiatives. In his doctrine, Sun had embraced the twin goals of rural reconstruction and urban development. He had also promised a future of economic growth without social inequality. He wanted the state to use taxation as an instrument for social equality, through the redistribution of wealth and public spending projects aimed at social welfare and education.

But it soon became clear, at least in the eyes of Zou Taofen, that the Nationalist government under Chiang Kaishek had preoccupied itself with military campaigns and political struggles, and had rearranged the priorities defined by the party's founding figure. The inauguration of the new government in 1927 marked the beginning, not the end, of the Nationalists' use of military force in its quest for national unification. After a series of regional wars with military governors based in northern Chinese provinces, Chiang Kaishek turned to his "extermination campaigns," targeting the rural soviets of the Chinese Communists in Jiangxi. Chiang's government made heavy demands on the Shanghai bourgeoisie to help pay for the staggering military expenses. There were few signs of the economic constructions that Sun Yatsen had outlined. To make matters even worse, the Nationalists, in response to criticism, further tightened their control over the formation of political associations. It also introduced new censorship laws to control the press.[65]

Shenghuo's commentaries on current events in the early 1930s reflected a growing disappointment with the Nationalists.[66] As the journal became increasingly critical of the government, it stressed the importance of self-cultivation to help improve the lives of petty urbanites. If the party-state was failing in its promise to fulfill its responsibilities to the nation, then members of the urban middle class, with their skills, virtue, knowledge, and discipline, should take it upon themselves to improve the country's prospects. To prepare themselves for such an undertaking, in addition to forming a viable urban political force, *Shenghuo* and the CSVE expanded their range of activities and inaugurated programs loosely referred to as "social" or "popular," along with the "vocational." These activities ranged from mass literacy programs, correspondence schools, evening classes, lending libraries, and reading clubs, to other forms of acculturation in music, drama, arts, and sports, in addition to the vocational training classes.[67]

Zou Taofen's relationship with the Nationalists soured all the more precipitously when the government, as part of its "Partification" *(danghua)* policies in education (see chapter 2), imposed regulations that pressured prospective students to enroll in state-accredited institutions. This effectively undercut the legitimacy of night schools, literacy classes, correspondence courses, and autodidactic studies sponsored by the social educators and entrepreneurial reformers of the CSVE.[68]

Editorial work at *Shenghuo* was encumbered, meanwhile, by new censorship rules requiring the government review of all manuscripts prior to publication. Zou Taofen responded angrily to Nanjing's attempt, through the Bureau of Social Affairs in Shanghai, to impose state control over the press. He spoke out repeatedly in favor of freedom of speech, and stressed the importance of unrestricted access to information and independent public opinion to a truly democratic political system. Before long *Shenghuo* was attacking top Nationalist officials on charges of corruption, accusing them of indulging in vices such as opium smoking, and suggesting that the self-styled followers of Sun Yatsen had betrayed their leader and degenerated into petty tyrants and ineffectual despots.[69]

A complete break with the government came with the Manchurian Incident of September 18, 1931. Under Zou Taofen, *Shenghuo zhoukan* embraced the cause of unqualified armed resistance against Japanese military encroachment.[70] The choices faced by the Chinese people, Zou commented grimly, were either death or dishonor. China must resist; otherwise, it risked condemning its citizens to a servile existence.[71] What the war represented was a total assault on the way of life that Shanghai's urbanites had aspired to build, something the Nationalists were not interested in defending. The journal printed eyewitness accounts of Japanese massacres of women and children, and photographs of captured Chinese soldiers in humiliation.[72]

Shenghuo readers responded with letters to the editor that were filled with fear and outrage toward both the Japanese and their own government. Readers also donated money, and the journal glorified the women and children who emptied their piggy banks.[73] Circulation soared to record sales of nearly one hundred and fifty thousand copies. Encouraged by such momentum, Zou Taofen and his friends began planning a newspaper, the "*Shenghuo Daily*," that promised to be even more responsive to street-level sentiments and concerns.[74]

In due course, the editorial voice grew shrill and defiant, and criticism of the Nationalists' appeasement policies crowded out discussions of most other subjects in *Shenghuo*'s pages. As the Nanjing government repeatedly ordered its troops to withdraw under Japanese military pressure, Zou Taofen openly declared that government incompetence and irresponsibility were "sowing the seeds of revolution."[75] *Shenghuo* began speaking of domestic classes of "oppressors" who were "beyond the touch of conscience and above the rule of the law," who stood in opposition to a vast majority of suffering people.[76] "We are but common civilians without arms or political power," Zou warned. With the nation in crisis and the Nationalists exhibiting not a trace of Sun Yatsen's ideals, the journal finally made a call to arms: "[F]or our self-defense as well as for the defense of the nation, we the people *(minzhong)* may have no choice but to rise up and take a last stand!"[77]

This radical turn in political inclination signified not so much an abandonment of Zou's earlier socio-moral philosophy as it did a shaken faith in creating a better society through individual efforts. His earlier beliefs had been predicated upon the assumption that socioeconomic construction could be brought about without resorting to political means. His encounter with the Nationalist regime had taught him, however, of the futility of attempting to preserve individual autonomy from political interference. Zou continued to advocate the necessity of striving to improve one's own lot in the world, but there was an element of resignation in his voice, born out of a bleak assessment of Chinese political realities. There was a belated recognition that no home or career was secure from the arbitrary power of an intrusive state. Nor were individual means adequate enough to stem the disastrous effects of irresponsible state policies on civilian lives. Revolutionary means for the creation of a new political system and society were thus necessary before anyone could peacefully enjoy the fruit of honest hard labor.[78]

"VOCATIONAL" OR "PROGRESSIVE"?

In June 1933 the Nationalist authorities shut down the journal.[79] Frustrated but undaunted, Zou Taofen and his colleagues set off to duplicate *Shenghuo*'s success and regain its interrupted momentum. Zou had previously attempted to publish a newspaper, the *Shenghuo Daily*. In an open letter to prospective supporters, he spoke of a paper that was to be "the daily, indispensable spiritual food for all 500 million Chinese . . . a collective enterprise by—and for—all producing members of this society, with news and commentaries contributed directly by workers, peasants, clerks, and students from all parts of the country."[80] Under Nationalist censorship, however, the *Shenghuo Daily* never saw the light of day.

After a two-year hiatus, Zou launched another weekly, the *Dazhong shenghuo* (The life of the masses). The new journal continued *Shenghuo*'s tradition with commentaries and a "Readers' Mailbox." Yet it was a publication that spoke in a different voice. *Dazhong shenghuo* featured contributions by an illustrious roster of left-wing intellectuals—Hu Sheng, Hu Qiaomu, Qian Junrui, Xia Yan, Mao Dun, and Zhang Youyu. It gave considerable space to theoretical issues about politics and economy, explaining the connections between the global and the local and prescribing the right course of action. To a former *Shenghuo* reader who urged

Zou Taofen to return to the personal voice and everyday concerns of the old journal, the editor, who now commanded the support of a whole network of publishers and contributors, replied that it was the goal of the new journal to take the nation down the path of "progressive" thinking. "The giant wheels of the epoch *(shidai)* roll on," Zou wrote. "The epoch for *Dazhong shenghuo* is utterly different from that for *Shenghuo*."[81] In the new epoch there was neither room nor time for individual concerns. Instead, a young person should endeavor to be "a brave and progressive fighter on behalf of the masses in step with the collectivity," because "to attain the autonomy of an individual, it is necessary to first achieve the emancipation of all."[82]

Dazhong shenghuo leveled categorical denunciations against the Nationalist regime and the system over which it presided. To those who were disturbed by the uncompromising demand for the democratization of the political process, Zou Taofen replied bluntly that their hesitations stemmed from their failure to become true "friends of the people."[83] With the editor passing judgments on the opinions submitted by his readers, the Readers' Mailbox took on a different nature. Instead of a lively forum covering the mundane and the extraordinary in personal lives, it became a lectern from which the enlightened leader sounded out his evaluation of the correctness of ordinary ways of thinking through a systematic application of scientific theories to everyday concerns.

Zou Taofen continued to agitate for a national policy of immediate armed resistance against Japanese military presence in China. He emerged, in 1936, as a major leader of the National Salvation Association (Jiuguo hui) in Shanghai. Zou was among the "seven gentlemen" arrested by the Nationalist authorities on the morning of November 23 for their vocal criticisms of Chiang Kaishek's policy of *annei rangwai* (first put down the internal [Communists], then expel the external [Japanese]).[84] He was put on trial and given a prison sentence. The following summer he was released, along with the other six, as the Nationalists prepared for war against Japan.

Zou Taofen warmed up to the Chinese Communist Party during the patriotic campaigns of the mid-1930s,[85] which coincided with a period of the latter's organizational disarray.[86] Zou helped to revitalize the underground communist movement with his vision and enthusiasm.[87]

As a prolific essayist, energetic publisher, innovative editor, and ingenious reporter, Zou Taofen was among the most talented and dynamic mass communicators of his generation. He freely interpreted ideas and practices from articles written in English, Russian, Japanese, and other languages. He honed his vernacular Chinese writing skills and styles in a highly competitive publishing market, in which over two thousand periodicals competed for the revenue and attention of a readership of a mere half million. *Shenghuo* emerged from the competition with flying colors, and the editor's public stature was founded upon the journal's success.

As the editor of *Shenghuo*, Zou Taofen projected a literary persona that combined earnest sincerity with sagely prudence. He empathized with distressed readers and encouraged contacts who were lawyers, doctors, accountants, and educators to contribute professional advice. He suggested courses of action and helped devise the means for feasible implementation. No issue concerning the younger generations was beneath his attention. Ultimately, Zou Taofen's success lay in his ability to articulate, in a colloquial style, the idea that individual dignity and personal happiness in working lives were the goals of an emerging society that combined knowledge, integrity, and prosperity. Through the medium of literacy, he brought into existence a veritable community in which a diverse range of individuals, otherwise separately mired in their own concerns, caught glimpses of a larger world beyond their immediate surroundings.

As the editor of *Shenghuo zhoukan*, Zou Taofen was engaged by the social educators and business entrepreneurs of the CSVE to persuade petty urbanites that the new economy promised a good life for everyone. It was only logical that Zou eventually turned his attention to political concerns. His brand of muscular patriotism began, understandably enough, with a humane concern for the devastation of lives in the war zone, and outrage over the injustice and humiliation inflicted upon civilians through means of force. In these discussions, Zou's literary persona acquired an additional dimension. He presented himself as a simple man armed with nothing but courage, who had been spurred to action by sheer moral indignation. For the petty urbanites, he drove home the personal relevance of the consequences of war or peace. He also directed their frustrations over endemic or systematic problems against the political authorities. Thanks to Zou's considerable talent, he infused the discussion of the Japan question with a particular pathos, exciting urban patriotism at the onset of a global recession.[88]

As the 1930s wore on, Zou Taofen took his reasoning to the conclusion that when war intervened, a just society for all was necessary before any individual could ever attain realistic opportunities to lead a good life. Instead of vocational education for the working youth, Zou turned his attention to the political awakening of the literate public. It was not enough for a journal like *Shenghuo* to give voices to the everyday people. It was imperative that the journal spearhead the transformation of the new economy's "vocational youth" into the "progressive youth" in an age of evolutionary struggle.

CHAPTER 6

Petty Urbanites
and Tales of Woe

In the 1930s, a new group of writers began contributing to the pages of Shanghai's journals and magazines. Consisting of shop clerks, office workers, trade apprentices, business trainees, elementary school teachers, and so forth, these were individuals whose formal education had ended before university, but who were working in jobs that required literacy. They found their public forum in the left-leaning journals, to which they contributed autobiographical accounts of personal circumstances. By and large, these authors recounted tales of hardship. They suggested preoccupations with the economic problems of the era and evoked an atmosphere of insecurity and fear.

There was hardly anything new about shop clerks and trade apprentices complaining about their anxieties (see chapter 5). The "*ku,*" or bitterness, in their lives was clichéd and proverbial. It was part of the normative expectation that success in business, whether in the sense of material accumulation or upward mobility, be predicated upon a capacity to "eat bitterness *(chiku).*"

But the descriptions of suffering in the 1930s broke new ground, both in their portrayal of the nature of their problems and in the medium of telling. Unlike the stories told in an earlier time, these accounts had little to do with violence or physical abuse. They were not about the kicking or beating of rickshaw pullers or bonded maids, nor about the undernourishment or mistreatment of teenage employees. The stories were told in the first-person voice with the narrative subject placed within his or her familial context. The hardships had as much to do with the self as with family members. For every description of what an individual had to endure, there were corresponding accounts of the misery that stemmed from an inability to look after one's own kin. It was the incapacity to act and the strains placed on the bonds of caring that was the ultimate cause of suffering.

The tales had become introspective, in other words, to sketch the inner workings of petty urbanite thinking. The acknowledged dimensions of hardship had been expanded to encompass the ethical and emotional in addition to the material. A hardship was not just about an unwelcome condition that had been inflicted, but also about a desired state that had been denied. The narrators of these stories were not passive victims. They were subjects incapacitated by circumstances and prevented from attaining a sense of being.

A second point of departure had to do with the public nature of this self-representation and the literary debut of the petty urbanites (xiao shimin) in the pages of Shanghai's popular magazines. Literary realism of the 1930s, inspired by Eastern European trends, had contributed to the rise of a journalistic genre of popular reporting. In Shanghai there were productions of major projects such as *One Day in China* and *One Day in Shanghai.*[1] The volumes were embodiments of the belief that social reality was fully representable. This occurred when large numbers of individuals recorded the actual happenings in their everyday lives. Popular journals set aside special columns for amateur contributions in order to present portraits of "society." Along with the "letters to the editor," such contributions were believed to offer accurate depictions of contemporary social conditions.

Petty urbanite tales of hardship were thus practices that stemmed from particular notions about the literary representability of social reality.[2] Individual tales of woe were anything but personal concerns. Detailed narratives about daily lives were the materials that made up "society." Journal editors set aside space and encouraged amateur contributions. The lines were purposefully crossed between truthful representations of social experience and mediated constructions in the service of social ideology. The very conditions that enabled the public representation of personal circumstances had placed the tales in a liminal space between the authentic and the fabricated. The characters and circumstances in the tales were read, more often than not, as categories and types rather than as individuals, despite their first-person voice and detailed specificity.

A TRAGEDY

On June 12, 1935, Yue Lin, a fifty-five-year-old clerk, was charged by the Shanghai Municipal Police for the murder of his wife and six children.

According to the local paper, Yue, who hailed from Tianjin, had recently lost his job, and his savings were quickly depleted. After several trips to the pawnshops and rounds of borrowing from relatives and friends, he persuaded his wife that they should kill themselves. The couple decided to use opium and served it in a meal. The woman and the children died that evening; Yue alone survived. Utterly distraught, he then threw himself into a river, but was fished out by the police. The latter promptly imprisoned him on charges of multiple counts of murder.

After the Yue story appeared in paper, another family jumped to their deaths from atop the sixth floor of the Great World amusement center. This family consisted of a woman in her fifties, her thirty-year-old son, his wife, and their three children, aged seven, ten, and fourteen. None survived.[3]

Little else is known about these individuals apart from their deaths. Their tragedies nonetheless touched a nerve among Shanghai's petty urbanites. "My wife wept uncontrollably after reading of these deaths," wrote one Zhou Fang in a letter to the editor that appeared in the popular journal *Dushu shenghuo* (Reading and Livelihood). "Neither was I able to hold back my tears." The shock and dismay had much to do with the knowledge that the Zhangs were, not so long ago, well off, and Yue had been making more than one hundred *yuan* a month. Both families had been saving conscientiously for rainy days; the Zhangs and Yues were among the salaried and respectable urban workers. "Who would have thought that they could end this way!" wrote Mr. Zhou. "And the children, too!"

Zhou's wife pleaded with him not to lose his job. "You are a father of three and you have a family to support," she said. "Please be sure to do everything to stay on the good side of your boss and coworkers." She pledged to cut back on family spending and to save the best she could. "I'll do the cooking and washing myself and dismiss the maid at the end of this month," she said, "and we will also set aside money for emergency." The critical factor remained, nonetheless, that Zhou should hold on to his income, regardless of whether this meant having to go out of his way to please his superiors to the point of making himself unhappy. No price was too high to pay if it meant job security. "Please always think of your responsibility as a father and a husband and please think of the family!" Zhou's wife pleaded.

These thoughts brought a sense of gloom to the evening hours after work. Zhou recognized what this meant for his pride and autonomy, which had to take second place to the needs of his family. "I looked at my three children: the newly born, asleep in the crib; the middle one, playing on the floor; and the oldest, doing his homework by the lamp." They all depended upon him as their father and provider. It was an unbearable thought how the bliss and tranquility in his children's lives would shatter if he were to lose his job. "How could I possibly ignore my wife's plea?" Zhou concluded.

But were his job prospects secure even with the compromise in personal pride and autonomy? When Zhou described his new resolve to a friend at work, the latter responded with a jeer. "It is very well that you wish to heed your wife's plea. But don't you see that there is no promise of security beyond the day? Where are you going to keep the money that you are to save? Banks go out of business all the time. The ones owned by foreigners close down too. Things change so quickly these days. You deposit one thousand *yuan* and it shrinks to five hundred. If you'd like some sensible advice from me, I say you spend your money and buy some pleasure when it lasts! Do you really believe that you can hold on to your job just by being pliant and even obsequious? People lose their jobs when business slows down, and you lose your job even if you are competent and helpful! People of our sort cannot afford to think about the future. We are like the sparrows in the spring. Let's sing our happiness and fill our stomachs when the sun shines. As for the winter, there is not much that any one of us can do!"[4]

Zhou Fang's purported dialogue with his wife and friend, prominently featured in *Dushu shenghuo,* was an attempt to spell out the significance of the two family suicides for Shanghai urbanites who saw themselves in these tragedies. It placed the primary emphasis on job security, linked it to family survival, and depicted the male heads of households as hostages both to the workplace and the marketplace thanks to their family obligations. It wasn't just that old-fashioned notions of pride and autonomy were out of place; when hard times hit, these dialogues suggested, middle class virtues such as thrift and diligence promised no reward. Because human factors had been removed from the processes controlling individual destinies, there was little that anyone could do either to steer one's own future or to save one's family.

Zhou Fang's letter to the editor thus was no mere reaction to the two cases of family suicides. Invoking issues of life and death, and obligation and capability, it was a dire prognosis concerning the viability of middle-class social existence in Shanghai's prevailing economic system. It pried open the question: will middle-class economic virtue save white-collar families? It answered, emphatically, that the logic of the economic system was such that it simply would not permit petty urbanites to earn the social rewards of their hard work. If virtue was rendered irrelevant, then what values were petty urbanites to live by? Was there any escape from a fate that seemed comparable to that of a spring sparrow caught in a winter storm? How was a father and husband to assure the survival of his family in the economic turmoil of the 1930s?

It is worth noting that Zhou's letter appeared in the pages of *Dushu shenghuo*, a leading left-leaning journal in 1935. The fate of the bourgeois nuclear family occupied a strategic position in the formulation of a left-wing rhetoric that called for a socialist transformation of Chinese society. This left-wing discourse was centered upon the family rather than the individual; in that sense it represented a distinct departure from the cultural agenda of the May Fourth Movement of 1919. While the May Fourth radicals harangued the educated to urge individual liberation, the 1930s leftists mobilized the urbanites to seek national emancipation. While the former stressed the importance of a radical intellectual awakening to break with the past, the latter sought individual commitment to build up collective security. And while the former gave birth to radical politics and a socialist agenda, the latter ultimately led to the expansion of the CCP to include Shanghai's petty urbanites.

Left-wing publishing in the 1930s was progressive in the sense that unlike the student journals of the May Fourth Movement, it included the less educated and barely literate in its literary representations. A journal such as *Dushu shenghuo* gave space not only to the intellectuals, but also to shop clerks, factory managers, office workers, elementary school teachers, pawnshop apprentices, and so forth, all with their own tales of hardship and woe. This latter group appeared in print as authors instead of readers, unveiling the fears and frustrations in their lives while expecting exoneration instead of shame.

There were close connections between the stories of middle-class nuclear families and the construction of a socialist rhetoric of revolution. To better place these tales of hardship in historical context, let us examine the journal in greater depth.

DUSHU SHENGHUO

Dushu shenghuo was a bi-weekly magazine of social commentary that made its first appearance in Shanghai in late 1934. It was the work of four men—Li Gongpu, Ai Siqi, Liu Ti, and Xia Zimei (Xia Zhengnong). All, except the editor in chief, Li Gongpu (1902–1946), were clandestine members of the CCP.[5] Li, who was noted previously for his editorial role with the "Dushu shenghuo" column in *Shenbao*, Shanghai's leading daily, had built a career under Shi Liangcai, the newspaper's owner.[6] Shi had fostered the paper's critical stance of Chiang Kaishek's Nationalist government, and was consequently gunned down on November 14, 1934 by Nationalist secret service agents on an open highway.[7] *Dushu shenghuo*, a publication of left-wing and dissenting intellectuals, was poised to be critical of the established order from the outset.

In the inaugural issue of the journal, the editors explained their goals and the editorial line. They had acted, first of all, in the spirit of a new era *(shidai)*. The "old era," in which access to the printed page was viewed as status-conferring and possible only for those with time on their hands, had now passed.[8] The time had come for publishing to be shared with everyone.[9]

Literacy, the editors continued, remained a skill available only to an educated minority. Yet even within this minority there was a numerically significant majority who had been denied, as a result of their life circumstances, continuous access to the printed page. This majority included many of Shanghai's petty urbanites—the tens of thousands of shop clerks and apprentices employed in Shanghai's trades and industries, who had been "locked out of the iron gates of modern-style schoolhouses."[10] The hunger and thirst for knowledge among these men, the editors noted, went far beyond what the elite imagined. Yet they had been forced to limit their reading to after-work hours only. These men sought, as they should, knowledge only "of the sorts of practical relevance" that would enable them to "open their eyes and awaken their consciousness." With their consciousness awakened, these individuals would then be able to "set the course of their own lives."[11]

If reading was to lead to an increased control for clerks and apprentices over their destinies, the editors reasoned, then it could not be an end in itself, but must be combined with the struggle to make a living. Seen from this perspective, not all publications in circulation would suit the needs of the petty urbanite readers; they required guidance in the selection of reading material, which would be the journal's function. Moreover, the journal would not only suggest suitable material, but also teach "the correct method" of reading. The editors would conduct themselves, in short, as "earnest and sincere schoolmasters" vis-à-vis their reading pupils, who would be following the journal's prescriptions for the sake of their own betterment and benefit.[12]

Dushu shenghuo would thus function as an educational forum *(jiaoyu yuandi)* that supplemented the formal school system. It would be a school without walls, transforming workplaces into classrooms whenever someone picked up a copy of the journal. In contrast to the lecture halls, the journal's forum would not be dominated by the articulate and the learned, but would feature voices from the "vast and silent masses" who had been forced to drop out of school. The literary section of the journal was thus devoted to printing readers' contributions. They were encouraged to "use the language and experience of . . . [their] own lives to express . . . [their] own thoughts and feelings." The shared experiences reflected in these contributions were to provide the basis for a community among *Dushu shenghuo*'s reading audience.

There were over two dozen articles (about sixty thousand characters) in each issue. To implement the editorial policy, the journal divided its content into approximately ten headings. These included social commentaries, news analyses, book reviews, and essays on the natural sciences and social philosophy, which gave the journal a serious tone. There were also literary contributions, both autobiographical and fictional, by the readers. These stories contributed a rich description of the petty urbanite lives. Above all, the journal featured a section entitled "Questions and Answers about Readings" that continued the *Shenbao* column edited by Li Gongpu. This section featured the readers and the editors as joint contributors in an ongoing dialogue.

CHINA IN CRISIS

Take, for example, the May 1935 issue of the journal. Ai Siqi, who had already published a series of six or seven "talks" *(jianghua)* on ontology in the pages of *Dushu shenghuo*, entitled the latest segment "Heaven knows!" *(Tian xiao de!)*. Ai treated "heaven" and "humanity" as opposites, and declared that consciousness was a product of humankind's own history and past practices. Heaven, according to Ai, "does not know, despite ancient aphorisms to the contrary." Knowledge and consciousness arose in the course of human action. Because so much learning came from experience, there could be no limits to a man's capacity to know,

Ai continued, if one simply applied the correct scientific method to gather knowledge with diligence. Take, for example, the current economic recession that had affected so many lives. A person following the proper scientific method of analysis would easily see how this was entirely the fault of mankind rather than heaven. It was neither fate nor bad luck but the acts of human beings that had led to the closure of factories and the dismissal of employees.[13]

Qian Yishi's account and analysis of current events in the international arena, paired with Ai's philosophy, were meant to call the readers' attention to "the mess that the world is in," which Qian attributed largely to "evil dealings by monstrous imperialist powers."[14] Qian saw imperialism in two areas: military buildup in preparation for war, and economic expansion through international interaction. His commentaries in the May 1935 issue began with reports of the European talks in Dresden and Geneva. He lambasted Great Britain—"all justice and integrity in talk yet whores and bandits at heart"—for its soft stance vis-à-vis Hitler's Germany. He juxtaposed the Polish-German non-aggression pact with the "unthinkable" alliance between imperialist France and the socialist Soviet Union, and confidently declared that Europe was on the brink of war. Qian also devoted considerable space to the Silver Purchase Act passed by the U.S. Congress, and linked it directly to the monetary crisis in China. He greeted the arrival of an American economic study commission in China with a sneer, declaring that the commission, despite its announced mission statement, had come, in fact, to "enhance America's trade benefits at the expense of the Chinese."[15]

In the social commentary section, Li Gongpu surveyed the domestic scene and drew attention to four dates: May 1, May 3, May 4, and May 9. May 1 and May 4, Li wrote, deserved to be marked in red, for these were moments of new beginnings. May 3 and May 9, by contrast, were anniversaries of tragedy and humiliation, and should be remembered in grief and anger. But commemorative rituals would not serve any productive goals; there should be action in lieu of ceremonies. It was only by taking firm action that "we wipe off the shame on the brows of our people" and create a new and improved environment for productive work.[16]

With the bankruptcy of its villages and the armed invasion by Japanese imperialists, Li went on, China was in the depth of an acute crisis. Furthermore, with the imminent outbreak of a second world war, China's future was inextricably connected with developments beyond its borders. The Chinese had to nonetheless act to assert control over their own destiny. All actions, whether private, public, individual, or collective, must be geared toward the survival of the Chinese nation through active resistance against the Japanese and all forms of imperialism.

The laborers' fight against foreign imperialists, however, must not prevent them from simultaneously engaging in a struggle against the exploitation of Chinese national capitalism in a time of recession. Workers, for example, should continue to insist on their demand for an eight-hour workday. They must see themselves as entitled not only to unemployment benefits, but also to legal protection for the right to organize and to strike. Those who could read and write must serve as the nation's cultural workers striving toward the forging of an iron will of resistance. These were the trends of a new era. Cultural workers had to exercise vigilance and show no mercy toward those who wished either to reverse the current trends or to restore the values and beliefs of an earlier era.

The top task facing the nation and the people, Li concluded, was thus the consolidation of an anti-Japanese resistance front that would dedicate itself to fighting imperialism in all its forms. He urged "all readers of this journal" to commemorate the four anniversaries with a new awareness of the significance of these dates. He called for action whenever possible, and urged the petty urbanites, who might see themselves as insignificant "ants," to form "an army of ants in defense of the nation."[17]

Li Gongpu, however, was careful to remind his readers that they must hold on to their jobs and families while engaging in these wars of resistance. The appropriate action for the moment was not to cast aside the established order, but simply to gain a new consciousness about the world via reading and writing. This was to be done by following the reading program that *Dushu shenghuo* promised to outline.

Li Chongji, in a separate essay in the same issue, picked up where Li Gongpu had left off. On "Why Study Philosophy?" he explained that to live like a man, one must never mechanically perpetuate tradition, but should, instead, always make conscious choices. The very making of these choices constituted a form of action that lay well within the power of the average person. But most urbanites often failed to do so, because they tended to be constrained by their beliefs and outlooks, which were in turn products of their social circumstances. Their "philosophy of life," inherited and unexamined, limited their ability to grasp social reality. This might not be too much of a problem if the times were good. But in a time of economic hardship, "erroneous thoughts," which stemmed from uninformed value systems, might even lead people to tragic choices such as suicide. Philosophy, then, was the most important subject in a person's life in order to lead the existence of a true human being. By acquiring the proper scientific method, one could gain new perspectives to see the world and thereby attain a new sense of being and purpose. Philosophical lessons were important for everyone, Chongji stated, and it was well within the capacity of all journal readers to pursue the subject. Once a person acquired a new consciousness, he would be well prepared for action when the right moment came.[18]

The Chinese people in the 1930s, according to the editors, lived in a world of imperialism and capitalist exploitation, both foreign and domestic. They had also been born into a time of recurrent national humiliation and widespread social misery. Factories and shops were closing, and unemployment was on the rise. With the rural economy on the brink of bankruptcy, large numbers of peasants were forced to leave their homes in search of food. Most found neither work nor support as they moved from town to town. Worse yet, under the relentless pressure of capitalist and imperialistic exploitation, even property owners and the educated felt the pinch of recession and the threat of unemployment. With dimming job prospects and an unpredictable marketplace, a growing proportion of college students began to grow restless. The Chinese state, constrained by its own resources and embroiled in domestic feuds, did little to provide guidance, planning, or relief. Those with the power and the means paid little attention to the well-being of the multitude at large. With the help of Chinese capitalists, much of the wealth produced by the hard work of the Chinese people went overseas into the pockets of foreign imperialists. Japan, meanwhile, had steadily stepped up its military pressure on China. The loss of Manchuria and Inner Mongolia to the Japanese further deprived the Chinese people of important natural resources for survival. As armed conflicts continued between the Nationalists and the Communists, villagers were forced to pay additional levies to help finance the war, which came on top of the rent, interest, and taxes that they had already been paying. Highways for military use were built at the expense of peasant lives along their path. China, in short, was in a dire state of crisis, and it was the Chinese people who were being asked to bear the entire brunt.

To lend visual components to this idea of widespread Chinese misery, the journal used ink-and-brush drawings and woodblock prints to provide powerful cover designs and pictorial illustrations.[19] One drawing entitled "Their Picnic," for example, depicted two barefoot peasants, their faces buried in rice bowls, squatting under a tree for a hurried meal.[20] Another sketch, entitled "Refugees," depicts an uprooted peasant family of four on the run. The man leads the way hauling two large sacks on his back that contain the family's belongings. The woman walks behind him carrying a toddler in one arm and a large bag of clothing in another. A small child walks alongside tugging his mother's blouse. None of the figures have distinct features—the drawing made little attempt to represent the individuals. It conveyed, in general terms, the idea of a peasant family in flight.[21]

The cover of the journal's October 1935 issue portrays a long line of refugees, mainly women and children, trying to board a train. On the cover of the next issue was yet another cluster of villagers leaving home under an open sky, this time wading across a flooded river, their personal belongings hanging from shoulder poles. In the same issue a woodblock print depicted a group of people huddled together aboard a small boat that was afloat in the midst of a raging stream. The darkened clumps of human figures were motionless and trapped in the tight frame, while white waves crashed violently against the fragile boat.[22]

Those who turned to the pages of *Dushu shenghuo* in the mid-1930s could not help but be reminded of the scenes of flood, famine, destitution, and despair. As the leading popular left-wing journal seeking to establish itself with the middle class, its serious tone and austere appearance contrasted sharply with other popular publications of this time. *Liangyou*, for instance, featured colorful portraits of Westernized young women and glamorized images of modern Shanghai (see chapter 3).

While journals such as *Liangyou* devoted considerable space to commercial advertisements of consumer products, *Dushu shenghuo* ran no advertisements, only printing announcements of a selected list of new books. For this reason, *Liangyou* and comparable journals have been widely seen as part of a broader phenomenon of middle-class consumerism.[23] *Dushu shenghuo* was, by contrast, ideologically opposed to capitalism and consumption. Of the six hundred some journals published in Shanghai in the 1930s, *Dushu shenghuo* and *Liangyou* can be seen as occupying the opposite ends of the radical-conservative ideological spectrum.

Yet it is noteworthy that despite the ideological oppositions and other differences, the two journals shared one important point in common. Both delivered their message by presenting images and narratives that evolved around an idealized construction of the nuclear family. The nuclear family, with its conjugal bonds, parent-child love, material wants, and ethical expectations, had become the unstated subject in both sets of presentations.

This is not to deny the differences between the two positions. While *Liangyou* presented the nuclear family as a locus of comfort and consumption in a system of private ownership, *Dushu shenghuo* depicted these same families as fragile institutions in a time of deep recession and imminent warfare. While *Liangyou* encouraged its readers to imagine a life of ease and fulfillment, *Dushu shenghuo* attacked that confidence and raised specters of hardship and insecurity. While *Liangyou* spoke of youth, health, and longevity, *Dushu shenghuo* dwelled upon illness, hunger, death, and poverty. The woodblock images featuring the peasants, for example, were more than simply reminders of the disturbance lying beyond the confines of the city; the plight of the peasants carried subtle hints that the security of urban existence could be subjected to severe tests as well.

Despite such differences in representation, the point remains that both in *Liangyou* and *Dushu shenghuo* there was a shared assumption about the unstated subject, which was not the individual per se, but an individual as a member of a nuclear family. *Liangyou*'s promotion of fashionable women was not quite so much a statement about women on their own, but about the way a beloved wife or a pampered daughter participated in the material benefits of modernity. *Dushu shenghuo*'s stories about hardship and poverty, similarly, were not quite so much about poverty in itself, but about how the orphaned or the widowed were deprived of support. Whether in bliss or in hardship, either in the representations of *Liangyou* or *Dushu shenghuo*, it was, in the final analysis, via the nuclear family that a multitude of individuals were linked to the global trends of their time. This was particularly evident in the literary sections and the "Questions and Answers" columns of *Dushu shenghuo*, where, in dialogues between the editors and the readers, the journal spelled out the broader relevance of events that were taking place throughout the world, and related them to the family.

THE PLIGHT

In the pages of *Dushu shenghuo*, a family—of the sort that seems effortlessly bourgeois—is both a haven and emotional unit of sharing and love. It is through the routines of home life that one gains a sense of self and proper place. The family also functions as an economic unit that provides its members with their material desires.

There is, meanwhile, a marked division of labor and a hierarchical distribution of authority, which reflects differences on the basis of gender and age. These divisions, accepted as natural and inviolable, shape a person's sense of worth and structure the expression of goals and ambition in the larger world.

Certain functions are attached to individual members of the family according to differences in sex and age. Those who assume these functions are expected, in turn, to display certain virtues. A mature man, who is the father and head of the household, is to assume responsibility as the decision maker, the breadwinner, and the protector. He is expected to be hard working as well as successful in his handling of the family's affairs with the outside world. A woman, meanwhile, is to take on the responsibility of caring, rearing, and nourishing. A good wife and mother is not only hard-working, but also frugal, loyal, and self-sacrificing. The children, meanwhile, are mainly passive and compliant in this structure. They do what they are told, and show loyalty and devotion by accepting whatever may seem to be the family's lot.

These bonds and duties, one learns in *Dushu shenghuo*, are fundamental and almost sacrosanct for both the individual and the whole of society. Virtuous families, with all members working hard, must be able to reap their just rewards and achieve their self-preservation. The happiness and prosperity of virtuous families are not just manifestations of a healthy society; they give proof to the soundness of the system as a whole. There is, in that sense, an implicit contract binding the family to the society. Should the connections between virtue and reward, and hard work and family preservation, ever be severed, this would not only bring attention to the suffering individuals, but must also raise fundamental questions about the fairness of the social system as a whole.

Several points are notable in *Dushu shenghuo*'s treatment of petty urbanite tales of personal woe. It accepted the ethical and material dimensions of middle-class constructions of nuclear families, and used first-person narrative voices to represent hardships that were believed to be real. These hardships were compelling presumably as they involved real people with names, jobs, families, and difficulties—real lives that could be situated in time and place. But few of the characters were meant to be exceptional or interesting in their own right. It was as illustrations of normative expectations (that were either fulfilled or betrayed) that the stories of these characters were told.

Take, for example, the story of Wang Ping, who came from Yancheng, in northern Jiangsu. When Wang Ping was barely six, famine spread across the region, and his parents decided to flee the area. They packed their belongings and set off walking south, moving from town to town.

Whenever they found an opportunity, the couple hired themselves out as day workers in the fields. They planted crops, harvested rice, and ground husks. They worked hard and spent little, saving as much as they could in order to support the family's journey to the next town south. In this manner they finally reached, after five years, a small town lying just south of the Yangzi River, where they settled down.

Two years went by. Wang's father had saved a small sum of money and used it to set himself up as a street vendor. The entire family participated in this new venture. Each morning Wang's father would make the twenty *li* (six mile) trip to the county seat before daybreak, where he would buy candies and miscellaneous household goods totaling fifty to sixty catties (sixty-five to eighty pounds) in weight. He would then head back to town, carrying the entire load in two baskets balanced on a shoulder pole.

Wang's mother, meanwhile, attended the stand that was set up at a street corner in town. To help reach more customers, especially those who were confined to their workplace during the day, Wang Ping walked the streets hawking candies. They did well, Wang recalled, because his parents were "congenial people of a caring nature," and his father was "frugal and hard working." The whole family toiled all day long. They received their just rewards and, for a while, saw improvement in their income.

Wang's parents then decided to trade in the street stand for a rented store. As before, his father made daily runs to the county seat while his mother watched the store and Wang sold candies in the street. To help pay for the rental of the shop, Wang's father added an additional route to his itinerary, selling to outlying villages out of his baskets. Twice a year, during the planting and harvesting seasons when everyone was out in the fields, Wang's father would get up at three in the morning, make the solitary trek over to the county seat to obtain a good supply of preserved meat and fish, and then hurry over to the villages, arriving just in time to provide breakfast to the farm workers. The meat and fish were always popular, and attentive observations of market behavior paid off. Diligence and acumen reaped rewards. The senior Wang brought material benefits to his entire family.

Wang Ping, who by then was fifteen, was able to attend literacy classes in the local public school. Sales at the family shop exceeded one thousand copper coins each day. Wang's father found himself trusted as an honest and hard-working man in his new hometown.

Wang's parents then decided to have a second child. Things went downhill for the family from this point onward. During his mother's pregnancy and childbirth, Wang's father took her place in the shop. He took his usual trek to the county seat each day, and he also took care of his wife and the new baby. But this turned out to be more than he could bear—before the baby had turned one, the father fell ill and died.

Wang's father received a respectable burial befitting his stature. The funeral, however, placed a considerable drain upon the family's resources and a downward spiral commenced at this point. Unable to keep up with the rental charges, Wang's mother closed down the shop and moved back to the street corner where the family had had their stand a few years earlier. It now fell upon Wang Ping to make the daily run to the county seat at daybreak in order to buy supplies.

With the livelihood for a family of three upon his shoulders, Wang Ping had to give up literacy classes at the local school. He strained under the weight of his burden each day, although he was barely carrying half of what his father used to haul. His mother came down with a chronic illness in addition to suffering from depression. She wept each time she saw her teenage son struggling under the weight of the shoulder pole.

Wang Ping wrote his story with pen and paper borrowed from his literacy class. Of his trip in the pre-dawn darkness, as he marched his aching legs over the hills with baskets dangling on each side, he would say, "I cannot help the tears that are rolling down my cheeks. I miss my father."[24]

There are no visible villains in Wang's story. But nevertheless a family of virtue ultimately failed to receive its just reward. Diligence and dedication had brought this refugee family from Jiangsu to the threshold of a respectable life. Yet, in the end, the family's hard-earned new prospects were too fragile. The decision that Wang's parents made to have a second child seemed innocent and natural; the new baby was an event that deserved celebration. Yet things were thrown so disastrously out of kilter thereafter that the family's entire trajectory was tragically reversed.

A conclusion like this runs against well-established narratives about the connections between honest people and good fortune, and exemplary deeds and felicitous results. If real people are shown, furthermore, to face depressing prospects in places like a small town south of the Yangzi River, this poses a threat to the confidence of all who pride themselves in the same diligence and dedication, with the hope that hard work will lead their families to a better future. Like the family suicides that disturbed Zhou Fang and his wife, Wang Ping's story shook the foundations of the petty urbanites most fundamental beliefs, because it underscored the vulnerability of nuclear families in the current economic system.

Wang Ping's story ends with the loss of his father. Given the gender-hierarchical nature of the nuclear unit, no greater disaster could have befallen the family other than the death of the patriarch. The removal of such a paternal presence deprived the family of its main source of support and protection, and forced the women and children to confront the harshness of society.

This social independence, of course, is hardly what a woman or child would have chosen had it been possible for either to remain under the protective wing of the husband and father. Women and children, furthermore, were by definition weaker members of the family and the society. When left on their own, they were bound to be taken advantage of or coerced against their will. The following account, which features a woman worker and her mother, underscores this sense of loss following the death of a father. It is beside the point whether Qiao Ying, the twenty-something-year-old narrator, is earning a full wage in lieu of her deceased father. The loss of the father represents such an irreparable injury inflicted upon the wholeness of the nuclear family that the surviving widow and daughter could not but labor under the conviction that they had been deprived of a happier lot.

Qiao Ying was employed in a Japanese-owned cotton mill, and had the following to say about her payday: "This morning, before I left for work, mother gave me fourteen copper coins and a box of cooked noodles. She said: 'Ying, we are again out of rice. The cash is for you to get some breakfast before work. Be sure to get some sugar to flavor your noodles for lunch.' My money paid for three buns, but I ate only two. I gave the third to Ju, who had even less for breakfast."[25]

That afternoon the workers received their quarterly wages. Ying's wages, after three months of work, were a mere four *yuan*. Her employers withheld six *jiao* (sixty cents) ostensibly for safe-keeping.

Upon returning home, Ying handed her wages to her mother. The landlady promptly showed up, demanding her three-*yuan* payment. In addition, she asked for a repayment on a two-*yuan* loan. "Mother pleaded with her long and hard. She finally agreed to take three *yuan* and left us with but one." That evening, with rice again at the table after many days, "I ate happily and hungrily. Mother looked on and hardly touched the food. She had tears in her eyes. She was thinking of father."[26]

It is remarkable that Ying showed little pride in independently supporting her mother with honest labor. Because of the circumstances, Ying had become the household breadwinner. The villains in the account were stereotypes rather than real people—the landlady as the vile rentier and the factory management as the exploitative capitalists. They had behaved in perfect accord with the logic of the economic system that was presumably in place. The removal of the father-protector exposed the women of Ying's family to the outside forces of hostility. It broke down the divisions separating the inner realm of the female from the outer domain of the male. A family run by women might be able to function adequately as an economic unit. Yet it could never hope to repair this sense of normative breach. The loss of the patriarch had reduced the surviving widow and children to a lesser state of existence. It was this knowledge that brought tears to the mother and resignation to the daughter.

Numerous other contributions to *Dushu shenghuo* traced the downturn in family fortune to the death of the father. Sun Shuzhi's hope to go to middle school and to become a teacher was dashed when he received news that his father had died in Shanghai. Sun was fifteen and had just finished elementary school in his home town. His maternal uncle then dutifully arrived to console the widowed sister and orphaned nephew. It now fell upon the uncle to look after the bereaved household. Using his personal connections, the uncle arranged to have Sun accepted in a county pawnshop as an apprentice. He was to learn a trade and to drop out of school. On the day Sun was due at work, his uncle came to perform the duties of the male head of the household. The uncle escorted Sun to the pawnshop and witnessed the initiation ceremony on behalf of the family. Both the ritual and the workplace were exclusively for men; Sun's mother had to stay behind. She tearfully saw her son off as he was led away from home. In the next three years he would be permitted to return but three times each year. How the teenage boy was to fare from that point onward became largely a matter in the hands of the new master-employer.[27]

Yuan Fangxi was thirteen when his father died. Yuan's father had been a private tutor, school master, and finally the principal of a public elementary school. Yuan had learned how to read and write sitting on his father's lap and hovering around his desk. He had also been a pupil at the school and had always wanted to become a man of letters.

With the death of his father, Yuan was withdrawn from school and sent away to a distant town, where he was apprenticed to a soy sauce shop. Yuan did manual work and was kept on his feet all day.

If he could muster the energy at the end of the day, Yuan would peruse a set of collected essays written by his father, which he treasured as a special text of wisdom. He hoped to absorb the learning they embodied and restore himself one day to the company of the educated.

Yuan had to keep his reading secret, however. It was a "must" that trade apprentices learn use of the abacus and bookkeeping. It was a "must not" that they read literature and hold literary aspirations. Yuan thus risked exposing himself to the ire of his master trying to read his father's essays.[28]

Jin Manhui of Huizhou was a twelve-year-old elementary school student when his father died. He was immediately withdrawn from school, and, thanks to an uncle, accepted as an apprentice by a fellow Huizhou merchant in Shanghai.

The night before Jin left home, his mother helped him pack. Jin wanted to take along his ink slab, brush, paper, and books. He also wanted his Tang poetry collections and English textbooks. His mother said no and took them away; they were objects that belonged to a literary life. They no longer suited him in trade and were bound to annoy his new master.

The boy burst into tears and said that he would rather stay home; he was apprehensive about the apprenticeship. But the resistance was futile and only brought tears to his mother's eyes. Without a father, the son was lucky to find an apprenticeship. The next morning the uncle picked him up and delivered him, "lonely and dejected, . . . gripped by fear and sadness," into the hands of his new master.[29]

Jiao Daqiu, a twenty-seven-year-old farm laborer who wrote to *Dushu shenghuo* by the light of a kerosene lamp in a corral, dated his hardship to the summer when his father died. Jiao was sixteen and a secondary school student when tragedy struck. The family owned a three-room dwelling and eight *mu* of land. But it also went into debt during his father's illness. In order to pay off the debt and support his mother and four younger siblings, it fell upon Jiao to work in the fields. He mortgaged the family land and indentured himself to his father's creditors. His mother and sisters helped too, knitting, washing, and mending whenever they could find such work. The family managed with barely enough for two meals each day. Ten years had gone by, and Jiao saw neither hope nor respite from his incessant toil.[30]

Numerous accounts of this sort filled the pages of *Dushu shenghuo* during its two years of publication. The formulaic representation encapsulates a central trauma consisting of the loss of the father, the end of a familiar way of life, the departure from home, and the beginning of a new life of dependency. The recurrence of this storyline in the journal produced, in the end, a distinct effect. It turned individual narratives into sample reports about the conditions of a whole class of people. In the language of the 1930s, those who had lost their fathers *(shifu)* were inevitably deprived, at the same time, of opportunities for an education *(shixue)*. Arrangements were made at the father's funeral between the widowed mother and a visiting male relative. The young man thus passed from his father's care into the home of a new master.

While the master-employer wielded patriarchal authority that was no less absolute than that of the father, it was power of a different sort. The teenager entered into a personal dependency that was not only contractual, but also entailed a loss of autonomy and a measure of degradation. As the relationship was based on a transaction, it was vulnerable to the changing tides of the marketplace. In that case the youngster was also likely to lose his apprenticeship—*shiye*, which along with *shifu* and *shixue* made up the complete picture of destitution.

All in all, for a "vocational youth" the new addition of a master and a vocation *(zhiye)* would hardly make up for the loss of a father and an education. These personal accounts in the pages of *Dushu shenghuo,* as they dwelled upon the hardships that awaited the orphaned, simultaneously idealized the sanctity of the nuclear family and underscored its centrality in the well-being of everyone.

This is not to suggest, of course, that all Shanghai apprentices had been traumatized by the loss of their fathers. Nor that, despite the high personnel turnover rate in trades and shops, all vocational youths were on the verge of losing their jobs. It does mean, however, that there was a latent frustration and insecurity among Shanghai's petty urbanites, and left-wing journals such as *Dushu shenghuo* either gave expression to it or persuasively suggested it. These individuals saw themselves as the underprivileged and disadvantaged who had been denied access to education, deprived of the benefits of a more beneficent patronage, and blocked from a future of career advancement. In a time of recognized hardship such as the mid-1930s, the petty urbanites saw themselves as being particularly vulnerable; they had been deprived of a social safety net. They were forced to face the incalculable forces of the global marketplace on their own.

Dushu shenghuo, by painting a catastrophic picture of flooding, drought, famine, recession, and warfare, amplified this voice of fear, destitution, and despair. By printing the stories submitted by the readers, it also allowed these individuals to see that they were not alone in their plights. The journal's message, repeatedly stated, stressed that there was no viable future for any single individual, and that the bourgeois dream of someday moving ahead into the warmth of comfort and the ranks of the respectable was destined to fail. For the widowed, the orphaned, and the unprotected, virtue and hard work would not guarantee their survival. Nor, given the real cause of misfortune, should anyone hope to escape the general fate that befell the Chinese nation in the face of imperialism and global capitalism. The only viable course of action open to the petty urbanites was to band together and transform themselves into patriots and warriors who fought foreign aggressors in defense of the nation. For those deprived of paternal patronage, it was futile to lament the loss of their fathers. It was all the more imperative, in an acute struggle for survival, that they become patriots. By giving life to the nation, they would then give a fighting chance to themselves.

STRUGGLE AND SURVIVAL

Those who read *Dushu shenghuo* and wrote to its editors for advice could not fail to learn that the key to self-help was a reformed way of life, which could be summed up in two words: survival and struggle. No one was safe from the forces of foreign imperialism, which subjected the Chinese nation to external aggression. Under such circumstances, career failures and personal frustrations were only to be expected. No one needed to personally take responsibility for his or her condition. By the same reasoning, no one could realistically hope to better his or her prospects under prevailing circumstances. Such improvements would not be possible until the Chinese nation and its people had won liberation from imperialism. The prospects of the individual—the material well-being of the wives and children of the petty urbanites—were inextricably linked to the struggle for the liberation of the nation *(minzu jiefang)*. This simple truth, as the editors of *Dushu shenghuo* endeavored to show, was founded on principles of social science. It was a truth for all to grasp. The campaign for national liberation must therefore begin with a refashioning of petty urbanite consciousness through reading and thinking. It would gather momentum only as the petty urbanites engaged in struggles *(shenghuo douzheng)* that concerned them in their daily lives.[31]

The notion of self-help, of course, had been prominent in Shanghai popular journals well before this time. It was a main theme developed in Zou Taofen's *Shenghuo zhoukan*, which enjoyed enormous popularity with petty urbanite readers. Although barely a decade apart, *Dushu shenghuo* had redefined the terms of the discussion as developed in *Shenghuo zhoukan*. It rejected self-help as a means to improve professional skills and promote career advancement. It directed attention emphatically to outright unemployment and the absence of job security, and displayed a strong skepticism about the relevance of competence, merit, and work ethics to the improvement of one's lot. A willingness to adhere to high professional standards, of course, had been the cornerstone of Zou Taofen's prescription to the job-seeking petty urbanites. Like Zou and many other reformers, *Dushu shenghuo* sought the betterment of individuals through their transformation. This betterment, however, was not to take place within the context of accepted workplace relationships within a corporate framework. It was to lead, instead, to a total refashioning of socio-political relationships in the larger society, including a thorough revision of the basic principles of economic operation.

What, then, should be an appropriate response to the family suicides that had so shaken Zhou Fang and his wife? What should be the proper course of action for petty urbanites during the recession of the 1930s? From the perspectives of *Dushu shenghuo*, both Zhou's wife and his friend had displayed "the narrowly self-centered perspectives of the small property owners." Zhou's wife, like all virtuous women of the past, believed that she could save her family with old-style frugality and good-natured docility. Zhou's friend, on the other hand, had given himself to modern man's hedonistic impulses, which were just as misdirected. What Zhou should do, advised the editors, is prepare himself for the challenges of a different kind of life. Was manual labor truly shameful? Was social degradation into the ranks of the laborers a condition worse than death? Was it truly justifiable that parents should kill their children so as to spare them the prospect of a "lower" status in life? The answer to each one of these questions clearly had to be "no." The Yues and the Zhangs, in that sense, were victims of their own erroneous thoughts, products of social circumstances. They made the mistake of doing little to fight their false values. The families were killed by their unreformed state of mind.

There was, *Dushu shenghuo* continued, a collective life above and beyond that of the mere individual, in the stream of which one man was but "as insignificant as an ant." This was the life of the masses, which would continue on even if the individuals were to perish. What the "spring sparrows"—petty urbanites at a time of economic recession—ought to do, then, was to regard the world in a new way, to join the life that flew in this powerful stream, and to fight to enrich and enhance the vitality of a larger collective existence. Those with jobs and families "need not take up the vanguard position, but . . . must join the camp." One could do so by training oneself to have the right kind of thoughts in everyday life.[32] Although no promise was offered that this would help guarantee the security of Zhou's employment, he was at least shown a way to cultivate a consciousness that would give him and his family a life without a white-collar job.

A critical number of individuals had come under the influence of journals such as *Dushu shenghuo* in the mid-1930s. As Japan intensified its attempt to gain control over northern China in 1935, Shanghai's petty urbanites mobilized for patriotic action. The Shanghai National Salvation Association of Vocational Youths was one of the most active divisions in the All-China Federation of National Salvation Associations.[33] The Ants Club (Yishe), which pledged to build "an army of ants" to struggle for the survival of the nation, developed a membership of over ten thousand people. After the outbreak of war in July 1937, the Shanghai branch of the Chinese Communist Party, led by the accountant Gu Zhun (see chapter 7), facilitated the formation of Society of Beneficial Friends (Yiyou she), which used cultural and social events as a front for political mobilization.[34] These organizations did much to draw the city's clerks, office workers, and apprentices out of the established networks of relationships centering upon their activities at home and work. These "ants" built new communities that evolved around their patriotic activities. They formed drama troupes, choirs, news clubs, and reading groups. Such mobilization profoundly altered the use of literacy and the dissemination of ideas in Shanghai's petty urbanite society.[35] The rise of the nation, in this sense, had stemmed from a deep-seated uneasiness at the workplace, and was concurrent with an acute sense of crisis within the nuclear family.

Pre-war left-wing discourse on the nuclear family is significant in several ways. As it shifted attention away from the individual to focus instead on the family, it directed concerns to issues of survival and familial obligations rather than to rights and individual happiness. It pushed aside the May Fourth agenda of the articulation of individuality and developed a gendered construction of "male" and "female" within the context of the family.

Ethical norms governing familial relationships, meanwhile, became closely intertwined with a consideration of material well-being. It was essential that as a father or a husband, a man should provide for and shield his family. It was in keeping with a time-honored Confucian teaching, similarly, that as a filial son a man must be able to provide for the comfort and support of his aging parents. An inability to provide was not only an economic hardship, but also a moral failure and an emotional misfortune. When a whole class of hard-working men found themselves unable to fulfill such obligations, the time had clearly come for there to be drastic changes within the entire society. There was, once again, an "economistic" turn that demanded a place in Chinese democracy.

Left-wing discourse of the 1930s presented individuals as the product of a web of ethical and material relationships, and thus laid the foundation for a systemic critique of the social system. The result was not only a radical rejection of a capitalist economy of private ownership and market mechanisms, but also an attack on the practical viability of the very idea of an idealized nuclear family.

As the heads of households were shown to dysfunction, there emerged at the same time an idealization of a paternalistic socialist state that institutionalized its functions both as a provider for and protector of the Chinese people. The state, in a sense, had taken over the tasks of the family. Familial bonds had not been rejected, they had been depersonalized. Under state management, Chinese modernity emerged as an economistic project of material comfort and moral conservatism, instead of a critical exercise in intellectual self-reflection.

Chinese modernity, as it had taken shape in the social and cultural context of Republican Shanghai, came to promise endless progress and sustained prosperity, and, at the same time, inspired demands for security and protection against the backdrop of recession and imminent warfare in the 1930s. During the War of Resistance these demands converged in a popular idealization of a paternalistic state powerful enough to look after individual well-being. Virtue and authority came to rest neither with the heads of the households nor with the corporate leaders. Neither would be able to live up to the moral obligations toward their dependents in the larger circumstances of the time. Worse yet, some would even be forced to compromise their principles. But the promises of a good life in a just society continued to inspire. In the end, Shanghai's petty urbanites pinned their hopes on the construction of a modernized, socialist state.

From Patriarchs to Capitalists

In July 1937, the Nationalist government declared the War of Resistance against Japan. In Shanghai, fighting broke out soon after in the city's outskirts on August 13, 1937. The war, which was to last for eight years (1937–45), went through three stages: intense fighting in the lower Yangzi region (August–December 1937), the isolation of the foreign concessions into "lone islets" (August 1937–December 1941) in occupied China, and, with the outbreak of war in the Pacific on December 7, 1941, the full occupation of the concessions under Japanese military authorities, aided by the Nationalist Wang Jingwei regime in Nanjing.[1]

R. H. Tawney, in *Land and Labor in China,* famously characterized the Chinese peasantry of the 1930s as being immersed up to their necks in water.[2] Even a single ripple would have drowned many. In the case of the petty urbanites in Shanghai, the fighting, siege, and occupation of the city, accompanied by violence, destruction, material scarcity, inflation, commodity control, and the slowing of business, proved to be a succession of such ripples. Those occupying the lower rungs of the "gowned" slipped off the social ladder. The number of those who were forced out of schools *(shixue)* and jobs *(shiye)* were lost as well, their ranks augmented by children and teenagers orphaned *(shihu)* by the war.

Preoccupation with issues of violence and survival, foremost on the minds of many, did more than simply distance the pre-war middle-class aspirations for a prosperous, white-collar nuclear family. They also placed new strain on the construction of the company as a family that ran on patriarchal authority and economic virtue. The war sent the natural families of the petty urbanites into a state of crisis. This condition at home led the employees to place new demands on the corporate family. The legitimacy of managerial power and executive privileges during the war hinged, in the end, not only on the new enterprises' claims to patriotism, but also on the perception of their social responsiveness to the destitute and the needy. If private mercantile wealth in these extraordinary times was to retain its respectability, it had to shift its legitimizing device from a mere identification with the interest of the nation to an added demonstration of its concern for the well-being of the people.

Workplace culture in Shanghai's modern sectors underwent significant transformation during the war. Managers and clerks survived by juggling different priorities. Whether on the floors of the stores or in the offices of banks and firms, new ideas about the corporate family took hold that were to refashion post-war urban politics at the workplace.

WARTIME SHANGHAI (1937–45): AN OVERVIEW

When fighting broke out on the outskirts of Shanghai in August 1937, Chinese troops put up a firm resistance and sustained heavy casualties.[3] Japanese troops concentrated their land and air power on townships north of the Shanghai concessions, destroying large parts of satellite towns such as Wusong, Hongkou, Dachang, and Zhabei and reducing Chinese industrial facilities by half. The invaders began a second offensive from the south, launched from Jinshanwei, a small town north of the Hangzhou Bay. The rural communities east of the Huangpu River (Pudong) thus found themselves directly exposed to enemy fire. Frightened, many families packed up and ferried across the river to the Nanshi district. From there, some tried to flee further south by taking the train, while others headed north and west in the hopes of entering the French Concession. One day in late August, Japanese war planes dropped eight bombs into the crowds waiting at the south train station. The explosions injured and killed seven to eight hundred people. The devastation was captured in a photograph of a lone toddler crying in the midst of the bombed-out station, which appeared in *Life Magazine* in September.

In late November, with losses estimated at upwards of a quarter of a million people, the Nationalist army abandoned the city and withdrew up the Yangzi toward Nanjing, the national capital. This second line of defense was crushed within two weeks. Japanese troops entered Nanjing on December 12 and perpetrated numerous violent acts—a strategic use of brutality now known as the controversial "Nanjing Massacre"—in which yet another estimated quarter of a million people perished.[4] With the Nationalist government forced to relocate increasingly farther up the Yangzi to Wuhan, Japanese forces were able to advance steadily into central China. By late December few lower Yangzi cities remained unoccupied, and few towns or villages were spared fire or looting. The bulk of China's industrial facilities, heavily concentrated in this region, were also laid to waste.[5]

Shanghai's foreign concessions had declared neutrality virtually as soon as armed conflict broke out.[6] On August 14, Chinese fighter planes, in a botched attempt to attack Japanese battleships in the Huangpu River, dropped bombs on the International Settlement, which resulted in deaths and damage. British and American consuls protested vehemently, demanding that fighter planes of both sides stay clear of concession skies. On August 23, Japanese planes nonetheless dropped bombs on the busiest intersections of Nanjing Road, killing and injuring hundreds in an area distinguished by over one hundred and sixty thousand square feet of merchandise displays, restaurants, theaters, bars, and fancy hotels belonging to the Wing On and the Sincere department stores.

The population displacement in the lower Yangzi was massive, reaching an estimated total of over 1.3 million people by late October 1937. Of these, an estimated seven hundred thousand sought refuge in Shanghai. Many women and children lived in the streets, the latter dying at a rate of over two hundred per day from hunger, illness, and exposure.[7]

As soon as the violence broke out, a multitude of local charitable organizations sprang to action. Among these were the Shanghai International Red Cross, the Chinese Buddhist Association, the Shanghai Chinese Charitable Relief Association, the International Red Sauvastika Association, and the Relief Committee of the Federation of Shanghai Charitable Associations. They joined forces under the International Relief Committee (IRC) led by prominent religious figures such as Yan Huiqing, R. P. Jacquinot, W. H. Plant, and G. E. Baker. The committee eventually received funding from the Nationalist government, the American Red Cross, and private individuals and organizations from all walks of Shanghai society. With the support of the foreign consular corps and the Shanghai municipal government, the IRC created an international relief zone in Nanshi, which employed Chinese police officers to maintain order. The zone bordered the Huangpu River on the east and the Nanyang Bridge, a gateway to the French Concession, on the west. It was an enclosure that included a large number of public buildings such as the Temple of the City Gods, the Yu Gardens, schools, guild halls, and other temples. Many shops had been closed or abandoned by then. On its first day of operation, the zone took in over twenty thousand people who were given basic care. In mid-November Japanese troops pushed toward Nanshi, bombing the area relentlessly; the wooden structures of the old city were quickly engulfed in flames. As Nanshi burned, many more were forced to flee. The total number of war victims sheltered in the zone was said to have reached between seventy thousand and one hundred thousand, who were accommodated in 104 to 130 sites.[8]

Shanghai Protestants, Catholics, Buddhists, and the business elite also launched relief operations inside the foreign concessions. The YMCA and the Shanghai Disaster Relief Society of the Federation of Charitable Associations (Shanghai cishan tuanti lianhe jiuzai hui)—convened by Mayor Wu Tiecheng in December 1936, chaired by prominent local lay Buddhists Xu Shiying, Huang Hanzhi, and Qu Yingguang, and headquartered at the Benevolence and Sustenance Charitable Hall (Renji shantang)—were among the most active in the International Settlement. Scores of theaters, cinema houses, hotels, guild halls, restaurants, night clubs, banks, and schools were converted into temporary shelters. Tents were pitched later on cemetery grounds that accommodated up to six thousand. Some of the charitable activities were mobilized on the basis of the networks that contributed to the National Salvation Movement in 1936. Young cadres staffing the relief camps were soon organizing literacy classes and political education for the teenagers at the camps. To relieve the population pressure on the concessions, war victims were encouraged either to rehabilitate or to move on, often to join the war efforts in the interior under the command either of Nationalist or Communist generals. When business resumed in 1938, a small number of these youths found jobs as trainees and junior clerks in Shanghai's offices and shops.[9]

In mid-November, with Nanshi under Japanese occupation, the foreign enclave, shaken as it was, became a haven and an oasis—a "lone islet" *(gudao)* of relative safety within a sea of massive conflict and extensive bombing. But the borders of the "lone islet" were permeable to the upheavals engulfing the continent. The war transformed business operations, cut off regular shipping and supplies, disrupted the circulation of currencies, and exposed travelers to exceptional hazards. Hardship ensued, and in the winter of 1940, when an exceptionally cold spell gripped the lower Yangzi region (Jiangnan), thousands died of starvation and exposure in Shanghai's streets. In the French Concession alone, municipal authorities documented hundreds of dead bodies that were removed from the streets each morning. The living, as contemporary photographs suggest, coped by averting their gaze from the dead lying at their doorsteps.[10]

The war sent Jiangnan's wealthy households into the concessions. Estimations varied, but by general accounts the total population had risen from three to four million.[11] Rent soared and living conditions deteriorated. Once the fighting subsided, the rich and idle began to fill bars, restaurants, theatres, hotels, dance parlors, movie houses, amusement halls, and stock exchanges, killing time and gambling on luck. Sales revenue at the Wing On Department Store rose sharply after a brief period of depression the previous fall.[12] The extravagant expenditure of the wealthy lit the wartime night sky ablaze in neon once again. Even as Shanghai's elite and civic associations rallied to offer relief for war refugees, the scene was being set for sharp contrasts between the rich and the poor, and the well-connected and the utterly destitute, who had come to coexist in close proximity on the "lone islet."

Wartime Chinese politics in Shanghai evolved, meanwhile, around the choice between collaboration or resistance vis-à-vis the Japanese. After the initial military action, occupation authorities embarked upon negotiations with individual Chinese who might collaborate to create local regimes.[13] Nationalist government authorities, in response, instructed their special agents to step up assaults on likely traitors. Media opinion by and large applauded state-sponsored violence as a necessary expression of wartime patriotism. To counter such attacks, the occupiers in turn exploited internal Chinese divisions to create "puppet" intelligence operations that would do their bidding. The result was the birth of a unit for action headquartered at 76 Jessfield Road, consisting of former Chinese Communist agents and Green Gang members. Known as "Number 76," the service soon earned notoriety for their ruthless brutality.[14] Both sets of Chinese agents were based outside the concessions, yet staged their rival action inside. The "lone islet," where financial, commercial, journalistic, educational, and entertainment establishments had amassed, became the site of countless incidents involving mail bombs, hand grenades, shootings, assassinations, and abductions. The "extra-boundary" "badland" on the western end of the International Settlement, where casinos and nightclubs relied upon gangster connections for security, degenerated into a scene of urban terrorism.[15]

In the summer of 1938 the Nationalist government relocated its wartime capital to Chongqing. In December, Wang Jingwei, the second highest ranking official in the Nationalist Government, left Chongqing for Hanoi under secret arrangements with the Japanese.[16] Wang then made his way to Shanghai after a failed assassination attempt. In Shanghai, Wang, a veteran follower of Sun Yatsen, declared himself the head of a reconstituted Nationalist government that would fight for peace. He returned to Nanjing and announced, on March 30, 1940, the "return" of the Nationalist government to its rightful capital. In April, on the traditional tomb-sweeping day, Wang appeared for a full ceremony before the Sun Yatsen Mausoleum. The establishment of the Wang regime, endorsed by the mayor of Shanghai, Fu Zongyao (Fu Xiao'an), was designated as "*huan du* (return to the capital)" and celebrated with parades, speeches, lantern processions, radio broadcasts, newsreels, special newspaper editions, and public gatherings.[17]

For the people of Shanghai and the lower Yangzi region, the establishment of the Wang regime was a watershed in wartime politics. The two Nationalist governments, in mirror images of each other, stood in different degrees of tension with the Japanese and the Chinese Communists. The Communists had declared, in August 1937, a second united front with the Nationalists in a Chinese war of national liberation against Japanese imperialism. The Communist's New Fourth Route Army, which was allowed to operate in the hilly region of southern Anhui, nonetheless competed aggressively with the Third Military Command of the Nationalists for the human and material resources that were flowing out of Shanghai. The two armies clashed in January 1941, breaking up the united front. The Wang regime in Nanjing, for its part, embraced as its goals "the unification and construction of China and the establishment of permanent peace in East Asia."[18] This meant suspending hostility toward Japan, declaring war on communism, and booting the European concessions out of China.[19] Yet it was under its watch that an underground network developed between Shanghai's ardently anti-Japanese petty urbanites and the Communist New Fourth Route Army, after the latter had reestablished its base in northern Jiangsu. The Communist army, marginalized in the rural hinterland, relied upon its underground connections with Shanghai for supplies such as medicine, radio transistors, steel pipes, communication equipment, and printing machines, in addition to skilled organizers and literate cadres.[20] Tension escalated, meanwhile, between the Wang regime and its Japanese backers as these presumed partners for peace quarreled over issues of puppet autonomy, the degree of Japanese interference, level of war contribution, and responsibilities for civilian security.[21] The multifaceted struggles between the Chinese and the Japanese, and the Nationalists and the Communists, cut across lines of nationhood and ideology. At critical junctures, local

politics, old-society values, petty vice, and individual corruption meant
as much as high-sounding rhetoric and grand strategy. Yet after the establishment of the Wang regime in 1939, no division seemed to matter
more than the systematic rivalries between Nanjing and Chongqing when
it came to the politics of patriotism, situated in the broader struggles between Anglo-American democracies, Central European fascism, and Eastern communism.

On December 7, 1941, Japan attacked Pearl Harbor. In Shanghai, John
Birge Sawyer, American Consul for the visa section, described the following day:

> Was awakened at 4:15 by distant gun firing and explosions. Got up and
> looked out of window; saw nothing; went back to bed and sleep. Arrived
> at office on time (9 A.M.) and was met by Harold Pease who said that state
> of war existed and several members of staff had already burned the confi-
> dential files and the code books. . . . Finally received word that the offices
> must be vacated by noon. Piled all records into safes and cabinets and went
> home to Cathay Mansions. . . . Saw Japanese military trucks drive up to
> the American Club, all bristling with bayonets and saw the Japanese flag
> unfurled from upper window and large notices pasted on pillars at the
> front entrance. Got word orally from various sources that the USS WAKE
> had been boarded and had surrendered and was now flying the Jap. Flag;
> that the British Naval vessel (PETREL) had been blown up to escape cap-
> ture; that the British and American installations of the oil companies had
> been seized. Saw the captain of the WAKE in uniform taken captive in front
> of our consulate entrance.[22]

At about 10:00 A.M. Japanese troops marched into the International
Settlement in a light drizzle. An invisible crowd watched in silence as the
invaders crossed the bridge spanning Suzhou Creek. The soldiers reached
the southern bank of the river and took up positions at street intersections. They deployed themselves from the Bund to the western end of the
Extra-Boundary Road. "Some of these men wore glasses. Others wore
a short mustache. A few were smoking cigarettes. All held their guns right
across their laps and none made a sound."[23] The French Concession,
which had earlier come under a municipal council appointed by the Vichy
regime, was spared this grim humiliation.[24]

Much discussion took place the following year between the Wang government and the Japanese occupation authorities. On August 1, 1943,
the International Settlement and the French Concession were formally
handed over to the Chinese government of the Shanghai Special Municipality. The two concessions were combined to form a single Number
One District Office.[25] Serving as the mayor of the larger Shanghai was

Chen Gongbo, a close colleague of Wang Jingwei.[26] Chen wrote the lyrics for a song called "The Greater Shanghai March," the performance of which filled the airwaves with eulogies for "the renaissance of China, the security of East Asia, and the completion of our independence and freedom."[27] Almost exactly one century after the Opium War (1839–42), European Shanghai had come to an end and the city was unified under a Chinese government, thanks to Japan's "friendship." The new district office would be staffed thereafter by an administrative team consisting of Chinese and Japanese administrators who were paired in functions and appointed in equal numbers. The busy mayor, for example, took the job as the district's director on a part-time basis (jian). To help him fulfill his duties, a full-time Japanese "advisor" was to work with him, wielding the ultimate power of decision-making.[28]

The fall of the concessions meant the silencing of Chinese resistance in the press and the end of the public activities of organizations. It also meant the end of Shanghai as a destination for people fleeing the Imperial Japanese Army. Occupation authorities introduced a system of household registration and pressured recent arrivals to depart either with or without the use of travel passes issued by the military authorities. Within a matter of months, three quarters of a million people had been returned to the countryside.[29] To help quell the urban population, Japanese military authorities turned off power supply, cut back tramway services, threw up road blocks, erected barbed wire fences, posted armed sentries at crossroads, and randomly subjected urban districts to blockades that lasted from days to weeks. The Wing On Department Store, for example, was blockaded twice, for three weeks and three days respectively. Such closures did not encourage business.

Currency and commodity control ensued, both with a devastating effect on the free-flow of goods. Shops and businesses were required to accept the paper currency issued by the Central Reserve Bank of the Wang regime. Moreover, by mid-1942, it had become illegal and punishable to carry the fabi, the legal tender issued by the Nationalist government in Chongqing.[30] The Chongqing notes were in wide circulation in the foreign concessions prior to 1941. Shanghai's civilians were ordered to exchange their fabi for Nanjing's Central Reserve notes at a rate of two to one. A ban was also placed on the use of the English pound, the American dollar, and the Hong Kong dollar in either cash, traveler's checks, or personal checks.[31] British or American registered companies such as Wing On fell into the category of "enemy properties." These firms were subjected to downright confiscation or Japanese administrative oversight, in addition to suffering from the economic consequences of wide-ranging restrictive measures on the movement of goods and limitations on pricing. With the buying, selling, pricing, and transport of rice placed under strict control, rice lines appeared days after the Imperial Japanese Army entered the concessions. Smugglers risked death to cross military checkpoints. Rampant black market dealings arose, which further disrupted the operation of the open market.

Corporate rhetoric of diligence and dedication continued from the prewar days. Yet under the changed circumstances of war, issues of violence and survival preoccupied the work force. In tacit defiance of the managerial authorities, employees launched, in the late 1930s, their own associations for mutual insurance and patriotic activism. Quoting classics such as Mencius, petty urbanites invoked historical memories and articulated their own notions of economic justice.

With the end of European Shanghai, the modern sector of Shanghai's businesses were further subjected to powerful pressure. To the extent that Shanghai had come under a Nationalist regime that promoted "peace," all business enterprises that continued their operations had implicitly accepted a political arrangement with the Japanese occupation authorities. Corporate leaders were seen compromising their patriotism for the preservation of their companies and complicit in the construction of the "Greater East Asian Co-Prosperity Sphere" of the invading authorities. In the War of Resistance the modernizing business elite of Shanghai lost their patriotic claims, which they had won decades earlier on a metaphorical war of trade.

The larger issue of collaboration and resistance eroded the moral authority of the corporate superiors, who had, in peace, presented themselves paternalistically as teachers, paragons, and providers. Shanghai's middle- and lower-level employees struck out on their own in the late 1930s beyond the confines of the corporate compound. Building on the momentum of the National Salvation Movement of the mid-1930s, they formed associations and joined support networks.[32] They met after work and appeared on stage, in the streets, and in the press. The participation of underground Communist activists was strategically critical, if not organizationally decisive and discursively indispensable. Shanghai's white-collar business employees, knowingly or not, ended up joining efforts with the Chinese Communist Party (CCP).

This does not mean that the familial ideal and the metaphor of a corporate family ceased to be relevant. It means, instead, that the war decisively changed the political dynamics within the "family," which in turn produced discursive consequences. Instead of loyalty to the hierarchical dependence between the superiors and the subordinates, young clerks and junior trainees, distanced from the moral authority of their belea- guered superiors, formed for themselves a kind of brotherhood based on the egalitarian bonds that joined fellow workers. Instead of workplace parents and managerial moral paragons, the corporate workforce took matters into its own hands; it demanded institutional attention to issues of care and assistance and provided support for each other. The old sys- tem had used language such as "*nian shang*" and "*fen hong*" to describe the gifts of benevolence and the sharing of blessings offered by the pa- triarchs to worthy members of the extended family. The new workforce now looked past the "gifts" and the "benevolence" to demand such re- wards as basic considerations in response to their needs. "Benevolence," once institutionalized and divorced from the charitable intent and dis- cretionary authority of the corporate patriarchs, became a system of de- personalized welfare. The transformation eventually eroded the defer- ence that was due to the patriarchs. Whether an employer deserved respect was subjected to the criteria of social justice: Were benefits and wealth equally distributed? Was there a larger assurance for the survival of worker families in times of stress?

SHANGHAI GLAMOUR DURING THE WAR

At almost exactly 1:00 P.M. on August 23, 1937, while bustling traffic and throngs of pedestrians jammed the intersections of Nanjing and Zhe- jiang roads, bombs fell from the sky. They hit a third floor balcony of the Sincere Department Store. Water cascaded down the building as the pipes were exposed to the streets. The explosion took out shop windows on either side of the Nanjing Road, including those belonging to a sev- enteen-story building that had just been finished for the Wing On De- partment Store. The flying pieces of glass rained down on the passersby before carpeting the streets. A Sikh policeman, who was directing traffic atop his box, vanished along with the rest of the intersection. Just to the east, a double-decker municipal bus, filled with passengers, caught fire. The next day there were still body parts sticking out of the bus's charred and mangled carapace. What was once the fanciest section of Nanjing Road had been transformed, within a matter of minutes, into a deadly scene of bloody chaos. Some seven hundred people were injured; over one hundred eventually died.[33]

Inside Wing On, the company's official bulletin board in the employee dining hall, which the week before had been urging everyone to sign up for smallpox immunizations and to watch out for over-extended credit accounts, was blank for the next two days. Fifteen people on the company's payroll had been killed. Over four hundred thousand *yuan* worth of company goods and decor had been destroyed. Merchandise like towels, lingerie, parasols, Western medicine, and quilts were among the most extensively damaged.[34] Scores of men picked up the brooms and began removing the debris in the summer heat. "It was hot and humid and I was quickly soaked through in a sweat," a Hongkou credit department clerk, ordinarily a desk worker, wrote in his request for sick leave. "There was no meal service in the dining hall. I was hungry after sweating for an entire day. I went to the lower level of the Great Eastern Hotel, ate some bread, and washed it down with cold water. Little did I realize that the chill of the water and the heat of the sun was to clash to cause me great sickness in the stomach!"[35] Zhao Zuyou, employee No. 570 in the fabrics department, fell to the floor bleeding from shrapnel that had entered his back. He was also to lose his left middle finger, which would later make him self-conscious when showing quality fabric to customers. Yao Zhaochun, security guard No. 1, survived only after undergoing several rounds of surgical operations to remove various bits and pieces of debris lodged in his face and neck.[36] Even Leon Kwok (also known as Guo Linshuang, Lam Shuen Kwok, or L. S. Kwok), Wing On's general manager, sustained cuts on his hands and sought remedy later in Hong Kong in the winter of 1939.

When Wing On's managerial voice was again heard on August 25, it announced that the company had engaged the service of Dr. Chen Daming to operate an onsite clinic, which would open daily at 2:00 P.M. Dr. Chen was to receive patients in the tearoom on the second floor of the company's Great Eastern Hotel. Guest rooms 218 to 220, ordinarily off-limits to employees, were now designated as sick wards.[37] By then the store had been shut down for two and a half days, which almost matched the vacation time granted for the Spring Festival. The management announced that business would resume the following day, August 26, at 8:00 A.M. The wheels of commerce had to again be set in motion.[38]

The store's board of directors, located in Hong Kong under the parent company, held urgent discussions to assess the damage and to consider appropriate steps. On August 31 the management formally communicated the board's decisions to the employees. Relief and compensations were in order, though offered in a way that honored seniority and hierarchy. The company would pay for the proper burial of all who had died.

It would also offer monetary compensation to the surviving families. The kin of those with "low salaries," junior clerks and trainees, would be offered two hundred *yuan*. The families of those receiving higher pay, like senior clerks and department heads, were to receive the equivalent of a full year's worth of the deceased person's salary. For those who had been injured, the company would cover all medical expenses. And, upon recovery, even the permanently maimed would be suitably employed and looked after to the best of possibilities.[39]

Wing On employees were generally appreciative. The measures earned Leon Kwok, in particular, a lasting reputation as a caring person and a benevolent patriarch. By and large, the parents of the "low-paid" teenage trainees would be awarded a lump sum that exceeded the equivalent of their sons' annual pay. And the wives and children of those drawing higher salaries—older men with responsibilities as heads of households—would be consoled with settlements in the thousands. For the security guard Yao, Wing On expended hundreds of dollars for medical treatments on company account. Yao was also comforted daily, during his recuperation, with special meal deliveries, including poached eggs, prepared in the kitchen of the Great Eastern Hotel. Upon recovery Yao received a promotion to become a squad leader in the company's security force. He was put on light duty to watch the newly completed dormitory building. The clerk Zhao, whose aching back distracted him from a job that required climbing up and down ladders to retrieve rolls of fabric, also received reassignment to a desk job.

Wing On management, in short, responded with caring concern to the crisis at hand. In the weeks after the bombing incident it spearheaded two initiatives. Employees were guided to contribute to a patriotic fund that would aid the Chinese troops at the front. They were also urged to join a communal fund for mutual assistance in case of unexpected death, an initiative that developed, in 1939, into a full-blown employee life insurance policy.

The bombing incident drove home to the members of the Wing On company, nonetheless, that despite the volume of business in luxury, war was at their doorsteps. The narrow encounter with death, bloodshed, and destruction had profoundly shaken the employees, producing a traumatic effect that was to outlast the cleanup of the debris. For the remainder of 1937, as Chinese and Japanese troops engaged in massive battles throughout Shanghai, business stagnated in the foreign concessions. A deep restlessness and anxiety gripped the minds even of those employed in the business of glamour and luxury.

TO THE WAR

One response from the workforce was a decision to join the war. Zhang Qingsheng enlisted in a military training camp in Changzhou, west of Shanghai. Jing Songbo and Yin Shouqu, of the blanket and sweater departments respectively, signed up in Jiangyin, a military port city south of the Yangzi. Lu Jinxi, Li Huanzhang, and Chen Jiang wrote, six months later, to inform their former colleagues that they had completed their military training and were waiting, in a temple in Wuchang, for assignment to the front.

Management attitude towards such initiatives was apparently supportive. When a candies department clerk decided to follow Nationalist troops into the interior, Leon Kwok contributed thirty *yuan* for her travel expenses. Similarly, Kwok granted the request of Wu Ganchun, a junior clerk, who asked for travel funding to head inland. A former trainee who joined Wing On in 1932, Wu saw his hometown fall into Japanese hands in late 1937. "My family has been broken up. Alone in Shanghai, grieving the crisis facing the nation and the loss of my hometown, I cannot but wish to join the fighting."[40]

Wu's sentiments resonated with those of many white-collar workers: that in a time of war, their rightful place was to join the war effort and "serve the nation." A Wing On network soon developed, consisting of clerks and trainees who chose to join paramilitary services in the unoccupied Chinese interior. In July 1938, Yang Mingde, an orphan raised by his uncle and a trainee in the hat department, decided to join a number of Wing On "classmates" in the interior. He signed up for wartime services with their help. He sent his resignation letter to the general manager, who responded with money for his travel. He bought a one-way passage and was about to set to sail, but the voyage was delayed by a storm that necessitated some last-minute repairs of the vessel. During the extra day on shore, Yang ran into his uncle, who was entirely ignorant of his plan. Instead of sailing away, Yang's plan came to an abrupt end when he was marched back to his managers.

Wing On workers in the interior generated a steady flow of war zone accounts. Li Yi took a leave to join the military. For nearly a full year between 1937 and 1938, he wrote, "I followed our troops as they pulled out of Shanghai. I had been to Jiangsu, Zhejiang, Anhui, Henan, Hubei, Jiangxi, Hunan, Guangdong, traversing tens of thousands of miles on foot. I received training in Nanchang, saw action in Lanfeng, and was in the siege of Jiujiang. I have been in and out of showers of bullets and forests of rifles on numerous occasions. Yet somehow I managed to survive."[41]

The clerk from the candies department traveled almost as far:

> "On April 7 I boarded the *Desheng* that was bound for Ningbo. From Ningbo I took the bus to Jinhua. There I worked for two months before boarding the bus again to Sui'an, where I worked for a month. From Sui'an I took the train to Hankou, where I remained for over a half month. I had wanted to carry on with my work there. Yet my parents in Shanghai became exceedingly worried that people might take advantage of a young woman traveling alone. They put relentless pressure on me and I finally gave in. On August 21 I began the return journey by boarding the train bound for Guangzhou. From Guangzhou I took the train to Kowloon. That same evening I ferried across to Hong Kong. The next morning I boarded the *Ji'nan* for Shanghai. I got back on September 1."[42]

Jinhua, Sui'an, and Wuhan were all major bases where Nationalist army units were recruiting and training before assigning young people to duties with military hospitals, logistics, propaganda, and civilian education. Other Wing On employees reported joining such operations in central China and farther up the Yangzi.

Those who returned after shorter stints recounted equally profound experiences. Zhang Qingsheng, who joined a training camp in Changzhou, witnessed the collapse of his unit in early December 1937 during the Japanese push for Nanjing. "A majority of my teammates had died. The rest had scattered and disappeared." Zhang, too, ran for his life and managed to get back to Shanghai a mere four months after he had first joined up.

THE ROAD HOME

Another response to the August bombing incident was simply to flee. A large number of Wing On employees fled the bombing and failed to report to work when the store reopened on August 26, 1937. Some were still attending to the funerary arrangements or injuries of colleagues. Many more simply abandoned their posts and ran home to their families. Work discipline became lax for much of the remainder of 1937. Active fighting, meanwhile, continued to grate urban nerves and spread terror and devastation throughout the city.

Citing "negligence of duty" and complaining about the fickleness of their loyalty at a time when the company needed it the most, Wing On announced in late September that all employees must report to work by the end of the month or else face termination of their employment on grounds of "resignation." Letters containing the announcement went out to home addresses across the lower Yangzi Delta. The threat of termination must have produced impressive results, for "all but one" of the dining room staff, hit hard during the bombing, reappeared shortly for work.

Still, during the following year, when active fighting moved westward up the Yangzi and a semblance of normalcy returned to Shanghai, no fewer than forty individuals surfaced to plead for their reinstatement—a figure that stood for nearly 10 percent of Wing On's workforce in the pre-bombing days. Some told stories of how they had accepted the termination and sought to eke out a meager existence elsewhere. Their failure with the alternatives had driven them back to Wing On's doorstep. Directly and indirectly, the testimonies of the expelled workers served as indicators of how the explosion had shaken the discipline and altered the managerial rationale at the company. One letter reads as follows:

> To the most esteemed manager:
>
> Last year's bombing incident resulted in injuries to both of my hands. I received treatment in a city hospital. Yet I was unable to either dress or feed myself, about which I felt most embarrassingly inconvenienced. Reluctantly I asked for leave, a request that you graciously granted, with a loan of thirty *yuan* against my future salaries. Gratefully I went home to recuperate. Unfortunately I came down with typhoid, which prevented my early return to Shanghai.
>
> When I was well enough I went in to town to catch the train. Japanese bombing raids however had cut off the railroad lines. I was turned back many times despite repeated attempts. With no other choice, I took a river boat heading to Shanghai. When the boat approached Zhouzhuang we encountered retreating Chinese forces falling back from the enemies. This encounter forced the boat to turn back to Wuxi. Yet we were barely a couple of days in Wuxi when the local people took to the road and began their flight from the fighting.
>
> With few options left, I gathered the old and the young in my family and crossed over to Baoying on the other bank of the Yangzi. My wife was about to give birth and unable to continue with the journey. We had to find a place to stay and to wait for the arrival of the baby. Luckily we ran into Mr. Cheng Jingsheng, a regular customer with Wing On and now the deputy director of the International Red Cross north of the Yangzi. Mr. Cheng took us in and bid us to stay until the baby was born. I would have asked Mr. Cheng to provide you with a letter to attest to the truth of all of these happenings except that he happens to be called to Hankou by the government for a meeting and thus is unavailable to write.
>
> Thereafter I took my mother, wife, son, and daughter to Shanghai to

report back to work. I learned meanwhile that the company has adopted a policy not to reinstate people who had deserted.

But in my case I had received formal permission to take leave as a result of my injuries. This makes my situation different from all those who took flight.

As I have long been favored with your instruction on business matters I dare to hope that you will grant me your special consideration. Please allow me to have my job back so that my family will not go hungry and cold.

With a tremulous heart I state and detail my situation for your consideration. I am barely able to bear the anxiety awaiting for your reply.[43]

Qiu Jinhai's two-page letter, written in a cursive calligraphy and phrased in semi-classical Chinese, was characteristic of the scores of other letters submitted to Leon Kwok for comparable purpose. The details of hardships varied, yet by and large all letter-writers spoke of their flight from Shanghai in order to rejoin their families at the first opportunity after the August bombing. Their delay reporting back to work was due to no fault of their own (Japanese sieges, Chinese military action, other family complications) and their desire to be given back their old jobs was great, as the income was now worth more than ever—the "lone islet" was a refuge in a sea of burning, looting, and killing.

Peng Baosheng, who had worked in the company's delivery department since 1929, labored on for five pages to plead for his reinstatement. He had fallen ill in April, well before the August bombing. He was granted sick leave by his department head. He had a written diagnosis provided by Dr. Chen Daming, the company physician. The doctor's diagnosis had been alarming, yet his multiple prescriptions of Western medicine had produced no relief. The employee's frustration with the Western-trained doctor led him to switch to an old-fashioned practitioner Dr. Yu Bomin, who dispensed herbal medicine and gave compelling advice. Yu's "alternative medicine" eased Peng's symptoms yet also complicated his routine, because the bagfuls of recommended herbs had to be boiled down daily to a drinkable brew, consumed along with soft foods to enhance the prescription's medicinal effect. Dr. Yu's treatment, in short, underscored the desirability of the presence of a caring and attentive wife, not to mention the benefits of breathing the hometown air. Thus fortified, Peng boarded a ship and headed home. Then came Wing On's certified mail on September 23.

Peng went on:

My wife opened the mail and read it. She saw that it was about dismissal, so she hid it to spare me the further aggravation that the notice might bring. It so happened that I opened her trunk the other day to look for something and I came upon this letter. Upon reading it I become utterly consumed by anxiety. All colleagues who had been terminated had fled from the scene after the bombing. Yet my situation is different because I have been on sick leave well before the outbreak of the war.[44]

He pleaded therefore for mercy—for "the great benevolence that all members of my family, old and young, will forever remember."

To save their jobs, all those who had taken off in August in the aftermath of the explosions were obliged to come up with plausible accounts that explained their conduct. Yu Zude explained, in a letter dated March 1938, that he had sustained knee injuries during the bombing and had sought treatment in Shanghai, only to find Shanghai doctors and hospitals overwhelmed by the wounded. He therefore headed home to Changzhou to seek treatment from a bone specialist who happened to be a relative. Xie Ji, formerly with the cosmetics department, said his August trip to Shaoxing was a long-planned journey to finalize the burial arrangements for his mother. Zhou Daxin, of the hardware department, stated that he was training with the army's special service *(biedong dui)* during his absence. The special service was unfortunately disbanded upon the Nationalist pullout from Shanghai. Zhou had only been away for a couple of weeks yet he had somehow neglected to first ask for leave. Yang Naizhen, a trainee in the silk blouse department, admitted in January 1938 that he had fled but did not believe that he was being irresponsible: "I am the only son in my family. . . . My seventy-two-year-old grandmother was staining her face daily with tears when she learned that war had broken out in Shanghai. . . . After the Sincere bombing incident my mother, too, became anxious and much desired my return. . . . My family sent a person to Shanghai to fetch me. . . . I boarded the ship with this person and bound for home without taking leave."[45]

Tan Fuyao, with the jewelry department, also insisted that it was not negligence that had taken him away from his station. For fourteen years, he wrote, he had worked with utmost diligence and had carefully observed the norms at work. He had "treaded gingerly and fearfully, without ever overstepping the bounds by even a crack." Yet with the outbreak of the war "the winds and the clouds had turned ominous. My family was in Shanghai. Women and children did not bear well their fear and anxiety." To set his mind at ease so as to be better able to concentrate on work, Tan left work to settle his family in the countryside.[46]

There were strong desires in the aftermath of the explosions for individuals to take time off from their work. Those with families in Shanghai wanted to move their dependents to safety. Those from the countryside wanted to allay the fears of their families concerning their own safety in the city. Almost all wanted solace with kin after having emerged from the debris of the explosions. The injured and frightened, in particular, desired respite in the embrace of their family. The violence and devastation had placed the population in a different frame of mind, producing needs that could not be readily satisfied by workplace relationships supplied by the corporate family.

In dozens of letters, Wing On workers informed their bosses that the last months of 1937 had been hazardous for those attempting to make their way back to Shanghai. Those traveling from Suzhou and Wuxi were cut off by Japanese troops. Those traveling from Ningbo were blocked by Chinese forces determined to prevent the departure of able-bodied men. Those coming from the extensive area along the Yangzi risked encountering bands of marching soldiers or local toughs, who had been pillaging and burning with impunity in a state of civil chaos. A dried goods trainee was in Jiangyin, escorting his mother and younger sister, when word came that enemy soldiers were approaching. Jiangyin authorities sought to evacuate the civilians across the Yangzi to Yangzhou on the northern bank. Sadly, the Jiangyin boats were hit by a shower of bombs in midstream. Many capsized, taking their unfortunate passengers into the river. The trainee, who survived to tell the story, reunited with his mother weeks later. He invoked the war-zone trauma to plead for special dispensation. Yet to keep the company solvent during the war, Wing On management resorted to personnel rules with even greater stringency than before.[47]

Despite their pleas, scores of clerks were dismissed in the last quarter of 1937. This was due, in no small measure, to how the war had further depressed the business prospects of the company, which had not fared well since the recession in the mid-1930s. Profit margins had been slim and the circulation of capital and merchandise had been seriously disrupted. Wing On's directors, when managing their delicate state of business, exercised caution to the point of penny-pinching precision.[48] Over the course of 1938, 386 trainees were hired to replace the dismissed clerks. The measure increased the number of available hands on the floor and reduced the expenses on salaries. But it also changed the ratio on the floor between experience and labor, thereby diluting the "teaching" of skills and knowledge, and the teacher-student bond between the supervisors and the subordinates—a bond that had been critical in the ethical construction of the corporate family.[49]

On matters of personnel, the war thus led to an emerging rift in the urban construction of an idealized harmony between the demands of work and home. Personal familial loyalty and filiality, so often lauded in company rhetoric in the 1930s, now competed with company demands for institutional loyalty and filiality that had been set in a pseudo-familial framework. Management demand for primary dedication, delivered with threats of termination, exposed, in the months after the bombing incident, the impersonal nature of company rules and discipline. The company dismissed, on grounds of negligence and questionable loyalty, those who walked out without first obtaining managerial permissions. By the same token those who demanded their reinstatement assembled leave letters, doctor's prescriptions, travel passes, train tickets, and other pieces of signed forms and certified documents of seeming relevance—papers that gave evidence to their stories every step of the way and demonstrating their careful compliance with formal rules and regulations—to prove their unfailing loyalty and personal integrity. Eventually the workforce came to believe that the company took disciplinary actions not to protect standards of diligence and integrity, but to alleviate the investors' concerns for the balance sheets. Such suspicion fueled angry cynicism and had a powerfully corrosive effect undermining the bonds constructed in the ideal of the corporate family, especially when wartime mobilization for charitable relief and patriotic contributions had encouraged, at the same time, the ethics of sharing and giving.

THE DISPLACED AND THE DESTITUTE

In the winter of 1938, fighting subsided in the Yangzi Delta. Those who had been running for their lives now returned home to take stock of the damage. Many had lost their businesses as well as their homes. The flow of refugees into Shanghai's foreign concessions continued in earnest in the early months of 1938. No fewer than an estimated one million extra people entered the concessions; about two hundred and fifty thousand sought shelter in refugee camps. By pooling private resources, the city operated, at one point, no fewer than two hundred such camps. The YMCA, with which Guo Shun and Guo Le, Wing On's senior directors, were associated, operated four such centers and provided food and accommodation to about two thousand and six hundred people.[50] The disparity between the haves and have-nots came into ever sharper relief in Shanghai at the conclusion of active fighting.

Jin Jun, a twenty-four-year-old graduate of Songjiang County Middle

School and five-year employee with the Songjiang Gas and Electric Company, now found himself destitute and dependent on an acquaintance in the French Concession for a mailing address.

> It is two months since I fled from the bombings and the explosions. My ancestral home in Songjiang, at about seventy-two kilometers from here, lay in complete ruins. I lost my mother and younger brother in the confusion. I pray to heaven that they are alive and well somewhere. . . . In Shanghai I am a total stranger. . . . Exposed to wind and frost and without the help or introduction of relatives or friends, I will soon become a pauper on the street. . . . Mr. Manager, please have pity on me. . . . All I am asking is three meals a day and a place to spend the night. You earn my infinite gratitude by granting my request.[51]

While Jin asked for a job, Wang Guoying, a graduate from a prestigious Zhejiang secondary school and a veteran editorial assistant with newspapers and businesses who felt the mounting pressure of inflation, simply asked for money. Wang went to Leon Kwok's office with a request for twenty *yuan*. He was met by an assistant who flatly refused him. Irate, the disappointed man vented his frustration by composing a long letter in which he invoked Mencius and Sun Yatsen, as well as British missionary relief workers. "What is the point of organizing charity events and staging fund-raising performances if you do not intend to part with your money?" Wang asked.[52]

Wang's humiliation seemed minor in comparison with the insult suffered by the elderly Mr. Gong Fuchu. A successful county-level civil service examination degree-holder *(xiucai)* from 1895 and a veteran in Zhejiang's provincial administration for two decades, the sixty-six-year-old Mr. Gong found himself stranded in Shanghai with his wife and daughters after the fall of Zhejiang. He had already been loaned money from Zhejiang provincials. Gong then applied to Wing On for a job. Leon Kwok directed his application to the advertising department, which presumably had some use for talents in calligraphy and poetry. Mr. Gong appeared for an interview. The advertising director asked him to write a poem on "To covet the fish while gazing into the stream from the bank" *(Lin yuan xian yu)*. The topic, the first half of a couplet from the classics, implied its second half: "Is never as smart as withdrawing from the site to knit a net" *(buru tui er jie wang)*. Mr. Gong worked on the assignment ignoring the subtext, producing a classical poem in but a few minutes. The director gave him one *yuan* for his trouble and sent him away.[53]

Other unlikely applicants for clerical jobs included a former employee with the Telegraph Bureau in the Ministry of Communications, a graduate of the Shanghai YMCA high school who had worked with the Bureau of Public Health of the Shanghai municipal government, elementary school teachers, and a former secretary with a gift company in Guangzhou. The latter called himself a "buffoon" *(yuren)* and wrote with the theatrical flare appropriate to the performance of a clichéd worthy-man-down-on-his-luck part in a popular *tanci* (storytelling) drama.[54]

Some applicants applied with exceptional intensity. Zhu Jielu, an "educated man with no money," wrote no fewer than seven letters between November 3, 1938 and May 1939 to beg for a job. A thirty-four-year-old native of Jiangsu and a high school graduate, Zhu had worked in various offices in Shanghai since 1923. He had "always been frugal and diligent," "never wasted a minute of time nor a bit of material," and gingerly maintained the livelihood of all members of his family. Then the war broke out and Zhu lost his job. He returned to the country home in Jinjiang, where he witnessed "tragic scenes" and heard "moans and groans":

> Struggling in deep water and hot fire, leading a life in the total darkness of grief and sorrow, I was terribly shaken and lost my usual state of mind. I would have killed myself had circumstances permitted. Faced with mounting debts and deepening destitution, I have exhausted all available resources: energy, strength, helpful support, friendly connections. My whole family's livelihood is in jeopardy.[55]

From his state of "nine deaths" the desperate Mr. Zhu saw the splendor and scale of Wing On, with its luxury hotel, amusement hall, textile factory, credit department, and the fancy department store beckoning to him like a beacon of hope. He would take any job so long it did not require knowledge of a foreign language. He would pray for Leon Kwok's good health and he would hail "long life" to the general manager as well as to the Wing On Company.

Citing "no opening" in a form letter issued on November 8, the company promptly rejected Zhu's request.[56]

Mr. Zhu refused to give up. He sent more letters describing how he had become "deeply anxious and worried," "grief-stricken to the point of near death," "thoroughly depressed," and "unable to get a moment's rest day and night." He meticulously numbered his submissions, referring to them as "tearful pleas" *(aiqiu)*, begged the company to keep his requests on active file, and anxiously waited for a response with each attempt. By May 1939 he was writing on borrowed stationery from a hotel room in the French Concession, where he was crammed with seven members of his family. The tragedy of death and separation for the old and young was imminent, he warned. Leon Kwok would earn his "eternal gratitude," Zhu pledged, if Wing On would take him in, which would cost the company so little. Kwok would thereby display compassion worthy of the Buddha, the benevolence of a sage, and the life-giving grace of the Almighty. No more was heard of Zhu after this date. It is not clear whether he had finally given up or was no longer able to write.

The glamour of Wing On radiated ever more magnificently into the provincial hinterland in the dark days of the war. Lu Xichao, a sales clerk and assistant cashier for an oil plant in Jiaxing, Zhejiang, dreamt of a bright future working for "the largest department store in all of China." The nineteen-year-old Lu, who had accumulated five years of work experience since his graduation from an elementary school, described himself as "healthy" and "willing to do hard work." His current employer thought so well of him, they gave him a promotion with a salary increase of 50 percent. His family was well off enough not to depend on his income. He could also offer as his business guarantor "a person of considerable substance." Lu would trade his present job for a trainee's position at Wing On nonetheless because "in the current environment there are various constraints about making a living in the interior."[57] "How can I be content with twelve *yuan* a month in the occupied zone?"[58] Yet if his co-workers were to learn of his application to Wing On "they will make such merciless fun of me that matters will be complicated in the future, especially if I am to fail." Lu therefore asked the company "not to write back—as they will see the mail bearing your logo—unless you are going to grant my request."[59] Lu ended up sending several certified letters to Wing On asking why there had not been a reply, sure as he was that a positive response was forthcoming. He had obtained the required permission for the purchase of train tickets to Shanghai. He would lose no time jumping aboard the train. His last missive reported that the travel pass was about to expire; the company's letter, he believed, was forthcoming.

THE APPLICANTS

As Jiangnan's wealthy inhabitants were also converging on the "lone islet," business momentum accelerated over the course of 1938. By the end of 1939, with the imminent inauguration of the Nationalist Wang regime in Nanjing, Wing On reported a profit of over 13 percent on a total revenue that was slightly below 10.5 million *yuan*. It did a thriving business selling exotic birds priced at 150 Hong Kong dollars each, the equivalent of eighteen catties of rice at market price. The popularity of the birds did little to comfort the employees, who were servicing up to sixty customers during twelve-hour business days. The profit margins for the company fluctuated between 13 and 17 percent in the next two years. The figure jumped to 25 percent in 1941 before Wing On's run with fortune was irreparably damaged by the outbreak of the Pacific War.[60]

All told, over a hundred clerks were added to Wing On's roster in 1939. The company's work force nearly doubled to eight hundred at the peak of its hiring during the war. The new employees nonetheless represented but a fraction of the skilled and experienced who had been applying to Wing On since 1938.

Wing On's applicants in 1938 consisted of a large number of experienced but displaced people—junior and senor clerks, and even proprietors of shops and firms destroyed by the war. They came from Hongkou, Zhabei, and Nanshi, from teashops, printing houses, candy stores, tobacco shops and more, telling stories of bombing, fighting, fire, and pillage. They also came from elsewhere in the Shanghai concessions—from the Modernhood Hat Company and the B. Joseph Photo Studio, for example, where the shops remained but the business had been ruined. They even came from other Nanjing Road department stores, including the National Goods Department Store that had cut back drastically in June, 1938, and the Sincere Company, which had never quite recovered from the August bombing.[61]

The flow of job inquiries at Wing On, meanwhile, rose and fell with the circumstances of war. The fall of Hangzhou brought letters from experienced workers in ginseng, tea, and herbal medicine. The fall of Tianjin brought requests from ice rink attendants to work at the YMCA. Japanese seizure of the Beijing-Nanjing railroad prompted the dining car waiters and busboys to apply to Wing On's Western-style restaurants. The fall of Hankou disrupted and scattered the sojourning mercantile community, sending senior clerks who had been managing the dry goods business for their Cantonese owners back to Shanghai. The fall of Guangzhou in October 1938 disrupted its mercantile community. Scores of department store and trading firm clerks arrived in Shanghai to recount their hardships to fellow provincials at Wing On.

Job applicants came, almost in equal numbers, from the Jiangnan region and from among the Guangdong sojourners in Shanghai. About a quarter of them had finished middle school. Another one-fifth had advanced further, attending or finishing high school. A handful might have attended junior college (the Francis Xavier College). Even graduates of teachers' normal schools and of the Sino-French language schools submitted applications, though their inexperience with the abacus and English doomed their chances.

About half the applicants were single, had an elementary school diploma or an advanced vocational training certificate, were between eighteen and twenty-two years old, and wanted to be trainees. They had gone to semi-charitable schools such as the Private Shaoxing Sojourners' Elementary School in Shanghai (Sili Shaoxing lü Hu xiaoxue), the Guangdong-Zhaoqing Charitable School (GuangZhao yixue), the Private Minsheng Elementary School (Sili Mingsheng xiaoxue), the Seven Star Vocational School (Qixing zhiye xuexiao), the YMCA School for evening English programs, the elementary school of the Chinese Vocational Education Association, and an assortment of business *(shangke)* or vocational programs. They came from the lower stratum of literate families, had learned basic reading, writing, counting, and vocational skills, and probably had rarely ventured beyond their neighborhood or provincial settings.

Another one-third of the applicants were older (between twenty-three and twenty-six), often married, sometimes better educated, had almost always worked elsewhere in clerical positions with firms dealing in trade, shipping, merchandising, gas, food, fabrics, and so forth, in areas that as diverse as sales, inventory, secretarial assistance, business correspondence, and accounting. Some were also sons or nephews of shop owners in their own right, who sought "on-the-job training" with a major modern-style retail operation such as Wing On. In more peaceful times, after working a dozen years with meager pay, long hours, watchful alertness, and dedicated hard work, the more savvy among the senior clerks would have built up business connections, accumulated some capital, learned how to broker deals, and acquired the marketing sophistication to advise a supplier about what would or would not sell. A certain Chen, son of a substantial Changzhou merchant family, worked briefly at Wing On before going home to run the family shops. Pang Jie'an from Changshou similarly went to Shanghai to train in a photo studio. He learned the technique as well as the business, and went home in 1932 to open his own studio. The outbreak of the war in 1937 unfortunately ruined his business. He thus returned to Shanghai and applied to Wing On.

Hundreds and thousands in Shanghai's merchandizing business looked upon the seventeen-story Wing On, lit in neon, as the pinnacle of their vocation. They slept in attics and on floors, in dimly lighted rooms, atop or behind wine shops, curio stores, fan shops, hardware stores, fabric shops, general stores, merchandizing outlets, and so forth in the downtown sections of the foreign concessions. They also shared rooms in crowded compounds, congested back alleys, along the putrid river banks, and behind the stately façades on the main roads in the French Concession. They lived their lives on the streets or in spaces that opened out onto the streets. They had ties with relatives, co-provincials, and classmates from home and school. They knew their suppliers, creditors, employers, fellow workers, and customers. They shared newspapers and magazines, rented novels and comic books, listened to storytelling programs on the radio, ate at roadside stands, played chess or other games, prayed to the gods of fortune, and dreamt of a better future.

In July 1938, the nineteen-year-old Yan Laigen, calling himself a "pitiable petitioner" *(aiqiu zhe)*, wrote to Leon Kwok to ask for a trainee position. A year earlier, through the introduction provided by a certain Mr. Zhao, Yan had taken Wing On's exams for prospective trainees and had been judged "eligible" by the examiner Guo Jiu, one of Kwok's relatives and Wing On's chief finance officer. There was, however, no immediate opening. War broke out the following month. Yan joined a service corps attached to the military and helped with the evacuation of wounded soldiers from the front line. When the Nationalist troops pulled out of Shanghai in November, Yan left the corps and moved in with a friend. For nearly a year he tried to make a living as a street peddler. The degradation was extremely humiliating for a former middle school student; Yan could hardly bear it. Then he ran into his friend Zhao Quanhui. Zhao, a Wing On employee, described Leon Kwok as a man who "bestows benevolence and cares for giving, a charitable man with much compassion for fellow compatriots in distress." His hope rekindled, Yan Laigen wrote to the company and begged to have his exam files reopened.[62]

Within a month, the "tearful," "pitiable" Yan was steering other teenagers to petition "pitiably" to Wing On.

Dear Esteemed Manager,

> I am Hong Ruquan, eighteen years old. I was a seventh grader at the Jinghua Middle School in Hongkou when the war broke out in August 1937. My home was destroyed. My family fled to the foreign concessions with scarcely any of our belongings. Overnight I was out of school [*shixue*] and without a job [*shiye*]. . . .
>
> My father worked for the postal service as a driver. . . . Around 7:00

P.M., on November 15, 1937, when my father was in the Kunshan area *en route* to deliver mail to Suzhou, his mail truck caught the attention of Japanese war planes. They trained their spot lights on his truck and dropped bombs. My father died in the bombing. . . .

Thereafter my loving mother, myself, my two younger brothers, and two younger sisters lost our only support [*shihu*]. My mother supported us by doing needle work.

Merciful, benevolent manager! Maybe it's a sign that my luck has turned? Last night I went past the North Xizang Road and ran into my former classmate Yan Laigen, whom I have not seen for years. He said he is now working in your company. With tears in my eyes I told Mr. Yan my story, which moved him to tears. He said that you, Great Manager, are the true great benefactor of our day. You have a heart full of compassion for compatriots who have fallen on hard times. Yan Laigen encouraged me to tell you of my pain. He said you are so full of mercy that you will surely take me in.

I was overjoyed to hear this. Unable to contain my excitement, I hope you will not mind my presumptuousness writing to you like this. I am a pitiable petitioner who pledges to you my utmost honesty, diligence, frugality, and dedication. Oh merciful Manager! You will surely show this pitiable petitioner your compassion and sympathy?[63]

Another eighteen-year-old, also orphaned, out of school, and without a job, tried his chance with Wing On, encouraged by the same Yan Laigen.

Dear Mr. Manager,

Yesterday Mr. Yan Laigen said that your company is recruiting trainees. He also said that you are a generous person with a big heart for the poor. I was deeply touched by what I heard and would like to tell you about myself.

My father died when I was very young. My mother raised the family with her hard work. Last year the war broke out and I was put out of my middle school. . . . Circumstances became difficult and . . . my mother, under a lot of stress, fell ill and died. . . . These days I make do with the help of my older sister and older brother. . . . With utmost respectfulness I beg of you to grant me a position. If you grant my wish I will be forever grateful!"[64]

Like Yan and Hong, Chen had graduated from a semi-charitable school (Shaoxing Sojourners' Shanghai Elementary School) in Hongkou. He was a student at the private Minsheng Middle School when the war put an end to his schooling. Former classmates and neighbors, all three had fled from their bombed-out homes and had lost a parent. Yan's employment with Wing On at this moment probably excited much hope as the three reunited after such travails. Hong and Chen's application letters bore remarkable resemblance to Yan's not only in tone and composition but even in handwriting. It may not be far-fetched to speculate that the lugubrious Yan Laigen had conducted himself as an involved advisor to his fellow refugees in distress.

GETTING INTO WING ON

Certain procedures governed the hiring practice at Wing On. Characteristically, a promising applicant would be summoned for an interview, during which he or she would be given written and verbal tests. If the results qualified the applicant as "eligible," a job offer would follow upon the availability of an opening. Yang Jing went for such an interview and was "utterly embarrassed" by his own performance. Knowing that there was no chance he'd be deemed "eligible," he did not wait for the company to inform him of the results.

> I love working for your company. That's why I came for the interviews. If you can trust my character, I will deposit three to four hundred *yuan* as my guarantee. . . . Also within the shortest period of time I will improve my English conversational skills. . . . I had studied abacus while in elementary school. . . . That was some time ago and I am no longer able to do things beyond the elementary addition, subtraction, multiplication and division. . . . But I just bought an abacus book and I will catch up in no time. . . . What if you grant me a suitable position at this moment and dock my pay until my performance meets your satisfaction?"[65]

But there was more to the interview than English, Chinese, arithmetic, and abacus use, as a certain Mr. Chen found out.

> To the Manager:
>
> Can you tell me why an applicant for a sales position needs to be tested on eyesight? Does this mean that those with myopia are not eligible to work as clerks? Educated men are often short-sighted while the illiterate are the ones with eyesight as sharp as a hawk!
>
> I came for an interview on May 27. I wrote a job application letter in English and answered a number of conversational questions in English. Then there was this test of eyesight, which was my undoing!
>
> Your company enjoys this great reputation as a compassionate employer. . . . Why are the tests so demanding? Does this mean that those who know no English deserve to starve? Those who cannot do their math deserve to starve? Those with short-sightedness deserve to starve?[66]

Wing On wanted its employees to be "sharp-eyed, quick in hearing, pleasantly engaging, smartly alert" (*er cong mu ming, huo po ling li*).

But the interviews were not foolproof in weeding out health factors that impaired job performance. Trainee Bi Tonglun came forward with his problems after struggling for three months in the fabrics and the suits departments:

> Ever since childhood I have had a hearing problem. This now hampers my work, especially when following orders given by Guangdong people [Cantonese] speaking Shanghainese. I have a hard time comprehending what is being said. Sometimes I would be absorbed doing my work and a shout of order would come out of the blue. It is a situation set for mis-understanding, because the person who was giving the order would get frustrated and irritated, whereas your pupil here remained utterly innocent and ignorant as to what was being said. People who know of my hearing problem may forgive me for my not being responsive. But those who don't are likely to take me as an indolent worker.[67]

Yet "good character,"—that is, "honesty" and "reliability"—ultimately trumped "adequate skills" and "perfect health" in personnel evaluation. The store's workers interacted daily with scores of others in departments where goods lay around, cash was handed back and forth, things got moved about, merchandise was delivered or returned, customers came and went, and accounts were opened or closed. As was common in the trade, all trainees thus had to supply guarantors who agreed to assume liabilities, and all clerks were to deposit a substantial sum with the company against probable future misdeeds. Wing On asked for no more than a few hundred *yuan* from a new clerk. The figure was thought of as show-ing magnanimity. The Sincere Company across the street, in contrast, op-erated on the principle of "unlimited liability" and asked the new hires each to deposit in the thousands.

WORKING FOR WING ON

Once on the payroll, Wing On trainees received room and board in com-pany housing units. By the mid-1930s they were also issued two sets of uniforms, for summer and winter, and a starting salary of 3.50 *yuan* a month. Junior clerks received uniforms, meals, and starting salaries in the range of twelve to fifteen *yuan* a month. Depending on the annual job performance evaluation, these figures would be raised over time. There were twelve clerks and trainees, for example, in the ivory depart-ment in 1939. The annual performance evaluation took into considera-tion factors such as performance ranking for the past year, sales revenue in the current year, performance ranking for the current year, and issues of character. Zhang Wengui, who ranked first in 1939, was in his twelfth year with the company. His base salary had risen from five *yuan* to fifty *yuan* a month. Judged "cordial, obedient, careful with company property," Zhang had "performed adequately in service and sales," for which he received the grade "A+."[68]

Those who performed poorly, of course, faced dismissal. As was customary, dismissal notes were issued at the conclusion of the festive banquet on the eve of the Spring Festival. Job security at Wing On was negligible during the war, thanks to the oversupply of qualified work force and latent tension within the ranks. Senior executives and department heads exercised the power of dismissal at will on minor provocations, although as a last resort there was sometimes the option of a final appeal to Leon Kwok.

Trainee Zou Jinbao, who earned 7.50 *yuan* each month, talked back one day when "insulted" by co-workers. He was dismissed. Trainee Du Weixing at the ice rink had a falling-out with colleagues. He was dismissed. Trainee Gu Zhihong was caught "taking a break" when business was slow in the furniture department. He was dismissed on the spot by Guo Yuewen, deputy general manager, on his routine tour of the floor.[69]

Clerk Xu Yayan, in the cashier's department, had been on the job for four years. On March 1, 1938 he "took issue" with Guo Jiu, his department head, over whether a ten-*yuan* note was a forgery. In all probability the chief had pronounced it a fake and the clerk had refused to agree—as the responsible party who had accepted the fake note, he would have had to make up the sum. The chief spoke in his native Guangdong dialect (Cantonese) and the clerk his native Shanghainese. "Language difficulty" did little to help the conversation, and the chief suspended the clerk on the spot. The irate clerk protested to the general manager and demanded his severance pay of fifty *yuan*.[70]

Clerk Tang Zhigao, a departmental cashier, made a mistake with a gift certificate one day. He was given a warning and transferred to the fourth floor. Tang then made another mistake. Pleading that he was not feeling well, he explained how he had accepted a fake ten-*yuan* note plus an uncollectible payment of thirteen *yuan*. Both mistakes became his personal liabilities. Tang borrowed eight *yuan* from relatives and tried to borrow the balance of fifteen *yuan* from the company cashier against his future pay. Mr. Yang, the cashier in charge, refused the request and reprimanded the clerk for his mistakes. He also ordered him to turn in his keys, seals, and employee identification cards. In all likelihood the supervisor had suspected that Tang, with his problematic record, was again devising deception. Clerk Tang did not report to work the following day. Supervisor Yang accused him of fleeing his unpaid debt. Tang was forced to return to clear the charges or otherwise risk rejections by future employers.[71]

INSIDE THE HALL OF MAGNIFICENCE

In the spring of 1939, Wing On advertised that it was hiring a number of saleswomen "of Guangdong descent" (*Yue ji*). Over thirty women submitted their applications. Among them was Grace Woo, who wrote her letter in English.

Dear Sir,

> I take the liberty to ask you if there is a vacancy in your firm. I should like to apply for the position.
> I have completed the second senior year middle of English in the Shanghai Moore Memorial Church, and I am a fair typist. Besides, I can speak Mandarin, Hankow [Hankou], and Shanghai dialects. Though I have no experience, I have had good training at school.
> My age is twenty-one. I am a native of Canton [Guangzhou], and not afraid of hard work. I am willing to do any kind of work in your company, for all that I wish to get a job to learn business. I will appreciate it.
> Awaiting for your favorable reply.[72]

Female employees were to staff the stationery, cosmetics, and candies departments. A certain Ms. Chen Peiqin wrote to apply:

> I am nineteen years old, from Huizhou, Guangdong. I graduated from Peicheng Women's Middle School. I am fluent in the dialects of Shanghai, Beijing, and Hubei. I am also fluent in English. Last year I was a sales woman in the candies department with the Huaxing Company on Hubei Street in Hankou. Then I moved with my older sister to Shanghai, and took a job as a sales person with the Wenhua Bookstore.
> Then the war broke out and I lost my job. Both of my parents have died. I have an older sister and an older brother . . . I hope to work for you.[73]

Chen gave her address as 54, Wuding Fang, Wuding Road, Xiao Shadu. Four months later, on June 4, 1939, the same Ms. Chen, from an identical address at Xiao Shadu, wrote again to apply:

Taipan Kwok,

> I am an employee with the hat department of the Sun Sun Department Store. . . . Company rules do not permit that I apply to other jobs while

being employed. So I have resigned in order to apply for a position with you. I am fond of Guangdong opera, but the job at Sun Sun left me little opportunity to practice. . . . I hope to work for your company so as to carry on with my theatrical passion while working at the same time. . . . I have given up a good job for the liberty to apply, and I hope my effort will not go wasted.[74]

Strictly speaking, there were no irreconcilable contradictions between Chen's two letters, though they appeared to give different impressions about who she was and what she had been doing. While the first application stressed relevant work experience selling candy, the second shifted the emphasis to leisure and passion—to a lack of commitment to clerical work and a taste for the limelight, as well as to Leon Kwok's favorite hometown opera.

As the hundreds who followed the company's application procedures anxiously awaited their replies, the specially connected, armed with letters of introduction, entered General Manager Leon Kwok's office by means of other channels.

One shareholder sent his brother-in-law over for a job.[75] Another shareholder nominated his seventeen-year-old nephew as a trainee.[76] Tao Guilin, Shanghai's famed general contractor, scribbled "please hire" in a perfunctory note presented by a candidate. So did Guo Linzhuo, Leon Kwok's brother and the general manager of the Wing On Textile Company, while presenting the daughter of an associate. A woman wrote from Hong Kong saying she was dispatching "two girls" to Wing On for work.[77] A business associate wrote about two relatives, "Yang Aimei, age nineteen, Yang Ailan, age seventeen, who had worked for two weeks in your company's promotional shows advertising fragrant soap." The sisters enjoyed what they did and they now wanted to occupy "proper positions so as to earn pocket money."[78] The eighteen-year old niece of the head detective in the Luza Police Station wrote in English to recommend herself "for a position suitable for my qualifications."[79] A young woman paid her first visit to Kwok's office *after* the latter had promised her employment to her father. Lu Zhenduo, son of a lawyer and director of a Cilianhui refugee relief program, sent over a young woman carrying her own résumé, accompanied by a note indicating that other candidates would be forthcoming.

Even in the shadow of war, Wing On juxtaposed velveteen Shirley Temple dolls (priced at fifty-two *yuan* each) and Huizhou clay figurines (less than ten *yuan*), Max Factor lipsticks and miniature pine trees (all over ten *yuan*)—goods that were several times the monthly income of its trainees and junior clerks.[80] As the men patiently served their time and awaited raises and promotions, young women with connections stepped into instant fame and glamour working as models in company-sponsored fashion shows and product displays.

Inside this "company with the most magnificent building and state-of-the-art amenities," a disgruntled employee complained, issues of personnel, whether with regard to hiring, compensation, assignment, evaluation, training, promotion, discipline, or dismissal, seemed "stagnant and archaic." There were too many reasons for working life to become "unhappy and unproductive" for Wing On's employees. There were rifts between men and women, Guangdong provincials and Shanghai natives, the English-speaking and the Chinese-educated, the young and the old, not to mention the supervisors and the subordinates. Promotion was slow and transfers were few. Hierarchy was upheld while loyalty went unrecognized. Sons of veteran employees who had put in many years of long service, unlike the relatives and friends of the shareholders and the investors, received no special consideration in hiring. Department heads and managerial supervisors took home hundreds of *yuan* each month whereas a majority of workers "do not even earn enough to maintain their wives."[81] Top managers availed themselves of luxury items at the company's expense. The clerks and trainees, on the other hand, were hardly ever able to afford the glamour that they were selling. Factions and cliques were rampant as people openly or covertly attempted to augment their income through a variety of means. Some workers complained, "Many who worked here have sunken into a downcast mood and become disappointed with their prospects. Not only that we cannot see any forward movement into the future, but that some people have even decidedly embarked upon a path of corruption and downfall."[82]

On August 12, 1938, the day before the first anniversary of the outbreak of fighting in Shanghai, Wing On employees wrote to Leon Kwok with a request. The staff, they reported, had raised three thousand *yuan* on their own from sales and customer donations as their "patriotic contribution" to aid the war effort of the Nationalist government. They were also well on their way to organizing a memorial gathering to commemorate the victims of August 23, 1937. They had contributed 1 percent of their monthly salaries to a communal fund that would be used to aid the widows, orphans, and parents of the victims. On the anniversary day of the bombing, furthermore, they would like the company's dining hall to serve vegetarian meals as a mourning gesture. Company funds thus saved from the regular meal budget should be added, they said, to the communal fund. The combined sum would then be distributed equitably to the families of all the deceased with no regard to distinctions of position or salary.[83]

The management granted the requests. These employee-initiated gestures became a company practice that was continued until a Japanese controller took over the accounts in 1941.

Other employee initiatives ensued in the following years. In August 1940, a group that described itself as "ardent supporters for the winter clothing movement" asked Wing On to contribute clothing to Chinese soldiers on the front line.[84] The soldiers turned out to be those belonging to the CCP's New Fourth Route Army. On April 1, 1941, the "Children's Day" that Wing On had used to promote toys, candies, food, and clothing for pampered children, staff demanded that the company contribute to the relief fund of China's war orphans.[85] The management again did what it was asked.

Certain issues, however, were more delicate in the pro-resistance atmosphere on the "lone islet." It also sounded vaguely ominous when voiced. Was Wing On in fact selling Japanese-manufactured goods under falsified Chinese labels? Did the company not allow its sponsored radio stations to laud the Japanese and endorse the collaborationist Chinese regime in Nanjing?[86] Anonymous accusations surfaced mysteriously from time to time. Even as the company made its contributions to the war effort and the relief missions, it had difficulty in the end dodging the suspicion that the self-styled patriarchs, by dint of doing well, must have betrayed the common good.

THE BANKING WAR

In the banking sector of Shanghai's modern economy, a comparable scenario unfolded during the war, which undercut the patriarchal authority of the corporate leaders and empowered the clerks and the trainees.

The bankers' war in Shanghai centered on the struggle between the Chongqing and the Nanjing governments over the circulation of legal tender in the lower Yangzi area.[87] The Bank of China maintained its operation in the International Settlement in Shanghai while the headquarters relocated to Chongqing. Branch offices in captured areas, meanwhile, became the basis of the Central Reserve Bank of the collaborationist Wang regime. The supporters of Chiang Kaishek's regime backed the *fabi*, Chongqing's legal tender. The Central Reserve Bank issued the *zhongchu-*

juan (central reserve notes), which the Wang regime sought to impose in Shanghai. Wang financiers resorted to speculation, hoarding, and the levying of special taxes on *fabi* holders in order to weaken the Chongqing-issued note. Wang's secret service mounted terrorist schemes, including assassination and bombing, to intimidate *fabi*-issuing banks. Chongqing assassins retaliated in kind, targeting Central Reserve Bank assets and operations with violent means. Shanghai's banking employees thus found themselves in the crossfire of a vicious war over currency.

In the chronicle of wartime terrorism, the night of March 21, 1941 stood out for bank workers. In a coordinated attack on three bank buildings, the night began with six gunmen dispatched by Number 76 (the collaborationist intelligence operation) pushing their way past the guards of the dormitory building of the Jiangsu Farmers Bank. The gunmen flipped on the lights and opened fire onto the beds, killing five bank clerks and leaving six more lying comatose in blood-soaked sheets.[88] Later that night Number 76 vehicles descended upon Centro Terrace, the residential compound of the Bank of China at 96 Jessfield Road. Japanese military police watched as plainclothes Chinese police dragged bank employees out of their beds at 3:00 A.M., to be thrown into the cells at 76 Jessfield Road.

The next day the Minister of Police acknowledged that his force had seized 128 employees of the Bank of China. The full roster was released to the press.[89] With these men as hostages, minister Li Shiqun denounced previous "Chongqing terrorists" for their attacks on Nanjing government personnel, and threatened to take "similar measures" against "the entire staff of all financial institutions" that supported the Chongqing government.[90] Nanjing special service forces meanwhile unleashed their bomb squads on pro-Chongqing banks. There were panicky phone calls from bank offices to the Shanghai Municipal Police force about mail packages with ticking sounds. There were explosions in bank buildings.[91] When the Nanjing authorities finally released the Bank of China hostages on April 8, they were sent home with severe warnings. A week later, when someone shot and hacked a deputy director of the Central Reserve Bank to death,[92] secret service agents from Number 76 seized nine senior officers from the Bank of China compound that same evening. The episode ended with the shooting of three managers in the head in full view of their families and colleagues in front of the Centro Terrace.[93] All seventy-seven families in the bank compound departed in the aftermath of the bloodshed. The now deserted premises of the much coveted compound was taken over by the rival Central Reserve Bank.[94]

LIFE ON THE STREET

As a multitude of banking institutions were singled out and separately attacked, financial employees throughout the industry joined together to form associations. The most active among these was the Shanghai Banking and Money Shop Employees After-Work Friendship Association (Shanghai shi yinqian ye yeyu lianyi hui; hereafter Banking Employees Association), which traced its founding to November 1936 as a constituent unit in the Shanghai National Salvation Association of the Vocational Circles (Shanghai zhiye jie jiuguo hui). It began with a total membership of about two hundred people. In two years it expanded into an organization of nearly seven thousand members, which amounted to over half of the city's financial employees. The members used their after-work hours to meet in classes, organize events, discuss concerns, and forge links across institutional divides. Instead of fostering the teacher-disciple norms that had existed within the corporate hierarchy since the 1920s, the association provided the forum and infrastructure for the construction of fraternal solidarity.[95]

The Banking Employees Association was among the most visible civil organizations in Shanghai on the "lone islet." It listed an "honorary board and advisory committee" of fifteen senior bankers and guild members. These men were heads and senior directors of leading institutions such as the Bank of China, the Shanghai Banking Association and the Money Guild—an impressive "who's who" of the remnants of the financial community after 1937. It was directed by a fifteen-member standing committee that reported to an elected board of directors of fifty-two members. Sun Ruihuang, the chief executive of the Xinhua Bank, chaired the board as well as the standing committee. He was assisted on the executive committee by Pan Yangyao, chief executive of the Siming Savings Bank. Sun and Pan dated their connections back to the early 1920s, when both men worked with Wang Zhixin, the founder of the Xinhua Bank, a former principal of the Chinese Vocational Educational School, and former editor of *Shenghuo Weekly*. Under the standing committee there were three departments (Secretariat, General Affairs, and Membership) plus nine functional committees: Scholarship, Sports, Entertainment, Employee Welfare, Cooperatives, Supplementary Education, Placement, Rules and Procedures, and Publications. Each featured scores of volunteers and a sizable roster. Each committee also featured its own sub-departments and committees of secretariat, finance, and general affairs.

The Employee Welfare Committee, for instance, consisted of a chair-

man, five vice-chairmen, thirty-five committee members, and three secretaries who worked through fourteen "divisions" and "sections" of general affairs, administration, accounting, social events, collegial service,
business services, reference, advice, forums, enterprises, medicine, hygiene, clinical services, and pharmaceutical services. The Publications
Committee, which published the association's newsletter, the *Yinqian-
bao* (Banking and Money Guild Report), and ran a news agency called
Yinqian shixi tongxun she (The Banking and Money Guild News Agency-
in-Training), similarly deployed over hundreds of people to serve as "correspondents" *(tongxunyuan)* in the association's various departments
and committees, in addition to the hundreds of institutions from which
the members had come. Competing in size and volume of activities with
the Publications Committee was the Entertainment Committee, which
consisted of divisions of "Beijing Opera," "Spoken Drama," "Music,"
"Chess," and "Amusements" (Kun Opera and storytelling). Those directing Beijing opera included the Bao brothers, Xiaodie and Youdie, all
famed opera performers with long-standing ties to the banking community. Those directing spoken drama were by and large clerks rather than
actors—figures such as Yang Shantong and Wang Jishen, whose growing involvement with acting eventually overtook their lives as clerks in
banking.[96] But none of the committees were as elaborately constructed
as the Membership Department, which, with its designated "resident rep-
resentatives" and "resident liaison" in all banks and money shops from
which the members came, had put in place an infrastructure with networks reaching far and wide throughout the industry.[97] The association
brought together financial workers from nearly four hundred institutions.[98] The activists among them appeared as directors or executives serving on multiple committees and subcommittees, departments and subde-
partments. Four individuals on the eleven-member Rules and Procedures
Committee, for example, fit that description. It is perhaps not altogether
surprising that among the most active participants were individuals who
surfaced, in the summer of 1949, as underground members on the "takeover" teams of the CCP.

The declared goals of the association were "to share knowledge" and
"to gain welfare." The Scholarship Committee offered courses on banking. It also organized sessions on calligraphy. Neither program, however,
attracted more than two dozen people at a time. The language program
taught English, Japanese, and Russian. But there appeared to be a general coolness towards "useful" knowledge that might advance one's career in a professional setting. In contrast, the committee's library drew

hundreds every week for guided discussions on issues of "economics" and "philosophy"—euphemisms for principles of justice in the distribution of wealth. The Entertainment Committee in particular drew several hundred to programs organized to "help the refugees."

The association's consumer co-op vowed, meanwhile, "to facilitate the distribution of national goods *(guohuo)*" and "to fight the effects of hoarding and inflation."[99] The co-op signed agreements with over a hundred retailers who agreed to supply, at a discounted rate, goods and services that included clocks, cosmetics, candies, Western medicine, writing instruments, sports equipment, fabrics, shoes, hats, books, tea, cameras, electrical appliances, coal, haircuts, laundry, and restaurant meals.[100] The co-op also launched a "Benefits Reserve Fund" *(fuli chujin)*. Subscribers to the fund made monthly individual payments. The money was managed with the advice of a select committee of Shanghai's leading bankers, accountants, and lawyers. It appeared to have done well enough to generate enough resources for the association's expenditures on charities, employee benefits, and unemployment subsidies.[101]

The most popular group was the spoken drama section under the Entertainment Committee. Its gatherings routinely drew three to four hundred participants. The most important rationale for its mobilization was the staging of public performances to help raise money for refugee relief. Activities conducted under the spoken drama section propelled the Banking Employees Association to high visibility on Shanghai's social calendar during the lone islet period. Little was openly stated about aiding Chinese troops on the front. Japanese military authorities nonetheless suppressed such activism through the authorities in the French Concession, where the theaters were located. The pressure merely stiffened the resolve of the young clerks who chose to remain with the spoken drama group.[102]

In all these activities the Banking Employees Association functioned, first of all, as an organization that redirected the energy and attention of Shanghai's bank employees toward their peers and counterparts in other units in the industry, instead of toward their superiors within the corporate hierarchy. "Friendship" *(lianyi)* and "collectivity" *(jiti)* supplanted words such as "diligence" and "professional improvement" in the lives of bank employees. Much of their after-work hours were spent mobilizing for events or fraternizing with each other instead of listening to their superiors preach on career subjects.

Bank employees who sought "knowledge" within the programs put together by the association, furthermore, looked for socioeconomic perspectives rather than vocational skills. Why did so many people starve and perish? Was it right for a small number to continue in their existence of luxury and indulgence? Did the city not become a den of vice where integrity and loyalty were traded for profits? Was it not an act of complicity if corporate leaders and school principals worked to maintain an order that served the enemy? These were among the questions enacted on stage or scripted in print by the members.

PERFORMING SOCIAL JUSTICE

"In this city of ten thousand vices," wrote Wu Limen, chair of the Entertainment Committee, "we stand on the brink of the abyss. . . . All our members work in the banking and money business. It is of extra importance that we cultivate our minds and hearts."[103]

Nightlife reached a new height of frenzy during the lone islet period. The "extra-boundary" Shanghai on the western edges of the concessions, where luxury gambling mixed with political intrigue, belonged to the city's gangs. Prostitution diversified into multiple forms as sex penetrated all venues of commercial entertainment.[104] Banking employees, as the elite of the middle class, wanted to keep themselves pure and clean. They wanted their "proper" entertainment with guitars, flutes, strings, and vocals in the company of each other. They championed just causes such as relief and edification. Beijing opera posed a high entry barrier: it required committed training before an amateur might walk or sing convincingly on stage. The spoken drama in the modern vernacular, by comparison, was ideally suited for amateur theater. Over one hundred people joined its activities in 1938. The membership more than tripled in the next twelve months. Members divided themselves into "teams" that looked after matters such as makeup, scripts, costumes, directing, production, reviews, and so forth. Professional actors joined the bankers as advisors. Rehearsals for major productions took months. One- or two-act plays were staged in between to debut the amateur actors.[105]

Among the amateur vernacular plays were *Yi bei niunai* (A Glass of Milk), *Sheng de yizhi* (The Will to Live) and *Bai cha* (White Tea). These plays dealt with the issue of "how people solve the bread-and-butter issues of daily existence" in wartime Shanghai.[106] A recurrent theme concerned the hard choices between material interest and moral integrity. In "The Will to Live," a hard-working young bank employee faced the difficult choice of whether to give up his job or his love, who was desired by the spoiled son of a senior manager of the bank. Those who wielded power and wealth, including the corporate leaders, were selfish people with neither principles nor responsibilities. Their status, wealth, and seniority enhanced their capacities to do harm rather than good. Wealthy individuals, in short, were unlikely to be agents of social justice. This contrasted sharply with the assumptions that informed the corporate community in the early 1930s. Few plays made explicit reference to the Japanese.[107] Yet there was no mistaking that the outbreak of the war had ushered in a new era.[108]

On the occasion of the fourth membership meeting of the Banking Employees Association, the spoken drama section, after four months of rehearsing, staged Cao Yu's play *Richu (Sunrise)* in late November 1938. *Richu* was selected for the occasion because it "exposed the dark side of society . . . as seen through the degenerate and indulgent style of existence prevalent in yesterday's banking circle." That previous state of moral corruption "contrasted sharply with the simple and frugal style that prevailed in today's banking circle." The goal of the performance was both to underscore those contrasts and to "deliver a warning."[109] The play, directed by Xia Feng and featuring bank employees as actors, concentrated on the evil character Jin Ba, a powerful financier who brought young men into his orbit only to corrupt them.[110] At the end of the play the heroine Chen Bailu intones her last lines: "The sun is risen, and the darkness is left behind. But the sun is not for us, for we shall be asleep." The audience drew from this that the new proletarian force was rising and the nocturnal revelers of the capitalist class were doomed.[111]

Yet the audience knew well that the "evil financier" in *Richu* was not a person of yesterday, but a privileged collaborator of today. Today was a time of vicious betrayal and criminal collaboration—a time of selling-out to the feared and despised enemy. The contrasts between wanton debauchery and purposeful discipline were not contrasts between past and present, but between the top leadership and the bank's average employees. Lao Yan, an association reporter, wrote after viewing the play: "It may seem superfluous to some that we stage *Richu* at this time and expose evil characters such as Jin Ba. I happen to believe, however, that many in the audience were able to read into the play another level of meaning. Just take a look around our lone islet! There are, indeed, sinister characters tens of thousands of times more powerful than Jin Ba in the play, who have taken our destinies into their evil hands! How should we, indeed, try to face up to this cruel reality?"[112]

The suicides and deaths in *Richu* in that sense were warnings delivered toward "all those who have sold their souls to the devil" and "all those who have capitulated without resistance." These losers should know that "there would be no room for [their] existence on this planet" unless they put up a fight to earn their place.[113] Given the context of its time, the play called for the meek to stiffen their backbones in a fight of resistance.

The association's staging of *Richu* was significant, furthermore, because it was "a play about banking . . . produced by those employed in the banking business for the consumption of their fellow members."[114] The actors were playing familiar figures in known circumstances, according to Lao Yan. They succeeded in capturing with authenticity "down to the minutest detail the darkness and wickedness of banking circles in an earlier time."[115] The performance delivered a loud denunciation of privately-owned wealth that failed to demonstrate its sensitivity to social responsibility; this message was not lost on the audience. Xu Jiqing, senior banker and president of the Banking Association, said of the play: "The casting was superb. The performance was moving and stirring. Bank workers were enacting the world of banking. Their message powerfully grabbed those of us who played the 'real' bankers in this business. To me it was like being hit in between the eyebrows!"[116]

The members of the Banking Employees Association saw themselves, meanwhile, as having seized the high moral ground. In the words of Pei Wei, "*Richu* and its denunciation of top financiers announced to the world that the sun has risen over the battlefield in this war of resistance. The darkness that had cast its shadow on the banking circles will soon be lifted."[117]

It was the employees rather than their superiors, Pei suggested, who were letting in the sunlight. So long as the war continued, bank leaders could not avoid striking their deals in some smoke-filled room with the collaborators and the enemies. Displacing the patriarchs as the guardians of the bankers' integrity were thus the junior clerks, who would not only remain patriotic in their resistance against the enemies, but would also uphold the ideal of social justice by opposing the "capitalists" who had betrayed the collectivity out of a selfish desire for material gains.

FROM PATRIARCHS TO CAPITALISTS

The end of the war in 1945 brought Nationalist government authorities who had spent over a half decade in Chongqing back to Shanghai. With the end of the foreign concessions, the Nationalist police force—including the secret service under the Military Bureau of Statistics and Investigation—was able to establish control over the entire city. The Nationalist government also brought back former executives and staff members of the state banks, whose return with their new recruits from Sichuan meant that there were duplicate sets of personnel in almost all branches of government-owned financial institutions.

Prominent financial figures such as Wu Yunzhai, the head of the wartime Bank of China in Shanghai, Qian Xinzhi, the head of the wartime Bank of Communications, and Lin Kanghou, the head of the Shanghai Bankers Association, were charged and prosecuted for collaboration. Private entrepreneurs who had collaborated with the Wang regime by serving on the commodity control boards, for example, were also fined and punished, usually with the confiscation of their property. Senior staff members in government enterprises were spared. But there was such a thorough personnel turnover in almost every office that the shakeup eventually reconstituted even the boards of the Shanghai YMCA. This distinct shift in local institutional power at the moment of the proclaimed national victory upset expectations, destabilized communities, and led to much tension and resentment among the Shanghai's war survivors. With the return of the Chongqing victors, the "non-Chongqing" locals found themselves facing rivals, competitors, and accusers who sought to impose a Nationalist order. Those with close ties to the Wang regime exiled themselves to Hong Kong. Chongqing power extended to all corners of Shanghai. There were, above all, no more foreign concessions to erect barriers between China's financial elite and its own government.

On October 5, 1945, Shu Yueqiao, an expelled former employee of the Sun Sun Department Store, went up to the store's main entrance and unfurled a homemade "big-character-poster" *(dazibao)* in which he accused Li Ze, the general manager of the company, of "ten cardinal crimes" of collaboration that made him a traitor *(hanjian)*.[118] The company called the police, who led the man away on charges of "disruption of business." Three days later the same man, undeterred, went to the police with a prepared statement to lay out his accusations.

Sun Sun clerks who were underground members of the CCP took note of Shu Yueqiao's accusations. They wrote to the left-leaning journal *Zhoubao* to publicize the incident and signed as "the Entire Staff of Sun Sun." They declared that Sun Sun's general manager had been a collaborator and a traitor. They threw in the additional charge that Nationalist authorities had been reluctant to take action against him—a reluctance that proved that the Nationalists were in collusion with the traitors.

The journal printed the letter. Copies were soon circulated around the company.

In early November 1945, Shu Yueqiao sent his written complaints against Li Ze to the Shanghai headquarters of the Command in the Third Front of the Nationalist Army (Di san fangmian jun). In late November 1945, the Nationalist government issued its official guidelines regarding the prosecution of traitors upon receiving such accusations from the public. In early December, Shu again went to the main entrance of Sun Sun. He harangued the crowd about the crimes committed by General Manager Li during the war. He was again led away by the police on "disruption of business." Shu then set up a roadside fortune-telling stand and used it as a pulpit to voice loud predictions. He wore a plaque around his neck that denounced Li Ze in big characters. He marched around the block wearing the plaque, thrusting his fist in the air and shouting denunciations.

In late December, Sun Sun clerks who were underground members of the CCP formed a group of ten to take up the task of bringing legal proceedings against General Manager Li. The group brought Mr. Shu into its midst. To document Li's collaborative activities, it researched the company's financial records, pored over wartime newspapers, and collected old photographs. Records concerning metal transactions during the war, for instance, appeared to have been altered. The metal could have gone to supply Japanese troops. There were newspaper articles listing Li as a member of the puppet Commodity Control Board. The group mobilized a campaign among their colleagues and garnered over 350 signatures. In the early weeks of January 1946, just weeks before the Spring Festival, the group plastered an entire stretch of Nanjing Road with anti-Li slogans, cartoons, and proclamations. The signs extended almost to the front door of Li's private residence. Similar posters were displayed in the shop windows at the Sun Sun Department Store. Underground CCP members at other department stores such as Wing On, Sincere, the Sun, National Goods, and Lihua showed their solidarity by displaying the anti-Li posters at their workplaces. The campaign, with its defiance of authority and disrespect for Manager Li, now drew in the entire Nanjing Road neighborhood.

These happenings were reported on the front pages of major Shanghai newspapers. The report caught the attention of the political elite. Sha Qianli, an attorney and one of the "seven gentlemen" jailed in 1936 (see chapter 5), came for a visit. Attorney Sha, trailed by photographers, volunteered his legal service to the Sun Sun employees. Sha contacted a

civic association, the "Hanjian Scrutiny Committee." The Hanjian re-
viewers convened a news conference on January 7, in which Sun Sun employees, with the support of the scrutinizers, denounced General Manager Li, demanded his prosecution, called for his wartime victims to come
forward with full complaints, and demanded the confiscation of Li's
properties so as to aid the unemployed. That same day Shanghai's mayor,
Qian Dajun, ordered the police chief, Xuan Tiewu, to take Li Ze into
custody.[119]

To keep the pressure on the case, the Shanghai branch of the CCP mobilized members of twenty-four trade unions to form the "Support Group
for the Prosecution of Traitor Li Ze." The union members included those
employed in department stores, car mechanics, tailors, hairdressers, waiters, bus boys, and noodle factory workers. The group charged that Guo
Shun, vice-president of the Wing On company, was also a *hanjian*, because Guo, like Li, had sat on the Commodities Control Board and had
made material contributions to the Japanese to supply war machines. Guo
Shun fled to the United States. Other employees—at businesses like the
Taikang Food Company, Kangyuan Canning Factory, and Shengsheng
Ranch—came forward as well to denounce their employers as "capitalists" and "traitors," and to demand court action.[120]

Was it an act of treason that Li Ze allowed his name to appear as a
director on the Commodity Control Board? The defense argued that it
was not, otherwise anyone who had ever been forced to bow to a Japanese soldier at a checkpoint would deserve *hanjian* prosecution. Was Li
Ze being justifiably accused for his wartime conduct? Or were his post-
1945 accusers principally motivated by material gains—by a "misun-
derstanding" between the "labor" and the "capital?" For a moment the
Nationalist municipal authorities, the court, and the police appeared to
be receptive to the latter thesis. They were willing to entertain the possibility that a majority of the workers at Sun Sun had been mobilized on
the false pretext of improving their living standards, and that clerk Shu,
who insisted that his life was ruined, would have walked away happily
had the general manager succumbed to his blackmail.[121] Yet the discourse
of patriotism, mixed with sentiments of aggrieved social justice, had
gained such force that it was beyond the power of the Nationalist authorities to buck the trend or voice its suspicion.

Li Ze was put on trial in 1946. The accusers engaged the legal service
of Sha Qianli and Shen Junru, veteran leaders the National Salvation Association and two of the "seven gentlemen." The defendant engaged the
service of Chen Ruiting and Zhang Shizhao, renowned legal experts and

Nationalist parliamentarians who had mastered the court systems under the foreign concessions and the Nationalist government in Chongqing. The trial went on for more than half a year, with the two sides engaging in pointed debates. Hundreds of members from the employee associations packed the courtroom at each session, shouting, hooting, and booing, while forty or fifty newspaper reporters covered the proceedings. In the words of Party historians with the Shanghai Municipal Committee who documented the case decades later, "The audience's emotions ran high. The atmosphere in the courtroom was intense. Even the defense attorneys felt the pressure." The hecklers booed and yelled "*Hanjian* attorney!" when Chen and Zhang defended Li Ze's patriotism. Party historians readily agreed that the audience was there "to show force." The strategy was designed to place the judge and the government prosecutor "under the weight" of the "rage of the people."[122]

In June 1946 the district court declared its judgment. It waded through the evidence and pronounced the defendant guilty for his association with the Commodity Control Board. Li's alleged "betrayal" was attenuated by his proven patriotism, however. The Bureau of Military Statistics and Investigations had provided solid evidence of Li Ze's instrumentality in aiding and sheltering Nationalist agents and guerrilla forces in Pudong during the war.[123] Li was thus punished with a three-year prison term and the confiscation of his property.

The verdict, unfortunately, did not please either side. Appeals were filed. More press conferences, rallies, and union mobilizations ensued. Li Ze's final sentencing was scheduled for the Jiangsu High Court in September 1947. Communist activists among Sun Sun employees again mobilized to "launch an assault campaign in the arena of public opinion."[124] The unions plastered the Nanjing Road department stores with slogans such as "Punish *hanjian* Li Ze! Justice for the sacrificed soldiers and people during the War of Resistance!" "Confiscate the traitor's property! Fill the coffer of the state! Relief for the unemployed!" "Do not allow *hanjian* Li Ze to slip through! Watch the sentencing on September 30!"[125] Li Ze was again pronounced guilty, sentenced to three years in prison with his property confiscated. He was quietly released shortly afterwards.[126] After the final verdict the employees confronted Sun Sun's board of directors, which had stood behind the general manager, and forced the members to drop Li from the payroll.[127]

In the late 1940s, with inflation once again on the rise, numerous incidents broke out in Shanghai's department stores and banking institutions. These typically involved protests by organized employees, who demanded salary raises and an improvement in living standards. Corporate employees rebelled against their superiors, however, not by arguing that the hierarchy ought to be done away with completely, but by drawing attention to the needs of their families—the ailing elders and the hungry children, undernourished trainees skipping breakfast and overburdened clerks incurring health risks by taking on extra work. It was not that the hierarchy had to be abolished, but that it had to be reformed. As the protestors made clear time and again, corporate leaders had lost their moral authority because they had allowed their employees to slip into hardships that prevented them from meeting basic needs. It was a matter of basic humanity that an adult son to be able to bury his dead parents, and that a working parent be able to treat his or her sick children. Corporate leaders who failed to see this point were not patriarchs but capitalists. They had placed the balance sheets ahead of the human costs, and they had forfeited their claims to respectability. What had to be put in place was thus a structure that would restore the moral principles of the economic system, thereby enabling the petty urbanites to fulfill their familial obligations with honest work.

FROM CLERKS TO COMMUNISTS

It is often observed that the CCP had gained significant influence by the late 1940s with employee associations. It is also often asserted that wartime conditions of underground resistance and open collaboration had done much to lay the groundwork for this development. The war had facilitated the development of many trends in Shanghai. But it was not the cause behind the city's turn to socialism. The seeds had been planted much earlier, well before the outbreak of the war in 1937. Even without the war, there would have been socialist sympathizers ready to join the cause. On the other hand, things might not have followed the trajectory and gained a mass following as they did in the 1940s had there not been the extraordinary disruption of the war, which dislodged a large number of educated youth from their circumstances and turned their thoughts to alternative courses of action.

It is therefore suggestive to sketch the life of Gu Zhun, who began as a trainee with the Lixin Accounting Firm under Pan Xulun in 1927, and rose to become, on Pan's recommendation, a professor of economics at the Shanghai College of Commerce. Gu left the city to enter the Communist base area in 1940, and returned, in 1949, as a member of the takeover team in the professional sector at the head of the triumphant CCP.

A native of Shanghai, Gu Zhun was born in 1915 in an outlying rural district called Lujiabang. He was the fifth child to his father, Chen Wenwei (1873–1944), and the third to his mother, Gu Qinglian (1885–1979). This was not because either parent had previously divorced, but because Chen had married two sisters. As the Gu sisters were the only heirs to their parents' fan shop, Chen agreed to have his children with the younger sister surnamed Gu.[128] (This explains how *Gu* Zhun might have been *Chen* Zhun.)

Chen went on to sire a large family. The older Gu, who died in 1916, gave birth to four sons and one daughter. The younger Gu, who survived her sister by another sixty-some years, had three sons and two daughters. The birthdates of the ten siblings spanned two dozen years, from 1902 to 1926. Gu Zhun saw himself as the first born to his "birth mother" and the fourth or fifth to his father and titular "mother."[129] He was also in the midst of a complex kinship web in which not all children received an equal opportunity.

Chen was unfortunately not very skilled in guarding the family fortune. He failed at one enterprise after another. By 1924 Grandfather Gu had died, Grandmother Gu had moved in, Chen was in debt, and the family was in crisis. The women did washing, sewing, and embroidering to pay for the meals. There were too many people and not enough opportunities. The grown-ups "bickered bitterly and relentlessly" over who owed what to whom.[130] Gu Zhun later described himself as coming from "the middle stratum of the propertied class in a state of bankruptcy" *(pochan de zhongdeng zichan jieji jiating)*, which would apply both to the ethical and the economic fiber of his family.[131]

The Gu family then moved to the southern part of Nanshi—near the seasonal markets of the nineteenth century, where there were no street lights or running water. Gu Zhun and his brothers attended a charitable school in a local Buddhist temple, and learned enough to pass the entrance examinations for the elementary school run by the CSVE. The CSVE curriculum promised to lead to a vocational career. But tuition and fees for books, at twenty *yuan* per term, remained expensive. After a mere two semesters, the ten-year-old Gu would have been forced to drop out had Principal Wang Zhixin, the future editor of the *Shenghuo Weekly* and head of the Xinhua Bank, not intervened to reduce the fees by half. Wang gave Gu's name to his friend Pan Xulun, the American-educated accountant (see chapter 2). In July 1927, at the age of twelve, Gu Zhun joined Pan's accounting firm as a trainee.[132]

The Pan Xulun Accounting Firm, which in the 1930s acquired national fame as the Lixin Accounting Firm, was in its early stage of development when Gu joined as its first trainee. Gu was responsible for reception and delivery. He learned to type, in English and Chinese, and was trained to handle registration matters in compliance of the codes of incorporation and trademarks. In the spring of 1928, Pan launched the Lixin Evening School of Accounting, where the trainee Gu took a course on bookkeeping. He also began working as a junior assistant in accounting and auditing.[133]

Gu's vocational development and Lixin's growth as an accounting school took place simultaneously. Under Pan's watch Gu assisted with the correction of homework assignments for students at the Lixin school. He then served as the scribe to prepare copies for Pan's lecture notes and teaching materials. He was the proofreader and the printing and publishing liaison for Pan's texts, published by the Shanghai Commercial Press as the *Lixin Accounting Series*. The school soon added a correspondence program that expanded to an instructional program offering multiple subjects. In 1931 Gu Zhun became an instructor; the following year he compiled his first textbook, on accounting for banking, which appeared in the *Lixin Accounting Series*. He took charge as Lixin's "Director of Instructional Affairs." He was elected to the board of the Lixin Alumni Association. Formed in 1929, the association published a quarterly accounting journal and an association newsletter. It also routinely organized company visits and alumni reunions. This placed him in a unique position to exploit the networking potential of Lixin's growing roster, which matured to include a large number of Shanghai's financial workers.

Gu Zhun's first payment in 1927 as a trainee was four *yuan* a month. By 1930 his monthly pay had risen to thirty *yuan*, a respectable sum that enabled the fifteen year old, who took all his meals at the firm, to support his family of seven.[134] In addition to his regular salary, he also brought home bonuses from the firm's profit-sharing scheme. By early 1932 Gu Zhun, no longer a trainee, was drawing monthly bonuses that exceeded his regular pay. For the compilation of his first textbook he received eight hundred *yuan* as royalties. By late 1934 Gu, barely twenty years of age, was taking home over one hundred *yuan* each month, which was more than enough to pay for his younger brother's tuition fees and to support his mother in comfort.[135]

A filial son, a hard worker, and a serious and unhappy youth disturbed by the vice and injustice surrounding him, Gu was also a voracious reader driven by pragmatic needs and existential questioning. His dealings with the Shanghai Commercial Press opened the doors to the publishing house's library, widely regarded as Shanghai's best, for both classical and modern publications. His liaison chores on behalf of the accounting series, furthermore, put him in touch with the press's young printers who were among the most radical of Shanghai's organized workers.[136] Gu spent long hours in the evenings reading in the library, to teach himself accounting for his compilation and teaching assignments, as well as to avoid the unpleasantness of home. His interest in the "economics" of banking and accounting soon expanded to include "philosophical" questions concerning social justice and the economic system. He taught himself English and Japanese. He borrowed his brother's copies of *China Forum* that carried reports about the Soviets. He followed the "social history" debates in the *Dushu Monthly*. He also worked his way through Kawakami Hajime's *Principles of Economics*. On weekends he visited former CSVE classmates who had gone on to the Labor University (Laodong daxue) in Jiangwan, a stronghold of anarchists and labor unionists. At Labor University he learned of Kropotkin and Ba Jin.[137] It rang true to him that it was labor rather than capital that had created value.[138] Yet in this firm run by the American-educated Pan, knowledge-based workers had to sign away their copyrights, allowing the firm, of which a single individual owned more than half, to profit exclusively from the sales of complied and translated books.

In the winter of 1934, Gu Zhun assembled ten of his former classmates and current associates from the CSVE elementary school, the Lixin Accounting School, the Lixin Accounting Firm, and the Lixin Alumni Association to launch the *Jinshe* (The Society for Progress), which met weekly in his kitchen to discuss books and current events. The group consisted of elite clerks with CSVE and Lixin credentials. They were also printers and radio technicians. All were interested in issues of "economics" and "philosophy." All, in other words, were serious-minded young people of the "middle stratum of the propertied class in a state of bankruptcy" who cared for knowledge and knew of poverty. All had harbored, in the words of Gu, aspirations at one point for an upwardly mobile "vocational life" *(zhiye shenghuo)*. They saw their prospects dimmed in the 1930s with the recession in the city and intensified tension with Japan.[139] They were not certain of the best solutions, though they were sure that the Nationalist authorities were not doing the right things.

This grassroots organization, which sprang up without the guiding light of the CCP, gathered momentum among the top students of the vocational programs (members of the Shangxue tuan—"Corps for Commercial Learning") and evening schools, including those run by the YMCA. Within half a year the society had more than doubled its membership. It had also set up a branch in the commercial town Changshou, west of Shanghai. But the secret gatherings of frustrated yet ambitious young people sharing left-wing reading materials soon attracted the attention of the Nationalist authorities. It was against the law to be in possession of banned materials. Late in 1934 Gu Zhun was forced to flee from his home in Nanshi to take refuge in the foreign concessions, where he took up a job, thanks to connections through Pan Xulun, in the auditing department at the head office of the Bank of China. The appointment certified his standing as an accountant and enormously enhanced his professional prestige. Gu spent more than half a year on the job, double-checking the transaction statements between hundreds of branches and devoting more than six hours each day to the abacus. Three decades later he told his Communist interrogators that bank assignments had been "tedious and demanding," his bank colleagues had been "docile and compliant," and that his bank superior was a "pompous bureaucrat": disparaging remarks that were no doubt appropriate under Communism for a premier bourgeois and Nationalist institution.[140] Gu described himself as a tardy and indolent bank worker who was hardly interested in his career advancement. He was totally absorbed, especially in the evenings, in keeping up with current events and the latest social philosophical tracts. This might well have been true at the moment. He went back to Pan, who was aware of his difficulties with the authorities. Pan placed him on traveling assignments to elude the police. He also encouraged Gu to continue with writing, compiling, translating, and publishing.

Gu Zhun and his Society for Progress came into being when the CCP was in total disarray. The central committee of the Party had been forced to move out of Shanghai in 1933 in the aftermath of the Gu Shunzhang incident, in which the turncoat disclosed CCP safe houses and secure contacts to his Nationalist captors and caused the total breakdown of the underground Communist organization. The central committee relocated itself to the Jiangxi soviet.[141] CCP members in Shanghai thereafter maintained but sporadic connections with the larger Party organization. It was not until 1936, with the arrival of Liu Changsheng and Pan

Hannian from the north, that a Jiangsu provincial CCP committee was established to reconnect the Shanghai Communists organizationally to the central committee in Yan'an. Gu Zhun's confirmation in the CCP thus took place through the remnants of the pre-1932 central committee—under the branch for writers (Wenwei) run by Zhou Yang, as Gu was a published author.

The Society for Progress, a "spontaneous Marxism-Leninism cell" that had sprung up (as Mao had predicted) "from within the masses" "of its own accord" at "a historical turning point" on the eve of the December 9 Movement of 1934,[142] "found the Party" in the guise of two organizations, the East Asian Anti-Japanese League (Yuandong renmin fanri da tongmeng) and the Committee for the Armed Self-Defense of the Chinese Nation (Zhonghua minzu wuzhuang ziwei weiyuanhui; hereafter Committee for Armed Self-Defense).[143] Decades later during the Cultural Revolution, Gu Zhun would learn that the Shanghai Party committee in the mid-1930s contained traitors who were responsible for the destruction of the underground Party in 1935, which led to massive arrests of members of the Committee for Armed Self-Defense, as well as the Party's provisional committee. These arrests, which took place a mere six months before the "high-tide" of anti-Japanese protests among college students, put the Shanghai Communists in an awkward position trying to catch up with the shifting political momentum on issues of patriotism.

Gu and his friends joined, in the summer of 1934, the first class of an evening reading group directed by Li Gongpu (see chapter 6) at the YMCA. The class enrolled five sections and a total of nearly two hundred readers, each doing the reading on proposed titles and meeting together on Saturdays for monitored discussions. Fellow participants included students of the Liangcai School of Supplementary Education—the evening school sponsored by *Shenbao* and named after the paper's assassinated publisher, Shi Liangcai. Many of the discussions evolved around the issue of China's future. Gu and his friends signed up for different sections and got themselves all elected as class leaders. These class leaders met as Society for Progress members on Sunday; the society thus gained a controlling voice in the reading class. At the commencement of the first session of the YMCA reading class, Gu Zhun revealed a "Six-Point Guideline on Resistance against Japan," which his fellow students adopted with enthusiasm. Some of these fellow readers were eventually funneled into the Committee for Armed Self-Defense.

With the intensification of Sino-Japanese conflicts and the worsening of the global economy in the mid-1930s, a growing number of Shanghai's petty urbanites came under the sway of critical viewpoints contained in the pages of the *Shenghuo zhoukan* and *Dushu shenghuo* (see chapters 5 and 6). Strident calls for armed resistance against Japan by Zou Taofen and Li Gongpu gave powerful impetus to the rise of muscular patriotism among the vocational youth. With reading groups functioning as the core of larger employee after-work activities, a whole host of associations such as the Shanghai Banking Employees Association, the Shanghai Department Store Employees Association, the Shanghai Trading Firm Employees Association, and the Shanghai Maritime Customs Employees Association came into being, the last of which contained a large number of former CSVE students. When the "high-tide" of patriotism surged in 1936, these associations contributed to the formation of the Shanghai Vocational Circles National Salvation Association (Shanghai zhiye jie jiuguo hui) in 1936.[144] Gu Zhun by then had become a high ranking underground cadre reporting directly to the Jiangsu Provincial Committee of the CCP. It fell upon him decades later to argue that the CCP, despite the destruction of satellite organizations such as the Committee for Armed Self-Defense and the Provincial Party in 1935, had played a significant role leading the patriotic movement.

While still a teenager, Gu Zhun, who later described himself as prone to "jump and react on the slightest irritation" (thereby testing the patience of his CCP superior, Liu Changsheng), once talked back sharply to Pan Xulun. At the end of the outburst the boss said to the trainee, "I have treated you with greater tenderness than your father has ever shown."[145] By Gu's own admission the "capitalist" accountant, who served for one term as deputy minister of finance with the Nationalist government, had indeed been consistently protective and indulgent. Pan was aware of the trainee's left-wing sympathies and activities in the 1930s, yet he chose to take the rebellious youth under his wing. The compensation package and fringe benefits that he offered were more than generous by contemporary standards. Pan was enthusiastic in his praise of Gu's talents and admired his relentless drive. He created opportunities for Gu to study, teach, read, and publish. He recommended him to college teaching positions and sent his essays to publishers of professional journals. With Pan's trust and support Gu rose quickly in the accounting firm. Pan continued to provide him with handsome salaries when Gu was running from the Nationalist police, making payments that permitted Gu to read and write in hiding. In the winter of 1940, Gu and Pan left the "lone islet" to find their ways respectively to Yan'an and Chongqing. Pan shed tears at the farewell party while Gu registered no emotion. These details emerged during the Cultural Revolution, when Gu was interrogated on account of his relationship with a powerful figure in the unreformed old society.

True enough, Pan Xulun had extended a hand to "lift" and "promote" Gu Zhun, a young trainee from an impoverished background. But this surely did not mean that Pan had failed to "exploit" him. It was also true that well into the 1950s, former Lixin workers, Gu Zhun included, maintained their decade-long habit and referred to Master Pan, in writing as well as in speech, as "Teacher" (shi). This was because almost all Lixin workers had studied, as Gu did, with Pan. When using the old salute, Gu was merely following the directives of the Party to show "some gesture of civility."[146] Nor did it imply, on Gu's part, any acknowledgement of having actually learned anything from Pan: "If I were to say that I had achieved anything at all within the framework of bourgeois accounting, I can say with certainty that . . . this was because I had learned from the students in my class and learned from the authors of a large number of books that I had read. It was absolutely not because I had learned anything from Pan Xulun."[147]

Gu Zhun returned to Shanghai triumphant as a member of the CCP. His association with Pan Hannian, deputy mayor of Shanghai, did not help his political prospects. In 1957 he was denounced as a "rightist." In 1966 he was again declared a rightist and interrogated for his activities during the 1930s.

In his self-examination documents Gu Zhun laid out his early life and explained his loyalty. There was no denial that Pan Xulun, the leading accountant in the Republican era, had been a major patron and employer, without whom Gu's life would have taken a different turn. There was also no denial that Pan had consistently been a source of support. Gu took pains to suggest that Pan's conduct had been motivated by economic gains, and that the compensations that he had drawn from the firm hardly matched the value of his real contribution. His patron, being a capitalist, was incapable, in other words, of conducting himself in ways that defied the logic of his class. He was bound to be economically calculating and exploitative, even if his deeds might lend the appearance of paternalistic kindness.

Pan and Gu met again shortly after the latter's return to Shanghai in 1949. The former patron nominated Gu to become the head of the Lixin Accounting School, which Gu declined. As a member of the Communist Party, Gu was no longer in a position to accept personal nominations. A new regime had been inaugurated, and Pan's gesture was seen not as an act of affirmation, but of self-preservation.

By the late 1940s the petty urbanites of Shanghai had found their new place and allegiance within the CCP. The victorious Party promised to uphold the principles of social justice and distribute its institutionalized benevolence to each according to his worth. The days of the patriarchs, who for decades had set the terms of Shanghai capitalism, were over.

The Return of the Banker

In May 1949, the People's Liberation Army (PLA) crossed the Yangzi River and marched into Shanghai, entering the undefended city on a bright spring day. Throngs of onlookers crowded the streets. Thousands of underground Party members, including the activists among the employee associations and publishing enterprises, staged celebrations for the liberation that they had so assiduously worked for. The city's elite faced a difficult decision with the takeover. Managers of Wing On chose to stay, as did the accountant Pan Xulun. A large number of senior bank executives, however, decided to either relocate to Hong Kong or New York, or to follow the Nationalist government to Taipei.

To those who had to choose between Nationalist or Communist affiliations, the regime shift marked a major watershed in China's twentieth century. The "New China" of Mao Zedong's communist revolution, to be sure, did not appear overnight. Nor was it able to devise means of governing that were totally different from those adopted by its Nationalist foes. In the 1950s, both Chinese governments proceeded to deepen the social reforms and revolutions that they had envisioned in earlier decades, seeing these as means as well as ends, as they sought to regenerate the war-torn economies under their respective governance. The 1950s witnessed, on both sides of the Taiwan Strait, land reforms, nationalization of major enterprises, and economic planning, along with ideological training, domestic surveillance, and campaigns of party rectification. Both states had turned economistic, measuring the success of their governance in terms of economic growth and material transformation.

There remained, nonetheless, fundamentally different ideas between the Nationalists and the Communists about strategies for growth and the functions of the private sectors in the economy. By the late 1950s a new perspective had taken hold in Shanghai, and what used to be prized as glamour now became a political liability. Shanghai before 1949 came to embody the corruption and humiliation of China in the age of European expansion. Under socialism the city was reorganized to become a center of manufacturing rather than commerce and finance; the inhabitants were workers, not consumers. The Communist government eliminated the social reproduction of the bourgeoisie by abolishing, through legislation, the rights of private ownership and space for mercantile activities. It took away foreign privileges and property by seizing or freezing the assets of international enterprises and institutions.[1] It eliminated the feminine presence in public *not* by sending women back to homemaking, but through a constitutional assurance of gender equality that desexualized the feminine. Public culture in Shanghai under socialism was no less than a reversal and critique of the dynamic mixture of the feminine, mercantile, and foreign, which had come to define the city's culture in the century after the Opium War.

THE BANKER

In the late 1980s, the writer Cheng Naishan began working on a novel entitled *Jin rong jia (The Banker)*.[2] Born and raised in Shanghai in the 1950s, Cheng was the granddaughter of Cheng Muhao, formerly a senior executive at the Bank of China. Cheng Muhao left for Hong Kong after the Communist takeover, and it was not until 1986 that Naishan finally met her grandfather for the first time. Based on the life story of Cheng Muhao, *The Banker,* completed shortly before 1989, was among the first post-1949 publications to break a long-kept literary silence on the subject of Shanghai's financial past.

Cheng's fictional "realistic account," based on three months of intensive interviews conducted with her ailing grandfather in Hong Kong in 1986, told the story of an eminent Shanghai banker (Zhu Jingchen) who led the "Bank of Cathay" and his own family through the dark days of the War of Resistance. Cheng reconstructed the Westernized social milieu in Shanghai's high society and financial circles before 1949. Using wartime trials and tribulations as a backdrop, she restored the senior

banker to the role of a patriarch and patriot instead of a collaborator
and capitalist. In the book, Manager Zhu looked after not only his own
children and employees, but also the children and widows of former colleagues and deceased employees. He also resisted Japanese intervention
into bank affairs. He stopped short of joining the socialists to fight capitalist institutions. Yet he displayed the sorts of economic sentiments that
were shorn of market instincts. Banker Zhu, in short, was *almost* as good
as a socialist in his dealings with money. Despite the watchful caution
and deep-seated ambivalence of the Communists who had taken the city
from him, the banker, after an exile of four decades, returned to Shanghai in the guise of an honorary socialist.

THE PAST IN THE PRESENT

As a forward-looking city that was being incessantly refashioned into
images of modernity, post–Opium War Shanghai hardly had the energy
for introspective searching into its own past. Whether in its pursuit of
capitalist splendor or socialist revolution, the city, for much of the twentieth century, measured its progress by negating its past.

In *Ziye (Midnight)*, Mao Dun's massive work of social realism of the
1930s, the writer famously represents the city as the transient material-
ization of "light, heat, power."[3] A vortex of market transactions swept
capitalist Shanghai into a state where the city was barely able to see beyond the immediate present. Modernity under capitalism, in Shanghai
as well as elsewhere, was incapable of either memory or reflection.

Similarly, for much of the mid-twentieth century, with its celebration
of the next wave of revolution and the wanton destruction of the feudal
past, socialist Shanghai showed hardly any sentimentality toward days
of old.

It is thus interesting to note how in the 1990s, Shanghai gave in to nostalgia, and devoted its energy to reconstructing the city's past. Shanghai
authorities reopened colonial mansions that had been gathering cobwebs,
restored historical landmarks, built urban history museums, and rein-
stated library collections of pre-1949 publications. Guidebooks appeared,
containing rave reviews of restaurants, shops, sights, and entertainment—
places were endorsed not for their revolutionary correctness, but for their
long reach and deep connections with pre-socialist distinctions. Teams
of researchers embarked upon massive local history compilation projects.
Quietly, yet unmistakably, through literature, memoirs, biographies,
posters, photographs, newspaper columns, magazine articles, and even

fashion accessories and restaurant décor, the city opened its doors to the return of its repressed and banished pre-revolutionary memories.

These initiatives, to be sure, hardly stemmed from a veneration of the past for its own sake. Instead, a main function of the new interest was instrumental. The reinvigoration of an urban historical narrative not only served to enrich the city's imagination of the future, but also bolstered its claim to the legitimacy of doing so.

THE USE OF HISTORY

In the 1980s, following the opening of Shenzhen as a Special Economic Zone under the new policies of the "Four Modernizations," Shanghai reported economic growth that lagged behind the Pearl River Delta. The latter was being rapidly transformed by its connections with Hong Kong while Shanghai continued to stagnate. In China's planned economy, Shanghai had functioned for decades as the country's main producer and supplier of industrial products. It had also contributed the lion's share of its revenue to the maintenance of the state in Beijing. Authorities were thus reluctant to tamper with an arrangement upon which they had come to depend. They argued that the strategic importance of Shanghai dictated extra caution and a gradual approach in the remaking of the city's state-owned enterprises. Shanghai's municipal authorities, however, showed less patience. They put together "Strategic Guidelines for Economic Development in Shanghai," which the State Council in Beijing finally approved in February 1985.[4]

Not much took place, however, until well into the 1990s, after Deng Xiaoping's reaffirmation, in 1992, of policies of economic openness.[5] Deng's open resolve, coming in the aftermath of the June 4, 1989 military crackdown against protestors at Tiananmen Square in Beijing, spurred a "second high tide" in the search for a developmental strategy for Shanghai. It also helped that Shanghai's erstwhile municipal leadership, Party Secretary Jiang Zemin and Mayor Zhu Rongji, were at this point the general secretary of the CCP and the vice-premier of the State Council respectively. Out of the "high tide" of the 1990s emerged the vision that twenty-first century Shanghai would function as an "international center for economy, finance, and trade." This engine of growth would develop "in leaps and bounds," and would drive not just the lower Yangzi Delta, but the entire Yangzi valley.

Under the joint chairmanship of the city's deputy mayor and deputy CCP general secretary, a team of Shanghai researchers worked on the articulation of this vision. Using "big," "fast," and "strategic" as key words, they produced statements that sketched out the city's place in the twenty-first century. The Shanghai of the future was "not only to be the Shanghai of China, but also the Shanghai of the world."[6] In policy terms this meant that Shanghai had to break away from the socialist mode of economic production and participate in the globalizing economic framework dominated by the G7. In strategic terms, the report called for the development of Shanghai as China's gateway to the world in the country's march into the new century.

Under the new guidelines the city would reorient itself to "face the world, face modernization, and face the twenty-first century."[7] Without explicitly stating it, Shanghai was also to turn its back on the corresponding opposites ("Chinese provinces," "socialist conservatism," "past practices in the twentieth century"). To "jump-start" so as to "ascertain a central place in international economy" within "as brief a period as possible," Shanghai would, in its planning for the future, adopt a "grand view encompassing its urban surroundings."[8] It would set off from "a high vantage point" in order to produce developmental results "in leaps and bounds." Through strategic concentrations of human, material, and economic resources, Shanghai would "allocate its limited resources differentially so as to better realize its comparative advantages in targeted areas."[9]

The farming counties east of the Huangpu River, known as Pudong, which until the 1980s had not been part of the established Shanghai municipality, represented, for instance, an enormous amount of property assets that could be "exchanged into more advanced modes of capital" for the development of a greater Shanghai. The 1993 project report concluded with the recommendation that Shanghai serve as the locus for a massive regional plan that would encompass a threefold addition to its existing area. It would also follow a "unique path" based on "the incremental secession of the usage rights of its land."[10] Shanghai was to lease or rent its land to international developers in exchange for much needed capital, which in turn would bankroll the city's leap into the new century. Under a massive regional developmental plan backed by the State Council during the presidency of Jiang Zemin, the "land grant" program in exchange for overseas capital and technology enclosed the entire lower Yangzi Delta, from the mouth of the Yangzi River to the mouth of the Qiantang River—an area that had been divided up under the jurisdiction of three counties under the Qing.

No land in the intensively cultivated lower Yangzi, of course, was without people. The more strategic the location was, the less favorable the population to land ratio tended to be. There were "social problems" that clearly would have to be addressed if such a developmental strategy was to materialize.

It was within this context that the planners of the Shanghai Academy of Social Sciences and the Shanghai CCP Propaganda Department set to work.[11] They identified, in 1995, ten major areas—demographic composition, social security, income distribution, urban communities, youth, environmental protection, housing, relocation, crime, and religion—for focused examination. The investigators found, not surprisingly, that four decades of socialism had done little to improve the living conditions in the city, and that major facilities—sewage, running water, heating, power, and public transportation—dated their construction well back to pre-revolutionary days. Housing and traffic had been acutely congested. In some parts of the city each inhabitant occupied, on average, a mere 38.7 square feet of living space. The city's prime real estate—Huangpu, Luwan, and Xujiahui—had been weighed down in particular by a maturing population consisting of multi-generational families. Shanghai, in short, had been bogged down by the working population and their residential households, which had been multiplying since Liberation.

To achieve the "leaps and bounds" and to make room for outside investors and their developmental capital, Shanghai simply scooped up established residents and relocated them to the urban peripheries. The ramifications were broad and far-reaching. It meant, for instance, breaking up the work unit system *(danwei)* that for decades had provided accommodations to workers in compounds nearby their workplace. It meant, furthermore, either relocating or shutting down Shanghai's state-owned manufacturing facilities in order to reduce pollution and make room at prime locations for commercial enterprises. It meant a thorough remaking of the city from an industrial center to a commercial and financial one, replacing the factories and the workers with shopping centers, restaurants, offices, hotels, expatriate apartments, public transportation systems, commercial employees, and, at times, even colonies of artists and enclaves of studios. It meant, in short, the construction of an outward-looking economy of consumption built on imported capital, reorganizing a city that had been based upon a rooted economy of industrial production. The social and political challenges of the transformation were to be matched only by the magnitude and audacity of the economic vision. In the cryptic language of the official reports and the recommendations, the best possible scenario for the city's leap into the new century was thus "a modernized international city of socialism, which achieves internationalism without betraying the principles of socialism."[12]

As a planned leap (which some have dubbed "the Great Leap Outward") that originated with the state and top party officials, full-time researchers in all disciplines—economics, sociology, international law, finance, science, urban planning, education, social psychology, demography, environmental studies, architecture—were mobilized to contribute. As the planners, architects, accountants, lawyers, project managers, general contractors, and so forth readied themselves for work, Shanghai historians rallied to throw their weight behind the city's modernization project and to make the intellectual case in favor of the outlined change.

The diligence of the historians produced, over the course of the next fifteen years, a large number of volumes and journals that filled multiple shelves in the libraries. This is not the place to engage in an examination of this massive corpus of work, which makes contributions on scholarly as well as other grounds.[13] At the risk of oversimplification, the point of relevance is simply that the historians, through their descriptions of the city's recent past, embraced Shanghai's modern history as a chronicle of Shanghai's uniqueness, if not China's pride. By doing so they had set aside an old-fashioned, revolutionary belief and refashioned the city's urban identity. They consequently supplied, wittingly or not, the critical historical justification in favor of the city's strategic repositioning in the 1990s.

As history has so often served as a handmaiden to ideology, Shanghai historians in the 1990s assumed a critical and delicate task. By and large they were firm in disposing of a narrative that stemmed from the old socialist orthodoxy. By shifting attention away from colonialism, capitalism, Nationalist betrayal, and Communist martyrdom, new images emerged that described a middle-class city of material comfort in everyday life that was making steady progress in the enhancement of wealth and health.[14] In lieu of the workers, martyrs, underground Communists, radical intellectuals, and ardent patriots who had occupied the center stage in the old historiography, women, merchants, foreigners, and entertainers were gaining in visibility. Instead of dwelling upon the structural injustice in the "social relationships of production" under capitalism, the more innovative historians chronicled the scientific and technological advancement in "modes of production" as the city underwent modernization.[15] There were plenty of achievements to be recorded in printing, publishing, journalism, education, architecture, fashion, theater, civil associations, local self-governance, custom reform, family life, women's status, migrant integration, merchandizing, shopkeeping, cuisine, advertising, and so forth.

Shanghai under foreign municipal councils, with its electric lights, comfort, civility, and sophistication, had long claimed itself to be the "Paris of the East." Shanghai regained its glamour in Chinese historical representations in the 1990s. Yet this was glamour with a difference. Pre-1949 Shanghai was the making, according to a new generation of Chinese historians, *neither* of the colonialists *nor* of the capitalists. It was, instead, the work of the petty urbanites who were the occupants, for example, of the *shikumen* residences. In the words of Zhang Zhongli, president of the Shanghai Academy of Social Sciences, "The bottom line is: Shanghai was Chinese, Shanghai was Shanghainese. The city developed as a result of the people in Shanghai making innovations on inspirations taken from the West."[16] Shanghai, from the mid-nineteenth century onward, has been a city of migrants coming from all parts of the lower Yangzi.[17] These individuals transformed the city into a place of glamour with their talent and labor. Shanghai *was* Chinese, because it was built on the labor of the Chinese people. It did not have to await 1949 to *become* Chinese with the triumphant victory march of the PLA.

The rewriting of the history of pre-Communist Shanghai thus reconstructed urban developmental genealogies and supplied indigenous grounding to the post-Mao policies of openness toward the outside world. The modern history of Shanghai supplied not only the hard evidence about the attainability of the municipal planners' lofty goals for the new century, but also assured the people in the city's back alleys of their natural ownership of that vision. Seen from Shanghai, the agenda for China's future was simply an agenda that had already been attained once in the city's past. It went without saying that no place was better poised or prepared to lead China's "leaps and bounds" into the new century.

In the mid-1990s, construction work in Shanghai took place at a frenetic pace. Building slowed down only after the Asian monetary crises reached the city in the late summer of 1997, choking up the influx of overseas capital from Hong Kong and Southeast Asia. The lure of the "old Shanghai," meanwhile, continued in full force. Nostalgia gripped the city, and residents adjusted to the new appearance of billboards flanking the boulevards, which depicted the good life as defined by elite products such as Courvoisier Cognac V.S.O.P. Fine Champagne.

Wang Anyi's *Changhen ge* (Song of Everlasting Sorrow), the winner for the 1995 Mao Dun Literary Prize, tells the story of a former "Miss

Shanghai" who leads her life unobtrusively in a back alley during the days of socialism.[18] A gentle soul, "Miss Shanghai" tugs at the heartstrings of ordinary men and women, friends and foes alike. Feminine and domestic, she brings a special touch that never fails to lighten up her surroundings. Before socialism she posed innocently for photo studios in bridal gowns; she also walked down the runway as a modest beauty in pageants. This past, of "color and light . . . rises from behind her . . . like a mirage" even in the darkest days of communist tedium.[19]

The woman's talent to transform the mundane into the exquisite is not passed on to her daughter, however, who was born and raised under the new regime. Yet unlike the mother who was a survivor from a tainted past, the daughter, a child of socialist China who cares little of her parentage, inhabits a changing world with its own abundance and rewards. Almost belatedly, "Miss Shanghai" dies in the story so as to yield her space to a new generation that ruthlessly demands their share of the better things in life.

Faded photos and yellow newsprints capture the key moments in Shanghai's alleyway lives.[20] In the same vein, *Changhen ge* commemorates, in lieu of the tree-lined boulevards, colonial mansions, glittering shops, and grand ladies of the foreign concessions, "the fine lines on . . . the carved wooden panes atop the alleyway houses." These fine lines come into view, Wang tells us, only as the morning sun dissolves the darkness and pales the lights that line the thoroughfares.[21] In total contrast to the soaring glass and steel skyscrapers that transformed the spatial dynamics on the ground, Shanghai nostalgia in the 1990s romanticized the crammed alleyways and cluttered courtyards that were ultimately destined for the bulldozers. *Changhen ge* relishes the salacious curiosities and reverberating gossip of the crammed existence of a suppressed past. It writes into the urban legend a new kind of tale, with soap-opera flare, that glamorizes the ins and outs of the alleyway houses in their closing days.

Between 1992 and 1996, over two thousand skyscrapers, financed largely on Hong Kong and Southeast Asian capital, went up in Shanghai. These buildings now flank the Huangpu River, rising up through the former foreign concessions and Pudong's nondescript farmland, transforming Shanghai into a forest of incongruous towers. Perhaps most tellingly, they dwarf the Bund's picturesque colonial mansions that once symbolized Shanghai's modernity. Besides all the usual attributes of an up-and-coming Asian city—a television tower, massive eating and shopping districts, a large international airport, freeways, new subway lines, waterfront parks, a deep-water port—Shanghai today has built a brand

new civic center and high-speed Maglev train, and boasts a world-class
art museum and futuristic opera house. There are numerous other museums, shops, and restaurants that enliven the city, not to mention additional parks and green spaces that dot the urban center.

REVOLUTION AS HEROIC TRAGEDY

As the new Shanghai rose on the eastern bank of the Huangpu, another
figure from Shanghai's repressed past made his return. This was Gu Zhun,
the accountant, self-taught socialist, and veteran member of the CCP (see
chapter 7). An entire corpus of Gu Zhun-related publications appeared
in the mid-1990s. These include Gu's essays in political economy, his diaries kept during the Anti-Rightist campaigns and the Cultural Revolution, his statements of self-examination while under interrogation, and
his notes on Marx, Engels, Hegel, Kant, Rousseau, Feuerbach, Keynes,
Strauss, and Rostow. In addition, Gu's life story was narrated into an
impassioned biography (Tearing Out His Rib Bone to Make a Torch: The
Life of Gu Zhun), in which Gu emerged, in the old-fashioned communist style, as an unbending champion fighting for the ideal of social justice in the distribution of wealth.[22]

Gu Zhun headed north after leaving Shanghai in 1941. He traveled
through the CCP base area in northern Jiangsu and arrived in Yan'an.
His experience and expertise made him unique among his rural-based
comrades. He emerged as an economist and returned to Shanghai in 1949
in that capacity, as a member of the triumphant Eastern China Military
Commission. Gu's many responsibilities under the military government
included the takeover of the financial sectors of Shanghai.[23]

Gu Zhun's star, however, fell swiftly. His party superiors found him
arrogant and indomitable. He was abruptly dismissed from his government post in 1952, and was transferred to an economic research institute,
where he published essays that argued against the theoretical pronounce-
ments of Stalin on commerce under communism.[24] He was twice labeled
a rightist. He would not slacken, however, in his study of Marx. He endured divorce and the later suicide of his ex-wife. His children denounced
him and denied him a deathbed reconciliation. He died of cancer in 1974,
attended by veteran Communists and fellow political economists who
had been his comrades from the Shanghai underground days. His estate
consisted of nothing but unpublished manuscripts.

The didactic points of the Gu story, against the backdrop of a liber-
alizing economy that was orienting towards the free market, seem ap-

parent enough. Here is a figure resurrected from the 1930s who had known the comforts of middle-class life. He abandoned it in pursuit of an intractable ideal that he believed was to serve a just society and died a lonely man. His surviving comrades fought for a place for his memories in the public arena in the 1990s, while a new generation of urban planners, state economists, civil engineers, municipal officials, and overseas developers were busily tearing down his old hometown in order to make room for what they hoped would be the glitziest city in the world.[25]

Shanghai at the beginning of the twenty-first century has once again captured its place as China's capital of glamour and sophistication. Able cadres and imported capital have revitalized a consumer culture that thrives on alluring images, while a relentless pursuit of development has produced the world's fastest-growing economy.

As the course toward the future was being boldly mapped, voices from the past grew correspondingly more audible yet less certain. For a city that for over a century had shown so little concern for the past, Shanghai in the 1990s had turned historically-minded in an unprecedented way. Different sets of characters had reemerged to claim their place in the city's collective memory.

The return of an exiled banker from Hong Kong was celebrated as a family reunion across political divides and a mending of kinship ties across generations. Through the inclusion of Hong Kong as an extension of space in Shanghai's urban awareness, parts of the city were able to acquire an origin and reclaim a genealogy. The commemoration of the life story of the revolutionary Gu Zhun, on the other hand, served as a strong reminder of the diametrically opposite urban narrative, in which the birth of the city was attributed to social forces and the ideological drive of proactive individuals who embodied idealism and rode the trends. These new tales of martyrdom suggested that it was Gu Zhun and his contemporaries who had given birth to an urban vision that accorded Shanghai its special place in history.

Shanghai, of course, thrived on migration. Urban identities in its history always involved a certain element of construction, in which the sense of "home" was as often asserted as experienced. In the 1990s, those who had been settled in Shanghai for decades were keen to claim the city as their home. An abundance of *shikumen* literature, with *Changhen ge* being the most celebrated example, invoked the intensity of lives lived under the roofs of overcrowded alleyway houses, where dense webs of gossip and emotional entanglements ultimately engendered a powerful sense of community and belonging. The "old Shanghainese," who had been rooted in the city for decades, pointed to Shanghai's famous dumplings and insisted that their accustomed ways of everyday life had not been without comfort or pleasure. Meanwhile, a growing contingent of "new Shanghainese," estimated to number no fewer than five hundred thousand by the end of the twentieth century, began to make their presence felt in the city. Unlike the traditional immigrants and migrant workers from the countryside, these traveling urbanites flew in from Hong Kong, Taiwan, Southeast Asia, and elsewhere, following the flow of capital. Some came as developers and shareholders of malls, shops, restaurants, entertainment venues, offices, apartments, hotels, and bars. Others came as affluent retirees, high-paid senior managers, skilled consultants, or even active philanthropists. They were the transnationals who helped to transform Shanghai into a fast-paced metropolis of multiple identities, where the dark, dank communal homes of old with peeling paint and cluttered hallways were razed to make room for new high-rises with air-conditioning, running water, flushing toilets, and lights that could be dimmed for ambience. Between the "new" and the "old" Shanghainese were contending ideas about what a "home" was to be: a rooted community that was eulogized in literature, or a prized construction built of glass and marble, which was the embodiment not only of proprietary ownership, but also of a certain freedom to dictate the terms in one's acquired space.

Both "home" and "birth," then, were in flux. What, then, was the place of history in Shanghai's supercharged quest for modernity? Where did the city, which gave birth to the Chinese Communist Party in 1921, stand in relation to its own past at the end of the twentieth century?

On one level, the past—or a specific sort of "past" that had been inscribed as such—had ceased to have much relevance in Shanghai's relentless drive to climb the heights of material transformation in its embrace of the world. The city, thanks to Shanghai historians, had liberated itself from the long-established master narrative of socialism against capitalism, and nationalism against colonialism. It had arrived happily at an almost "weightless" state free of the burden of its past. There were no more obligatory denunciations against the evils of capitalism or colonialism. Instead, what was materially beneficial for Shanghai had to be ethically good and historically right.

The "lightness" of the present, meanwhile, opened up in public discourse a space for a multiplicity of lesser accounts. These divergent accounts pertained to remembered pasts authenticated by eyewitness experience. All vied for a place in urban memories. All impinged, ultimately, upon the issue: who owns Shanghai and has a right to speak in its voice?

How do we know, then, that we have come to an epochal moment in Shanghai's—or China's—modern experience, if so much of what we hear, said or unsaid, seems reminiscent, in bits and pieces at least, of century-old descriptions?

Much of Shanghai's century following the Opium War acquired its significance within a certain discursive framework, which the city depended upon for its special place in the construction of China's larger history of nationalism and anti-colonialism. That history was set aside when Shanghai authorities and scholars engineered, in the 1990s, the city's push to become the leading city in East Asia. A parallel shift in urban discursive constructions, from an emphasis on the temporal to the spatial, has opened up space for Shanghainese to confront the significance of their contentious yet shared memories. It is perhaps not without some measure of irony that the remembered pasts of Shanghai urbanites finally earned their due share of expression only when Shanghai was shedding the weight of its history in order to become a destination of global distinction.

Notes

INTRODUCTION

1. Wen-hsin Yeh, "Republican Origins of the *Danwei:* The Case of Shanghai's Bank of China," in *Danwei: The Changing Chinese Workplace in Historical and Comparative Perspective,* ed. Xiaobo Lu & Elizabeth J. Perry, (Armonk, NY: M. E. Sharpe, 1997), 60–88.

2. See chapter 3.

3. Raymond Williams defines these issues in *The Country and the City* (New York: Oxford University Press, 1975).

4. Frederic E. Wakeman, Jr., "China and the Seventeenth Century Crisis," *Late Imperial China* 7, no. 1 (June 1986): 1–23.

5. Frederic E. Wakeman, Jr., "The Canton Trade and the Opium War," in *The Cambridge History of China* vol. 10, pt. 1, *Late Ch'ing, 1800–1911,* ed. Denis Twichett and John K. Fairbank, (New York: Cambridge University Press, 1978), 163–212; Jonathan Spence, "Opium Smoking in Ch'ing China," in *Conflict and Control,* ed. Wakeman and Carolyn Grant, 143–73; Lin Man-houng, *China Upside Down: Currency, Society, and Ideologies, 1808–1856* (Cambridge, MA: Harvard University Press, 2006).

6. James Hevia, *Cherishing Men From Afar: Qing Guest Ritual and the Macartney Embassy of 1793* (Durham: Duke University Press, 1995); Timothy Brook and Robert Tadashi Wakabayashi, eds., *Opium Regimes: China, Britain, and Japan, 1839–1952* (Berkeley: University of California Press, 2000).

7. Marketing strategies, business networks, migration patterns, and the flow of images and information characteristically cut across national borders, political divisions, ideological rivalries, formal regulations legislated by various states, and so forth. See Sherman Cochran, *Big Business in China: Sino-Foreign Rivalry in the Cigarette Industry (*Cambridge, MA: Harvard University Press, 1980), *Encountering Chinese Networks: Western, Japanese, and Chinese Corporations in*

China, 1880–1937 (Berkeley: University of California Press, 2000), and "Marketing Medicine and Advertising Dreams in China, 1900–1950," in *Becoming Chinese: Passages to Modernity and Beyond,* ed. Wen-hsin Yeh (Berkeley: University of California Press, 2000), 62–97; Parks M. Coble, Jr., *Chinese Capitalists in Japan's New Order: The Occupied Lower Yangzi, 1937–1945* (Berkeley: University of California Press, 2003); "Chinese Capitalists and the Japanese: Collaboration and Resistance in the Shanghai Area, 1937–1945," in *Wartime Shanghai,* ed. Wen-hsin Yeh (New York: Routledge, 1998), 62–85; Aihwa Ong, *Flexible Citizenship: The Cultural Logics of Transnationality* (Durham: Duke University Press, 1999); and Rebecca Karl, *Staging the World: Chinese Nationalism at the Turn of the Twentieth Century* (Durham: Duke University Press, 2002), 53–115. For a provocative and eloquent statement about acknowledged strangers—Jews and Chinese included—functioning as professional merchants (with the Chinese doing so in Southeast Asia), see Yuri Slezkine, *The Jewish Century* (Princeton, NJ: Princeton University Press, 2003), 5–39.

8. See chapter 1.

9. On institutional features in the relationships between the Chinese state and its modernizing economy in the Republican era, see William C. Kirby, *Germany and Republican China* (Stanford, CA: Stanford University Press, 1986); Lloyd Eastman, *Seeds of Destruction: Nationalist China in War and Revolution, 1937–1949* (Stanford, CA: Stanford University Press, 1984), 172–202; Brett Sheehan, *Trust in Troubled Times: Money, Banks, and State-Society Relations in Republican Tianjin* (Cambridge, MA: Harvard University Press, 2003); Georgia Mickey, "The Politics of Reform: The Bank of China and Its Shareholders, 1904–1916" (PhD diss., Columbia University, 2004); and Man-bun Kwan, *The Salt Merchants of Tianjin: State-Making and Civil Society in Late Imperial China* (Honolulu: University of Hawaii Press, 2001).

10. Leo Ou-fan Lee, *Shanghai Modern: The Flowering of a New Urban Culture in China, 1930–1945* (Cambridge, MA: Harvard University Press, 1999); David Der-Wei Wang, *Fin-de-Siècle Splendor: Repressed Modernities of Qing Fiction, 1849–1911* (Stanford, CA: Stanford University Press, 1997); Perry Link, *Mandarin Ducks and Butterflies: Popular Fiction in Early Modern Chinese Cities* (Berkeley: University of California Press, 1981); Brian Martin, *The Shanghai Green Gang: Politics and Organized Crime, 1911–1937* (Berkeley: University of California Press, 1996).

11. Bryna Goodman, *Native Place, City, Nation: Regional Networks and Identities in Shanghai, 1853–1937* (Berkeley: University of California Press, 1995); and "Democratic Calisthenics: The Culture of Urban Associations in the New Republic, " in *Changing Meanings of Citizenship in Modern China,* ed. Merle Goldman and Elizabeth J. Perry (Cambridge, MA: Harvard University Asia Center, 2002), 70–109.

1. THE MATERIAL TURN

1. Leah Greenfeld, *The Spirit of Capitalism* (Cambridge, MA: Harvard University Press, 2002).

2. Benjamin Schwartz, *In Search of Wealth and Power: Yen Fu and the West* (Cambridge, MA: Harvard University Press, 1964).

3. On the steady decline of government finance under the Qing from the 1830s to the 1900s amidst warfare, reform measures, indemnity payments and inept fiscal administration see Zhou Yumin, *Wan Qing caizheng yu shehui bianqian* (Shanghai: Renmin chuban she, 2000). See also Madeleine Zelin, *The Magistrate's Tael: Rationalizing Fiscal Reform in Eighteenth-Century China* (Berkeley: University of California Press, 1984).

4. Mary C. Wright, *The Last Stand of Chinese Conservatism: The T'ung-Chih Restoration, 1862–1874* (Stanford, CA: Stanford University Press, 1962).

5. Emma Rothschild, *Economic Sentiments: Adam Smith, Condorcet, and the Enlightenment* (Cambridge, MA: Harvard University Press, 2001).

6. There is a large body of literature on business organizations and long-distance commodity trade in late imperial China. For the purpose of this chapter see Yen-ping Hao, *The Commercial Revolution in Nineteenth-Century China* (Berkeley: University of California Press, 1985); Evelyn Rawski, *Agricultural Change and the Peasant Economy of South China* (Cambridge, MA: Harvard University Press, 1972); Madeleine Zelin, Jonathan A. Ocko, and Robert Gardella, eds., *Contract and Property in Early Modern China* (Stanford, CA: Stanford University Press, 2004); Andrea McElderry, *Shanghai Old-Style Banks (Chien-chuang), 1800–1935: A Traditional Institution in a Changing Society* (Ann Arbor: Center for Chinese Studies, University of Michigan, 1976); Robert Gardella, *Harvesting Mountains: Fujian and the Chinese Tea Trade, 1757–1937* (Berkeley: University of California Press, 1994); Lillian M. Li, *China's Silk Trade: Traditional Industry in the Modern World, 1842–1937* (Cambridge, MA: Council on East Asian Studies, Harvard University, 1981).

7. Yu Ying-shih, *Zhongguo jinshi zongjiao lunli yu shangren jingshen* (Taipei, Lianjing chuban she shiye gongsi, 1987), 97–99.

8. Ibid., 104.

9. Ibid., 108.

10. Ibid., 97.

11. Ye Xian'en, *Ming Qing Huizhou nongcun shehui yu dianpu zhi* (Hefei: Anhui renmin chuban she, 1983); Guo Qitao, *Exorcism and Money: The Symbolic World of the Five-Fury Spirits in Late Imperial China* (Berkeley: Institute of East Asian Studies Publications, University of California, 2003).

12. Yu Ying-shih, *Zhongguo*, 139. Quoted Gu Yanwu.

13. Robert E. Hegel, *The Novel in Seventeenth-Century China* (New York: Columbia University Press, 1981); Wilt Idema and Lloyd Haft, *A Guide to Chinese Literature* (Ann Arbor: University of Michigan, 1997), 205–207.

14. Yu Ying-shih, *Zhongguo*, 143; Idema, *Guide to Chinese Literature;* Po Sung-nien and David Johnson, eds., *Domesticated Deities and Auspicious Emblems: The Iconography of Everyday Life in Village China* (Berkeley: Chinese Popular Culture Project, University of California, 1992).

15. Cynthia J. Brokaw, *The Ledgers of Merit and Demerit: Social Change and Moral Order in Late Imperial China* (Princeton, NJ: Princeton University Press, 1991).

16. Tetsuo Najita, *Visions of Virtue in Tokugawa Japan: The Kaitokudo Merchant Academy of Osaka* (Chicago: University of Chicago Press, 1987).

17. Robert Bellah, *Tokugawa Religion: The Values of Pre-Industrial Japan*

(Glencoe, IL: Free Press, 1957); Peter Berger, *In Search of an East Asian Development Model* (New Brunswick, NJ: Transaction Books, 1988).

18. Hao Yen-ping, *The Comprador in Nineteenth-Century China: Bridge Between East and West* (Cambridge, MA: Council on East Asian Studies, Harvard University, 1970), 44–48, 208.

19. Ibid., 99–101.

20. In 1854 there were 120 foreign merchant houses in Shanghai, each with a resident house comprador. Shanghai had approximately the same number of foreign merchant houses as all other treaty ports combined, thus putting the total number of compradors at about 250 for China. In 1870 there were 550 foreign merchant houses in China, including 203 in Shanghai and 202 in Hong Kong. Among these houses there were about 350 major compradors. The case of Jardine, Matheson & Co. suggests that there were at least an equal number of former compradors who were active in trade. There were thus about seven hundred major comprador merchants operating in China in 1870, each likely to have amassed one hundred thousand taels. Foreign firms in 1899 numbered 933. Most firms had branch offices in treaty ports other than Shanghai, each staffed with a comprador. The estimated total number of compradors by the end of the nineteenth century thus may have exceeded ten thousand, with another ten thousand former compradors remaining active in the field. Hao, *Comprador*, 102.

21. Ibid., 213.

22. Ibid., 180–86.

23. Hao Yen-ping's research unearthed the following exchange between Augustine Heard, Jr., and his comprador on December 10, 1856 (at the time of the second Opium War), when a rumor went around Hong Kong that Chinese authorities in Guangzhou had bribed a bakery to poison the foreigners: "Comprador, what's all this row? . . . Who is the cook?" "He's a good man, a connection of mine." . . . With great emphasis and indignation, "He's an honest man. He could not be bought. I *secure*." "Now, Comprador, you know this is a serious matter. *You* are the responsible man here. You know if anything goes wrong, we shan't look to the cook, but to you. You are the first . . . I give you my word, that on the first symptom of anything of this kind, we'll blow your brains out." "All right," he replied, "I understand," and it was understood. Hao, *Comprador*, 171–72.

24. Ibid., 1–2.

25. Ge Yuanxu, *Hu you zaji* (original preface 1875; repr. Shanghai: Shanghai guji chuban she, 1989), 14.

26. Hao, *Comprador*, 197–8; Wang Tao, *Gezhi shuyuan* (Shanghai: Tao yuan, Guangxu bing shugui si, 1886–1893); Wang Tao, *Yinghuan zazhi* (Shanghai: Shanghai guji chuban she, 1988), 44. How China acquired English is a subject beyond the scope of this chapter. Early Chinese students of English were not just traders and missionary school students but also diplomats. Guo Songtao, China's ambassador to England and France in the 1860s, taught himself English (and French) by memorizing entire dictionaries and grammar books, often while being transported to various places in the sedan chair. It took him nearly two years to master the basics; see Guo's diary, *Guo Songtao riji* (repr. Changsha: Hunan renmin chuban she, 1980–83), 4 vols. English-Chinese wordbooks were

first written in the Fujian (Min) dialect rather than Mandarin. This was because of the intermediate functions assumed by overseas Fujianese in British Malaya and elsewhere in Southeast Asia.

27. Hao, *Comprador,* 196.

28. Liu Kwang-ching, "Tang Tingshu zhi maiban shidai" [Tang Tingshu: Comprador years], in *Jingshi sixiang yu xinxing qiye* [Statecraft thinking and new-style enterprises], ed. by Liu Kwang-ching (Taipei: Lianjing chuban shi ye gongsi, 1990), 391.

29. On the publishing and educational activities of Taishan communities with extensive links to the United States, see Madeline Y. Hsu, "Migration and Native Place: *Qiaokan* and the Imagined Community of Taishan County, Guangdong, 1893–1993," *Journal of Asian Studies* 59, no. 2 (May 2000): 312–17. Other sponsors included coastal trading firms and companies, which traded as far away as Tianjin and Southeast Asia. Other supporters included a restaurant, a salted fish shop, a print shop, an herbal medicine shop, and a dried goods store. A majority of the journal's sponsors were Cantonese merchants based in Hong Kong. Ningbo merchants, through their chamber of commerce, steamship company, and railroad company, also contributed their share. Ningbo participation spoke of the broad appeal of the journal that went beyond a handful of fellow provincials. *Shangwu kaocha bao,* no. 1–3 (October 1907), 34.

30. The friends had planned to write up their interviews and present translated articles on various topics. Publishing, however, turned out to be a more challenging task than the young merchants realized. The first issue, listed as issues one through three, was a thin volume filled mainly by the contributions by Huang Jingqing, the HSBC accountant, and Chen Zhuoting, who had previously worked as a comprador for the branch office of a foreign bank in Canton. These two men offered detailed descriptions of a variety of foreign coins and currencies, especially gold coins and silver coins minted in Western countries. Life-size photos and close-ups showing inscriptions and designs in detail accompanied the descriptions. The writings were meant to be useful, in other words, as illustrated manuals or reference charts when dealing with the use of these coins. *Shangwu kaocha bao,* no. 1–3 (October 1907), 23.

31. Zeng Guofan sent a letter to Hunan Governor Mao Hongbin in 1862, in which he coined the phrase *shangzhan* as a modern-day equivalent to the Warring States' *gengzhan.* See Wang Ermin, "Shangzhan guannian yu zhongshang sixiang," in *Zhongguo jindai sixiang shilun,* ed. Wang Ermin (repr. Taipei: Taiwan shangwu yinshu guan, 1995), 240.

32. The term derives from Shang Yang (Gongsun Yang), in the classic *Shangzi,* a text the completion of which is dated to the third century B.C. In the original it is phrased as *nongzhan* (agricultural warfare). "*Guo zhi suo yi xing zhe, nong zhan ye* (How nations rise: this depends on winning the war in farming)." See volume 1, chapter 3 of *Shangzi.*

33. See, for example, Xue Fucheng's treatises on *shangzheng,* written in 1865. Xue was a member of Zeng Guofan's staff. Wang, "Shangzhan," 240.

34. Wang Ermin, "Shangzhan," 238–40.

35. The term *shang,* generally translated "merchant," was used quite loosely in late Qing documents. The term encompassed persons who engaged in any sort

of commercial, financial, or industrial pursuits. It referred, in other words, to importers and exporters, wholesalers and retailers, bankers, brokers, manufacturers and industrialists, old-style money exchangers and new-style bank executives all at once. Presumably only the "comprador class" or treaty-port merchants who had frequent dealings with foreign traders, financers, and institutions could claim new knowledge and special patriotic contribution. See Albert Feuerwerker, *China's Early Industrialization: Sheng Hsuan-huai (1844–1916) and Mandarin Enterprise* (Cambridge, MA: Harvard University Press, 1958), 17.

36. Wright, *Last Stand*.

37. Grand Secretary Song Jin authored the memorial attacking the Fuzhou Arsenal and Shipyard. Feuerwerker, *China's Early Industrialization*, 97.

38. Feuerwerker, *China's Early Industrialization*, 12, 97–98; Liu Kwang-ching, *Anglo-American Steamship Rivalry in China, 1862–1874* (Cambridge, MA: Harvard University Press, 1962).

39. Du Xuncheng, *Minzu ziben zhuyi yu jiu Zhongguo zhengfu, 1840–1937* [National Capitalism and the Chinese Ancien Régime] (Shanghai: Shanghai shehui kexue yuan chuban she, 1991), 40. The classic study is Liu's *Anglo-American Steamship*. The most recent contribution is by Lai Chi-Kang, based on extensive consultation of Sheng Xuanhuai's private papers held at the Shanghai Municipal Library.

40. Major projects of this period include the Kaiping Coal Mines (1877), the Shanghai Cotton Cloth Mill (later the Huasheng Cotton Mill, 1878), the Imperial Telegraph Administration (1881), the Mohe Gold Mines (1887) in Heilongjiang, the Hanyang Ironworks (1896), the Daye Iron Mines (1898), the Imperial Bank of China (1896), and the Pinxiang Coal Mines (1898). Capital investment for these projects ranged from over 6.9 million silver dollars for the Hanyang Ironworks to eight hundred and forty thousand silver dollars for the Steamship Company, and two hundred and eighty thousand silver dollars for the Gansu Woolen Factory. See Feuerwerker, *China's Early Industrialization*, 9, and Du Xuncheng, *Minzu*. Also Kuo Ting-yee, "Self-Strengthening: The Pursuit of Western Technology," in *The Cambridge History of China* vol. 10, pt. 1, ed. Denis Twichett and John K. Fairbank (New York: Cambridge University Press, 1978), 491–542.

41. Feuerwerker, *China's Early Industrialization*, 12–16.

42. Ibid., 16–21.

43. Liu Kwang-ching, "Tang Tingshu," 327–400; Feuerwerker, *China's Early Industrialization*,110–18.

44. For a succinct biography of Sheng Xuanhuai, see Feuerwerker, *China's Early Industrialization*, 58–95. Feuerwerker subscribes to the notion of "regionalism" and has placed much emphasis on the regional character of Li Hongzhang's power base and its potential capacity to challenge the will of the imperial court. Liu Kwang-ching disagrees with this reading of late Qing politics and draws attention to the fact that the Qing court continued to have full control over personnel appointments in the Qing bureaucracy. Individuals such as Zeng Guofan, Zuo Zongtang, and Li Hongzhang, powerful as they might be, continued to adhere to a Confucian ideology of loyalty to the imperial ruler. See Liu Kwang-ching, "Wan Qing dufu quanli wenti shangque" [The power of the

governors-general in late Qing], in *Jingshi sixiang yu xinxing qiye* [Statecraft thinking and new-style enterprises], ed. Liu Kwang-ching (Taipei: Lianjing chuban she, 1990), 247–293. On regionalism see also Stanley Spector, *Li Hung-chang and the Huai Army: A Study in Nineteenth-Century Chinese Regionalism* (Seattle: University of Washington Press, 1964), and Philip A. Kuhn, *Rebellion and Its Enemies in Late Imperial China: Militarization and Social Structure, 1796–1864* (Cambridge, MA: Harvard University Press, 1970).

45. Feuerwerker, *China's Early Industrialization*, 112, 161–62.

46. Ibid., 123.

47. Du Xuncheng, *Minzu*, passim.

48. On Zhang Jian, see Elizabeth Koll, *From Cotton Mill to Business Empire: The Emergence of Regional Enterprises in Modern China* (Cambridge, MA: Harvard University, Asia Center, 2003).

49. See Feuerwerker, *China's Early Industrialization*, 8–12. He claims over two hundred enterprises were incorporated by 1905 under the new Company Law.

50. Liu Kwang-ching, "Tang Tingshu," 420; Hao, *Comprador*, 205. After the Boxers fiasco and with the launching of the New Policies, political dynamics changed dramatically at the center. Negotiations over the Boxers indemnities clause, which led to a scrutiny of state finance, coincided with the application of the American Chinese Exclusion Act to the Philippines, which severely curtailed Chinese rights and activities there. Merchant groups in coastal Chinese cities rallied to launch anti-American protests and boycotts. These developments powerfully shaped Chinese views of the role of the state in commerce.

51. Shan Huafeng, *Shangwu kaocha bao*, no. 1–3, 18; Huang Qishi, "Preface," ibid., 10.

52. Wang Ermin, "Shangzhan," 240–61.

53. Ibid., 326–31.

54. Wang Ermin, "Shangzhan," 331; Sheng Xuanhuai, *Yu zhai cun gao* 3, no. 61.

55. Wang Ermin, "Shangzhan," 331; Sheng Xuanhuai, *Yu zhai cun gao* 3, no. 61.

56. On the application of the company law see William C. Kirby, "China Unincorporated: Company Law and Business Enterprise in Twentieth-Century China," *Journal of Asian Studies* 54, no. 1 (February 1995): 43–63.

57. *Shangren tongli* (1903; repr. Ministry of Agriculture and Commerce, 1914).

58. The author, Yang Yinhang, vigorously argued that commerce had become a "specialized discipline" and a "sophisticated branch of special knowledge and learning." In the old days, Yang wrote, "commerce was backward; people valued agriculture and circumstances. But in the modern West people learned business in schools." He cited Germany and America as the most advanced countries in the development of such education. Yang's roster of distinguished business schools included those at the universities of Berlin, Leipzig, and Frankfurt in Germany, and at the universities of Pennsylvania, Chicago, Illinois, California, Wisconsin, Michigan, Vermont, and New York. Yang Yinhang, "Geguo shangye daxue zhi zhuangkuang," *Shangwu guanbao*, no. 7 (1907): 1–4.

59. Karl Gerth, *China Made: Consumer Culture and the Creation of the Nation* (Cambridge, MA: Harvard University Asia Center, 2003), 125–33.

60. Quoted from David Der-Wei Wang, *Fin-de-Siècle Splendor: Repressed Modernities of Qing Fiction, 1849–1911* (Stanford, CA: Stanford University Press, 1997), 235.

61. Ibid., 236.

62. Ibid.

63. Ji Wen, *Shisheng* (Shanghai: Shanghai wenhua chuban she, 1957), 34.

64. Ibid., 191–218.

65. Yu Ying-shih, *Zhongguo,* 142.

66. David Wang, *Fin-de-Siècle Splendor,* 235.

67. Ji Wen, *Shisheng,* 80.

68. Ibid., 38.

2. THE STATE IN COMMERCE

1. Li Yunliang, "Gongsi zhidu yu xinshi kuaiji zhi guanxi," *Shanghai zong shanghui yuebao* 5, no. 4 (April 1925): 4–6.

2. Ibid.

3. Min Zhishi, "Kexue de guanli," *Shanghai zong shanghui yuebao* 5, no. 3 (March 1925): 1–3.

4. Jiang Mingqi, "Jingshang shibai de yuanyin," *Shanghai zong shanghui yuebao* 6, no. 1 (January 1926): 1–2.

5. "Duzhe luntan," *Shanghai zong shanghui yuebao* 5, no. 5 (May 1925): 3. The journals include the monthly journal of the Shanghai General Chamber of Commerce, *Textile Quarterly* of the Federation of Textile Mills, *Economic Weekly* of the Association for Economic Research, *Journal of Industry and Commerce (Gongshang xuebao)* of the Chinese Association of Industry and Commerce, the Hankou, Shanghai, and Beijing banking association weeklies, the journal of the Money Guild Association, the *Shangxue Quarterly* of Chinese University, and the *Shangda Weekly* of Wuchang University. Other periodicals were published either by provincial authorities or by newspapers.

6. Gu Zhun, who worked in the Lixin Accounting School, later revealed that he had authored a large number of the textbooks issued in Pan Xulun's name in the 1930s. See Gu Zhun, *Gu Zhun zishu* (Beijing: Zhongguo qingnian chuban she, 2002), 56–64.

7. To name but a few: Kong Di'an, born in 1900, attended Keio University and taught at several Shanghai colleges. He also held various positions as secretary of a trust company, editor with the Commercial Press, and secretary in the Ministry of Finance on the commission on tax rules. Kong compiled several textbooks on insurance, commercial law, commodity exchange, and corporate finance.

Li Quanshi, born in 1895, graduated from Qinghua University in Beijing, studied in the United States, received his MA from the University of Chicago, and his PhD from Columbia University. Li was a member of the Chinese Economics Study Society. He chaired the department of commerce at Fudan University and later became dean of Fudan's college of commerce. He was also the chief editor of the highly influential *Shanghai Bankers' Weekly.* Li's publications include books on finance, economics, business cycles, commercial education, commercial tax codes, economic principles of commerce (written in English and based on lectures delivered at Fudan University), commercial statistics (also in English and from lectures at Fudan), and a translation into Chinese of Ricardo's *Economics and Rent*.

Jin Guobao, a native of Jiangsu (b. 1892), received his MA in statistics from Columbia University. Jin was a member of the Chinese Statistics Study Association and also of the Banking Study Association. He taught classes at China College, Fudan University, Ji'nan University, and was an acting dean of Shanghai College of Commerce. He was the director of statistics, Ministry of Finance; deputy director, Bank of Communications; and professor of statistics at Shanghai College of Commerce. He authored textbooks on statistics, currency, pricing, and income tax.

Tang Qingzeng received his MA from Harvard and chaired the economics department of Daxia University. His book was titled *History of International Trade Policy.* He was the Chinese translator of John Stuart Mill's *Principles of Economics.*

Wang Xiaotong, a specialist in commercial law and commercial history, was born in Anqing in 1894. He graduated from St. John's University in Shanghai and received a master's degree in commerce from Beijing University. He taught commercial law at China College, Guanghua University; Shanghai Institute of Law and Politics, Shanghai College of Law, Daxia University, Fudan University, and worked as an attorney as well as account. He authored books on history of Chinese commerce and commercial law.

8. Pan Xulun and Gu Zhun, *Zhongguo zhengfu kuaiji zhidu* (Shanghai: Lixin kuaiji tushu yongpin she, 1941), 185–95.

9. Lixin Accounting School is alive and well in China today, one of the first institutions revived in the 1980s under the Modernizations policies of Deng Xiaoping.

10. These included Sanyu, "Women's Commerce College," Yuandong University; Dalu commercial training institute; Donghua University; Shanghai Accounting school; Nanyang Business College; Shanghai Commerce School; Guangming University; Xinmin University (also known as Jiangnan College), Hongcai University; Shanghai English College; Guomin University, east of Jing'an Temple; and Chunshen University, on Qingyun Road, Zhabei. Most of these were no more than a name and an address. The locals referred to them as "back alley" college and fly-by-night events. These operations were the targets of Ministry of Education regulators.

11. Li Chunkang, "Shanghai de gaodeng jiaoyu," in *Shanghai tongzhi guan qikan* (Shanghai: Shanghai tongzhi guan, 1934), 618.

12. For an in-depth discussion of the National Products Promotion Association and its campaigns, see Karl Gerth, *China Made: Consumer Culture and the Creation of the Nation* (Cambridge, MA: Harvard University Asia Center, 2003).

13. Sheng Langxi, "Shinian lai Jiangsu Zhongdeng xuexiao biyesheng chulu tongji," parts 1–2. *Jiaoyu zazhi* (reprinted 1975) 17.4 (April 1925) & 17.5 (May 1925), 25695–25730, 25875–25904.

14. Ernest P. Schwintzer, "Education to Save the Nation: Huang Yanpei and the Educational Reform Movement in Early Twentieth Century China" (PhD

diss., University of Washington, 1992); Zhu Zongzhen, "Huang Yanpei he rushang lunli," *Tansuo yu zhengming,* no. 8 (August 2003); and also Roxanne Prazniak, "Weavers and Sorceresses of Chuansha: The Social Origins of Political Activism among Rural Chinese Women," *Modern China* 12, no. 2 (April 1986): 202–229.

15. Cai Xingtao, *Kangzhan qian de Zhonghua zhiye jiaoyu she, 1917–1937* (Taipei: Dongda tushu gongsi, 1988).

16. Xu Hansan, ed., *Huang Yanpei nianpu* (Beijing: Beijing wenshi ziliao chuban she, 1985), 10.

17. Ibid., 10–17.

18. Ibid., 31–32.

19. Cai Xingtao, *Kangzhan,* 105–13.

20. Zou Weixin, "Zhonghua zhiye xuexiao chuzhong bu xuesheng shanshi xiankuang," *Zhiye shi shikan,* no. 1 (June 1934), 1–4.

21. Cai Xingtao, *Kangzhan,* 105–13.

22. The figure, coming in the depth of a recession, compared favorably with the employment rate of many colleges and universities. Some of the association's graduates worked in teaching positions in county schools. Others (about 56 percent) became administrators in the agricultural bureaus of county governments. The best jobs went to those who had knowledge in fields such as civil engineering, road construction, electrical engineering, and mechanical engineering. The graduates of Vocational Education took in salaries that surpassed those with degrees in general education. See He Qingru, "Zhiye xuexiao xuesheng chulu diaocha," *Jiaoyu yu zhiye,* no. 168 (October 1935): 535–54.

23. Xu Hansan, *Huang Yanpei,* 50.

24. Sun Jianqiu, "Tongchang chehang shixi baogao," *Zhiye shi shikan,* no.1 (November 1934), 54–61.

25. In Mao's China, students were sent down to the countryside to learn from the peasants; such experience was deemed an indispensable part of their learning.

26. Zhonghua zhiye jiaoyu she, ed., *Quanguo zhiye xuexiao gaikuang* (Shanghai: Commercial Press, 1934), 4, 260.

27. Ibid., 68.

28. Xu Hansan, *Huang Yanpei,* 40–48. In 1929 the CSVE paid for Liu Zhan'en's trip to Japan and the United States. Liu was the president of the Shanghai Baptist College.

29. A Ministry of Education report, produced in 1934, showed that there were a total of 330 vocational schools in twenty-four provinces outside Jiangsu, Sichuan, Guangxi and Xinjiang. Another report showed about 710 vocational schools throughout the country. See Zhong Daozan, "Zhiye xuexiao xiaozhang zhi xueli yu jingyan," *Jiaoyu yu zhiye,* no. 169 (November 1, 1935), 639–43. A majority of the principals of vocational schools had started their career as high school teachers or college lecturers. A large number of Jiangsu vocational school principals had been trained in industry or agricultural economy in Japan. A majority of commerce department heads in Shanghai, by contrast, had been trained in the United States. Ibid., 68.

30. Chen Jiaxuan, "Zixu," in *Shiyong shangye cidian* (Shanghai: Commercial Press, 1935).

31. The categories include the following: commercial activities, merchants, commercial organizations, business management, money, merchandise, notes, measurements, bookkeeping, accounting, banking, finance, commercial mathematics, the railroad, business documents, shipping, insurance, warehouse, exchanges, industry, advertisement, international law, civil law, commercial codes, history of commerce, geography of commerce, economics, finance, statistics, customs, municipal government, international trade, agriculture, fishing, mining, forestry, transportation, office equipment, government offices, and successful businessmen.

32. These terms include the following: *shangye shiyong ren* (trade assistants); *shangren tongli* (the code promulgated in 1914); *shangren tongli shixing xize* (the statute announced in 1914); *shangren nengli* (legal capacity to act as a merchant); *shang xingwei* (commercial transactions as legislated by the Beijing government in 1914); *shang xingwei fa* (legislation governing commercial transaction); *shangpin* (merchandise); *shangye* (commerce as defined in commercial laws); *shangban zaochuan chang zhuce guize* (registration rules governing merchant ship-building enterprises, as announced by the Nationalist government in 1932); *shangbiao* (trademark as defined by law); *shangbiao fa* (trademark law); *shangbiao fa shixing xize* (trademark law implementation guidelines); *shangbiao zhuce* (trademark registration); *shangbiao zhuce fei* (trademark registration fee); *shangshi* (commercial matter); *shangfa* (commercial law); *shangpin jianyan fa* (the 1932 merchandize inspection law of the Nationalist government); *shangpin jianding fa* (quality test); *shanglü* (commercial code); *shangyue* (commercial treaty); *shanggang* (trading port); *shanggang tiaoli* (trading port statutory regulations governing foreign ships; announced by the Nationalist government in 1933); *shanghao* (trade or firm name); *shanghao zhuanyong quan* (proprietary right); *shanghao zhuce* (trademark registration); *shanghao zhuce fei* (fee for trademark registration); *shang xiguan* (commercial usage or custom); *shang xiguan fa* (customary commercial law).

33. Such as *shangmin xiehui* (merchant civilian association as legislated by the Nationalist government); *shanghui* (chamber of commerce); *shanghui fa* (law governing merchant associations; promulgated in 1915); *shanghui lianhe hui* (federation of merchant associations); *shangye baohu zuhe* (trade protection); *shangtuan* (merchant corps).

34. The terms include *shangye si* (commercial section under the Ministry of Economics); *shangbiao ju* (trademark bureau); *shangshi gongduan chu* (the mediation office under the chamber of commerce); *shangshi caipan chu* (commercial adjudication office); *shangye diaocha chu* (bank office for the investigation of market conditions); *shangpin jiaoyi suo* (merchandise exchange); *shangpin chenlie suo* (merchandise exhibition); *shangpin chenlie shi* (merchandise display room); *shangpin jianyan ju* (merchandise inspection office); *shangye buzhu jiguan* (organizations that aid the development of commerce).

35. New terms in this connection include *shangye chenzhi* (commercial depression), *shangye xunhuan* (business cycle), *shangye zhengce* (commercial policy), *shangye jinrong* (commercial financing), *shangye ziben* (commercial capital), and *shangzhan* (trade war).

36. Such as *shangye buxi xuexiao* (schools that offer after-work training in

commerce); *shangye zhiye xuexiao* (commercial vocational school); *shangchuan xuexiao* (advanced level navigation school for the training of officers); *shangke daxue* (college of commerce); *shangye zhuanmen xuexiao* (commercial school), and *shangye jiaoyu* (commercial education). Chen Jiaxuan, *Shiyong shangye cidian*, 605–624. Other long entries in the dictionary, in descending order of overall volume, include terms that begin with the following characters: "gong" (public) (pp. 103–123); "gong" (work) (pp. 58–76); "hui" (remit) (pp. 840–858); "yin" (silver) (pp. 979–995); "hai" (maritime) (pp. 530–546); "bao" (protect or guarantee) (pp. 434–448); "guo" (nation) (pp: 624–639); "chuan" (ship or shipping) (pp. 687–699); "huo" (merchandise) (pp. 704–713); "nong" (agriculture) (pp. 909–917); "ying" (manage) (pp. 1092–1100); "tie" (iron) (pp. 1161–1169); "jiao" (transact) (pp. 230–237); "xin" (credit or integrity) (pp. 448–455); "mai" (pp. 805–812). In light of scholarly debates in the 1990s about the nature of modern Chinese "public sphere" and "civil society," it is interesting to note that while *gong* (public) tops the list along with *shang* (commerce), neither *guan* (official) nor *si* (private) leads to significant number of entries in Republican Chinese business usage.

37. The description of shop floor arrangement is based upon Zhang Shijie, ed., *Zengding shangren baojian* (Shanghai: Commercial Press, 1938), chap. 1, secs. 1–28.

38. Ibid., 1–28, 81–107.

39. Cai Xingtao, *Kangzhan*, 15–16, 32–33.

40. Ibid., 40–44.

41. "Zhonhua zhiye jiaoyu she zhangcheng cao'an," sec. 3, article 10; Guoshiguan Jiaoyubu dang, 196/188-1, 196/188-2.

42. Wen-hsin Yeh, "Progressive Journalism and Shanghai's Petty Urbanites: Zou Taofen and the Shenghuo Enterprise, 1926–1945," in *Shanghai Sojourners*, ed. Frederic Wakeman, Jr. and Wen-hsin Yeh (Berkeley: Institute of East Asian Studies, University of California, 1992), 205–214.

3. VISUAL POLITICS AND SHANGHAI GLAMOUR

1. Ge Yuanxu, *Hu you zaji* (1876; repr. Shanghai: Shanghai guji chuban she, 1998), 22.

2. Ibid.

3. James Soong, "A Visual Experience in Nineteenth-Century China: Jen Po-nien (1840–1895) and the Shanghai School of Painting," PhD diss., University of California, Berkeley, 1977; Britta L. Erickson, "Uncommon Themes and Uncommon Subject Matters in Ren Xiong's *Album after Poems by Yao Xie*," in *Visual Culture in Shanghai, 1850s–1930s*, ed. Jason Kuo (Washington, D.C.: New Academia Publishing, 2007); also Li Tang, "Art for the Market. Commercialism in Ren Yi's (1840–1895) Figure Painting," (MA thesis, University of Maryland, 2003); Britta L. Erickson, "Patronage and Production in the Nineteenth-Century Shanghai Region: Ren Xiong (1823–1857) and His Sponsors," (PhD diss., Stanford University, 1977).

4. Wu Youru, *Wu Youru huabao,* 3 vols. rev. ed. (1908; repr., Shanghai: Shanghai shudian, 1983).

5. Ge Yuanxu, *Hu you zaji,* 23.

6. On the images of late Qing Shanghai courtesans see Catherine Vance Yeh, "Creating the Urban Beauty: The Shanghai Courtesan in Late Qing Illustrations," in *Writing and Materiality in China: Essays in Honor of Patrick Hanan*, ed. Judit T. Zeitlin and Lydia H. Liu with Ellen Widmer (Cambridge, MA.: Harvard University Asia Center, 2003), 397–447.

7. An often featured example was Qiu Jin, beheaded by the state in 1907 for conspiring to assassinate the Anhui governor. Mary Rankin, *Early Chinese Revolutionaries: Radical Intellectuals in Shanghai and Chekiang, 1902–1911* (Cambridge, MA: Council on East Asian Studies, Harvard University, 1971).

8. The first women's school organized by the Chinese was Aiguo nüxue, in 1892, with funding by Jing Ziyuan.

9. These writers allegedly came from Jiangnan townships. In the aftermath of the Taiping uprising they arrived in large numbers and were eager for gainful employment. They were instrumental in bringing the Jiangnan courtesan culture to the foreign concessions. Xu Min, "Shi, chang, you: Wan Qing Shanghai shehui shenghuo yi pie," in *Shanghai: Chengshi, shehui yu wenhua*, ed. Wang Hui and Yu Guoliang (Hong Kong: The Chinese University Press, 1998), 113–126; Zhou Wu and Wu Guilong, *Shanghai tongshi*, vol. 5, *Wan Qing Shehui* (Shanghai: Shanghai renmin chuban she, 1999), 367–372.

10. Gail Hershatter, *Dangerous Pleasures: Prostitution and Modernity in Twentieth-Century Shanghai* (Berkeley: University of California Press, 1997).

11. Ge Yuanxu, *Hu you zaji*, 3.

12. Li Boyuan, *Wenming xiaoshi* [A Short History of Civilization] (Beijing: Tongsu wenyi chuban she, 1955), 99–105.

13. Ibid., 100.

14. Ibid., 101.

15. Ibid., 102.

16. Ibid., 103.

17. Ibid.

18. Sherman Cochran, ed., *Inventing Nanjing Road: Commercial Culture in Shanghai, 1900–1945* (Ithaca, NY: East Asian Center, Cornell University, 1999).

19. Shanghai baihuo gongsi, Shanghai shehui kexueyuan jingji yanjiu suo, Shanghai shi gongshang xingzheng guanli ju, eds., *Shanghai jindai baihuo shangye shi* (Shanghai: Shanghai shehui kexue yuan chuban she, 1988), 26–32, 51–114; Zhu Guodong and Wang Guozhang, eds., *Shanghai shangye shi* (Shanghai: Caijing daxue chuban she, 1999), 131–140, 395–430; Shangye bu baihuo ju, ed., *Zhongguo baihuo shangye* (Beijing: Beijing daxue chuban she, 1989), 4–15; Cao Juren, *Bei xing xiao yu* (Beijing: Sanlian shudian, 2002), 332–346.

20. Xu Dingxin, "Ershi sanshi niandai Shanghai guohuo guanggao cuxiao ji qi wenhua tece" [National goods advertising in Shanghai and its distinguishing features, 1920s and 1930s], paper presented at the seminar on Consumer Culture in Shanghai, Cornell University Press, July 1995; also Cochran, *Inventing Nanjing Road*.

21. Wen-hsin Yeh, "Shanghai Modernity: Commerce and Culture in a Chinese City," *The China Quarterly*, no. 150 (June 1997): 375–394.

22. On Huang Huan'nan, the cofounder and general manager of the Shanghai Sincere Company, see Deng Yikang, "Shanghai Xianshi gongsi chuangjian

ren Huang Huan'nan," *Shanghai wenshi ziliao xuanji,* no. 48 (November 1984): 46–51.

23. Shanghai shehui kexue yuan jingji yanjiu suo, ed., *Shanghai Yong'an gongsi de chansheng, fazhan he gaizao* (Shanghai: Renmin chuban she, 1981).

24. Ibid., 34.

25. Ibid., 17.

26. This requirement was dropped when young employees, encouraged by the rising tide of Chinese nationalism that swept across Chinese cities in the late 1920s, protested against the practice. Wing On management nonetheless strongly discouraged its employees to spend their Sundays partaking in frivolous activities or sheer idleness.

27. Shanghai shehui, *Shanghai Yong'an gongsi,* 18; Émile Zola, *The Ladies' Paradise* (Berkeley: University of California Press, 1992), 37.

28. Michael B. Miller, *The Bon Marché: Bourgeois Culture and the Department Store, 1869–1920* (Princeton: Princeton University Press, 1994), 19–72.

29. The medium ones, on other roads and in Nanshi, hired about thirty to forty people. The remaining, which constituted a majority, kept but two to three apprentices to work with the owner-masters and were located far away from Nanjing Road. The "clothing business" *(yizhuo ye)* of Republican Shanghai consisted of single-product retailers of fabrics in satin, cotton, and wool, the makers of dresses and of suits, and the dealers in second-hand clothing. They addressed the pragmatic needs of local consumers while selectively adopting the practices of the department stores. Vulnerable to the forces of the market, a multitude of these shops came and went in the 1930s and '40s. In 1949, the new Communist authorities counted over thirty-three hundred enterprises of this sort all over the city, with a work force of over nineteen thousand clerks and apprentices—a figure that broke down to one "clothing shop" for every one thousand persons in Shanghai. See Yu Kun, "Shanghai yizhuo hangye gaikuang," in *Shanghai yizhuo ye zhigong yundong shiliao,* ed. Zhonggong Shanghai shiwei dangshi ziliao zhengji weiyuan hui (unpublished manuscript, Shanghai, 1984), 5–6.

30. See Gloria Tseng, "Chinese Pieces of the French Mosaic: The Chinese Experience in France and the Making of a Revolutionary Tradition" (PhD diss., University of California at Berkeley, 2002), for treatment of Chinese sojourning in Paris in the inter-war years.

31. Vimalin Rujivacharakul, "Architects as Cultural Heroes," in *Cities in Motion,* ed. Sherman Cochran, David Strand, and Wen-hsin Yeh (Berkeley: Institute of East Asian Studies Publications, University of California, 2007).

32. Its opening was noted as an event in the pages of the *North China Herald.* Lenore Hietkamp, "The Park Hotel, Shanghai, and its Architect Laszlo Hudec (1893–1958)" (MA thesis, University of Victoria, 1989).

33. On the use of posters and calendars for advertising see Sherman Cochran, "Marketing Medicine and Advertising Dreams in China, 1900–1950," in *Becoming Chinese: Passages to Modernity and Beyond, 1900–1950,* ed. Wen-hsin Yeh (Berkeley: University of California Press, 2000), 62–97.

34. On "disembedding," see Anthony Giddens, *A Contemporary Critique of Historical Materialism,* vol. 1, *Power, Property, and the State* (Berkeley: Univer-

sity of California Press, 1981), 129–156; Stjepan G. Meštrović, *Anthony Giddens: The Last Modernist* (New York: Routledge, 1998), 15, 155, 173.

35. Christopher Reed, *Gutenberg in Shanghai: Chinese Print Capitalism, 1876–1937* (Honolulu: University of Hawaii Press, 2004).

36. Yan Juanying, "Buxi de biandong: Yi Shanghai meishu xuexiao wei zhongxin de meishu jiaoyu yundong," in *Shanghai meishu fengyun: 1872–1949 shenbao yishu ziliao tiaomu suoyin,* ed. Yan Juanying (Taipei: Zhongyang yanjiuyuan lishi yuyuan yanjiu suo, 2006), 48–56.

37. On poster paintings for commercial advertisements, see Cochran, "Marketing Medicine," 62–97. Also see Cochran, *Big Business in China: Sino-Foreign Rivalry in the Cigarette Industry, 1890–1930* (Cambridge, MA: Harvard University Press, 1980), on the operation of the advertising department of the British American Tobacco Company.

38. In the last decades of the Qing, in response to a sense of crisis about the loss of competitiveness of Chinese silk fabric in world market, Jiangsu gentry reformers sponsored study trips and sent Chinese artisans to Japan to study patterns and designs. Back home in Jiangnan, these reformers funded institutes of sericulture as well as vocational training schools, and supplied graduates to an emerging Chinese-owned textile industry. Textile designs were no longer home-based, but became instead part of an industrial process. See Bai Wei, "Wo toudao wenxue quan de chuzhong," in *Minguo cainu meiwen ji,* vol. 1, ed. Lan Yunyue (Beijing: Yanshan chuban she, 1995), 146–56. Also Dorothy Ko, "Between the Boudoir and the Global Marketplace: Shen Shou, Embroidery and Modernity at the Turn of the Twentieth Century," (paper presented at the Center for Chinese Studies, University of California at Berkeley, September 30, 2005).

39. Julia Andrews, "Judging a Book by Its Cover: Book Cover Design in Shanghai," (paper presented at the annual meeting of the Association for Asian Studies, Chicago, March 14, 1997).

40. Chen Ruilin, "'Yuefenpai' hua yu Haipai meishu," in *Haipai huihua yanjiu wenji,* Shanghai shuhua chuban she, ed. (Shanghai: Shanghai shuhua chuban she, 2001), 472.

41. Sakamoto Hiroko, "Shiseido," (paper presented at international conference on Urban Popular Culture and Social Changes in Modern History, East China Normal University, Shanghai, December 2005).

42. Ding Hao. "Jiang yishu caihua fengxian ge shangye meishu," in *Lao Shanghai guanggao,* ed. Yi Bin, Liu Youming, and Gan Zhenhu (Shanghai: Shanghai huabao chuban she, 1995), 15.

43. Chen Rulin, "'Yuefenpai'", 477.

44. Ding Hao, "Jiang yishu caihua," 15–17.

45. Ellen Johnston Laing, *Selling Happiness: Calendar Posters and Visual Culture in Early Twentieth-Century Shanghai* (Honolulu: University of Hawaii Press, 2004).

46. Chen Ruilin, "'Yuefenpai'", 477.

47. On traditional woodblock prints in book printing see Julia K. Murray, "Didactic Illustrations in Printed Books," in *Printing and Book Culture in Late Imperial China,* ed. Cynthia J. Brokaw and Kai-wing Chow (Berkeley: Univer-

sity of California Press, 2005), 417–450; also Cynthia J. Brokaw, "Reading the Best-Sellers of the Nineteenth Century: Commercial Publishing in Sibao" in *Printing and Book Culture*, 184–231; Craig Clunas, *Pictures and Visuality in Early Modern China* (Princeton: Princeton University Press, 1997).

48. Chen Ruilin, "'Yuefenpai'", 472–73.

49. Ibid., 473–75.

50. On the teaching of craftsmanship and techniques in religious art at the Jesuit-run orphanage at Tushanwan, see Shen Yuyuan, "Tushanwan yu guer yuan," in *Shanghai yishi*, ed., Tang Weikang, Zhu Dalu, and Du Li (Shanghai: Shanghai wenhua chuban she, 1987), 196–204.

51. Shanghai huabao chuban she, ed., *Lao yuefenpai* (Shanghai: Shanghai huabao chuban she, 1997), 27.

52. Chen Ruilin, "'Yuefenpai'", 475.

53. Shanghai huabao, *Lao yuefenpai,* 143.

54. His brothers, Liang Youming and Liang Zhongming, were also famous painters.

55. Chen Ruilin, ibid., pp.475–77. On Hang Zhiying see Ellen Johnston Laing, *Selling Happiness.*

56. Chen Ruilin, "'Yuefenpai'", 477.

57. Jin Xuechen, preface to *Lao Shanghai guanggao* by Yi Bin, Liu Youming, and Gan Zhenhu (Shanghai: Shanghai huabao chuban she, 1995), 1.

58. Laing, *Selling Happiness,* 61–77.

59. Wu Youru, *Wu Youru huabao*, vol. 13, *Huabao buyi,* 5 (bottom). Daiyu is the heroine in the Qing novel *Dream of the Red Chamber,* attributed to Cao Xueqin. In Wu's pictorial depiction of Daiyu, the woman directs her gaze towards mid-space in defiance of domination.

60. Yi Bin, *Lao Shanghai guanggao,* 15. See also Francesca Del Lago, "How 'Modern' is the Modern Woman? Crossed Legs and Modernity in 1930s Shanghai Calendar Posters, Pictorial Magazines and Cartoons," *East Asian History* 19 (2000): 103–44.

61. Carlton Benson, "Story-Telling and Radio Shanghai," *Republican China* 20, no. 2 (April 1995): 117–46; also Xu Dingxin, "Guohuo guanggao yu xiaofei wenhua," in *Shanghai bainian fenghua,* ed. Ye Wenxin (Taipei: Yaosheng wenhua chuban she, 2001), 137–38. For an original and full treatment of the subject, see Benson, "From Teahouse to Radio: Storytelling and the Commercialization of Culture in 1930s Shanghai," (PhD diss., University of California at Berkeley, 1996).

62. Susan Glosser, "The Business of Family: You Huaigao and the Commercialization of a May Fourth Ideal," *Republican China* (April 1995).

63. Helen Schneider, "Home Economics and its American Connections: The Case of Yenching University in the 1920s" (paper presented at the conference on the American Context of China's Christian Colleges, Wesleyan University, September 5–7, 2003).

64. Karl Gerth, *China Made: Consumer Culture and the Creation of the Nation* (Cambridge, MA: Harvard University Asia Center, 2003).

65. A Society for the Use of National Goods (Quanyong guohuo hui) was formed by the leaders of Shanghai's twenty major guilds on March 23, 1915, less than two months after it became public knowledge that Japan had presented

its Twenty-One Demands to China. See Cochran, "Marketing Medicine," 70–73; also Wen-hsin Yeh, "Shanghai Modernity: Commerce and Culture in a Chinese City," *The China Quarterly,* no. 150 (June 1997): 390–91.

66. On the boycotts see Cochran, *Sino-Foreign Rivalry,* and Parks M. Coble, *Facing Japan: Chinese Politics and Japanese Imperialism, 1931–1937* (Cambridge, MA: Council on East Asian Studies, Harvard University, 1991).

67. Cochran, *Marketing Medicine.*

68. Xu Dingxin, *Guohuo guanggao,* 138.

69. Ibid., 138–39.

70. Luo Suwen, *Shikumen: Xun chang renjia* (Shanghai: Shanghai renmin chuban she, 1991); Lou Chenghao, *Lao Shanghai shikumen* (Shanghai: Tongji daxue, 2004); Lu Hanchao, *Beyond the Neon Lights: Everyday Shanghai in the Early Twentieth Century* (Berkeley: University of California Press, 1999), 167–85.

71. On the discursive, legal, economic, and social constructions of the *xiao jiating* in China's twentieth century see Susan Glosser, *Chinese Visions of Family and State, 1915–1953* (Berkeley: University of California Press, 2003).

72. Yi Bin, *Lao Shanghai guanggao,* 65.

73. Ibid., 66.

74. Ibid., 104.

75. Ibid., 72.

76. Shanghai baihuo gongsi, *Shanghai jindai,* 72–98, 145–46, 178.

77. Shanghai shehui, *Shanghai Yong'an gongsi,* 128–35.

78. Between 1927 and 1937, machine-manufactured products made in China increased their market share by about thirty times on the floors of Wing On. In the context of the global recession of the 1930s and the imminent outbreak of war between China and Japan, Wing On reversed the distribution in value between domestic and imported goods to an unprecedented 65:35, remaking its image to become a provider of top-quality national goods made in China. Shanghai shehui, *Shanghai Yong'an gongsi,* 136–41.

79. Shanghai huabao, *Lao yuefenpai,* 28–29.

80. Wu Youru, *Wu Youru huabao,* vol. 3, *Haishang baiyan tu:* 12 (bottom).

81. Ibid., 5 (top).

82. Ibid., 9 (top). See also Don J. Cohn, *Vignettes from the Chinese: Lithographs from Shanghai in the Late Nineteenth Century* (Hong Kong: Research Center for Translation, the Chinese University of Hong Kong, 1987).

4. THE CLOCK AND THE COMPOUND

1. The Shanghai Maritime Customs was opened in 1846. The first building was burned down in the Small Swords Rebellion in 1853. In 1857 the Customs Service, under Inspector General Horatio Nelson Lay, relocated to the Bund. In 1893, during the service of Robert Hart (1835–1911) as inspector general, the service constructed a three-story building in Western style, with a clock tower in the middle section that raised it to five stories. In 1925 the old building was torn down and a new one put up in its place. The new building, built in the Neoclassical style, was inaugurated in December 1927. See Shanghai Library, ed., *Lao Shanghai: Jianzhu xunmeng juan* (Shanghai: Shanghai wenhua chuban she, 1998), 42. The clock was made in Great Britain and was the largest in Asia in

its time. In August 1966 the chime was altered to play the tune of "The East is Red." *Shanghai Star,* March 22, 2001.

2. On the collectivizing force of "public" time versus the heterogeneity, fluidity, and reversibility of a modern sense of "private" time, see Stephen Kern, *The Culture of Time and Space, 1880–1918* (Cambridge: Harvard University Press, 1983), 33–35.

3. David S. Landes, *Revolution in Time: Clocks and the Making of the Modern World* (Cambridge, MA: Harvard University Press, 1983), 42.

4. Carlo M. Cipolla, *Clocks and Culture, 1300–1700* (New York, London: W. W. Norton, 1977), 87.

5. This trade, however, was restricted largely to the Guangzhou area, and attracted customers who saw the timepieces more as status symbols and decorative items than anything else. Ibid., 92.

6. Chiang Monlin, *Tides from the West: A Chinese Autobiography* (New Haven, CN: Yale University Press, 1947), 34–35.

7. Cipolla, *Clocks,* 89.

8. Landes, *Revolution,* 29.

9. Jacques le Goff, *Time, Work, and Culture in the Middle Ages,* trans. Arthur Goldhammer (Chicago: University of Chicago Press, 1980), 43, 48–49.

10. Joseph Levenson, *Confucian China and Its Modern Fate: The Problem of Intellectual Continuity* (Berkeley, University of California Press, 1958), 15–43, 51–53. Levenson placed emphasis on the "amateur ideal" supposedly espoused by the landed gentry-elites of late imperial China, which led them to diminish the value of technical expertise and professional precision. This suggestion has been challenged by scholars who draw attention to the Statecrafts School and its emphasis on pragmatic expertise. None has gone so far as to suggest, nonetheless, that clocks were used in connection with the development of any particular aspect of Neo-Confucianism.

11. This is not to suggest, of course, that Shanghai's white-collar employees in the early decades of the twentieth century came either *directly* or *exclusively* from landowning gentry-merchant families, but rather, in contrast with the city's industrial laborers, white-collar employees came from backgrounds of means and literacy—the sort of setting characterized, from the 1860s onward, increasingly by the rise of "gentry-merchants" as a new social type and by the fusion of mercantile and landed wealth in response to new economic opportunities. On the gentry-merchants see Mary Rankin, *Elite Activism and Political Transformation in China: Zhejiang Province, 1865–1911* (Stanford, CA: Stanford University Press, 1986). See also Susan Mann Jones, "The Ningpo Pang and Financial Power at Shanghai," in *The Chinese City Between Two Worlds,* ed. Mark Elvin and G. William Skinner (Stanford: Stanford University Press, 1974), 73–96; and Marie-Claire Bergère's important work, *The Golden Age of the Chinese Bourgeoisie, 1911–1937* (Cambridge, U.K.: Cambridge University Press, 1989).

12. On the localized armed conflicts see Parks Coble, *Facing Japan: Chinese Politics and Japanese Imperialism, 1931–1937* (Cambridge, MA: Council on East Asian Studies Publications, Harvard University, 1991).

13. On Tianjin banking see Brett Sheehan, *Trust in Troubled Times* (Cambridge, MA: Harvard University Press, 2004).

14. Hong Jiaguan, *Zhongguo jinrong shi* (Chengdu: Xinan caijing daxue chuban she, 2001), 167–251. Also Wu Jingping, *Song Ziwen pingzhuan* (Fuzhou: Fujian renmin chuban she, 1992), 5–89.

15. On the Board of Revenue Bank and the founding of the Da Qing Bank see Georgia A. Mickey, "Politics of Reform: The Bank of China and Its Shareholders, 1904–1919," (PhD dissertation, Columbia University, 2004), 38–111. Mickey argues that British pressure on Chinese currency reform was partially responsible for the founding of the Da Qing Bank. Merchant shareholders were crucial in the reorganization of the Da Qing to become the Bank of China after the 1911 Revolution.

16. Numerous proposals were drafted in the second half of the nineteenth century for the creation of a Chinese-owned Western-style bank. The first such bank was the *Zhongguo tongshang yinhang* (Commercial Bank of China), inaugurated in 1897 in Shanghai by Sheng Xuanhuai, minister of railroad affairs, on the formula of "official supervision, merchant management" (*guandu shangban*). Out of this origin eventually came the Bank of China. See Hong Jiaguan, et al., *Zhongguo jinrong shi* [History of Chinese Finance] (Chengdu: Xinan caijing chuban she, 1993), 171–77; and also Wen-hsin Yeh, "Corporate Time, Communal Space: The Making of Everyday Life in Shanghai's Bank of China," *The American Historical Review* 100, no. 1 (February 1995): 97–122.

17. "Editorial remark," *Zhonghang shenghuo* [Life in the Bank of China] 1, no. 3 (July 15, 1932): 48 (*ZS* hereafter); Cao Erlong, "Wo suo yujian de guke" [My experience with customers], *ZS* 2, no. 16 (August 1, 1933): 319. See also Man Bun Kwan, *The Salt Merchants of Tianjin: State-making and Civil Society in Late Imperial China* (Honolulu: University of Hawaii Press, 2001).

18. Zhang Gongquan, "Women de chulu" [Our way out], *ZS* 2, no. 21 (December 1, 1933): 429. Zhang Gongquan was also known by his courtesy name (*zi*) Zhang Jia'ao. He lived in New York for many years after 1949, and published in English under the name Kia-ngau Chang.

19. This is not to be confused with the suggestion that the bank achieved a high degree of national integration in actual operation during the first decades of the twentieth century. Hong Jiaguan, "Minguo shiqi jinrong jigou zai shehui bianhua zhong de zuoyong" [The role of financial institutions in social change in the Republican era] (paper presented at the Luce Seminar on Modern Shanghai, University of California, Berkeley, March 6–7, 1992); and also Wen-hsin Yeh, "Corporate Space, Communal Time."

20. The Bank of China, which until then had functioned as a semi-official bank under the toppled government in Beijing, was cut off from its handling of state funds, and granted a new charter by the Ministry of Finance to become a "special institution" to handle foreign exchanges. Zhongguo yinhang zonghang and Zhongguo dier lishi dang'an guan, eds., *Zhongguo yinhang hangshi ziliao huibian, shang bian, 1912–1949* [Collected materials on the history of the Bank of China, first edition, 1912–1949] (Beijing: Dang'an chuban she, 1991), 6–17.

21. Although the economy of the Nanjing decade (1927–1937) has received a considerable amount of scholarly attention in the West, much of that has been focused on the agrarian sector. For insightful accounts about banking and money in this period, see relevant sections in Frank H. H. King, *A Concise Economic*

History of Modern China (1840–1961) (New York: Praeger, 1968); Arthur N. Young, *China's Nation-building Effort, 1927–1937: The Financial and Economic Record* (Stanford: Hoover Institution, 1971); Frank M. Tamagna, *Banking and Finance in China* (New York: Institute of Pacific Relations, 1942); and Ramon H. Myers, ed., *Selected Essays in Chinese Economic Development* (New York: Garland Publishing, 1980). The most significant recent publication in this area is Frank H. H. King, *The History of the Hongkong and Shanghai Banking Corporation* (New York: Cambridge University Press, 1987–1991), 4 vols.

22. The bank reorganized its board and increased the commercial shares in its capital structure. It also reoriented its business towards private accounts, factory loans, and foreign exchange service. On the reorganization of the Bank of China in 1928 see Hong Jiaguan, *Minguo shiqi*, 380–82; Tan Yuzuo, *Zhongguo zhongyao yinhang fazhan shi* [History of the development of major Chinese banks] (Taipei: Lianhe chuban zhongxin, 1961), 173, 219–26; Hong Jiaguan, *Zai jinrongshi yuandi li manbu* [A stroll in the field of the history of finance] (Beijing: Zhongguo jinrong chuban she, 1990), 261–64; Zhongguo renmin yinhang zonghang jinrong yanjiu suo jinrong lishi yanjiu shi, ed., *Jindai Zhongguo jinrong ye guanli* [Management practices in modern China's financial industry] (Beijing: Renmin chuban she, 1990), 354–56. Also see Kia-ngau Chang, *The Inflationary Spiral* (Cambridge, MA: MIT Technology Press, 1958), and Arthur Young, *China's Wartime Finance and Inflation, 1937–1945* (Cambridge, MA: Harvard University Press, 1965).

23. Zhang Gongquan, "Women de chulu," 430. On the history and operation of the *qianzhuang* or native banks, see Andrea McElderry, *Shanghai Old-style Banks (Ch'ien-chuang), 1800–1935: A Traditional Institution in a Changing Society* (Ann Arbor: Center for Chinese Studies, University of Michigan, 1976).

24. Yao Songling, *Zhang Gongquan xiansheng nianpu chugao* [Draft chronological biography of Mr. Zhang Gongquan], vol. 1 (Taipei: Zhuanji wenxue chuban she, 1982), 10. On Tang Wenzhi see Wen-hsin Yeh, *The Alienated Academy: Culture and Politics in Republican China* (Cambridge, MA: Council on East Asian Studies Publications, Harvard University, 1990), 97–102.

25. Yao Songling, *Zhang Gongquan,* 11–12.

26. Sheng Xuanhuai, *Sheng Xuanhuai riji* (Yangzhou: Jiangsu guangliang guji keyin she, 1998).

27. In 1913, back in Beijing, Zhang became one of the executive secretaries of Liang's Progressive Party, which after the 1911 Revolution came to enjoy extensive connections with the new government. On politics in the warlord period, see Andrew Nathan, *Peking Politics: Factionalism and the Failure of Constitutionalism, 1918–1923* (Berkeley, University of California Press, 1976). Zhang formed important friendships in Shanghai's banking circles. See Yao Songling, *Zhang Gongquan,* 21–28. On the Anglo-Chinese patronage network in Shanghai's financial circles at this time see especially Zhang Zhongli and Chen Zengnian, *Shaxun jituan zai jiu Zhongguo* [The Sassoons in Old China] (Shanghai: Renmin chuban she, 1983), 127–44.

28. Tang Yusun, "Ruhe chengwei benhang de jinglü" [How to become a crack unit at our bank]," *ZS* 3, no. 22 (January 15, 1934): 459. The number of branches

was increased to 203 by the end of 1934. See Zhongguo renmin yinhang, *Jindai Zhongguo*, 359.

29. Bianzhe, *Zhongguo yinhang Shanghai fenhang shi 1912–1949* [History of the Shanghai Branch of the Bank of China 1912–1949] (Shanghai: Jingji kexue chuban she, 1991), 84–85; Tan Yuzuo, *Zhongguo zhongyao yinhang*, 174, 193; Zhongguo renmin yinhang, *Jindai Zhongguo*, 358, 362–63.

30. Tan Yuzuo, *Zhongguo zhongyao yinhang*, 209–11; Bianzhe, *Zhongguo yinhang*, 77–79.

31. Bank of China, *Zhongguo yinhang hangyuan shouce* [Bank of China employee handbook], 3–9. From the Number Two State Archives.

32. In the case of Japanese corporations of the mid-twentieth century, Ezra Vogel offers the following observation: "Superiors do not promote someone who cannot win the liking and cooperation of his peers, for an individual's value to his unit is determined by his capacity to work effectively with his peers, his superiors, and his subordinates." Ezra Vogel, *Japan as Number One* (Cambridge, MA: Harvard University Press, 1970), 56.

33. See the insightful discussion in Brett Sheehan, *Trust in Troubled Times: Money, Banks, and State-Society Relations in Republican Tianjin* (Cambridge, MA: Harvard University Press, 2003), 45–75.

34. Mickey, "Politics of Reform," 193–328.

35. "News Brief" in *ZS* 2, no. 17 (September 1, 1933): 379; Zhang Gongquan, "Zhongguo yinhang zhi jichu anzai?" [Where does the Bank of China lay its foundation?] *ZS* 2, no.14 (June 15, 1933): 271–72.

36. In the Shanghai Branch, the first such ceremony was held on August 2, 1931. See *ZS* 1, no. 6 (October 15, 1932): 89, 95.

37. It is instructive in this connection to consider Alfred Chandler's presentation of the development of managerial hierarchy in the United States, which he saw primarily as a result of division of labor by function and specialty in response to a major expansion of markets and significant advancement in modern technology. Alfred D. Chandler, Jr., *The Visible Hand: The Managerial Revolution in American Business* (Cambridge, MA: Harvard University Press, 1977), 381–414.

38. *ZS* 1, no. 6 (October 15, 1932): 89, 95.

39. *ZS* 2, no. 15 (July 1, 1933): 304. Diary-keeping as part of an employee's moral training was apparently a common practice in those days. See Zhang Jia'ao [Zhang Gongquan], *Yinhang hangyuan de xin shenghuo* [New life for a bank employee] (Nanjing, 1934), 36–38; and Dai Ailu [Dai Zhiqian], *Yinhang jia, yinhangyuan zuoyouming* [Rules of thumb for bankers and bank employees] (Shanghai, 1932), 178–79, on diary-keeping in Japanese banks, and Barry Keenan, *Imperial China's Last Classical Academies: Social Change in the Lower Yangzi, 1864–1911* (Berkeley, University of California Press, 1994), on diary-keeping by Tongcheng School academics.

40. *ZS* 2, no.11 (March 15, 1933): 197.

41. Former employees with the Bank of Communications in Shanghai spoke of similar experiences. Interview with Lu Shengzu in the dormitory of the Bank of Communications, Shanghai, January 12, 1991.

42. Yihou, "Gongtong shenghuo zhi yiban—Jinzhongli" [Communal life in

the Jinzhongli], *ZS* 1, no. 4 (August 15, 1932): 60; Xiaoyi, "Gongtong shenghuo zhi yiban, jiushisi hao" [Communal life at number 94], *ZS* 2, no. 13 (May 15, 1933): 259; Li Jin, "Wuren yingdang xingcha ziji de bingtai" [We ought to examine our own shortcomings], *ZS* 2, no. 12 (April 15, 1933): 233.

43. On urban housing see Luo Suwen, *Da Shanghai: Shikumen, xunchang renjia* (Greater Shanghai: *Shikumen*, homes of ordinary households) (Shanghai: Renmin chuban she, 1991), 3–38.

44. Yihou, "Gongtong shenghuo," *ZS* 1, no. 4:58–60.

45. On the rise of the *xiao jiating* (nuclear family) in Republican cities and its significance, defined in opposition to the *da jiazu* or extended lineages that continued to be the norm in the countryside, see Wen-hsin Yeh, "Progressive Journalism and Shanghai's Petty Urbanites: Zou Taofen and the Shenghuo Enterprise, 1926–1945," in *Shanghai Sojourners*, ed. Wakeman and Yeh, 205–214; and also Susan Glosser, "The Business of Family," (paper presented at the annual meeting of the Association for Asian Studies, March 25–27, 1994, Boston). Past scholarship on the twentieth-century Chinese "family revolution" stressed the influence of Western liberal ideology and romantic individualism. Recent studies show the conservative dimensions of the new family in the context of urban economy and the rise of the Chinese nation-state. See also Gary Hamilton, ed., *Business Networks and Economic Development in East and Southeast Asia* (Hong Kong: Center of Asian Studies, University of Hong Kong, 1991).

46. Yihou, "Gongtong shenghuo," *ZS* 1, no. 4:58–60. The dinner party was apparently the most common form of socializing among these families. Interview with Li Wenquan, Shanghai, January 12, 1991.

47. Yihou, "Gongtong shenghuo," *ZS* 1, no. 4:58–60.

48. Pierre Bourdieu, "Sport and Social Class," in *Rethinking Popular Culture: Contemporary Perspectives in Cultural Studies*, ed. Chandra Mukerji and Michael Schudson (Berkeley: University of California Press, 1991), 368.

49. Shen Shuyu, "Huhang qiuyi bu zhi guoqu ji qi jinkuang" [Past and present of the team sports department of the Shanghai Branch]," *ZS* 2, no. 17 (September 1, 1933): 386–88; Peiguan, "Huhang tongren gongyu shenghuo xiezhen" [A realistic depiction of after-work life at the Shanghai branch], *ZS* 2, no. 16 (August 1933): 327–329. On the modern nature of Western-style sports see Wen-hsin Yeh, *The Alienated Academy: Culture and Politics in Republican China, 1919–1937* (Cambridge, MA: Council on East Asian Studies, Harvard University, 1990), 72–74, 101.

50. For illustration, see the account in *ZS* 1, no. 6 (October 15, 1932): 86–89; also Zhang Gongquan, "Zhongguo yinhang," *ZS* 2, no.14:272.

51. Leo Ou-fan Lee, "In Search of Modernity: Some Reflections on a New Mode of Consciousness in Twentieth Century Chinese History and Literature," in *Ideas Across Cultures: Essays on Chinese Thought in Honor of Benjamin I. Schwartz*, ed. Cohen and Goldman (Cambridge, MA: Council on East Asian Studies, Harvard University, 1990), 109–35.

52. Li Jilu, "Wo duiyu tongren de liangju hua" [A few words to my colleagues], *ZS* 1, no. 5 (September 15, 1932): 82.

53. On the tension between individual heroism and organizational emphasis on the "anonymous hero" see Wen-hsin Yeh, "Dai Li and the Liu Geqing Affair:

Heroism in the Chinese Secret Service during the War of Resistance," *The Journal of Asian Studies* 48, no. 3 (August 1989): 545–62.

54. Li Jilu, "Wo duiyu tongren," *ZS* 1, no. 5:37–38.

55. Zeng Runshan, "Tantan yinhang shenghuo" [On working for a bank], *ZS* 1 no. 6 (October 15, 1932): 119; Xiao Fusheng, "Dalian minzhong yule ji wohang tongren shenghuo" [Popular recreation in Dalian and employee life in the Bank], *ZS* 2, no. 15 (July 1, 1933): 302–3; Bao Wenzao, "Wo duiyu zhiwu diaoyi zhi ganxiang ji gongzuo jingguo de xingqu" [My thoughts on job transfer and interest in such work experience], *ZS* 3, no. 25 (April 1, 1934): 565.

56. For examples, see report on "Benhang ruhe faxian Shanghai yinhang Chen an de jingguo" [How we exposed the Chen case of the Shanghai Bank], *ZS* 3, no. 32 (November 1, 1934): 800–802. Also interview with Li Wenquan, January 12, 1991, Shanghai. Several cases filed with the Number One Special District Court of the Shanghai Municipality concern white-collar crimes of this nature. See Shanghai Municipal Archives, Min-31-Su-Gong-832, Min-31-Su-Gong-390. While these crimes were apparently rampant in smaller commercial banks, few of the Bank of China's employees were involved in such cases.

57. Some proposed that high-ranking managers should lead physical exercise sessions for twenty to thirty minutes everyday. Others suggested switching off electrical power supply to all dormitory units by 11:00 P.M. See Lan, "Wo suo xiwang benhang shixian de jijian shi" [What I'd like to see being realized in this bank], *ZS* 3, no. 22 (January 15, 1934): 474–75.

58. One man put it this way: "Individuals have lost control over their destiny. Mind and reasoning have lost their relevance." It was useless trying to find solace in reading and exercises, because "one loses interest in all things. Only numbness is felt. A restlessness grips us all." The problem appeared to be a lack of opportunity to "look beyond the institutional walls" and "think about the meaning of life and universe." Bank life was declared "monotonous and mechanical." See Yimin, "Tichu yige dushu shangde wenti" [To raise a question about reading and learning], *ZS* 3, no. 32 (November 1, 1934): 774–75.

59. In the word of a young cashier, "What youth like ourselves want to see is something potent and forceful: actions that demonstrate, not rhetoric that soothes." His fellow cashiers agreed with him, and demanded "truthful descriptions of the problems that exist for us," "concrete proposals for change," and "real improvement in the conditions under which we work." Xu Zongze, "Xiwang geyu youli de dongxi zaocheng hao de huanjing" [Hope for a powerful push in creating a better environment], *ZS* 2, no. 13 (May 15, 1933): 239.

60. Yao Songling, *Zhang Gongquan xiansheng nianpu chugao* [Draft chronological biography of Mr. Zhang Gongquan], vol. 1, (Taipei: Zhuanji wenxue chuban she 1982), 119. For the full text of this annual report, see Zhongguo dier lishi, *Zhongguo yinhang*, vol. 3, 2097–2132.

61. Yao Songling, *Zhang Gongquan*, 127.

62. China was on a silver standard until 1934. On the impact of the U.S. Silver Purchase Act see Frank King, *A Concise Economic History*, 135–38; Milton Friedman, *Money Mischief: Episodes in Monetary History* (New York: Harcourt Brace Jovanovich, 1992), 157–81. On inflation and Nationalist collapse see Chang Kia-ngau, *The Inflationary Spiral*.

63. "Gejie duiyu benhang ershiyi niandu baogao zhi pinglun" [Public comments and reactions to the 1932 annual report of the Bank of China: news digest], ZS 2, no. 13 (May 15, 1933): 265–66.

64. On the role of the Green Gang and the "Association of Bond Holders" see Bianzhe, Zhongguo yinhang Shanghai fenhang shi, 67. On the gang itself, see Frederic E. Wakeman, Jr., "Policing Modern Shanghai," The China Quarterly 115 (September 1988): 408–440; Brian G. Martin, "'The Pact with the Devil': The Relationship between the Green Gang and the Shanghai French Concession Authorities, 1925–1935," in Shanghai Sojourners, 266–304.

65. Bianzhe, Zhongguo yinhang Shanghai fenhang shi, 66–67.

66. Wang Shumei, "Jianku zhong delai de shengming" [Survival through hardship and struggle], ZS 2, no. 12 (April 15, 1933): 216; Zhu Yangchen, "Yige houjin hangyuan de zili yu xiwang" [A junior employee's experience and hope], ZS 2, no. 12 (April 15, 1933): 220.

67. On business strategies in Shanghai versus smaller provincial towns see Sherman Cochran, "Three Roads into Shanghai's Market: Japanese, Western, and Chinese Companies in the Match Trade, 1895–1937," in Shanghai Sojourners, 35–75; also Cochran, Big Business in China: Sino-Foreign Rivalry in the Cigarette Industry, 1890–1930 (Cambridge, MA: Harvard University Press, 1980), chap. 1.

68. Both the Dingxian experiment and the Zouping project aimed to combat rural poverty by mobilizing the peasantry to self-help, with emphasis either on Western agricultural and medical technology or moral cultivation and communal bonds. Charles W. Hayford, To the People: James Yen and Village China (New York: Columbia University Press, 1990); Guy S. Alitto, The Last Confucian: Liang Shu-ming and the Chinese Dilemma of Modernity (Berkeley: University of California Press, 1979).

69. The exchange rate between the Chinese yuan and the U.S. dollar fluctuated considerably between 1929 and 1936. See Frank King, A Concise Economic History, 136–37; Friedman, Money Mischief, 171–74.

70. Zhongguo renmin yinhang, Jindai Zhongguo, 371, 375–78; Yao Songling, Zhang Gongquan, 123–24, 128–29, 139.

71. Chen Bingtie, "Xiwang fenzhi jiguan bianshe guo nei wai" [Hope to see branch offices all over the country and the world], and Cao Zhibai, "Women yao zou shang xinlu qu" [We need to embark upon a new path], both appearing in ZS 3, no. 22 (January 15, 1934): 466.

72. Ye Boyan, "Xiangcun banshi chu zhi yipie" [A glimpse of a rural bank office], ZS 3, no. 22 (January 15, 1934): 464.

73. Ibid.

74. Ibid.

75. Ibid., 464–65.

76. Ibid.

77. Ibid.

78. The American Silver Purchase Act of May 1934 "directed the Secretary of the Treasury to purchase silver at home and abroad until the market price reached $1.29 an ounce, or until the monetary value of the silver stock held by the Treasury reached one-third of the monetary value of the gold stock." China went off

the silver standard in November 1935 and embarked upon a sweeping currency reform. See Friedman, *Money Mischief*, 163–64, 175. On Nationalist government control of the Bank of China see Coble, *Facing Japan*, chaps. 6 and 7.

79. On the "salaried man" in industrializing Japan, see Ezra Vogel, *Japan's New Middle Class: The Salary Man and His Family in a Tokyo Suburb* (Berkeley: University of California Press, 1963).

5. ENLIGHTENED PATERNALISM

1. For a comparable social landscape, see William T. Rowe, *Hankow: Commerce and Society in a Chinese City, 1796–1889* (Stanford, CA: Stanford University Press, 1984), pt. 2, and *Hankow: Conflict and Community in a Chinese City, 1796–1895* (Stanford, CA: Stanford University Press, 1989), pt. 1. On native-place ties in Shanghai's work force, see Emily Honig, *Sisters and Strangers: Women in the Shanghai Cotton Mills, 1919–1949* (Stanford, CA: Stanford University Press, 1986), 57–78.

2. On popular literacy in late imperial and modern China, see Evelyn Rawski, *Education and Popular Literacy in Ch'ing China* (Ann Arbor: University of Michigan Press, 1979); Leo Lee and Andrew Nathan, "The Beginnings of Mass Culture: Journalism and Fiction in the Late Ch'ing and Beyond," in *Popular Culture in Late Imperial China*, ed. Johnson, Nathan, and Rawski (Berkeley: University of California Press, 1985), 360–417.

3. On the fragmentation of the Chinese cultural and intellectual landscape in the early twentieth century see Wen-hsin Yeh, *The Alienated Academy: Culture and Politics in Republican China, 1919–1937* (Cambridge, MA: Council on East Asian Studies, Harvard University, 1990).

4. Wang Zhixin, "Chuan changshan ren de kutong," *Shenghuo zhoukan* 2, no. 47 (September 25, 1927): 348–50.

5. Under its first editor Wang Zhixin, the journal in its initial year of existence adopted a didactic tone and commented dutifully on Shanghai's employment scene. Circulation was under two thousand copies, most of which were distributed free of charge.

6. Zou Taofen's involvement with the CSVE began in 1922, when he was recommended by Huang Yanpei to become the society's editor and English secretary. Fudan daxue xinwen xi yanjiu shi, ed., *Zou Taofen nianpu* (Shanghai: Fudan daxue chuban she, 1982), 22. Also Zhou Tiandu, ed., *Qi junzi zhuan* (Beijing: Zhongguo shehui kexue chuban she, 1989), 309–89. Zou Taofen's oldest son, Zou Jiahua, served as China's deputy premier in the 1990s. Zheng Yi, *Zou Jiahua he ta de fuqin* (Taipei: Kaijin wenhua, 1994).

7. On the students see the section on Gu Zhun in chapter 7.

8. Zou Taofen, *Jingli*, 296–99.

9. Ibid., 21–23.

10. Ibid., 42–43, 54–58, 64–65. Zou Taofen graduated from the Episcopalian St. John's University in Shanghai in July 1921. His first job was English secretary to Mu Ouchu, owner of the Housheng Cotton Mill and founder of the Shanghai Textile Exchange. Thereafter he was also an English secretary, a teacher, and a lecturer at *Shenbao*, the YMCA Middle School, and the Baptist Shanghai College. Ibid., 21. On St. John's University, see Wen-hsin Yeh, *Alienated Academy,*

31, 49–128. Also Yeh, "Progressive Journalism and Shanghai's Petty Urbanites: Zou Taofen and the *Shenghuo* Enterprise, 1926–1945," in *Shanghai Sojourners,* ed. Wakeman and Yeh (Berkeley: Institute of East Asian Studies, University of California, 1992), 205–214.

11. See, for example, Yang Xianjiang, "Qingnian xiuyang lun-faduan," *Shenghuo* 1, no. 1 (October 11, 1925): 4–6; Yang Dinghong, "Qingnian congshi zhiye yihou yingyou de taidu," *Shenghuo* 1, no. 33 (June 6, 1926): 195; Enrun, "Gongzuo yu pinxing zhi guanxi," *Shenghuo* 2, no. 2 (October 31, 1926): 8–9. In the 1940s Zou Taofen refashioned *xiuyang* to denote the raising of the political consciousness of the masses for the creation of a new society. See Yeh, "Progressive Journalism," 205–214.

12. Wu Weizhong, "Liu Bannong suo quxing jinxiang de xuetu ku," *Shenghuo* 2, no. 9 (December 19, 1926): 54.

13. Ibid.

14. Ibid.

15. Ibid.

16. Ibid.

17. Ibid.

18. Hong Gengyang, "Kai hu yan zhi," *Shenghuo* 2, no. 49 (October 9, 1927): 383–84.

19. Bianzhe, "Ruhe chushi," *Shenghuo* 2, no. 10 (December 26, 1926): 60.

20. Bianzhe, "Zheng zai ci, zhongzhong nan kan chu," *Shenghuo* 2, no. 8 (December 12, 1926): 50.

21. Bi Yuncheng, "Qingnian zhi chenggong," *Shenghuo* 2, no. 11 (January 16, 1927): 65–66. Wang Zhixin, "Chuxu de yichu," *Shenghuo* 2, no. 11 (January 16, 1927): 68–69; Lu Guiliang, "Tian ye zuo shenghuo," *Shenghuo* 2, no. 11 (January 16, 1927), 68.

22. Yangyi, "Dexing—fuwu zhi dier tiaojian," *Shenghuo* 2, no. 11 (January 16, 1927), 66–67.

23. Zou Taofen, "Ji," *Shenghuo* 3, no. 25 (May 6, 1928): 269; Bi Yuncheng, "Huiwei," *Shenghuo* 3, no. 34 (July 8, 1928): 381–86.

24. Bi Yuncheng, "Yi ge fuche," *Shenghuo* 3, no. 12 (January 22, 1928): 129–30.

25. See Wang Zhiyi, "Zhengdang de yule fangfa," *Shenghuo* 2, no. 1 (October 24, 1926): 1–2, on "musts" and "must-nots" in recreation.

26. Luoxia, "Fanhua Shanghai zhong de qijian zhe," *Shenghuo* 3, no. 33 (July 1, 1928): 371–73.

27. On *xiao jiating* see Susan Glosser, *Chinese Visions of Family and State, 1915–1953* (Berkeley: University of California Press, 2003).

28. Chow Tse-tsung, *The May Fourth Movement: Intellectual Revolution in Modern China* (Cambridge, MA: Harvard University Press, 1960), 306; Jonathan D. Spence, *The Gate of Heavenly Peace: The Chinese and Their Revolution, 1895–1980* (New York: Penguin, 1981), 259–61; Glosser, *Chinese Visions,* 27–80; Wen-hsin Yeh, *Provincial Passages: Culture, Space, and the Origins of Chinese Communism* (Berkeley: University of California Press, 1996), 174–82; Wang Zheng, *Women in the Chinese Enlightenment: Oral and Textual Histories* (Berkeley: University of California Press, 1999), 67–116.

29. Zou Taofen, "Wu ai," *Shenghuo* 3, no. 44 (September 16, 1929): 521–22.

30. Bianzhe, "Tianmi de chenghu," *Shenghuo* 4, no. 31 (June 30, 1929): 347.

31. Xizhen, "Xiangxia ren bing bu wangu," *Shenghuo* 4, no. 29 (June 16, 1929): 319–20.

32. Zou Taofen, "Yifeng wanfen poqie qiujiu de xin," *Shenghuo* 4, no. 46 (October 13, 1929): 519.

33. Mao Jindao, "Fumu cuihun shenji," *Shenghuo* 3 no. 33 (July 1, 1928): 377–78.

34. Bianzhe, "Women lianxi Huang Huiru nüshi" *Shenghuo* 4, no. 3 (December 2, 1928): 24–26; Bianzhe, "Women lianxi Huang Huiru nüshi," *Shenghuo* 4, no. 4 (December 9, 1928): 36–38.

35. Ibid.

36. Zou Taofen, "Yihou she qu Huang nüshi de bianshi 'hero'," *Shenghuo* 4, no. 5 (November 16, 1927): 41.

37. Ibid.

38. Hu Yaochang, "Shehui duiyu Huang nüshi he ruci zhi canku," *Shenghuo* 4, no. 11 (January 27, 1929): 111–12.

39. Zou Taofen, ed., *Duzhe xinxiang waiji* 1:80–83.

40. See, for instance, Bi Yuncheng, "Yige heyu lixiang de jiating," *Shenghuo* 3, no. 8 (December 25, 1927): 81.

41. Baoyi, "Lixiang de jiating," *Shenghuo* 2, no. 7 (December 5, 1926): 42. See also Xinshui, "Jieshao jiating yule fangfa de xinjianyi," *Shenghuo* 2, no. 20 (March 20, 1926): 136–38.

42. Sheng Peiyu and Wu Shen, "Liangwei nüshi duiyu da jiazu de yijian," *Shenghuo* 2, no. 50 (October 16, 1927): 394.

43. Hu Shi, "Shijian bu zhiqian," *Shenghuo* 2, no. 7 (December 5, 1927): 43–44; Sheng Peiyu, "Shu kan hao tan," *Shenghuo* 3, no. 2 (November 13, 1927): 15; Wang Jianrui, "Shanghai funü li de maotouying," *Shenghuo* 3, no. 3 (November 20, 1927): 26.

44. Wang Xiaochong, "Yige nande de nüzi," *Shenghuo* 2, no. 2 (November 1, 1926): 12.

45. Too much education in reality could sometimes pose a problem, though, as was evidenced by, for example, "the undeniable fact that the Jinling College for Women has a large number of old spinsters among its graduates." Cai Xiyue, "Dakai Jinling nüda xiaokan kankan," *Shenghuo* 4, no. 31 (June 30, 1929): 348.

46. Glosser, *Chinese Visions*, 134–66.

47. Zhuang Zexuan, "Hunyin de xianjue wenti," *Shenghuo* 2, no. 16 (February 12, 1927): 103–4.

48. Yin, "Shou jingji yapo er xiangdao jieyu de yiwei qingnian," *Shenghuo* 2, no. 7 (December 5, 1927): 54–55.

49. The term *tuoli* (extricate, break away from, separate oneself from) occurs repeatedly in the family literature of this period.

50. The two stories are "Yiwei Meiguo ren jia gei yiwei Zhongguo ren de zishu," adapted from Mae Franking, *My Chinese Marriage* (New York: Duffield, 1922), and "Yiwei Yingguo nüshi yu Sun xiansheng de hunyin," adapted from Louise Jordan Miln, *Mr. and Mrs. Sen* (New York: Frederick A. Stokes Co., 1923).

The former was serialized in *Shenghuo zhoukan* vols. 2–3, the latter in vols. 3–4. See Michael Hsu, "Domesticating the Foreign Western Women and Mixed Marriages in Republican China," MA thesis, University of California, Berkeley, 2007.

51. Sun Li, "Liangnan," *Shenghuo* 4, no. 5 (December 16, 1928): 50.

52. Li Guochong, "Ying peng ying," *Shenghuo* 4, no. 6 (December 23, 1928): 59.

53. Qian Zhuanggong, "Nongcun shenghuo jiyi gailiang zhi duan," *Shenghuo* 2, no. 1 (October 24, 1926): 4–5.

54. Yang Chizhi and Bianzhe, "Nongmin yundong yu baodong," *Shenghuo* 2, no. 13 (January 30, 1927): 82–83; Zou Taofen, "Tianzai renhuo," *Shenghuo* 6, no. 34 (August 15, 1931): 725; Xueshi, "Hankou shuihuan zhong zhi shehui xiaoxian guan," *Shenghuo* 6, no. 34 (August 15, 1931): 733–35.

55. Wang Zhiyi, "Zhengdang de yule fangfa," *Shenghuo* 2, no. 1 (October 24, 1926): 1–2; and "Gaizao dushi de yanjiu," *Shenghuo* 2, no. 2 (October 31, 1926): 9–10.

56. Sheng Peiyu and Wu Shen, "Liangwei nüshi duiyu da jiazu de yijian," *Shenghuo* 2, no. 50 (October 16, 1927): 394.

57. On Lu Xun, see Leo Ou-fan Lee, *Voices from the Iron House: A Study of Lu Xun* (Bloomington: Indiana University Press, 1987).

58. Mengsheng, "Jiujiu wo jiejie de xingming," *Shenghuo* 3, no. 40 (August 19, 1928): 476–77.

59. Kathryn Bernhardt, "Women and the Law: Divorce in the Republican Period" (paper prepared for the Conference on Civil Law in Chinese Society, University of California at Los Angeles, August 1991, 1–2).

60. Zou Taofen, *Duzhe xinxiang waiji*, 1:218–19.

61. Ibid.

62. Ibid., 57–58.

63. Li Gongpu, "Quan Zhongguo zhiyou yizhong guoqi le," *Shenghuo* 4, no. 17 (March 24, 1929): 174.

64. Zou Taofen, "Kanle Sun zongli guozang dianli yingpian," *Shenghuo* 4, no. 34 July 21, 1929): 375.

65. The most infamous case of this sort was the assassination of Shi Liangcai, the publisher of *Shenbao*. See Frederic Wakeman, Jr., *Policing Shanghai, 1927–1937* (Berkeley: University of California Press, 1995), 257–59.

66. On the government's bureaucracy, see Qiuxing, "Women jinri suo zui xuyao de shi shenme?" *Shenghuo* 4, no. 15 (March 10, 1929): 148; Zou Taofen, "Bukan shexiang de guanhua," *Shenghuo* 5, no .1 (December 1, 1929): 1; on selfishness and irresponsibility, see "Mou yuanlao de liumang wenti," *Shenghuo* 5, no. 8 (January 19, 1930): 113; on famine in Shanxi, "Ji Zha Liangzhao jun tao Shan zaishi," *Shenghuo* 6, no. 12 (March 14, 1931): 253–54; on popular protest, "Minyi suozai," *Shenghuo* 6, no. 25 (June 13, 1931): 509; on the state of gloom, "Guoqing yu guoai," *Shenghuo* 6, no. 42 (October 10, 1931): 893; on Nationalist appeasement of the Japanese, "Guonan yu xuechao," *Shenghuo* 6, no. 52 (December 19, 1931): 1153.

67. See, for example, Zou Taofen, "Qingkan jiaoyu jijin de gongxiao," *Shenghuo* 6, no. 14 (March 28, 1931): 285; Zhu Jin, "Women de dushu hezuo," *Shenghuo* 6; no. 14 (March 28, 1930): 299–300.

68. On the Nationalists and higher education see Yeh, *Alienated Academy,* chap. 5.

69. Zou Taofen, "Yapian gongmai minyi ceyan," *Shenghuo* 7, no. 42 (October 22, 1932): 825. Also Parks M. Coble, "Chiang Kai-shek and the Anti-Japanese Movement in China: Zou Tao-fen and the National Salvation Association, 1931–1937," *Journal of Asian Studies* 44, no. 2 (February 1985): 293–310.

70. Zou denounced Chinese military commanders in the field for cowardice and attacked the Nationalist government for non-resistance. Zou Taofen, "Wu ke yanshi de jiduan wuchi," *Shenghuo* 6, no. 41 (October 3, 1931): 873. Zou Taofen, "Dui quanguo xuesheng gongxian de yidian yijian," *Shenghuo* 6, no. 40 (September 26, 1931): 854.

71. Zou Taofen, "Yizhi de yanli jiandu," *Shenghuo* 6, no. 40 (September 26, 1931): 854.

72. Jizhe, "Shangxin canmu," *Shenghuo* 6, no. 42 (October 10, 1931): 913–14; Zou Taofen, "Guoqing yu guoai," *Shenghuo* 6, no. 42 (October 10, 1931): 893; "Shenghuo guonan canxiang huabao," *Shenghuo* 6, no. 44 (October 24, 1931): 991–94.

73. See, for instance, "Benshe wei choukuan yuanzhu Heisheng weiguo jianèr jinji qishi," *Shenghuo* 6, no. 48 (November 21, 1931): 1071-72; "Juankuan zhuxiang zhe laihan zhi yiban," *Shenghuo* 6, no. 48 (November 21, 1931): 1080.

74. Zou Taofen, "Chuangban *Shenghuo Ribao* zhi jianyi," *Shenghuo* 7, no. 9 (March 5, 1932): 114–16.

75. Zou Taofen, "Zhengfu guangbo geming zhongzi," *Shenghuo* 6, no. 49 (November 28, 1931): 1081.

76. Ibid.

77. Ibid.

78. Zou Taofen's response to Liang Shaowen, in "Hangao lüci," *Shenghuo* 5, no. 32 July 20, 1930): 541. For further elaboration on this theme, see Yeh, "Progressive Journalism."

79. Zou was forced to travel to the United States and elsewhere. The success of *Shenghuo zhoukan* had laid the foundation of Zou Taofen's larger publishing enterprise, the Shenghuo Bookstore. Du Chongyuan, Zou's colleague and deputy, took charge of much of the publishing business while Zou was away.

80. Fudan daxue, *Zou Taofen nianpu,* 90.

81. For "epoch" (*shidai*), see Lung-kee Sun, "Chinese Intellectuals' Notion of 'Epoch' *(Shidai)* in the Post–May Fourth Era," *Chinese Studies in History* 20, no. 22 (Winter 1986–87): 32; and Leo Ou-fan Lee, "In Search of Modernity: Some Reflections on a New Mode of Consciousness in Twentieth-Century Chinese History and Literature," in *Ideas Across Cultures: Essays on Chinese Thought in Honor of Benjamin I. Schwartz,* ed. Cohen and Goldman (Cambridge, MA: Council on East Asian Studies Publications, Harvard University Press, 1990), 120–21.

82. Ku Fengshi, "Qiwang," *Dazhong Shenghuo* 1, no. 2 (November 23, 1935): 62–64.

83. Liang Ziqi, "Yanlun de lichang he taidu," *Dazhong Shenghuo,* no. 6 (June 21, 1941): 140–43.

84. Parks M. Coble, *Facing Japan: Japanese Politics and Japanese Imperial-*

ism, 1931–1937 (Cambridge: Council on East Asian Studies Publications, Harvard University Press, 1991), 289–97.

85. On progressive publishers and Communist sympathy see Xu Xuehan, "Huiyi quanguo gejie jiuguo lianhehui pianduan qingkuang," in *"Yi er jiu" yihou Shanghai jiuguohui shiliao xuanji,* ed. Zhonggong Shanghai shiwei (Shanghai: Shanghai shehui kexue yuan chuban she, 1987), pp. 405–6; Wu Dakun, "Dang yu jiuguohui," in *"Yi er jiu,"* 407–8. On vocational youths and the National Salvation Association (NSA) see Wang Han, "Yi er jiu yundong hou Shanghai dixia dang gongzuo luxian de zhuanbian," in *"Yi er jiu,"* 315; Lu Zhiren, "Guanyu Shanghai zhiye jie jiuguohui de yixie qingkuang," in *"Yi er jiu,"* 417–18; Yong Wentao, "Huiyi Dang dui zhijiu de lingdao he Shanghai renmin de kangri jiuwang yundong, in *"Yi er jiu,"* 411–12.

86. On Communist disarray in the 1930s see Li Fanfu, "Guanyu yijiusanwu hou yijiusanqi qian Shanghai dixiadang douzheng de yixie qingkuang," in ibid., 379–80; Qian Junrui, "Jiuguohui nei de dang zuzhi qingkuan," in *"Yi er jiu,"* 387; Wu Dakun, "Dang yu jiuguohui," 408. Also Wang Yaoshan, "Yijiusanqi nian qian Shanghai de kangri jiuwang yundong he dixia dang zuzhi de zhengli gongzuo," in *"Yi er jiu,"* 382; Hu Yuzhi, "Pan Hannian tongzhi yu jiuguohui," in *"Yi er jiu,"* 386.

87. Patricia Stranahan, *Underground: The Shanghai Communist Party and the Politics of Survival, 1927–1937* (Lanham, MD: Rowman & Littlefield Publishers, 1998).

88. During the Cultural Revolution, Zou Taofen, though dead, was accused of having collaborated with the enemy. Zou Jiahua, Zou Taofen's son, was sent to prison. Zou Jiahua's father-in-law, Marshall Ye Jianying, also came under suspicion. See Zheng Yi, *Zou Jiahua he ta de fuqin* (Taipei: Kaijin wenhua, 1994).

6. PETTY URBANITES AND TALES OF WOE

1. Sherman Cochran and Andrew C. K. Hsieh with Janis Cochran, trans. and ed., *One Day in China: May 21, 1936* (New Haven, CN: Yale University Press, 1982).

2. On realism in literature as practiced by the leading writers see David Der-Wei Wang, *Fictional Realism in Twentieth-Century China: Mao Dun, Lao She, Shen Congwen* (New York: Columbia University Press, 1992).

3. Liu Ti, "Tong gui yu jin," *Dushu shenghuo* 2, no. 4 (June 1935): 135–136.

4. Bianzhe, "Xiao quezi yao renshi shijie le," *Dushu shenghuo* 2, no. 4 (June 1935): 152–156.

5. On Ai Siqi, see Joshua A. Fogel, *Ai Ssu-ch'i's Contribution to the Development of Chinese Marxism* (Cambridge, MA: Council on East Asian Studies, Harvard University, 1987). See also Patricia Stranahan, *Underground: The Shanghai Communist Party and the Politics of Survival, 1927–1937* (Lanham, MD: Rowman & Littlefield Publishers, 1998).

6. On Li Gongpu see Zhou Tiandu, ed., *Qi junzi zhuan* (Beijing: Zhongguo shehui kexue chuban she, 1989): 393–462. On the death of Li Gongpu see John Israel, *Lianda: A Chinese University in War and Revolution* (Stanford, CA: Stanford University Press, 1998), 378–379.

7. On the death of Shi Liangcai see Frederic Wakeman, *Policing Shanghai: 1927–1937* (Berkeley: University of California Press, 1995), 257–259.

8. On "shidai," see Leo Lee, "In Search of Modernity: Some Reflections on a New Mode of Consciousness in Twentieth-Century Chinese History and Literature," in *Ideas Across Cultures,* ed. Cohen and Goldman, (Council on East Asian Studies, Harvard University, 1990) 109–135.

9. Tongren, "Chuangkan ci," *Dushu shenghuo* 1, no. 1 (November 1934): 1.

10. Ibid.

11. Ibid.

12. Ibid., 2.

13. Ai Siqi, "Tian xiaode," *Dushu shenghuo* 2, no. 1 (May 1935): 27–28.

14. Qian Yishi, "Siyue houbanyue de guoji dashi," *Dushu shenghuo* 2, no. 1 (May 1935): p.4.

15. Ibid., 6.

16. Li Gongpu, "Zenyang jinian sige weidai de rizi," *Dushu shenghuo* 2, no. 1 (May 1935): 1.

17. Ibid., 1–2.

18. Li Chongji, "Zenyang yanjiu zhexue," *Dushu shenghuo* 2, no. 1 (May 1935): 19.

19. Over half of all issues published in 1935 featured cover designs done in woodblock prints. Special sections were included, in addition, that used woodblock prints to tell the story of Lu Xun's "Kong Yiji" over several issues. Li Ti, "Muke teji," *Dushu shenghuo* 3, no. 1 (November 1935): 31; Tang Ke, "Muke luetan," *Dushu shenghuo* 3, no. 1 (November 1935): 32–38. On left-wing leanings in woodblock prints see Chang-tai Hung, *War and Popular Culture: Resistance in Modern China, 1937–1945* (Berkeley: University of California Press, 1994), 239–244.

20. *Dushu shenghuo* 2, no. 12 (October 1935): 511.

21. Ibid., 528.

22. These pictures were intended to be read as visual texts that capture scenes in contemporary lives. Li Ti, "Muke teji," 31.

23. On the pictorial journal *Liangyou* (The Young Companion), see Leo Ou-fan Lee, *Shanghai Modern: The Flowering of a New Urban Culture in China, 1930–1945* (Cambridge, MA: Harvard University Press, 1999), 64–74.

24. Wang Ping, "Yige xiaofan de shenghuo," *Dushu shenghuo* 1, no. 7 (Feb. 1935): 13–14.

25. Qiao Ying, "Fa gongqian de yitian," *Dushu shenghuo* 2, no. 2 (May 1935): 73–74.

26. Ibid., 74.

27. Sun Shuzhi, "Wode diandang shenghuo," *Dushu shenghuo* 1, no. 2 (November 1934): 23.

28. Yuan Fangxi, "Xiao yangdeng xia," *Dushu shenghuo* 1, no. 1 (November 1934): 24.

29. Jin Manhui, "Yadian nei," *Dushu shenghuo* 1, no. 4 (December 1934): 16–17.

30. Jiao Daqiu, "Yige yonggong de shenghuo jilu," *Dushu shenghuo* 1, no. 3 (December 1934): 16–17.

31. *"Shenghuo douzheng"* and *"minzu jiefang"* were adopted by the journal as its official slogan beginning January 1936.

32. Bianzhe, "Xiao quezi yao renshi shijie le," *Dushu shenghuo* 2, no. 4 (June 1935): 152–56.

33. On Zou Taofen, Li Gongpu, and the national salvation organizations of the vocational youths see Parks M. Coble, *Facing Japan: Chinese Politics and Japanese Imperialism, 1931–1937* (Cambridge, MA: Council on East Asian Studies, Harvard University, 1991), 289–297; John Israel, *Student Nationalism in China, 1927–1937* (Stanford, CA: Stanford University Press, 1966); Israel and Donald W. Klein, *Rebels and Bureaucrats: China's December 9ers* (Berkeley: University of California Press, 1976). See also Zhonggong Shanghai shiwei dangshi ziliao zhengji weiyuan hui, ed., *"Yi er jiu" yihou Shanghai jiuguo hui shiliao xuanji* (Shanghai: Shanghai shehui kexue yuan chuban she, 1987), 97–104, and 311–372 on the "Seven Gentlemen."

34. Zhonggong Shanghai shiwei dangshi ziliao zhengji weiyuan hui, Yiyoushe shiliao zhengji zu, eds., *Yiyoushe shier nian, 1938–1949* (Shanghai: unpublished ms., 1985).

35. The Ants Club moved to Wuhan in late 1937. It was active there in the Second United Front directed by Wang Ming. The Nationalist government disbanded the club in 1938. Club activists went on to join the CCP in Yan'an.

7. FROM PATRIARCHS TO CAPITALISTS

1. Wen-hsin Yeh, "Shanghai Besieged, 1937–45," in *Wartime Shanghai,* ed. Yeh (New York: Routledge, 1998), 1–17.

2. Richard Henry Tawney, *Land and Labor in China* (New York: Octagon Books, 1972).

3. Yeh, "Shanghai Besieged," 1–17; Christian Henriot and Wen-hsin Yeh, eds., *In the Shadow of the Rising Sun: Shanghai under Japanese Occupation* (New York: Cambridge University Press, 2004); Frederic Wakeman, Jr., *Shanghai Badlands: Wartime Terrorism and Urban Crime, 1937–1941* (New York: Cambridge University Press, 1996); and Poshek Fu, *Passivity, Resistance, and Collaboration: Intellectual Choices in Occupied Shanghai, 1937–1945* (Stanford, CA: Stanford University Press, 1993), and *Between Shanghai and Hong Kong: The Politics of Chinese Cinemas* (Stanford, CA: Stanford University Press, 2003).

4. There is a growing body of literature concerning the "Nanjing Massacre," which has followed the publication of Iris Chang's best-selling *The Rape of Nanjing.* Notable titles include Joshua Fogel, ed., *The Nanjing Massacre in History and Historiography* (Berkeley: University of California Press, 2000); Timothy Brooks, ed., *Documents on the Rape of Nanjing* (Ann Arbor: University of Michigan Press, 1999); and Zhang Kaiyuan, ed., *Eyewitnesses to Massacre: American Missionaries Bear Witness to Japanese Atrocities in Nanjing* (Armonk, NY: M. E. Sharpe, 2001).

5. Christian Henriot, "Shanghai Industries under Japanese Occupation: Bombs, Boom, and Bust, 1937–1945," in *In the Shadow,* 20–25.

6. Robert Bickers, "Settlers and Diplomats: The End of the British Hegemony in the International Settlement, 1937–1945," and Christine Cornet, "The

Bumpy End of the French Concession and French Influence in Shanghai, 1937–1946," in *In the Shadow,* 229–56, 257–76.

7. Luo Yijun, "Nanshi nanmin qu shu lue," *Shanghai wenshi ziliao xuanji,* no. 51 (April 1985): 172.

8. Luo Yijun, "Nanshi nanmin," 173–76.

9. Zhao Puchu, "Kangzhan chuqi Shanghai de nanmin gongzuo," *Shanghai wenshi ziliao xuanji,* no. 51 (April 1985): 149–63; Zhou Ke, "Nanmin gongzuo he dixia jun gongzuo huiyi pianduan," *Shanghai wenshi ziliao xuanji,* no. 51 (April 1985) 164–71; Wu Dakun, "Kang'ri zhanzheng zhong dui xin si-jun de weiwen," *Shanghai wenshi ziliao xuanji,* no.51 (April 1985): 124–31; Shen Yi, "Yunsong renyuan he wuzi qu kang'ri genjudi de qingkuang," *Shanghai wenshi ziliao xuanji,* no. 51 (April 1985): 132–44.

10. Christian Henriot, "Death in Shanghai" (paper presented at conference on visual documentations, jointly organized by the Institut d'Asie Orientale, Lumière-Lyon 2 University and the University of California at Berkeley, in Tokyo, September 2004).

11. Zou Yiren, *Jiu Shanghai renkou bianqian de yanjiu* (Shanghai: Shanghai renmin chuban she, 1980), 3–4, 47, 53–55.

12. Henriot, "Shanghai Industries," 26–35.

13. Timothy Brook, "The Great Way Government of Shanghai," in *In the Shadow,* 157–86; Brook, "Collaborationist Nationalism in Occupied Wartime China," in *Nation Work: Asian Elites and National Identities,* ed. Brook and Schmid (Ann Arbor: University of Michigan Press, 2000), 159–90; and Brook, *Collaboration: Local Elite and Japanese Agents in Wartime China* (Cambridge, MA: Harvard University Press, 2005).

14. Wen-hsin Yeh, "Dai Li and the Liu Geqing Affair: Heroism in the Chinese Secret Service during the War of Resistance," *The Journal of Asian Studies* 48, no. 3 (August 1989): 552–53.

15. Frederic Wakeman, *Shanghai Badlands: Wartime Terrorism and Urban Crime, 1937–1941* (New York: Cambridge University Press, 1996).

16. Yamada Tatsuo, *Chugoku kokuminto saha no kenkyu* (Tokyo: Keio Tsushin, 1980).

17. Shanghai shi dang'an guan, ed., *Ri wei Shanghai shi zhengfu* (Beijing: Dang'an chuban she, 1986), 851–58.

18. Ibid., 856.

19. Yeh, "Shanghai Besieged," 1–17.

20. Allison Rottmann, "Crossing Enemy Lines: Shanghai and the Central China Base," in *In the Shadow,* 90–115.

21. Gerald E. Bunker, *The Peace Conspiracy: Wang Ching-wei and the China War, 1937–1941* (Cambridge, MA: Harvard University Press, 1972).

22. John Birge Sawyer diaries, volume 6, p. 36. Bancroft Library, University of California, Berkeley. Transcribed by Robert Bodde, September 2004.

23. Tao Juyin, *Gudao jianwen: Kangzhan shiqi de Shanghai* (Shanghai: Shanghai renmin chuban she, 1979), 99.

24. On the end of the French Concession in China see Cornet, "The Bumpy End," 257–76; and Marie-Claire Bergère, "The Purge in Shanghai: The Sarly

Affair and the End of the French Concession, 1945–1946," in *Wartime Shanghai*, ed. Wen-hsin Yeh, 157–78.

25. Shanghai shi, *Ri wei Shanghai,* 119–23.

26. Chen Gongbo was a founding member of the CCP in Shanghai in 1921.

27. Shanghai shi, *Ri wei Shanghai,* 989–90.

28. Shanghai shi, *Ri wei Shanghai,* 119–23.

29. On wartime Japanese military control of the Chinese civilian population, see Brook, *Collaboration.*

30. Shanghai shi, *Ri wei Shanghai,* 593–97.

31. Shanghai shi, *Ri wei Shanghai,* 654–55.

32. Zhonggong Shanghai shiwei dangshi ziliao zhengji weiyuan hui, ed., *Shanghai sihang erju zhigong yungdong shiliao* (Shanghai: Zhongguo Renmin yinhang Shanghai shi fenhang, 1987), 2 vols; Zhonggong Shanghai shiwei dangshi ziliao zhengji weiyuan hui, ed., *Shanghai Nanshi liuye zhigong yungdong shi* (Shanghai: 1986); Zhonggong Shanghai dangshi ziliao zhengji weiyuan hui, ed., *Shanghai yizhuo ye zhigong yundong shiliao* (Shanghai: 1984).

33. Tao Juyin, *Gudao jianwen,* 7–8.

34. Shanghai shehui kexue yuan jingji yanjiu suo, ed., *Shanghai Yong'an gongsi de chansheng, fazhan he gaizao* (Shanghai: Renmin chuban she, 1980), 147–48.

35. Shanghai Yong'an baihuo gongsi dang'an, "Renshi xinhan," Shanghai Municipal Archives (hereafter SMA), Q-235, February 22, 1938.

36. Ibid.

37. Shanghai Yong'an baihuo gongsi dang'an, "Bugao," SMA, Q-235, Aug. 25, 1937, no. 241.

38. Ibid., no. 242.

39. Ibid., no. 244.

40. Shanghai Yong'an baihuo gongsi dang'an, "Renshi xinhan," SMA, Q-235, 1937.

41. Ibid., 1937–38.

42. Ibid., 1938.

43. Ibid.

44. Ibid.

45. Ibid.

46. Ibid.

47. Ibid.

48. Shanghai shehui, *Shanghai Yong'an gongsi.*

49. Ibid., 192.

50. *Shanghai Qingnian* [Shanghai youth], 1939.

51. Shanghai Yong'an baihuo gongsi dang'an, "Renshi xinhan," SMA, Q-235, Jan. 26, 1938.

52. Ibid., 1938.

53. Ibid., Sept. 14, 1938.

54. Ibid., 1938.

55. Ibid., Nov. 3, 1938.

56. Ibid., 1938.

57. Ibid., Jan. 10, 1938.

58. Ibid., Feb. 17, 1938.

59. Ibid., Jan. 10 and Mar. 3, 1938.

60. Shanghai shehui, *Shanghai Yong'an gongsi,* 150–51.

61. Shanghai Yong'an baihuo gongsi dang'an, "Renshi xinhan," SMA, Q-235, Feb. 26, June 6, June 12, June 29, and July 22, 1938.

62. Ibid., July 22 and July 25, 1938.

63. Ibid., Aug. 1938.

64. Ibid.

65. Ibid., Aug. 14, 1939.

66. Ibid., June 9, 1939.

67. Ibid., Nov. 4, 1939.

68. Shanghai Yong'an gongsi dang'an, "Gebu zhiyuan chengji baogao zongbiao ji geji baogao biao, 1939," SMA, O-225-2-101.

69. Shanghai Yong'an baihuo gongsi dang'an, "Renshi xinhan," SMA, Q-235, 1938.

70. Ibid., May 7, 1938.

71. Ibid., 1938.

72. Ibid., 1939.

73. Ibid., Feb. 1939.

74. Ibid., June 4, 1939.

75. Ibid., Aug. 10, 1938.

76. Ibid., Sept. 7, 1938.

77. Ibid., Feb. 23, 1939.

78. Ibid., Sept. 23, 1939.

79. Ibid., Aug. 8, 1939.

80. Shanghai shehui, *Shanghai Yong'an gongsi,* 41.

81. Shanghai Yong'an baihuo gongsi dang'an, "Renshi xinhan," SMA, Q-235, Sept. 1939.

82. Ibid., Aug. 1939.

83. Shanghai Yong'an baihuo gongsi dang'an, "Quan ti tong ren shangshu," SMA, Q225-2-46, Aug. 12, 1938.

84. Ibid., Aug. 25, 1940.

85. Ibid., Apr. 1, 1941.

86. Shanghai Yong'an baihuo gongsi dang'an, "Nanjing lu shangjie lianhe hui han Yong An," SMA Q225-2-49, March 28, 1939.

87. The following discussion of bank wars is largely based upon chap. 10 in Wakeman, *Shanghai Badlands.*

88. *North China Herald,* March 26, 1941, 483; cited in Wakeman, *Shanghai Badlands.*

89. Zhongguo yinhang zonghang, Zhongguo dier lishi dang'an guan, eds., *Zhongguo yinhang hangshi ziliao huibian, shang bian, 1912–1949* (Beijing: Dang'an chuban she, 1991), 1:433–35.

90. Confidential U.S. State Department Central Files. China: Internal Affairs, 1940–1944. See 893.108, March 24, 1941, 296. Cited in Wakeman, *Shanghai Badlands.*

91. This account is based on Wakeman's reconstruction in chap. 10, *Shanghai Badlands.*

92. *China Weekly Review,* April 26, 1941, 267; *North China Herald,* April 23, 1941. Cited in Wakeman, *Shanghai Badlands.*

93. Zhongguo yinhang zonghang, *Zhongguo yinhang hangshi,* 435–37.

94. Anonymous letter signed "A Banker," dated April 22, 1941, in *China Weekly Review,* April 26, 1941, 242, 267. Cited in Wakeman, *Shanghai Badlands.*

95. Pei Yunqing, "Di san jie huiyuan dahui de shiming he fazhan" [The mission and future of the third annual membership meeting], *Yinqianjie* [Banking circle] 2, no. 1 (June 12, 1938): 1; "Shanghai shi yinqianye yeyu lianyihui chengli sanzhounian jinian ji diwujie huiyuan dahui tekan" [Special issue on the third anniversary of the Shanghai banking and *qianzhuang* after-work friendship association and the fifth membership meeting], October 29, 1939, 35.

96. "Shanghai shi yinqianye" (Shanghai: 1939), 50–58.

97. Ibid., 58–69.

98. Registration figures compiled in October 1938 showed that the association's seven thousand members were drawn from ninety-seven banks, 101 *qianzhuang,* 164 insurance and trust companies, and thirty-four other women's organizations. See ibid., 38.

99. Wu Yaqin, "Fa qi yinqian ye xiaofei hezuo she de yiyi" [The significance of launching a consumer co-op in banking and money circles], *Yinqianjie* 2, no. 8 (October 1938): 155.

100. Ibid., 41.

101. Huang Dinghui, "Jianyi tongren fuli chujin" [Fellow-worker benefits reserve fund—a proposal], *Yinqianjie* 2, no. 4 (August 1938), 69.

102. On the spoken drama as *the* artistic medium of resistance during the lone islet period, see Poshek Fu, *Passivity, Resistance, and Collaboration.*

103. Wu Limen, "Yule de jituan," *Yinqianjie,* no. 11 (November 20, 1938), 215.

104. Wakeman, *Shanghai Badlands.*

105. Wu Limen, "Yule de jituan," 215–16.

106. Pingzi, "Sanshi yu danwei huiyuan jiaoyi dahui texie" [Special report on the friendship gathering of members of thirty-some *danwei*], *Yinqianjie* 2, no. 10 (November 1, 1938): 195.

107. Popular urban fiction in this period, like spoken drama, also made little explicit reference to the Japanese. See Edward Gunn, *Unwelcome Muse: Chinese Literature in Shanghai and Peking, 1937–1945* (New York: Columbia University Pres, 1980). Whether there was a literary resistance movement in wartime Chinese writings is the subject of Poshek Fu's *Passivity, Resistance, and Collaboration.*

108. Nicole Huang argues, for example, that there was hardly a literature of overt resistance in Shanghai during the war. Women writers (Zhang Ailing, Su Qing, and Gu Lu) dominated the literary scene. They portrayed the seemingly domestic subjects of women, marriage, and everyday life. Their work, in the end, underscored the extraordinary circumstances of wartime upheaval. Nicole Huang, *Women, War, and Domesticity: Shanghai Literature and Popular Culture of the 1940s* (Boston: Brill, 2005).

109. "Yule xinwen" [Entertainment news], *Yinqianjie* 2, no. 4 (August 1938), 71.

110. There are obviously numerous other interpretations of *Sunrise*. Cao Yu himself would have preferred a different interpretation than Xia Feng's. See Cao Yu [Wan Jiabao], *Richu* [Sunrise] (Shanghai: wenhua shenghuo chuban she, 1936), "postscript," i-xxxii; Tian Benxiang, *Cao Yu zhuan* [A biography of Cao Yu] (Beijing: Shiyue wenyi chuban she, 1988), 174–87; Sichuan daxue zhongwen xi, ed., *Cao Yu zhuanji* [Special selections on Cao Yu] (Sichuan: Renmin chuban she, 1979), vol.1, 410–14; vol. 2, 415–95.

111. Leo Lee, *Shanghai Modern*, 226–27.

112. Lao Yan, "Kan *Richu*" [Watching *Sunrise*], *Yinqianjie* 2, no. 12 (December 1938), 245.

113. Ibid.

114. Ibid.

115. Huang Yingzi, in "Kan *Richu*," 245.

116. Photographic copy of Xu Jiqing's calligraphy, in *Yinqianjie* 2, no. 12 (December 1938): 244.

117. Pei Wei, "Kan le *Richu* yi hou" [After viewing *Sunrise*], *Yinqianjie* 2, no. 12 (December 1938): 247.

118. On *hanjian* see Frederic Wakeman, "*Hanjian*" in *Becoming Chinese: Passages to Modernity and Beyond*, ed. Wen-hsin Yeh (Berkeley: University of California Press, 2000), 298–341.

119. "Jian ju Hanjian Li Ze," in *Shanghai baihuo ye zhigong yundong shiliao*, ed. Zhonggong Shanghai shiwei dangshi ziliao zhengji weiyuan hui (Shanghai: 1986), 93–99.

120. Ibid., 102–3.

121. Ibid., 103–4.

122. Ibid., 107–8.

123. Ibid., 107–8.

124. Ibid., 109.

125. Ibid., 109–10.

126. Ibid., 104–10.

127. Ibid., 110.

128. Gu Zhun, *Gu Zhun zishu* (Beijing: Zhongguo qingnian chuban she, 2002), 1.

129. Ibid., 2–3.

130. Ibid., 3.

131. Ibid., 16.

132. Ibid., 3–4.

133. Ibid., 8–9.

134. Ibid., 4–5, 8.

135. Ibid., 9–10.

136. Elizabeth Perry, *Shanghai on Strike: The Politics of Chinese Labor* (Stanford, CA: Stanford University Press, 1993). Also Wen-hsin Yeh, *Provincial Passages: Culture, Space, and the Origins of Chinese Communism* (Berkeley: University of California Press, 1996).

137. On Labor University see Yeh, *The Alienated Academy: Culture and Politics in Republican China, 1919–1937* (Cambridge, MA: Council on East Asian Studies, Harvard University, 1990).

138. Gu Zhun, *Gu Zhun zishu*, 18–19.
139. Ibid., 18.
140. Gu Zhun, 30.
141. Gu Zhun, 399–400.
142. Gu Zhun, 400.
143. Gu Zhun, *Gu Zhun zishu*, 400.
144. Gu Zhun, ibid, 403–7.
145. Gu Zhun, ibid., 58, 457.
146. Gu Zhun, ibid., 62–63.
147. Gu Zhun, ibid., 63.0

EPILOGUE

1. Party-centered narratives of Shanghai continued to hold forth throughout the 1980s. See Shanghai shi dang'an guan, ed., *Wu san yundong*, vol. 1 (Shanghai: Shanghai renmin chuban she, 1991), 1. Other archival selections publicized by the Shanghai Municipal Archives concern the Federation of Shanghai Workers' Association (Shanghai gonghui lianhe hui), the "Three Armed Uprisings" in 1927, the Merchant Association in 1927, and so forth. Also Zhonggong Shanghai shiwei dangshi yanjiu shi, ed., *Shanghai kangri jiuwang shi* (Shanghai: Shanghai shehui kexue yuan chuban she, 1995), 351–399, 407–412. See also Zhonggong Shanghai shiwei dangshi ziliao zhengji weiyuan hui, ed., *"Yi er jiu" yihou Shanghai jiuguo hui shiliao xuanji* (Shanghai: Shanghai shehui kexue yuan chuban she, 1987).

2. Cheng Naishan, *Jinrong jia* (Shanghai: Shencheng wenyi chuban she, 1990). English translation and introduction by Britten Dean, *The Banker* (San Francisco: China Books and Periodicals, 1992).

3. Mao Dun, *Ziye* [*Midnight*] (Beijing: Renmin chuban she, 1977).

4. Cai Laixing, Zhang Guangsheng, and Xu Qiang, eds., *Shanghai: Chuangjian xin de guoji jingji zhongxin chengshi* (Shanghai: Shanghai renmin chuban she, 1995), 2.

5. This discussion is based on Cai Laixing et al., *Shanghai*. A later text discussing the specifics of Shanghai's development into a global financial center is Shanghai shi jinrong xuehui, ed., *Lun xin shiji Shanghai guoji jinrong zhongxin jianshe* (Shanghai: Shanghai sanlian shudian, 2002.)

6. Cai Laixing et al., *Shanghai*, 5.

7. Ibid., 4.

8. Ibid.124–125.

9. Ibid.

10. Ibid. 244.

11. Shanghai "jiuwu" shehui fazhan wenti sikao keti zu, *Shanghai kua shiji shehui fazhan wenti sikao* (Shanghai: Shanghai shehui kexue yuan chuban she, 1997).

12. Shanghai "jiuwu," *Shanghai kua shiji*, 168. On urban neighborhood collective enterprises see Zhonggong Shanghai shiwei bangong ting shiqu chu, ed., *Chengshi jiedao banshi chu jumin weiyuan hui gongzuo shouce* (Shanghai: Shanghai renmin chuban she, 1988); Beijing shi renshi ju and Beijing shi xicheng qu renshi ju, eds., *Chengshi jiezheng guanli* (Beijing: Zhongguo gongren chuban she,

1990); Quanguo bufen chengshi jiedao tizhi gaige di wu ci tantao hui mishu chu, ed., *Jiedao gongzuo yu gaige: quanguo bufen chengshi jiedao tizhi gaige di wu ci tantao hui wenji* (Jinan, Shandong: Xinwen chuban ju, 1990); and Beijing shi Haidian qu zhengfu jiedao gongzuo bangong shi, *Haidian qu jiedao gongzuo yanjiu* (Beijing: Haidian qu jiedao gongzuo bangong shi, *neibu faxing,*1991). Urban reform moved up in scope and scale structurally and conceptually in the 1990s. See Zhou Yihu and Yang Xiaomin, *Zhongguo danwei zhidu* (Beijing: Zhongguo jingji chuban she, 1999).

13. The Institute of History, Shanghai Academy of Social Sciences has been a major force behind the development of an entire field of Shanghai historical studies in China. Between the late 1980s and the late 1990s it hosted several major international conferences on the urban history of the city. It regularly publishes the *Shanghai yanjiu luncong* (Papers on Shanghai Studies) and *Shanghai shi* (Shanghai History) and acts as an academic host facilitating research projects undertaken by international scholars and students. Research findings were written and compiled, in 1999, into a monumental fifteen-volume *Shanghai tongshi* (General History of Shanghai). Under the general editorship of Xiong Yuezhi, then director of the Institute of History, the project pooled the contributions of three generations of institute researchers and encompassed the entire span of Shanghai history from antiquity to the late twentieth century. Each volume, with text, graphs, illustrations, notes, and bibliography, comes to nearly six hundred pages. The volumes add up to a richly textured and comprehensively conceptualized representation of the modern and contemporary development of the city based on a wealth of empirical materials. Published by the Shanghai People's Publishing House in 1999, it was presented as the academy's contribution in celebration of the fiftieth anniversary of the founding of the People's Republic. Important works on Shanghai history are also carried out at Fudan University, Eastern China Normal University, the Office for the Compilation of Shanghai Local Gazetteer, and the Shanghai Municipal Archives.

14. The groundbreaking work in this regard is Zhang Zhongli, ed., *Jindai Shanghai chengshi yanjiu* (Shanghai: Shanghai renmin chuban she, 1990). The volume contains twenty chapters and includes contributions from researchers of the Institutes of History and Economics of the Shanghai Academy of Social Sciences. Significant interpretive themes in this volume have been anticipated in Tang Zhenchang, ed., *Shanghai shi* (Shanghai: Shanghai renmin chuban she, 1989), which forcefully argues in favor of the hybrid quality of Shanghai culture.

15. For a quick overview of major shifts in economic thinking that developed in Shanghai from 1978 to 1998 see Shanghai shehui kexue yuan, ed., *Shanghai shehui kexue yuan jingxuan zhuzuo jianjie, 1958–1998* (Shanghai: Shanghai shehui kexue yuan chuban she, 1998), 77–269.

16. Ibid., 83–84.

17. A selected sample of the growing body of significant works along these interpretive lines include Xiong Yuezhi, *Zhongguo jindai minzhu sixiang shi* (Shanghai: Renmin chuban she, 1986); Xiong Yuezhi, *Xixue dongjian yu wan Qing shehui* (Shanghai: Renmin chuban she, 1994); Du Xuncheng, *Minzu ziben zhuyi yu jiu Zhongguo zhengfu (1840–1937)* (Shanghai: Shanghai shehui kexue chuban she, 1990); Xu Dingxin and Qian Xiaoming, *Shanghai zong shanghui*

shi (1902–1929) (Shanghai: Shanghai shehui kexue yuan chuban she, 1991); Luo Suwen, *Nüxing yu jindai Zhongguo shehui* (Shanghai: Renmin chuban she, 1996); Zheng Zu'an, *Bainian Shanghai cheng* (Shanghai: Xuelin chuban she, 1999); Zhou Yumin, *Wan Qing caizheng yu shehui bianqian* (Shanghai: Renmin chuban she, 2000); and Li Changli, *Wan Qing Shanghai shehui de bianqian: shenghuo yu lunli de jindai hua* (Tianjin: Tianjin renmin chuban she, 2002).

    18. Wang Anyi, *Changhen ge* (Beijing: Zuojia chuban she, 1996).

    19. Ibid., 190.

    20. Edward S. Krebs, "Old in the Newest New China: Photographic History, Private Memories and Individual Views of History," *The Chinese Historical Review* 11, no. 1 (Spring 2004): 87–116.

    21. Wang Anyi, *Changhen ge,* 3–4.

    22. Gu Zhun, *Gu Zhun riji,* ed. Chen Minzhi and Ding Dong (Beijing: Jingji ribao chuban she, 1997); Gu Zhun, *Gu Zhun wengao,* ed. Chen Minzhi and Gu Nanjiu (Beijing: Zhongguo qingnian chuban she, 2002); Gu Zhun, *Gu Zhun zishu* (Beijing: Zhongguo qingnian chuban she, 2002); Gu Zhun, *Gu Zhun biji* (Beijing: Zhongguo qingnian chuban she, 2002); and Gao Jianguo, *Chaixia legu dang huoba—Gu Zhun quan zhuan* (Shanghai: Shanghai wenyi chuban she, 2000).

    23. Pan Xulun and Gu Zhun, *Zhongguo zhengfu kuaiji zhidu* (Shanghai: Lixin kuaiji tushi yongpin she, 1941; revised 1944).

    24. Gu Zhun, "Shi lun shehui zhuyi zhidu xia de shangpin shengchan he jiazhi guilu" [On merchandise production and the laws of value under socialism], *Jingji yanjiu* [Economic research] no. 3 (1957).

    25. Gu Zhun, *Cong lixiang zhuyi dao jingyan zhuyi* (Taipei: Shulin, 1994), viii.

Bibliography

Ai Siqi. "Tian xiaode." *Dushu shenghuo* 2, no. 1 (May 1935): 27–28.

Alitto, Guy. *The Last Confucian: Liang Shu-ming and the Chinese Dilemma of Modernity.* Berkeley: University of California Press, 1979.

Andrews, Julia. "Judging a Book by Its Cover: Book Cover Design in Shanghai." Paper presented at the annual meeting of the Association for Asian Studies, Chicago, March 14, 1997.

Bai Wei. "Wo toudao wenxue quan de chuzhong." In *Minguo cainü meiwen ji,* Vol. 1, edited by Lan Yunyue, 146–156. Beijing: Yanshan chuban she, 1995.

Zhongguo yinhang hangyuan shouce [Bank of China Employee Handbook]. Number Two State Archives, Nanjing.

Bao Wenzao. "Wo duiyu zhiwu diaoyi zhi ganxiang ji gongzuo jingguo de xingqu" [My thoughts on job transfer and interest in such work experience]. *Zhonghang shenghuo,* no. 25 (April 1, 1934): 565.

Baoyi. "Lixiang de jiating." *Shenghuo zhoukan* 2, no. 7 (December 5, 1926): 42.

Beijing shi Haidian qu zhengfu jiedao gongzuo bangong shi. *Haidian qu jiedao gongzuo yanjiu.* Beijing: Haidian qu jiedao gongzuo bangong shi, neibu faxing, 1991.

Beijing shi renshi ju, and Beijing shi xicheng qu renshi ju, eds. *Chengshi jiezheng guanli.* Beijing: Zhongguo gongren chuban she, 1990.

Bellah, Robert. *Tokugawa Religion: The Values of Pre-Industrial Japan.* Glencoe, IL: Free Press, 1957.

Benson, Carlton. "From Teahouse to Radio: Storytelling and the Commercialization of Culture in 1930s Shanghai." PhD diss., University of California, Berkeley, 1996.

———. "Story-Telling and Radio Shanghai," *Republican China* 20, no. 2 (April 1995): 117–146.

Berger, Peter. *In Search of an East Asian Development Model.* New Brunswick, NJ: Transaction Books, 1988.

Bergère, Marie-Claire. *The Golden Age of the Chinese Bourgeoisie, 1911–1937.* Translated by Janet Lloyd. Cambridge, U.K.: Cambridge University Press, 1989.

———. "The Purge in Shanghai: The Sarly Affair and the End of the French Concession, 1945–1946." In *Wartime Shanghai,* edited by Wen-hsin Yeh, 157–178. London: Routledge, 1998.

Bernhardt, Kathryn. "Women and the Law: Divorce in the Republican Period." Paper prepared for the Conference on Civil Law in Chinese Society, University of California at Los Angeles, August 1991.

Berninghausen, John. "Mao Dun's Early Fiction, 1927–1931: The Standpoint and Style of His Realism," PhD diss., Stanford University, 1980.

Bi Yuncheng. "Huiwei." *Shenghuo* 3, no. 34 (July 8, 1928): 381–386.

———. "Qingnian zhi chenggong." *Shenghuo* 2, no.11 (January 16, 1927): 65–66.

———. "Yige fuche." *Shenghuo* 3, no. 12 (January 22, 1928): 129–130.

———. "Yige heyu lixiang de jiating." *Shenghuo* 3, no. 8 (December 25, 1927): 81.

Bianzhe. "Ruhe chushi." *Shenghuo* 2, no. 10 (December 26, 1926): 60.

———. "Tianmei de chenghu." *Shenghuo* 4, no. 31 (June 30, 1929): 347.

———. "Women lianxi Huang Huiru nüshi." *Shenghuo* 4, no. 3 (December 2, 1928): 24–26; 4, no. 4 (December 9, 1928): 36–38.

———. "Xiao quezi yao renshi shijie le." *Dushu shenghuo* 2, no. 4 (June 1935): 152–156.

———. "Zheng zai ci, zhongzhong nan kan chu." *Shenghuo* 2, no. 8 (December 12, 1926): 50.

———. *Zhongguo yinhang Shanghai fenhang shi, 1912–1949* [History of the Shanghai Branch of the Bank of China, 1912–1949]. Shanghai: Jingji kexue chuban she, 1991.

Bickers, Robert. "Settlers and Diplomats: The End of the British Hegemony in the International Settlement, 1937–1945." In *In the Shadow of the Rising Sun: Shanghai under Japanese Occupation,* edited by Christian Henriot and Wen-hsin Yeh, 229–256. New York: Cambridge University Press, 2004.

Bourdieu, Pierre. "Sport and Social Class." In *Rethinking Popular Culture: Contemporary Perspectives in Cultural Studies,* edited by Chandra Mukerji and Michael Schudson. Berkeley: University of California Press, 1991.

Brokaw, Cynthia J. *The Ledgers of Merit and Demerit: Social Change and Moral Order in Late Imperial China.* Princeton, N.J: Princeton University Press, 1991.

———. "Reading the Best-Sellers of the Nineteenth Century: Commercial Publishing in Sibao." In *Printing and Book Culture in Late Imperial China,* edited by Cynthia J. Brokaw and Kai-wing Chow, 184–231. Berkeley: University of California Press, 2005.

Brook, Timothy. "Collaborationist Nationalism in Occupied Wartime China." In *Nation Work: Asian Elites and National Identities,* edited by Timothy Brook and Andre Schmid, 159–190. Ann Arbor: University of Michigan Press, 2000.

———. "The Great Way Government of Shanghai." In *In the Shadow of the Rising Sun: Shanghai under Japanese Occupation,* edited by Christian Henriot and Wen-hsin Yeh, 157–186. New York: Cambridge University Press, 2004.

Brook, Timothy, and Robert Tadashi Wakabayashi, eds. *Opium Regimes: China, Britain, and Japan, 1839–1952.* Berkeley: University of California Press, 2000.

Bunker, Gerald E. *The Peace Conspiracy: Wang Ching-wei and the China War, 1937–1941.* Cambridge, MA: Harvard University Press, 1972.

Cai Laixing, Zhang Guangsheng, and Xu Qiang, eds., *Shanghai: Chuangjian xin de guoji jingji zhongxin chengshi.* Shanghai: Shanghai renmin chuban she, 1995.

Cai Xingtao. *Kangzhan qian de Zhonghua zhiye jiaoyu she, 1917–1937.* Taipei: Dongda tushu youxian gongsi, 1988.

Cai Xiyue. "Dakai Jinling nüda xiaokan kankan." *Shenghuo* 4, no. 31 (June 30, 1929): 348.

Cao Erlong. "Wo suo yujian de guke" [My experience with customers]. *Zhonghang shenghuo,* no. 16 (August 1, 1933): 319.

Cao Juren. *Beixing xiaoyu: yige xinwen jizhe yanzhong de xin Zhongguo.* Beijing: Sanlian shudian, 2002.

Cao Yu [Wan Jiabao]. *Richu* [Sunrise]. Shanghai: wenhua shenghuo chuban she, 1947.

Cao Zhibai. "Women yao zoushang xinlu qu" [We need to embark upon a new path]. *Zhonghang shenghuo,* no. 22 (January 15, 1934): 466.

Chandler, Alfred Dupont. *The Visible Hand: The Managerial Revolution in American Business.* Cambridge, MA: Harvard University Press, Belknap Press, 1977.

Chang, Iris. *The Rape of Nanjing: The Forgotten Holocaust of World War II.* New York: Basic Books, 1997.

Chang, Kia-ngau [Zhang Gongquan; Zhang Jia'ao]. *The Inflationary Spiral: The Experience in China, 1939–1950.* Cambridge, MA: MIT Technology Press, 1958.

Chang Yen-hsien, ed. *Zhongguo haiyang fazhan shi lunwen ji.* Taipei: Sun Yat-sen Institute of Philosophy and Social Sciences, Academia Sinica, 1997.

Chen, Joseph T. *The May Fourth Movement in Shanghai: The Making of a Social Movement in Modern China.* Boston: Brill, 1971.

Chen, Yung-fa. *Making Revolution: The Communist Movement in Eastern and Central China, 1937–1945.* Berkeley: University of California Press, 1986.

Chen Bingtie. "Xiwang fenzhi jiguan bianshe guo nei wai" [Hope to see branch offices all over the country and the world]. *Zhonghang shenghuo,* no. 22 (January 15, 1934): 466.

Chen Jiaxuan, ed. "Zixu." In *Shiyong shangye cidian.* Shanghai: Commercial Press, 1935.

Chen Ruilin. "'Yuefenpai' hua yu Haipai meishu." In *Haipai huihua yanjiu wenji,* edited by Shanghai shuhua chuban she, Shanghai: Shanghai shuhua chuban she, 2001.

Chen Xihe, and Wang Xiaoming. "'Chongxie wenxue shi' zhuanlan zhuchi ren de duihua." In *Shanghai wushi nian wenxue piping congshu,* vol. 4, edited by Xu Junxi, 127–153. Shanghai: Huadong shifan daxue chuban she, 1999.

Chen Yu-shih. *Realism and Allegory in the Early Fiction of Mao Tun.* Bloomington: Indiana University Press, 1985.

Chen Ziying, and Lin Jiahe, eds. *Shiji fenghua: Hongxi meishuguan cang haishang meishu bainian zhan (1840–1940)* [A Vibrant Century: Shanghai Painting (1840s–1940s) from the Chang Foundation]. Kaohsiung, Taiwan: Kaohsiung shili meishuguan, 2003.

Cheng Naishan. *The Banker.* Translated by Britten Dean. San Francisco: China Books & Periodicals, 1992.

———. *Jin rong jia.* Shanghai: Shanghai wenyi chuban she, 1990.

Chengshi jiedao tizhi gaige di wu ci tantao hui, ed., *Jiedao gongzuo yu gaige: quanguo bufen chengshi jiedao tizhi gaige di wu ci tantao hui wenji.* Ji'nan, Shandong: Xinwen chuban ju, 1990.

Chiang Monlin. *Tides from the West: A Chinese Autobiography.* New Haven, CN: Yale University Press, 1947.

Chow Tse-tsung. *The May Fourth Movement: Intellectual Revolution in Modern China.* Cambridge, MA: Harvard University Press, 1960.

Cipolla, Carlo M. *Clocks and Culture, 1300–1700.* New York: W. W. Norton, 1967.

Clark, Hugh R. *Community, Trade, and Networks: Southern Fujian Province from the Third to the Thirteenth Century.* Cambridge, New York: Cambridge University Press, 1991.

Clifford, Nicholas Rowland. *Shanghai, 1925: Urban Nationalism and the Defense of Foreign Privilege.* Ann Arbor: Center for Chinese Studies, University of Michigan, 1979.

———. *Spoilt Children of Empire: Westerners in Shanghai and the Chinese Revolution of the 1920s.* Hanover, NH: Middlebury College Press, 1991.

Clunas, Craig. *Pictures and Visuality in Early Modern China.* Princeton, NJ: Princeton University Press, 1997.

Coble, Parks M. "Chiang Kai-shek and the Anti-Japanese Movement in China: Zou Tao-fen and the National Salvation Association, 1931–1937." *Journal of Asian Studies* 44, no. 2 (February 1985): 293–310.

———. "Chinese Capitalists and the Japanese: Collaboration and Resistance in the Shanghai Area, 1937–1945." In *Wartime Shanghai,* edited by Wen-hsin Yeh, 62–85. New York: Routledge, 1998.

———. *Chinese Capitalists in Japan's New Order: The Occupied Lower Yangzi, 1937–1945.* Berkeley: University of California Press, 2003.

———. *Facing Japan: Chinese Politics and Japanese Imperialism, 1931–1937.* Cambridge, MA: Council on East Asian Studies, Harvard University, 1991.

———. *The Shanghai Capitalists and the Nationalist Government, 1927–1937.* Cambridge, MA: Council on East Asian Studies, Harvard University, 1980.

Cochran, Sherman. *Big Business in China: Sino-Foreign Rivalry in the Cigarette Industry, 1890–1930.* Cambridge, MA: Harvard University Press, 1980.

———. *Encountering Chinese Networks: Western, Japanese, and Chinese Corporations in China, 1880–1937.* Berkeley: University of California Press, 2000.

———, ed. *Inventing Nanjing Road: Commercial Culture in Shanghai, 1900–1945.* Ithaca, NY: East Asian Program, Cornell University, 1999.

———. "Marketing Medicine and Advertising Dreams in China, 1900–1950."

In *Becoming Chinese: Passages to Modernity and Beyond,* edited by Wen-hsin Yeh, 62–97. Berkeley: University of California Press, 2000.

———. "Three Roads into Shanghai's Market: Japanese, Western, and Chinese Companies in the Match Trade, 1895–1937." In *Shanghai Sojourners,* edited by Frederic Wakeman, Jr., and Wen-hsin Yeh, 35–75. Berkeley: Institute of East Asian Studies, University of California, 1992.

Cochran, Sherman, and Andrew C. K. Hsieh, trans. and eds., with Janis Cochran. *One Day in China: May 21, 1936.* New Haven: Yale University Press, 1983.

Cohn, Don J., trans. and ed. *Vignettes from the Chinese: Lithographs from Shanghai in the Late Nineteenth Century.* Hong Kong: Research Centre for Translation, Chinese University of Hong Kong, 1987.

Cornet, Christine. "The Bumpy End of the French Concession and French Influence in Shanghai, 1937–1946." In *In the Shadow of the Rising Sun: Shanghai under Japanese Occupation,* edited by Christian Henriot and Wen-hsin Yeh, 257–276. New York: Cambridge University Press, 2004.

Crossley, Pamela Kyle. *The Manchus.* Malden, MA: Blackwell, 2002.

———. *Orphan Warriors: Three Manchu Generations and the End of the Qing World.* Princeton, NJ: Princeton University Press, 1990.

Dai Ailu [Dai Zhiqian]. *Yinhang jia, yinhangyuan zuoyouming* [Rules of Thumb for Bankers and Bank Employees]. Shanghai, 1932.

Del Lago, Francesca. "How 'Modern' is the Modern Woman? Crossed Legs and Modernity in 1930s Shanghai Calendar Posters, Pictorial Magazines, and Cartoons." *East Asian History* 19 (2000): 103–144.

Deng Yikang. "Shanghai Xianshi gongsi chuangjian ren Huang Huan'nan." *Shanghai wenshi ziliao xuanji,* no. 48 (November 1984): 46–51.

Ding Hao. "Jiang yishu caihua fengxian ge shangye meishu." In *Lao Shanghai guanggao,* edited by Yi Bin, Liu Youming, and Gan Zhenhu, 13–17. Shanghai: Shanghai huabao chuban she, 1995.

Dong, Madeleine Yue. *Republican Beijing: The City and its Histories.* Berkeley: University of California Press, 2003.

Du Xuncheng. *Minzu ziben zhuyi yu jiu Zhongguo zhengfu, 1840–1937* [National Capitalism and the Chinese Ancien Régime]. Shanghai: Shanghai shehui kexue yuan chuban she, 1991.

Dushu shenghuo Vol. 2, no. 12. (October 1935): 511.

Duara, Prasenjit. *Rescuing History from the Nation: Questioning Narratives of Modern China.* Chicago: University of Chicago Press, 1995.

Eastman, Lloyd E. *Family, Fields, and Ancestors: Constancy and Change in China's Social and Economic History, 1550–1949.* New York: Oxford University Press, 1988.

———. *Seeds of Destruction: Nationalist China in War and Revolution, 1937–1949.* Stanford, CA: Stanford University Press, 1984.

Elliott, Mark C. *The Manchu Way: Eight Banners and Ethnic Identity in Late Imperial China.* Stanford, CA: Stanford University Press, 2001.

Elvin, Mark, and G. William Skinner, eds. *The Chinese City between Two Worlds.* Stanford, CA: Stanford University Press, 1974.

Enrun. "Gongzuo yu pinxing zhi guanxi." *Shenghuo zhoukan* 2, no. 2 (October 31, 1926): 8–9.

Erickson, Britta Lee. "Patronage and Production in the Nineteenth-Century Shanghai Region: Ren Xiong (1823–1857) and His Sponsors." PhD diss., Stanford University, 1977.

———. "Uncommon Themes and Uncommon Subject Matters in Ren Xiong's *Album after Poems by Yao Xie*." In *Visual Culture in Shanghai, 1850s–1930s,* edited by Jason Kuo, 29–54. Washington, D.C.: New Academia Publishing, 2007.

Fairbank, John K. "The Creation of the Treaty System." In *The Cambridge History of China,* vol. 10 part 1, edited by Denis Twichett and John K. Fairbank, 213–263. New York: Cambridge University Press, 1978.

———. "The Early Treaty System in the Chinese World Order." In *The Chinese World Order: Traditional China's Foreign Relations,* edited by John K. Fairbank, 257–275. Cambridge, MA: Harvard University Press, 1968.

———. "A Preliminary Framework." In *The Chinese World Order: Traditional China's Foreign Relations,* edited by John K. Fairbank, 1–19. Cambridge, MA: Harvard University Press, 1968.

———. *Trade and Diplomacy on the China Coast: The Opening of the Treaty Ports, 1842–1854.* Cambridge, MA: Harvard University Press, 1953.

Fei, Hsiao-tung. *China's Gentry: Essays on Rural-Urban Relations.* Chicago: University of Chicago Press, 1953.

Feuerwerker, Albert. *China's Early Industrialization: Sheng Hsuan-huai (1844–1916) and Mandarin Enterprise.* Cambridge, MA: Harvard University Press, 1958.

Fewsmith, Joseph. "In Search of the Shanghai Connection." *Modern China* 11, no. 1 (January 1985): 111–144.

———. *Party, State, and Local Elites in Republican China: Merchant Organizations and Politics in Shanghai, 1890–1930.* Honolulu: University of Hawaii Press, 1985.

Fogel, Joshua A. *Ai Ssu-ch'i's Contribution to the Development of Chinese Marxism.* Cambridge, MA: Council on East Asian Studies, Harvard University, 1987.

Friedman, Milton. *Money Mischief: Episodes in Monetary History.* New York: Harcourt Brace Jovanovich, 1992.

Fudan daxue xinwen xi yanjiu shi, ed. *Zou Taofen nianpu.* Shanghai: Fudan daxue chuban she, 1982.

Fu, Poshek. *Between Shanghai and Hong Kong: The Politics of Chinese Cinemas.* Stanford, CA: Stanford University Press, 2003.

———. *Passivity, Resistance, and Collaboration: Intellectual Choices in Occupied Shanghai, 1937–1945.* Stanford, CA: Stanford University Press, 1993.

Furth, Charlotte. "Intellectual Change: From the Reform Movement to the May Fourth Movement." In *An Intellectual History of Modern China* edited by Merle Goldman and Leo Ou-fan Lee, 13–96. New York: Cambridge University Press, 2002.

Galik, Marian. *Mao Tun and Modern Chinese Literary Criticism.* Wiesbaden, Germany: F. Steiner, 1969.

Gang Deng. *Maritime Sector, Institutions, and Sea Power in Premodern China.* Westport, CN: Greenwood Press, 1999.

Gao Jianguo. *Chaixia legu dang huo ba: Gu Zhun quanzhuan*. Shanghai: Shanghai wenyi chuban she, 2000.

Gardella, Robert. *Harvesting Mountains: Fujian and the Chinese Tea Trade, 1757–1937*. Berkeley: University of California Press, 1994.

Ge Yuanxu. *Hu you zaji*. Original preface in 1876. Reprinted Shanghai: Shanghai guji chuban she, 1998.

Gerth, Karl. *China Made: Consumer Culture and the Creation of the Nation*. Cambridge, MA: Harvard University Asia Center, 2003.

Giddens, Anthony. *A Contemporary Critique of Historical Materialism*. Vol. 1, *Power, Property, and the State*. Berkeley: University of California Press, 1981.

———. *The Consequences of Modernity*. Stanford, CA: Stanford University Press, 1990.

Glosser, Susan. "The Business of Family: You Huaigao and the Commercialization of a May Fourth Ideal," *Republican China* 20, no. 2 (April 1995): 55–79.

———. "The Business of Family." Paper presented at the Annual Meeting of the Association for Asian Studies, Boston, March 25–27, 1994.

———. *Chinese Visions of Family and State, 1915–1953*. Berkeley: University of California Press, 2003.

Goodman, Bryna. "Democratic Calisthenics: The Culture of Urban Associations in the New Republic." In *Changing Meanings of Citizenship in Modern China*, edited by Merle Goldman and Elizabeth J. Perry, 70–109. Cambridge, MA: Harvard University Press, 2002.

———. *Native Place, City, and Nation: Regional Networks and Identities in Shanghai, 1853–1937*. Berkeley: University of California Press, 1995.

Gu Fengshi. "Qiwang." *Dazhong shenghuo* 1, no. 2 (November 23, 1935): 62–64.

Gu Zhun. *Cong lixiang zhuyi dao jingyan zhuyi*. Taipei: Shulin, 1994.

———. *Gu Zhun biji*. Beijing: Zhongguo qingnian chuban she, 2002.

———. *Gu Zhun riji*. Edited by Chen Minzhi and Ding Dong. Beijing: Jingji ribao chuban she, 1997.

———. *Gu Zhun wengao*. Edited by Chen Minzhi and Gu Nanjiu. Beijing: Zhongguo qingnian chuban she, 2002.

———. *Gu Zhun zishu*. Beijing: Zhongguo qingnian chuban she, 2002.

———. "Shi lun shehui zhuyi zhidu xia de shangpin shengchan he jiazhi guilü." *Jingji yanjiu*, no. 3 (1957).

Gunn, Edward M. *Unwelcome Muse: Chinese Literature in Shanghai and Peking, 1937–1945*. New York: Columbia University Press, 1980.

Guo Qitao. *Exorcism and Money: The Symbolic World of the Five-Fury Spirits in Late Imperial China*. Berkeley: Institute of East Asian Studies, University of California at Berkeley, 2003.

Guo Songtao. *Guo Songtao riji*. 4 vols. Changsha: Hunan renmin chuban she, 1980–83.

Greenfeld, Leah. *The Spirit of Capitalism: Nationalism and Economic Growth*. Cambridge, MA: Harvard University Press, 2002.

Hamilton, Gary, ed. *Business Networks and Economic Development in East and Southeast Asia*. Hong Kong: Centre for Asian Studies, University of Hong Kong, 1991.

Hao Yen-ping. *The Commercial Revolution in Nineteenth-Century China: The*

Rise of Sino-Western Mercantile Capitalism. Berkeley: University of California Press, 1986.

———. *The Comprador in Nineteenth Century China: Bridge between East and West.* Cambridge, MA: Harvard University Press, 1970.

Harrison, Henrietta. *The Making of the Republican Citizen: Political Ceremonies and Symbols in China, 1911–1929.* New York: Oxford University Press, 2000.

Hayford, Charles Wishart. *To the People: James Yen and Village China.* New York: Columbia University Press, 1990.

He Qingru. "Zhiye xuexiao xuesheng chulu diaocha." *Jiaoyu yu zhiye,* no. 168 (October 1935): 535–554.

Hegel, Robert E. *The Novel in Seventeenth Century China.* New York: Columbia University Press, 1981.

Henriot, Christian. "Death in Shanghai." Paper presented at the conference on visual documentations, jointly organized by the Institut d'Asie Orientale, Lumiere-Lyon 2 University and the University of California at Berkeley, in Tokyo, September 2004.

———. "Shanghai Industries under Japanese Occupation: Bombs, Boom, and Bust, 1937–1945." In *In the Shadow of the Rising Sun: Shanghai under Japanese Occupation,* edited by Christian Henriot and Wen-hsin Yeh, 26–35. New York: Cambridge University Press, 2004.

———, ed. "Virtual Shanghai." http://virtualshanghai.ish-lyon.cnrs.fr/

Henriot, Christian, and Wen-hsin Yeh, eds., *In the Shadow of the Rising Sun: Shanghai under Japanese Occupation.* New York: Cambridge University Press, 2004.

Hershatter, Gail. *Dangerous Pleasures: Prostitution and Modernity in Twentieth-Century Shanghai.* Berkeley: University of California Press, 1997.

———. *The Workers of Tianjin, 1900–1949.* Stanford, CA: Stanford University Press, 1986.

Hevia, James. *Cherishing Men from Afar: Qing Guest Ritual and the Macartney Embassy of 1793.* Durham: Duke University Press, 1995.

Hietkamp, Lenore. "The Park Hotel, Shanghai, and its Architect Laszlo Hudec (1893–1958)" MA thesis, University of Victoria, 1989.

Hong Gengyang. "Kai hu yan zhi." *Shenghuo zhoukan* 2, no. 49 (October 9, 1927): 383–384.

Hong Jiaguan. "Minguo shiqi jinrong jigou zai shehui bianhua zhong de zuoyong." Paper presented at Luce Seminar on Modern Shanghai, University of California, Berkeley, March 6–7, 1992.

———. *Zai jinrongshi yuandi li manbu.* Beijing: Zhongguo jinrong chuban she, 1990.

Hong Jiaguan et al., *Zhongguo jinrong shi.* Chengdu: Xinan caijing chuban she, 1993.

Honig, Emily. *Sisters and Strangers: Women in the Shanghai Cotton Mills, 1919–1949.* Stanford, CA: Stanford University Press, 1986.

Hsu, Michael. "Domesticating the Foreign Western Women and Mixed Marriages in Republican China." MA thesis, University of California, Berkeley, 2007.

Hu Shi. "Shijian bu zhiqian." *Shenghuo zhoukan* 2, no. 7 (December 5, 1927): 43–44.

Hu Yaochang. "Shehui duiyu Huang nüshi he ruci zhi canku." *Shenghuo zhoukan* 4, no. 11 (January 27, 1929): 111–112.

Hu Yuzhi. "Pan Hannian tongzhi yu jiuguohui." In *"Yi er jiu" yihou Shanghai jiuguohui shiliao xuanji*, edited by Zhonggong Shanghai shiwei dangshi ziliao zhengji weiyuan hui, 386. Shanghai: Shanghai shehui kexue yuan chuban she, 1987.

Huang, Nicole. *Women, War, and Domesticity: Shanghai Literature and Popular Culture of the 1940s*. Boston: Brill, 2005.

Huang Dinghui. "Jianyi tongren fuli chujin." *Yinqianjie* 2, no. 4 (August 1938): 69.

Huang Yifeng et al. *Jiu Zhongguo minzu zichan jieji*. Nanjing: Jiangsu guji chuban she, 1990.

Hung, Chang-tai. *War and Popular Culture: Resistance in Modern China, 1937–1945*. Berkeley: University of California Press, 1994.

Hsu, Madeline Y. "Migration and Native Place: *Qiaokan* and the Imagined Community of Taishan County, Guangdong, 1893–1993." *Journal of Asian Studies* 59, no. 2 (May 2000): 312–317.

Idema, Wilt, and Lloyd Haft. *A Guide to Chinese Literature*. Ann Arbor: University of Michigan, 1997.

Israel, John. *Lianda: A Chinese University in War and Revolution*. Stanford, CA: Stanford University Press, 1998.

———. *Student Nationalism in China, 1927–1937*. Stanford, CA: Stanford University Press, 1966.

Israel, John, and Donald W. Klein. *Rebels and Bureaucrats: China's December 9ers*. Berkeley: University of California Press, 1976.

Johnson, Linda Cooke, ed. *Cities of Jiangnan in Late Imperial China*. Albany: State University of New York Press, 1993.

Ji Wen. *Shisheng*. Shanghai: Shanghai wenhua chuban she, 1958.

Jiao Daqiu. "Yige yonggong de shenghuo jilu." *Dushu shenghuo* 1, no. 3 (December 1934): 16–17.

Jiaoyu zazhi. Shanghai: Commercial Press, 1909–48. Reprinted in 80 volumes, Taipei: Commercial Press, 1975.

"Jianju Hanjian Li Ze." In *Shanghai baihuo ye zhigong yundong shiliao*, edited by Zhonggong Shanghai shiwei dangshi ziliao zhengji weiyuan hui, 93–99. Shanghai: 1986.

Jiang Mingqi. "Jingshang shibai de yuanyin." *Shanghai zong shanghui yuebao* 6, no. 1 (January 1926): 1–2.

Jin Manhui. "Yadian nei." *Dushu shenghuo* 1, no. 4 (December 1934): 16–17.

Jin Xuechen. Preface to *Lao Shanghai guanggao*, by Yi Bin, Liu Youming, and Gan Zhenhu. Shanghai: Shanghai huabao chuban she, 1995.

Jizhe. "Shangxin canmu." *Shenghuo zhoukan* 6, no. 42 (October 10, 1931): 913–914.

Karl, Rebecca E. *Staging the World: Chinese Nationalism at the Turn of the Twentieth Century*. Durham, NC: Duke University Press, 2002.

Keenan, Barry. *Imperial China's Last Classical Academies: Social Change in the Lower Yangzi, 1864–1911*. Berkeley, University of California Press, 1994.

Kern, Stephen. *The Culture of Time and Space, 1880–1918.* Cambridge, MA: Harvard University Press, 1983.

King, Frank H. H. *A Concise Economic History of Modern China (1840–1961).* New York: Praeger, 1969.

King, Frank H. H., with Catherine E. King and David J. S. King. *The History of the Hongkong and Shanghai Banking Corporation.* 4 vols. New York: Cambridge University Press, 1987–1991.

Kirby, William C. "China Unincorporated: Company Law and Business Enterprise in Twentieth-Century China." *Journal of Asian Studies* 54, no. 1 (February 1995): 43–63.

———. "Engineering China: Birth of the Developmental State, 1928–1937." In *Becoming Chinese: Passages to Modernity and Beyond,* edited by Wen-hsin Yeh, 137–160. Berkeley: University of California Press, 2000.

———. *Germany and Republican China.* Stanford, CA: Stanford University Press, 1984.

Koll, Elizabeth. *From Cotton Mill to Business Empire: The Emergence of Regional Enterprises in Modern China.* Cambridge, MA: Harvard University Asia Center, 2003.

Krebs, Edward S. "Old in the Newest New China: Photographic History, Private Memories and Individual Views of History." *The Chinese Historical Review* 11, no. 1 (Spring 2004): 87–116.

Ku Hung-ting. *Urban Mass Movement: The May Thirtieth Movement in Shanghai.* Taipei: Institute of Three Principles of the People, Academia Sinica, 1983.

Kuhn, Philip A. *Rebellion and its Enemies in Late Imperial China: Militarization and Social Structure, 1796–1864.* Cambridge, MA: Harvard University Press, 1970.

Kuo, Ting-yee. "Self-Strengthening: The Pursuit of Western Technology." In *The Cambridge History of China,* vol. 10, pt. 1, edited by Denis Twichett and John K. Fairbank, 491–542. New York: Cambridge University Press, 1978.

Kwan, Man Bun. *The Salt Merchants of Tianjin: State-making and Civil Society in Late Imperial China.* Honolulu: University of Hawaii Press, 2001.

Laing, Ellen Johnston. *Selling Happiness: Calendar Posters and Visual Culture in Early Twentieth-Century Shanghai.* Honolulu: University of Hawaii Press, 2004.

Lan. "Wo suo xiwang benhang shixian de jijian shi." *Zhonghang shenghuo,* no. 22 (January 15, 1934): 474–475.

Landes, David S. *Revolution in Time: Clocks and the Making of the Modern World.* Cambridge, MA: Harvard University Press, 1983.

Lao Yan. "Kan *Richu*" [Watching *Sunrise*]. *Yinqianjie* 2, no. 12 (December 1938): 245.

le Goff, Jacques. *Time, Work, and Culture in the Middle Ages.* Translated by Arthur Goldhammer. Chicago: University of Chicago Press, 1980.

Lee, Leo Ou-fan. "In Search of Modernity: Some Reflections on a New Mode of Consciousness in Twentieth Century Chinese History and Literature." In *Ideas Across Cultures: Essays on Chinese Thought in Honor of Benjamin I. Schwartz,* edited by Paul A. Cohen and Merle Goldman, 109–135. Cambridge, MA: Council on East Asian Studies, Harvard University, 1990.

———. *Shanghai Modern: The Flowering of a New Urban Culture in China, 1930–1945*. Cambridge, MA: Harvard University Press, 1999.

———. *Voices from the Iron House: A Study of Lu Xun*. Bloomington: Indiana University Press, 1987.

Lee, Leo Ou-fan, and Andrew Nathan. "The Beginnings of Mass Culture: Journalism and Fiction in the Late Ch'ing and Beyond." In *Popular Culture in Late Imperial China*, edited by David Johnson, Andrew J. Nathan, and Evelyn S. Rawski, 360–417. Berkeley: University of California Press, 1985.

Leonard, Jane Kate. *Wei Yuan and China's Rediscovery of the Maritime World*. Cambridge, MA: Council on East Asian Studies, Harvard University, 1984.

Levenson, Joseph R. *Confucian China and Its Modern Fate: The Problem of Intellectual Continuity*. Berkeley: University of California Press, 1958.

———. *Confucian China and Its Modern Fate: The Problem of Monarchical Decay*. Berkeley: University of California Press, 1964.

Li, Lillian M. *China's Silk Trade: Traditional Industry in the Modern World, 1842–1937*. Cambridge, MA: Council on East Asian Studies, Harvard University, 1981.

Li Boyuan. *Wenming xiaoshi* [A Short History of Civilization]. Beijing: Tongsu wenyi chuban she, 1955.

Li Changli. *Wan Qing Shanghai shehui de bianqian: shenghuo yu lunli de jindai hua*. Tianjin: Tianjin renmin chuban she, 2002.

Li Chongji. "Zenyang yanjiu zhexue." *Dushu shenghuo* 2, no.1 (May 1935): 19.

Li Chunkang. "Shanghai de gaodeng jiaoyu." In *Shanghai shi tongzhi guan qikan*, 618. Shanghai: Shanghai tongzhi guan, 1934.

Li Fanfu. "Guanyu yijiusanwu hou yijiusanqi qian Shanghai dixiadang douzheng de yixie qingkuang." In *"Yi er jiu" yihou Shanghai jiuguohui shiliao xuanji*, edited by Zhonggong Shanghai shiwei dangshi ziliao zhengji weiyuan hui, 379–80. Shanghai: Shanghai shehui kexue yuan chuban she, 1987.

Li Gongpu. "Quan Zhongguo zhiyou yizhong guoqi le." *Shenghuo zhoukan* 4, no. 17 (March 24, 1929): 174.

———. "Zenyang jinian sige weidai de rizi." *Dushu shenghuo* 2, no. 1 (May 1935): 1.

Li Guochong. "Ying peng ying." *Shenghuo zhoukan* 4, no. 6 (December 23, 1928): 59.

Li Jilu. "Wo duiyu tongren de liangju hua." *Zhonghang shenghuo* 1, no. 5 (September 15, 1932): 82.

Li Jin. "Wuren yingdang xingcha ziji de bingtai" [We ought to examine our own shortcomings]. *Zhonghang shenghuo*, no. 12 (April 15, 1933): 233.

Li Tang. "Art for the Market. Commercialism in Ren Yi's (1840–1895) Figure Painting." MA thesis, University of Maryland, 2003.

Li Ti. "Muke teji." *Dushu shenghuo* 3, no. 1 (November 1935): 31.

Li Wenquan. Interview with author. Shanghai, January 12, 1991.

Li Yunliang. "Gongsi zhidu yu xinshi kuaiji zhi guanxi." *Shanghai zong shanghui yuebao* 5, no. 4 (April 1925): 4–6.

Li Xiu, ed. *Mao Dun yanjiu zai guowai*. Changsha: Hunan renmin chuban she, 1984.

Liang Ziqi. "Yanlun de lichang he taidu." *Dazhong Shenghuo*, no. 6 (June 21, 1941): 140–143.

Liangyou huabao [The Young Companion]. Shanghai: Shanghai shudian, reprinted 1986. (Original: Shanghai: Liangyou yinshua gongsi, Feb. 1926–Oct. 1945)

Lin Man-houng. *China Upside Down: Currency, Society, and Ideologies, 1808–1856.* Cambridge, MA: Harvard University Press, 2006.

Link, Perry. *Mandarin Ducks and Butterflies: Popular Fiction in Early Twentieth-Century Chinese Cities.* Berkeley: University of California Press, 1981.

Liu Kwang-ching. "Tang Tingshu zhi maiban shidai" [Tang Tingshu: Comprador years]. In *Jingshi sixiang yu xinxing qiye* [Statecraft thinking and new-style enterprises], edited by Liu Kwang-ching, 327–400. Taipei: Lianjing chuban shiye gongsi, 1990.

———. "Wan Qing dufu quanli wenti shangque" [The power of the governors-general in late Qing]. In *Jingshi sixiang yu xinxing qiye*, edited by Liu Kwang-ching, 247–293. Taipei: Lianjing chuban shiye gongsi, 1990.

———. *Anglo-American Steamship Rivalry in China, 1862–1874.* Cambridge, MA: Harvard University Press, 1962.

Liu Ti. "Tong gui yu jin." *Dushu shenghuo* 2, no. 4 (June 1935): 135–136.

Lou Chenghao. *Lao Shanghai shikumen.* Shanghai: Tongji daxue, 2004.

Lu Guiliang, "Tian ye zuo shenghuo." *Dushu shenghuo* 2, no. 4 (June 1935).

Lu Hanchao. *Beyond the Neon Lights: Everyday Shanghai in the Early Twentieth Century.* Berkeley: University of California Press, 1999.

Lu Zhiren. "Guanyu Shanghai zhiye jie jiuguo hui de yixie qingkuang." In *"Yi er jiu" yihou Shanghai jiuguohui shiliao xuanji*, edited by Zhonggong Shanghai shiwei dangshi ziliao zhengji weiyuan hui, 417–418. Shanghai: Shanghai shehui kexue yuan chuban she, 1987.

Luo Suwen. *Da Shanghai: Shikumen, xunchang renjia* [Greater Shanghai: *Shikumen*, homes of ordinary households]. Shanghai: Shanghai renmin chuban she, 1991.

———. *Nüxing yu jindai Zhongguo shehui.* Shanghai: Shanghai renmin chuban she, 1996.

Luo Yijun. "Nanshi nanmin qu shulue," *Shanghai wenshi ziliao xuanji*, no. 51 (April 1985): 172.

Luoxia. "Fanhua Shanghai zhong de qijian zhe." *Shenghuo* 3, no. 33 (July 1, 1928): 371–373.

Ma Min. *Guan shang zhi jian: shehui jubian zhong de shenshang.* Wuhan: Huazhong shifan daxue chuban she, 2003.

Mann, Susan. *Local Merchants and the Chinese Bureaucracy, 1750–1950.* Stanford, CA: Stanford University Press, 1987.

Mann Jones, Susan. "The Ningpo Pang and Financial Power at Shanghai." In *The Chinese City between Two Worlds*, edited by Mark Elvin and G. William Skinner, 73–96. Stanford, CA: Stanford University Press, 1974.

Mao Dun. *Zi ye* [Midnight]. Beijing: Renmin wenxue chuban she, 1977.

Mao Jindao. "Fumu cuihun shenji." *Shenghuo zhoukan* 3, no. 33 (July 1, 1928): 377–378.

Martin, Brian G. "'The Pact with the Devil': The Relationship between the Green Gang and the Shanghai French Concession Authorities, 1925–1935." In *Shanghai Sojourners*, edited by Frederic Wakeman, Jr. and Wen-hsin Yeh, 266–304. Berkeley: Institute of East Asian Studies, University of California, 1992.

———. *The Shanghai Green Gang: Politics and Organized Crime, 1919–1937.* Berkeley: University of California Press, 1996.

McElderry, Andrea Lee. *Shanghai Old-style Banks (Chi'en-chuang), 1800–1935: A Traditional Institution in a Changing Society.* Ann Arbor: Center for Chinese Studies, University of Michigan, 1976.

Mengsheng. "Jiujiu wo jiejie de xingming." *Shenghuo zhoukan* 3, no. 40 (August 19, 1928): 476–477.

Meštrović, Stjepan G. *Anthony Giddens: The Last Modernist.* New York: Routledge, 1998.

Mickey, Georgia. "The Politics of Reform: the Bank of China and Its Shareholders, 1904–1916." PhD diss., Columbia University, 2004.

Miller, Michael Barry. *The Bon Marché: Bourgeois Culture and the Department Store, 1869–1920.* Princeton, NJ: Princeton University Press, 1981.

Min Zhishi. "Kexue de guanli." *Shanghai zong shanghui yuebao* 5, no. 3 (March 1925): 1–3.

Murray, Julia K. "Didactic Illustrations in Printed Books." In *Printing and Book Culture in Late Imperial China,* edited by Cynthia J. Brokaw and Kai-wing Chow, 417–450. Berkeley: University of California Press, 2005.

Myers, Ramon H., ed. *Selected Essays in Chinese Economic Development.* New York: Garland Publishing, 1980.

Najita, Tetsuo. *Visions of Virtue in Tokugawa Japan: The Kaitokudo Merchant Academy of Osaka.* Chicago: University of Chicago Press, 1987.

Naquin, Susan. *Peking: Temples and City Life, 1400–1900.* Berkeley: University of California Press, 2000.

Nathan, Andrew. *Peking Politics, 1918–1923: Factionalism and the Failure of Constitutionalism.* Berkeley: University of California Press, 1976.

Ong, Aihwa. *Flexible Citizenship: The Cultural Logics of Transnationality.* Durham, NC: Duke University Press, 1999.

Orrù, Marco, Nicole Woolsey Biggart, and Gary G. Hamilton, eds. *The Economic Organization of East Asian Capitalism.* Thousand Oaks, CA: Sage Publications, 1997.

Pan Xulun, and Gu Zhun. *Zhongguo zhengfu kuaiji zhidu.* Shanghai: Lixin kuaiji tushu yongpin she, 1941. Reprint 1944.

Pang Pu. *Tan maodun de pubian xing he teshu xing.* Beijing: Tongsu duwu chuban she, 1956.

Pei Wei. "Kan le *Richu* yi hou" [After viewing *Sunrise*]. *Yinqianjie* 2, no. 12 (December 1938): 247.

Pei Yunqing. "Di san jie huiyuan dahui de shiming he fazhan" [The mission and future of the third annual membership meeting]. *Yinqianjie* 2, no. 1 (June 12, 1938): 1.

Peiguan. "Huhang tongren gongyu shenghuo xiezhen" [A realistic depiction of after-work life at the Shanghai branch]. *Zhonghang shenghuo,* no.16 (August 1933): 327–329.

Perry, Elizabeth. *Shanghai on Strike: The Politics of Chinese Labor.* Stanford, CA: Stanford University Press, 1993.

Pingzi. "Sanshi yu danwei huiyuan jiaoyi dahui texie" [Special report on the friendship gathering of members of thirty-some *danwei*]. *Yinqianjie* 2, no. 10 (November 1, 1938): 195.

Po Sung-nien, and David Johnson, eds. *Domesticated Deities and Auspicious Emblems: The Iconography of Everyday Life in Village China*. Berkeley: Chinese Popular Culture Project, University of California, 1992.

Prazniak, Roxanne. "Weavers and Sorceresses of Chuansha: The Social Origins of Political Activism among Rural Chinese Women." *Modern China* 12, no. 2 (April 1986): 202–229.

Pudong kaifa [Pudong development]. Shanghai: Pudong kaifa zazhi she.

Qian Junrui. "Jiuguohui nei de dang zuzhi qingkuang." In *"Yi er jiu" yihou Shanghai jiuguo hui shiliao xuanji*, edited by Zhonggong Shanghai shiwei dangshi ziliao zhengji weiyuan hui, 387. Shanghai: Shanghai shehui kexue yuan chuban she, 1987.

Qian Yishi. "Siyue houbanyue de guoji dashi." *Dushu shenghuo* 2, no. 1 (May 1935): 4.

Qian Zhuanggong. "Nongcun shenghuo jiyi gailiang zhi qian." *Shenghuo zhoukan* 2, no. 1 (October 24, 1926): 4–5.

Qiao Ying. "Fa gongqian de yitian." *Dushu shenghuo* 2, no. 2 (May 1935): 73–74.

Qiu Wenzhi, and Han Yinting, eds. *Mao Dun yanjiu liushi nian*. Tianjin: Tianjin jiaoyu chuban she, 1990.

Qiuxing. "Women jinri suo zui xuyao de shi shenme?" *Shenghuo zhoukan* 4, no. 15 (March 10, 1929): 148.

Rankin, Mary Backus. *Early Chinese Revolutionaries: Radical Intellectuals in Shanghai and Chekiang, 1902–1911*. Cambridge, MA: Harvard University Press, 1971.

——. *Elite Activism and Political Transformation in China: Zhejiang Province, 1865–1911*. Stanford, CA: Stanford University Press, 1986.

Rankin, Mary Backus, John K. Fairbank, and Albert Feuerwerker. "Introduction: Perspectives on Modern China's History." In *The Cambridge History of China*, vol. 13, *Republican China*, edited by John K. Fairbank and Albert Feuerwerker, 1–73. Cambridge: Cambridge University Press, 1986.

Rawski, Evelyn. *Agricultural Change and the Peasant Economy of South China*. Cambridge, MA: Harvard University Press, 1972.

——. *Education and Popular Literacy in Ch'ing China*. Ann Arbor: University of Michigan Press, 1979.

Reed, Christopher A. *Gutenberg in Shanghai: Chinese Print Capitalism, 1876–1937*. Honolulu: University of Hawaii Press, 2004.

Rothschild, Emma. *Economic Sentiments: Adam Smith, Condorcet, and the Enlightenment*. Cambridge, MA: Harvard University Press, 2001.

Rottmann, Allison, "Resistance, Urban Style: The New Fourth Army and Shanghai, 1937–1945," PhD diss., University of California, Berkeley, 2007.

——. "Crossing Enemy Lines: Shanghai and the Central China Base." In *In the Shadow of the Rising Sun*, edited by Henriot and Yeh. 90–115. New York: Cambridge University Press, 2004.

Rowe, William T. *Hankow: Commerce and Society in a Chinese City, 1796–1889*. Stanford, CA: Stanford University Press, 1984.

————. *Hankow: Conflict and Community in a Chinese City, 1796–1895.* Stanford, CA: Stanford University Press, 1989.

Rujivacharakul, Vimalin. "Architects as Cultural Heroes." In *Cities in Motion*, edited by Sherman Cochran, David Strand, and Wen-hsin Yeh. Berkeley: Institute of East Asian Studies Publications, University of California, 2007.

Sawyer, John Birge. Diaries, volume 6. Bancroft Library, University of California, Berkeley. Transcribed by Robert Bodde, September 2004.

Schneider, Helen. "Home Economics and its American Connections: The Case of Yenching University in the 1920s." Paper presented at the conference on the American Context of China's Christian Colleges, Wesleyan University, September 5–7, 2003.

————. "Keeping the Nation's Home: Domesticity and Home Economics in Republican China." PhD diss., University of Washington, 2004.

Schwartz, Benjamin. "The Chinese Perception of World Order, Past and Present," in *The Chinese World Order: Traditional China's Foreign Relations*, edited by John K. Fairbank, 276–288. Cambridge, MA: Harvard University Press, 1968.

————. *In Search of Wealth and Power: Yen Fu and the West.* Cambridge, MA: Harvard University Press, Belknap Press, 1964.

Schwintzer, Ernest P. "Education to Save the Nation: Huang Yanpei and the Educational Reform Movement in Early Twentieth Century China." PhD diss., University of Washington, 1992.

Shanghai baihuo gongsi, Shanghai shehui kexueyuan jingji yanjiu suo, and Shanghai shi gongshang xingzheng guanli ju, eds. *Shanghai jindai baihuo shangye shi.* Shanghai: Shanghai shehui kexue yuan chuban she, 1988.

Shanghai gonggong zujie shigao. Shanghai: Renmin chuban she, 1980.

Shanghai "jiuwu" shehui fazhan wenti sikao keti zu. *Shanghai kua shiji shehui fazhan wenti sikao.* Shanghai: Shanghai shehui kexue yuan chuban she, 1997.

Shanghai Library, ed. *Lao Shanghai: Jianzhu xunmeng juan.* Shanghai: Shanghai wenhua chuban she, 1998.

Shanghai lishi bowuguan, ed. *Shanghai bainian lüeying, 1840s–1940s* [Survey of Shanghai 1840s–1940s]. Shanghai: Shanghai renmin meishu chuban she, 1992.

Shanghai Lu Xun jinian guan, and Jiangsu guji chuban she, eds. *Banhua jicheng: Lu Xun cang Zhongguo xiandai muke quanji.* Nanjing: Jiangsu guji chuban she, 1991.

Shanghai Municipal Archives, Min-31-Su-Gong-832, Min-31-Su-Gong-390.

Shanghai Qingnian (Shanghai youth), 1939.

Shanghai shehui kexue yuan, ed. *Shanghai shehui kexue yuan jingxuan zhuzuo jianjie, 1958–1998.* Shanghai: Shanghai shehui kexue yuan chuban she, 1998.

Shanghai shehui kexue yuan jingji yanjiu suo, ed. *Shanghai Yong'an gongsi de chansheng, fazhan he gaizao.* Shanghai: Shanghai renmin chuban she, 1981.

Shanghai shi dang'an guan, ed. *Ri wei Shanghai shi zhengfu.* Beijing: Dang'an chuban she, 1986.

————, ed. *Wu san yundong.* Shanghai: Shanghai renmin chuban she, 1991.

Shanghai shi jinrong xuehui, ed. *Lun xin shiji Shanghai guoji jinrong zhongxin jianshe.* Shanghai: Shanghai sanlian shudian, 2002.

"Shanghai shi yinqianye yeyu lianyihui chengli sanzhounian jinian ji diwujie huiyuan dahui tekan" [Special issue on the third anniversary of the Shanghai banking and *qianzhuang* after-work friendship association and the fifth membership meeting], published on October 29, 1939.

Shanghai Yong'an baihuo gongsi dang'an. "Bugao" [Bulletin announcements]. Shanghai Municipal Archives (SMA), Q-235, 1937.

Shanghai Yong'an baihuo gongsi dang'an. "Gebu zhiyuan chengji baogao zongbiao ji geji baogao biao, 1939." SMA, O-225-2-101.

Shanghai Yong'an baihuo gongsi dang'an. "Renshi xinhan" [Personnel affairs, internal correspondence]. SMA, Q-235, 1937–38.

Shanghai Yong'an baihuo gongsi dang'an. "Nanjing lu shangjie lianhe hui han Yong An." SMA, Q225-2-49, March 28, 1939.

Shanghai Yong'an baihuo gongsi dang'an. "Quanti tongren shangshu." SMA, Q225-2-46, August 8, 1938, August 25, 1940, April 1, 1941.

Shanghai zong shanghui yuebao 5, no. 5. "Duzhe luntan," (May 1925): 3.

Shangren tongli, 1914.

Shangwu kaocha bao, no.1–3 (October 1907).

Shangye bu baihuo ju, ed. *Zhongguo baihuo shangye.* Beijing: Beijing daxue chuban she, 1989.

Sheehan, Brett. *Trust in Troubled Times: Money, Banks, and State-society Relations in Republican Tianjin.* Cambridge, MA: Harvard University Press, 2003.

Shen Shuyu. "Huhang qiuyi bu zhi guoqu ji qi jinkuang" [Past and present of the team sports department of the Shanghai branch]. *Zhonghang shenghuo,* no. 17 (September 1, 1933): 386–388.

Shen Yi. "Yunsong renyuan he wuzi qu kang'ri genjudi de qingkuang," *Shanghai wenshi ziliao xuanji,* no. 51 (April 1985): 132–144.

Shen Yuyuan. "Tushanwan yu guer yuan." In *Shanghai yi shi,* edited by Tang Weikang, Zhu Dalu, and Du Li, 196–204. Shanghai: Shanghai wenhua chuban she: Xinhua shudian jingxiao, 1987.

Sheng Langxi. "Shinian lai Jiangsu zhongdeng xuexiao biyesheng chulu tongji," parts 1–2. *Jiaoyu zazhi* 17.4 (April 1925) and 17.5 (May 1925): 25695–25730, 25875–25904. Reprinted Taipei: Commercial Press, 1975.

Sheng Peiyu. "Shu kan hao tan." *Shenghuo zhoukan* 3, no. 2 (November 13, 1927): 15.

Sheng Peiyu, and Wu Shen. "Liang wei nüshi duiyu da jiazu de yijian." *Shenghuo zhoukan* 2, no. 50 (October 16, 1927): 394.

Sheng Xuanhuai. *Sheng Xuanhuai riji* [*Yuzhai dongyou riji*]. Yangzhou: Jiangsu guangliang guji keyin she, 1998.

Shenghuo zhoukan 6, no. 48. "Benshe wei choukuan yuanzhu Heisheng weiguo jian'er jinji qishi." (November 21, 1931): 1071–1072.

Shenghuo zhoukan 4, no. 1. "Dafu yifeng yanli zebei de xin." (November 18, 1928): 6–8.

Shenghuo zhoukan 6, no. 52. "Guonan yu xuechao." (December 19, 1931): 1153.

Shenghuo zhoukan 6, no. 42. "Guoqing yu guoai." (October 10, 1931): 893.

Shenghuo zhoukan 6, no. 12. "Ji Zha Liangzhao jun tao Shan zaishi." (March 14, 1931): 253–254.

Shenghuo zhoukan 6, no. 48. "Juankuan zhuxiang zhe laihan zhi yiban." (November 21, 1931): 1080.

Shenghuo zhoukan 6, no. 25. "Minyi suozai." (June 13, 1931): 509. *Shenghuo* 5, no. 8. "Mou yuanlao de liumang wenti." (January 19, 1930): 113.

Shenghuo zhoukan 6, no. 44. "Shenghuo guonan canxiang huabao." (October 24, 1931): 991–994.

Shi Meiding. *Zhui yi: jindai Shanghai tushi.* Shanghai: Shanghai guji chuban she, 1996.

Shi Meiding, Ma Changlin, and Feng Shaoting, eds. *Shanghai zujie zhi.* Shanghai: Shanghai shehui kexue chuban she, 2001.

Sichuan daxue Zhongwen xi, ed. *Cao Yu zhuanji* [Special selections on Cao Yu]. Chengdu: Sichuan daxue Zhongwen xi, 1979.

Skinner, G. William, ed. *The City in Late Imperial China.* Stanford, CA: Stanford University Press, 1977.

Slezkine, Yuri. *The Jewish Century.* Princeton, NJ: Princeton University Press, 2004.

So, Billy K. L. *Prosperity, Region, and Institutions in Maritime China: The South Fukien Pattern, 946–1368.* Cambridge, MA: Published by the Harvard University Asia Center, 2000.

Song Jialin. *Lao yuefenpai.* Shanghai: Shanghai huabao chuban she, 1997.

Soong, James. "A Visual Experience in Nineteenth-Century China: Jen Po-nien (1840–1895) and the Shanghai School of Painting." PhD diss., University of California, Berkeley, 1977.

Spector, Stanley. *Li Hung-chang and the Huai Army: A Study in Nineteenth-Century Chinese Regionalism.* Seattle: University of Washington Press, 1964.

Spence, Jonathan D. *The Gate of Heavenly Peace: The Chinese and Their Revolution, 1895–1980.* New York: Penguin Books, 1982.

———. *God's Chinese Son: The Taiping Heavenly Kingdom of Hong Xiuquan.* New York: W. W. Norton, 1996

———. "Opium Smoking in China." In *Conflict and Control in Late Imperial China,* edited by Frederic E. Wakeman Jr. and Carolyn Grant, 143–173. Berkeley: University of California Press, 1975.

Stapleton, Kristin. *Civilizing Chengdu: Chinese Urban Reform, 1895–1937.* Cambridge, MA: Harvard University Asia Center, 2000.

Stranahan, Patricia. *Underground: The Shanghai Communist Party and the Politics of Survival, 1927–1937.* Lanham, MD: Rowman & Littlefield Publishers, 1998.

Strand, David. *Rickshaw Beijing: City People and Politics in the 1920s.* Berkeley: University of California Press, 1989.

Sun, Lung-kee. "Chinese Intellectuals' Notion of 'Epoch' *(Shidai)* in the Post-May Fourth Era." *Chinese Studies in History* 20, no. 22 (Winter 1986–87): 32.

Sun Jianqiu. "Tongchang chehang shixi baogao." *Zhiye shi shikan,* no. 1 (November 1934): 54–61.

Sun Li. "Liangnan." *Shenghuo zhoukan* 4, no. 5 (December 16, 1928): 50.

Sun Shuzhi. "Wode diandang shenghuo." *Dushu shenghuo* 1, no. 2 (November 1934): 23.

Sun Zhongtian. *"Ziye" daodu*. Beijing: Zhonghua shuju, 2002.

Tamagna, Frank M. *Banking and Finance in China*. New York: International Secretariat, Institute of Pacific Relations, 1942.

Tan Yuzuo. *Zhongguo zhongyao yinhang fazhan shi* [History of the development of major Chinese banks]. Taipei: Lianhe chuban zhongxin, 1961.

Tang Ke. "Muke luetan." *Dushu shenghuo* 3, no. 1 (November 1935): 32–38.

Tang Yusun. "Ruhe chengwei benhang de jinglü" [How to become crack units of our bank]. *Zhonghang shenghuo*, no. 22 (January 15, 1934): 459.

Tang Zhenchang, ed. *Shanghai shi*. Shanghai: Shanghai renmin chuban she, 1989.

Tang Zhongxin. *Zhongguo chengshi shequ jianshe gailun*. Tianjin: Tianjin renmin chuban she, 2000.

Tao Juyin. *Gudao jianwen: Kangzhan shiqi de Shanghai*. Shanghai: Shanghai renmin chuban she, 1979.

Tawney, Richard Henry. *Land and Labor in China*. White Plains, NY: M. E. Sharpe, 1977.

Tian Benxiang. *Cao Yu zhuan* [A Biography of Cao Yu]. Beijing: Beijing shiyue wenyi chuban she, 1988.

Tongren. "Chuangkan ci." *Dushu shenghuo* 1, no. 1 (November 1934): 1.

Tseng, Gloria. "Chinese Pieces of the French Mosaic: The Chinese Experience in France and the Making of a Revolutionary Tradition." PhD diss., University of California, Berkeley, 2002.

Turner, Victor W., and Edward M. Bruner, eds. *The Anthropology of Experience*. Urbana: University of Illinois Press, 1986.

UNESCO Quanzhou International Seminar on China and the Maritime Routes of the Silk Roads (1991: Quanzhou Shi), *Zhongguo yu haishang sichou zhi lu: Lianheguo jiaokewen zuzhi haishang sichou zhi lu zonghe kaocha Quanzhou guoji xueshu taolun hui lunwen ji*. Fuzhou: Fujian renmin chuban she, 1991.

Vermeer, E. B., ed. *Development and Decline of Fukien Province in the 17th and 18th Centuries*. Boston: Brill, 1990.

Vogel, Ezra. *Japan as Number One: Lessons for America*. Cambridge, MA: Harvard University Press, 1979.

———. *Japan's New Middle Class: The Salary Man and His Family in a Tokyo Suburb*. Berkeley: University of California Press, 1963.

Wakeman, Frederic E., Jr., "The Canton Trade and the Opium War." In *The Cambridge History of China*. Vol. 10, pt. 1, *Late Ch'ing, 1800–1911,* edited by Denis Twichett and John K. Fairbank, 163–212. New York: Cambridge University Press, 1978.

———. "China and the Seventeenth Century Crisis." *Late Imperial China* 7, no. 1 (June 1986): 1–23.

———. "Hanjian." In *Becoming Chinese: Passages to Modernity and Beyond,* edited by Wen-hsin Yeh, 298–341. Berkeley: University of California Press, 2000.

———. "Policing Modern Shanghai." *The China Quarterly* 115 (September 1988): 408–440.

———. *Policing Shanghai: 1927–1937*. Berkeley: University of California Press, 1995.

———. *Shanghai Badlands: Wartime Terrorism and Urban Crime, 1937–1941*. New York: Cambridge University Press, 1996.

———. *Strangers at the Gate: Social Disorder in South China, 1839–1861*. Berkeley: University of California Press, 1966.

Wan Han. "Yi er jiu yundong hou Shanghai dixia dang gongzuo luxian de zhuanbian." In *"Yi er jiu" yihou Shanghai jiuguohui shiliao xuanji*, edited by Zhonggong Shanghai shiwei dangshi ziliao zhengji weiyuan hui, 315. Shanghai: Shanghai shehui kexue yuan chuban she, 1987.

Wan Ruijun. *Taiwan ren hengsao Shanghai*. Taipei: Shimao chuban she, 2001.

Wang, David Der-Wei. *Fin-de-Siècle Splendor: Repressed Modernities of Qing Fiction, 1849–1911*. Stanford, CA: Stanford University Press, 1997.

Wang, Te-wei [David Der-Wei Wang]. *Fictional Realism in Twentieth-Century China: Mao Dun, Lao She, Shen Congwen*. New York: Columbia University Press, 1992.

Wang Anyi. *Changhen ge*. Beijing: Zuojia chuban she, 1996.

Wang Di. *Street Culture in Chengdu: Public Space, Urban Commoners, and Local Politics, 1870–1930*. Stanford, CA: Stanford University Press, 2003.

Wang Ermin. *Zhongguo jindai sixiang shilun*. Reprint Taipei: Taiwan shangwu yinshu guan, 1995.

Wang Gungwu. *The Nanhai Trade: The Early Chinese Trade in the South China Sea*. Singapore: Eastern Universities Press, 2003.

———. *China and the Chinese Overseas: From Earthbound China to the Quest for Autonomy*. Singapore: Eastern Universities Press, 2003.

———. *China's Place in the Region: The Search for Allies and Friends*. Jakarta, Indonesia: Panglaykim Foundation, 1997.

Wang Jianrui. "Shanghai funü li de maotouying." *Shenghuo zhoukan* 3, no. 3 (November 20, 1927): 26.

Wang Ping. "Yige xiaofan de shenghuo." *Dushu shenghuo* 1, no. 7 (Feb. 1935): 13–14.

Wang Shumei. "Jianku zhong delai de shengming" [Survival through hardship and struggle]. *Zhonghang shenghuo*, no.12 (April 15, 1933): 216.

Wang Tao. *Gezhi shuyuan*. Shanghai: Tao yuan, Guangxu bing shugui si, 1886–1893.

———. *Yinghuan zazhi*. Shanghai: Shanghai guji chuban she, 1988.

Wang Xiaochong. "Yige nande de nüzi." *Shenghuo zhoukan* 2, no. 2 (November 1, 1926): 12.

Wang Yaoshan. "Yijiusanqi nian qian Shanghai de kangri jiuwang yundong he dixia dang zuzhi de zhengli gongzuo." In *"Yi er jiu" yihou Shanghai jiuguo hui shiliao xuanji*, edited by Zhonggong Shanghai shiwei dangshi ziliao zhengji weiyuan hui, 382. Shanghai: Shanghai shehui kexue yuan chuban she, 1987.

Wang Yuanhua. Preface to *Cong lixiang zhuyi dao jingyan zhuyi*, by Gu Zhun, iii–v. Hong Kong: Sanlian shudian youxian gongsi, 1992.

Wang Zheng. *Women in the Chinese Enlightenment: Oral and Textual Histories*. Berkeley: University of California Press, 1999.

Wang Zhixin. "Chuan changshan ren de kutong." *Shenghuo zhoukan* 2, no. 47 (September 25, 1927): 348–350.

———. "Chuxu de yichu." *Shenghuo zhoukan* 2, no. 11 (January 16, 1927): 68–69.

Wang Zhiyi. "Zhengdang de yule fangfa." *Shenghuo zhoukan* 2, no. 1 (October 24, 1926): 1–2.

———. "Gaizao dushi de yanjiu." *Shenghuo zhoukan* 2, no. 2 (October 31, 1926): 9–10.

Weber, Max. *Economy and Society: An Outline of Interpretive Society.* Edited by Guenther Roth and Claus Wittich. Berkeley: University of California Press, 1978.

———. *The Religion of China: Confucianism and Taoism.* Translated and edited by Hans H. Gerth. Glencose, IL: Free Press, 1951.

Wei Shaochang. *Li Boyuan yanjiu ziliao* [Research materials on Li Boyuan]. Shanghai: Guji chuban she, 1980.

Wenqing et al., eds., *Chouban yiwu shimo: Daoguang chao,* no. 551 in *Jindai Zhongguo shiliao congkan,* vol. 56. Taipei: Wenhai chuban she, 1970.

Wills, John E. "Maritime Asia: 1500–1800: The Interactive Emergence of European Domination." *American Historical Review* (February 1993): 83–105.

Wright, Mary C., ed. *China in Revolution: The First Phase, 1900–1913.* New Haven, CN: Yale University Press, 1968.

———. *The Last Stand of Chinese Conservatism: The T'ung-Chih Restoration, 1862–1874.* Stanford, CA: Stanford University Press, 1962.

Wu Dakun. "Dang yu jiuguohui." In *"Yi er jiu" yihou Shanghai jiuguohui shiliao xuanji,* edited by Zhonggong Shanghai shiwei dangshi ziliao zhengji weiyuan hui, 407–408. Shanghai: Shanghai shehui kexue yuan chuban she, 1987.

———. "Kang'ri zhanzheng zhong dui xin sijun de weiwen." *Shanghai wenshi ziliao xuanji,* no. 51 (April 1985): 124–131.

Wu Jingping. *Song Ziwen pingzhuan.* Fuzhou: Fujian renmin chuban she, 1992.

Wu Liang. *Lao Shanghai.* Nanjing: Jiangsu meishu chuban she, 1998.

Wu Limen. "Yule de jituan." *Yinqianjie,* no.11 (November 20, 1938): 215.

Wu Weizhong. "Liu Bannong suo quxing jinxiang de xuetu ku." *Shenghuo zhoukan* 2, no. 9 (December 19, 1926): 54.

Wu Yaqin. "Fa qi yinqian ye xiaofei hezuo she de yiyi" [The significance of launching a consumer co-op in banking and money circles]. *Yinqianjie* 2, no. 8 (October 1938): 155.

Wu Youru. *Wu Youru huabao,* 3 vols. Shanghai: Wenrui lou, 1908. Reprint, Shanghai: Shanghai shudian, 1983.

Xiao Fusheng. "Dalian minzhong yule ji wohang tongren shenghuo" [Popular recreation in Dalian and employee life in the Bank]. *Zhonghang shenghuo,* no.15 (July 1, 1933): 302–303.

Xiao Linsen. *Tizhi zhuangui qi chengshi gaige zhanlue ji caozuo.* Beijing: Jingji kexue chuban she, 1992.

Xiaoyi. "Gongtong shenghuo zhi yiban, jiushisi hao" [Communal life at number 94]. *Zhonghang shenghuo,* no. 13 (May 15, 1933): 259.

Xiong Yizhong. *Ming Qing guanxiang huatu lu.* Taipei: Guoli Taiwan yishu jiaoyu guan, 1998.

Xiong Yuezhi, ed. *Shanghai tongshi.* 15 vols. Shanghai: Shanghai renmin chuban she, 1999.

———. *Xixue dongjian yu wan Qing shehui*. Shanghai: Shanghai renmin chuban she, 1994.

———. *Zhongguo jindai minzhu sixiang shi*. Shanghai: Shanghai renmin chuban she, 1986.

Xinshui. "Jieshao jiating yule fangfa de xinjianyi." *Shenghuo zhoukan* 2, no. 20 (March 20, 1926): 136–138.

Xizhen. "Xiangxia ren bing bu wangu." *Shenghuo zhoukan* 4, no. 29 (June 16, 1929): 319–320.

Xu Dingxin. "Ershi sanshi niandai Shanghai guohuo guanggao cuxiao ji qi wenhua tese" [National goods advertising in Shanghai and its distinguishing features in the 1920s and 1930s]. Paper presented at the seminar on Consumer Culture in Shanghai, Cornell University, July 1995.

———. "Guohuo guanggao yu xiaofei wenhua." In *Shanghai bainian fenghua*, edited by Ye Wenxin, 111–144. Taipei: Yaosheng wenhua chuban she, 2001.

Xu Dingxin, and Qian Xiaoming, eds. *Shanghai zong shanghui shi, 1909–1929* [History of the Shanghai General Chamber of Commerce, 1909–1929]. Shanghai: Shanghai shehui kexue chuban she, 1991.

Xu Hansan, ed. *Huang Yanpei nianpu*. Beijing: Beijing wenshi ziliao chuban she, 1985.

Xu Junxi, ed. *Shanghai wushi nian wenxue piping congshu, Sichao juan*. Shanghai: Huadong shifan daxue chuban she, 1999.

Xu Mao, Gu Guanlin, and Jiang Tianying, eds. *Zhongguo shi yinhang jia*. Shanghai: Shanghai renmin chuban she, 1997.

Xu Min. "Shi, chang, you: Wan Qing Shanghai shenghui shenghuo yi pie." In *Shanghai: chengshi, shehui yu wenhua*, edited by Wang Hui and Yu Guoliang, 113–126. Hong Kong: Zhongwen daxue chuban she, 1998.

Xu Xuehan. "Huiyi quanguo gejie jiuguo lianhehui pianduan qingkuang." In *"Yi er jiu" yi hou Shanghai jiuguo hui shiliao xuanji*, edited by Zhonggong Shanghai shiwei dangshi ziliao zhengji weiyuan hui, 405–406. Shanghai: Shanghai shehui kexue yuan chuban she, 1987.

Xu Zongze. "Xiwang geyu youli de dongxi zaocheng hao de huanjing" [Hope for a powerful push in creating a better environment]. *Zhonghang shenghuo*, no. 13 (May 15, 1933): 239.

Xueshi. "Hankou shuihuan zhong zhi shehui xiaoxian guan." *Shenghuo zhoukan* 6, no. 34 (August 15, 1931): 733–735.

Yamada Tatsuo. *Chugoku kokuminto saha no kenkyu*. Tokyo: Keio Tsushin, 1980.

Yan Juanying. "Buxi de biandong: Yi Shanghai meishu xuexiao wei zhongxin de meishu jiaoyu yundong." In *Shanghai meishu fengyun: 1872–1949 shenbao yishu ziliao tiaomu suoyin*, edited by Yan Juanying, 47–117. Taipei: Zhongyang yanjiu yuan lishi yuyuan yanjiu suo, 2006.

Yang, Lien-sheng. "Historical Notes on the Chinese World Order." In *The Chinese World Order: Traditional China's Foreign Relations*, edited by John K. Fairbank, 20–33. Cambridge, MA: Harvard University Press, 1968.

Yang Chizhi, and editor. "Nongmin yundong yu baodong." *Shenghuo zhoukan* 2, no. 13 (January 30, 1927): 82–83.

Yang Dinghong. "Qingnian congshi zhiye yihou yingyou de taidu." *Shenghuo zhoukan* 1, no. 33 (June 6, 1926): 195.

Yang Dongping. *Chengshi jifeng: Beijing he Shanghai de bianqian yu duizhi*. Taipei Lianjing chuban shiye gongsi, 1996.

Yang Xianjiang. "Qingnian xiuyang lun faduan." *Shenghuo zhoukan* 1, no. 1 (October 11, 1925): 4–6.

Yang Xiaomin, and Zhou Yihu, ed. *Zhongguo danwei zhidu*. Beijing: Zhongguo jingji chuban she, 1999.

Yang Yinhang. "Geguo shangye daxue zhi zhuangkuang." *Shangwu guanbao*, no. 7, (1907): 1–4.

Yao Songling. *Zhang Gongquan xiansheng nianpu chugao* [Draft chronological biography of Mr. Zhang Gongquan]. Taipei: Zhuanji wenxue chuban she, 1982.

Ye Boyan. "Xiangcun banshi chu zhi yipie" [A glimpse of a rural bank office]. *Zhonghang shenghuo*, no. 22 (January 15, 1934): 464.

Ye Shanghai 20 jing [20 Views of Shanghai at Night]. Shanghai: Shanghai renmin meishu chuban she, 2002.

Ye Wenxin, ed. *Shanghai bainian fenghua*. Taipei: Yaosheng chuban she, 2001.

Ye Xian'en. *Ming Qing Huizhou nongcun shehui yu dianpu zhi*. Hefei: Anhui renmin chuban she, 1983.

Ye Xiaoqing. *The Dianshizhai Pictorial: Shanghai Urban Life, 1884–1898*. Ann Arbor, University of Michigan, 2003.

Ye Ziming, ed. *Lun Mao Dun sishinian di wenxue daolu*. Shanghai: Shanghai wenyi chuban she, 1959.

Yeh, Catherine Vance. "Creating the Urban Beauty: The Shanghai Courtesan in Late Qing Illustrations." In *Writing and Materiality in China: Essays in Honor of Patrick Hanan*, edited by Judith T. Zeitlin and Lydia H. Liu, with Ellen Widmer, 397–447. Cambridge, MA: Harvard University Asia Center for Harvard-Yenching Institute, 2003.

———. *Shanghai Love: Courtesans, Intellectuals, and Entertainment Culture, 1850–1910*. Seattle: University of Washington Press, 2006.

Yeh, Wen-hsin. *The Alienated Academy: Culture and Politics in Republican China, 1919–1937*. Cambridge, MA: Council on East Asian Studies, Harvard University, 1990.

———. "Corporate Time, Communal Space: The Making of Everyday Life in Shanghai's Bank of China." *The American Historical Review* 100, no. 1 (February 1995): 97–122.

———. "Dai Li and the Liu Geqing Affair: Heroism in the Chinese Secret Service during the War of Resistance." *The Journal of Asian Studies* 48, no. 3 (August 1989): 545–562.

———. "Organizing Recreation." Paper presented at the annual meeting of the Association for Asian Studies, 1990.

———. "Progressive Journalism and Shanghai's Petty Urbanites: Zou Taofen and the *Shenghuo* Enterprise, 1926–1945." In *Shanghai Sojourners*, edited by Frederic Wakeman, Jr., and Wen-hsin Yeh, 205–214. Berkeley: Institute of East Asian Studies, University of California, 1992.

———. *Provincial Passages: Culture, Space, and the Origins of Chinese Communism*. Berkeley: University of California Press, 1996.

———. "Republican Origins of the *Danwei:* The Case of Shanghai's Bank of China." In *Danwei: The Changing Chinese Workplace in Historical and Comparative Perspective,* edited by Xiaobo Lu and Elizabeth J. Perry. Armonk, NY: M. E. Sharpe, 1997.

———. "Shanghai Besieged, 1937–45." In *Wartime Shanghai,* edited by Wenhsin Yeh, 1–17. New York: Routledge, 1998.

———. "Shanghai Modernity: Commerce and Culture in a Chinese City." *The China Quarterly,* no. 150 (June 1997): 375–94.

Yi Bin, Liu Youming, and Gan Zhenhu, eds. *Lao Shanghai guanggao.* Shanghai: Shanghai huabao chuban she, 1995.

Yihou. "Gongtong shenghuo zhi yiban—Jinzhongli" [Communal life in the Jinzhongli]. *Zhonghang shenghuo* 1, no. 4 (August 15, 1932): 60.

Yimin. "Tichu yige dushu shang de wenti" [To raise a question about reading and learning]. *Zhonghang shenghuo,* no. 32 (November 1, 1934): 774–75.

Yin. "Shou jingji yapo er xiangdao jieyu de yiwei qingnian." *Shenghuo zhoukan* 2, no. 7 (December 5, 1927): 54–55.

Yinqianjie 2, no. 4. "Yule xinwen" [Entertainment news]. (August 1938): 71.

Yong Wentao. "Huiyi Dang dui zhijiu de lingdao he Shanghai renmin de kangri jiuwang yundong." In *"Yi er jiu" yihou Shanghai jiuguo hui shiliao xuanji,* edited by Zhonggong Shanghai shiwei dangshi ziliao zhengji weiyuan hui, 411–412. Shanghai: Shanghai shehui kexue yuan chuban she, 1987.

Young, Arthur N. *China's Nation-building Effort, 1927–1937: The Financial and Economic Record.* Stanford, CA: Hoover Institution Press, 1971.

———. *China's Wartime Finance and Inflation, 1937–1945.* Cambridge, MA: Harvard University Press, 1965.

Yu Kun. "Shanghai yizhuo hangye gaikuang." In *Shanghai yizhuo ye zhigong yundong shiliao,* edited by Zhonggong Shanghai shiwei dangshi ziliao zhengji weiyuan hui, 5–6 (unpublished manuscript, Shanghai, 1984).

Yu Ying-shih, *Zhongguo jinshi zongjiao lunli yu shangren jingshen.* Taipei: Lianjing chuban she shiye gongsi, 1987.

Yuan Fangxi. "Xiao yangdeng xia." *Dushu shenghuo* 1, no. 1 (November 1934): 24.

Zelin, Madeleine. *The Magistrate's Tael: Rationalizing Fiscal Reform in Eighteenth-Century China.* Berkeley: University of California Press, 1984.

Zelin, Madeleine, Jonathan K. Ocko, and Robert Gardella, eds. *Contract and Property in Early Modern China.* Stanford, CA: Stanford University Press, 2004.

Zeng Runshan. "Tantan yinhang shenghuo" [On working for a bank]. *Zhonghang shenghuo* 1, no. 6 (October 15, 1932): 119.

Zhang Gongquan. "Women de chulu" [Our way out]. *Zhonghang shenghuo,* no. 21 (December 1, 1933): 429.

———. "Zhongguo yinhang zhi jichu anzai?" [Where does the Bank of China lay its foundation?] *Zhonghang shenghuo,* no.14 (June 15, 1933): 271–272.

Zhang Jia'ao [Zhang Gongquan]. *Yinhang hangyuan de xin shenghuo* [New life for a bank employee]. Nanjing, 1934.

Zhang Shijie, ed. *Zengding shangren baojian.* Shanghai: Commercial Press, 1938.

Zhang Yuzhi. *Zhuanxing zhong de shequ fazhan: zhengfu yu shehui fenxi shi-jiao*. Shanghai: Shanghai shehui kexue yuan chuban she, 2003.

Zhang Zhongli, ed. *Jindai Shanghai chengshi yanjiu*. Shanghai: Shanghai renmin chuban she, 1990.

Zhang Zhongli, and Chen Zengnian, eds. *Shaxun jituan zai jiu Zhongguo* [The Sassoons in Old China]. Beijing: Renmin chuban she, 1985.

Zhao Nianguo. Interview with author. Shanghai, May 20, 1990.

Zhao Puchu. "Kangzhan chuqi Shanghai de nanmin gongzuo." *Shanghai wenshi ziliao xuanji*, no. 51 (April 1985): 149–163.

Zheng Yi. *Zou Jiahua he ta de fuqin*. Taipei: Kaijin wenhua shiye youxian gongsi, 1994.

Zheng Zu'an. *Bainian Shanghai cheng*. Shanghai: xuelin chuban she, 1999.

Zhong Daozan. "Zhiye xuexiao xiaozhang zhi xueli yu jingyan." *Jiaoyu yu zhiye*, no. 169 (November 1, 1935): 639–643.

Zhong Guisong, ed. *Er shi shiji Mao Dun yanjiu shi*. Hangzhou: Zhejiang renmin chuban she, 2001.

Zhonggong Shanghai shiwei bangongting shiqu chu, ed. *Chengshi jiedao banshi chu jumin weiyuan hui Gongzuo shouce*. Shanghai: Shanghai renmin chuban she, 1988.

Zhonggong Shanghai shiwei dangshi yanjiu shi, ed. *Shanghai kangri jiuwang shi*. Shanghai: Shanghai shehui kexue yuan chuban she, 1995.

Zhonggong Shanghai shiwei dangshi ziliao zhengji weiyuan hui, ed. *"Yi er jiu" yihou Shanghai jiuguo hui shiliao xuanji*. Shanghai: Shanghai shehui kexue yuan chuban she, 1987.

———. *Shanghai si hang er ju zhigong yundong shiliao*. 2 vols. Shanghai: Zhongguo renmin yinhang Shanghai shi fenhang, 1987.

———. *Shanghai Nanshi liu ye zhigong yundong shi*. Shanghai, 1986.

———. *Shanghai yizhuo ye zhigong yundong shiliao*. Shanghai, 1984.

Zhonggong Shanghai shiwei dangshi ziliao zhengji weiyuan hui, and Yiyoushe shiliao zhengji zu, eds. *Yiyoushe shi er nian, 1938–1949*. Shanghai, unpublished manuscript, 1985.

Zhongguo renmin yinhang zonghang jinrong yanjiu suo jinrong lishi yanjiu shi, ed. *Jindai Zhongguo jinrongye guanli* [Management practices in modern China's financial industry]. Beijing: Renmin chuban she, 1990.

Zhongguo yinhang zonghang, and Zhongguo di er lishi dang'an guan, eds. *Zhongguo yinhang hangshi ziliao huibian, shang bian*. Beijing: Dang'an chuban she, 1991.

Zhonghang shenghuo, no. 32. "Benhang ruhe faxian Shanghai yinhang Chen an de jingguo" [How we exposed the Chen case at the Shanghai Bank]. (November 1, 1934): 800–802.

Zhonghang shenghuo 1, no. 3. "Editorial remark." (July 15, 1932): 48.

Zhonghang shenghuo, no. 13. "Gejie duiyu benhang ershiyi niandu baogao zhi pinglun" [Public comments and reactions to the 1932 annual report of the Bank of China: news digest]. (May 15, 1933): 265–266.

Zhonghang shenghuo, no.17. "News Brief." (September 1, 1933): 379.

Zhonghua zhiye jiaoyu she, ed. *Quanguo zhiye xuexiao gaikuang*. Shanghai: Shangwu, 1934.

Zhou Ke. "Nanmin gongzuo he dixia jun gongzuo huiyi pianduan." *Shanghai wenshi ziliao xuanji*, no. 51 (April 1985): 164–171.

Zhou Tiandu, ed. *Qi junzi zhuan*. Beijing: Zhongguo shehui kexue chuban she, 1989.

Zhou Wu, and Wu Guilong. *Shanghai tongshi*. Vol. 5, *Wan Qing shehui*. Shanghai: Shanghai renmin chuban she, 1999.

Zhou Yumin. *Wan Qing caizheng yu shehui bianqian*. Shanghai: Shanghai renmin chuban she, 2000.

Zhu Guodong, and Wang Guozhang, eds. *Shanghai shangye shi*. Shanghai: Shanghai caijing daxue chuban she, 1999.

Zhu Jin. "Women de dushu hezuo." *Shenghuo* 6, no. 14 (March 28, 1930): 299–300.

Zhu Xueqin. "1998 nian guanyu Chen Yinke, Gu Zhun, Wang Xiaobo." In *Zhishi fenzi lichang. Ziyou zhuyi zhi zheng-yu Zhongguo sixiang jie de fenhua*, edited by Li Shitao, 215–220. Changchun, Jilin: Shidai wenyi chuban she, 2000.

Zhu Yangchen. "Yige houjin hangyuan de zili yu xiwang" [A junior employee's experience and hope]. *Zhonghang shenghuo* no. 12 (April 15, 1933): 220.

Zhu Zongzhen. "Huang Yanpei he rushang lunli." *Tansuo yu zhengming*, no. 8 (August 2003).

Zhuang Zexuan. "Hunyin de xianjue wenti." *Shenghuo zhoukan* 2, no. 16 (February 12, 1927): 103–104.

Zhuang Zhongqing. *Mao Dun shishi fawei*. Changsha: Hunan renmin chuban she, 1985.

Zola, Émile. *The Ladies' Paradise*. Berkeley: University of California Press, 1991.

Zou Taofen. "Bukan shexiang de guanhua." *Shenghuo zhoukan* 5, no. 1 (December 1, 1929): 1.

———. "Chuangban *Shenghuo Ribao* zhi jianyi." *Shenghuo zhoukan* 7, no. 9 (March 5, 1932): 114–116.

———. "Dui quanguo xuesheng gongxian de yidian yijian." *Shenghuo zhoukan* 6, no. 40 (September 26, 1931): 854.

———, ed. *Duzhe xinxiang waiji* 1: 80–83.

———. "Guoqing yu guoai." *Shenghuo zhoukan* 6, no. 42 (October 10, 1931): 893

———. "Hangao lüci." *Shenghuo zhoukan* 5, no. 32 (July 20, 1930): 541.

———. "Kanle Sun zongli guozang dianli yingpian." *Shenghuo zhoukan* 4, no. 34 (July 21, 1929): 375.

———. "Ji." *Shenghuo zhoukan* 3, no. 25 (May 6, 1928): 269.

———. "Tianzai renhuo." *Shenghuo zhoukan* 6, no. 34 (August 15, 1931): 725.

———. "Qingkan jiaoyu jijin de gongxiao." *Shenghuo zhoukan* 6, no. 14 (March 28, 1931): 285.

———. "Wo de muqin." *Jingli*: 296–299.

———. "Wu ai." *Shenghuo zhoukan* 3, no. 44 (September 16, 1929): 521–522.

———. "Wu ke yanshi de jiduan wuchi." *Shenghuo zhoukan* 6, no. 41 (October 3, 1931): 873.

———. "Yapian gongmai minyi ceyan." *Shenghuo zhoukan* 7, no. 42 (October 22, 1932): 825.

———. "Yifeng wanfen poqie qiujiu de xin." *Shenghuo zhoukan* 4, no. 46 (October 13, 1929): 519.

————. "Yihou she qu Huang nüshi de bianshi 'hero'." *Shenghuo zhoukan* 4, no. 5 (November 16, 1927): 41.

————. "Yizhi de yanli jiandu." *Shenghuo zhoukan* 6, no. 40 (September 26, 1931): 854.

————. "Zhengfu guangbo geming zhongzi." *Shenghuo zhoukan* 6, no. 49 (November 28, 1931): 1081.

Zou Weixin. "Zhonghua zhiye xuexiao chuzhong bu xuesheng shanshi xiankuang." *Zhiye shi shikan,* no. 1 (June 1934): 1–4.

Zou Yiren. *Jiu Shanghai renkou bianqian de yanjiu.* Shanghai: Shanghai renmin chuban she, 1980.

Glossary

Aiguo nüxue 爱国女学
aiqiu zhe 哀求者
Ai Siqi 艾思奇
Anhui 安徽
annei rangwai 安内攘外
Anqing 安庆
Ba Jin 巴金
Bai cha 白茶
baihuo 百货
bao 保
baoshang 保商
Baoying 宝应
Bi Tonglun 毕同伦
biedong dui 别动队
buru tui er jie wang 不如退而结网
Cai Yuanpei 蔡元培
can guohuo 掺国货
Cao Yu 曹禺
Changhen ge 长恨歌
Changsha 长沙
Changshou 常熟
Changzhou 常州
Chen Bailu 陈白露
Chen Gongbo 陈公博
Chen Minzhi 陈敏之
Chen Peiqin 陈沛芹
Chen Ruiting 陈锐霆

Chen Zengnian 陈曾年
Chen Zhuping (Choping) 陈竹平
chenggong de bangyang 成功的榜样
Cheng Jingsheng 程兢生
Cheng Muhao 程慕颢
Cheng Naishan 程乃珊
Chiang Kaishek 蒋介石
Chongqing 重庆
chuan 船
Cilianhui 慈联会
Dachang 大厂
da jiazu 大家族
Dalu 大陆
Dazhong shenghuo 大众生活
Dai Ailu 戴霭庐
danwei 单位
Danghua 党化
dao (way) 道
daotai 道台
Deng Xiaoping 邓小平
Di san fangmian jun 第三方面军
Diaocha 调查
Dingxian 定县
Dongnan daxue 东南大学
Du Zhongyuan 杜重远
Dushu shenghuo 读书生活
Du Yuesheng 杜月笙

Duzhe xinxiang 读者信箱
er cong mu ming, huo po ling li
  耳聪目明，活泼伶俐
Eryouxuan 二友轩
Fabi 法币
Fan Li 范蠡
Fan Muli 范慕蠡
Fan Yuanlian 范源濂
fen hong 分红
Fujian 福建
fuli chujin 福利储金
Fu Xiao'an 傅晓庵
Fuzhou 福州
Fu Zongyao (Fu Xiaoan) 傅宗耀
Gao Jianfu 高剑父
Gao Qifeng 高奇峰
Ge Yuanxu 葛元煦
Gezhi shuyuan 格治书院
gengzhan 耕战
gong (artisan) 工
gong (public) 公
gong (work) 工
gongfu 功夫
Gong Fuchu 龚复初
Gong Mujiu 官慕九
Gongshang xuebao 工商学报
Gongsi lü 公司律
Gudao 孤岛
Gu Shunzhang 顾顺章
Gu Qinglian 顾青莲
Gu Zhun 顾准
guan (official) 官
guandu shangban 官督商办
Guangdong 广东
GuangZhao yixue 广肇义学
Guangzhou (Canton) 广州
guishen 鬼神
Guizhou 贵州
guo 国
Guo Bingwen 郭秉文
Guofu lun 国富论
guohuo 国货
Guohuo baihuo gongsi 国货百货
  公司
guohuobu 国货部
Guo Jiu 郭就
Guo Le 郭乐

Guo Linshuang (Lam Shuen Kwok,
  L. S. Kwok, Taipan Kwok) 郭琳爽
Guo Linzhuo 郭琳卓
Guo Linzong 郭琳宗
Guomin canzheng huiyi 国民参政
  会议
Guo Shun 郭顺
Guo Songtao 郭嵩焘
Guo Yuewen 郭悦文
Guo zhi suo yi xing zhe, nong zhan
  ye 国之所以兴者，农战也
hai (maritime) 海
Hanjian 汉奸
Hankou (Hankow) 汉口
hangyuan shouce 行员手册
Hang Zhiying 杭稚英
Hangzhou 杭州
Harbin 哈尔滨
Hebei 河北
Henan 河南
Heilongjiang 黑龙江
heng (persistence) 恒
Hu Xueyan 胡雪岩
He Yuseng 贺屿僧
Hong Gengyang 洪庚阳
Hongkou 虹口
Hong Ruquan 洪茹泉
houbu 候补
hua (Chinese) 华
huahui 花会
Huashang 华商
hua yang fenju 华洋分居
hua yang za chu 华洋杂处
hua yang zahuo 华洋杂货
huan du 还都
huanqiu 环球
Huang Guomin 黄国民
Huang Huan'nan 黄焕南
Huang Huanzhi 黄焕之
Huang Huiru 黄慧如
Huang Jingcun 黄兢存
Huangpu River 黄浦江
Huang Yanpei 黄炎培
Hubao 沪报
Hubei 湖北
Hu Dingyi 胡定一
Hu Sheng 胡绳

Hu Shi 胡适
Hu Qiaomu 胡乔木
Huqiu 虎丘
Hu Xueyan 胡雪岩
hui (remit) 汇
huiyuan 会员
Huizhou 徽州
huo (merchandise) 货
jinian 纪念
jiti 集体
Ji Wen 姬文
Jiating xingqi 家庭星期
Jiaxing 嘉兴
jian (part time) 兼
jian li wang yi 见利忘义
jianghua 讲话
Jiang Menglin (Chiang Monlin)
  蒋梦麟
Jiangnan 江南
Jiangsu 江苏
Jiangwan 江湾
Jiangxi 江西
Jiangyin 江阴
Jiang Zemin 江泽民
jiao (transact) 交
Jiaoyu yu zhiye 教育与职业
jiaoyu yuandi 教育园地
Jin (dynasty) 晋
Jin Ba 金八
Ji'nan daxue 暨南大学
Jinchen yinhang 金城银行
Jin Guobao 金国宝
Jinhua 金华
Jinshanwei 金山卫
Jinshan zhuang 金山庄
Jinshe 进社
Jin Xuechen 金雪尘
jing (reverence) 敬
Jingdezhen 景德镇
Jing Guang zahuo 京广杂货
Jingyin huiye tu 净因慧业图
Jing Ziyuan 经子渊
Jiuguo hui 救国会
Jiujiang 九江
juren 举人
Juntong 军统
Kaiping 开平

Kong Di'an 孔涤庵
kongqian de 空前的
Kowloon 九龙
ku (bitterness) 苦
kuai (monetary) 块
Kuaijishi tiaoli 会计师条例
Kunshan 昆山
Laodong daxue 劳动大学
Laojiuhe 老九和
li (profit) 利
li (unit of length) 里
Li Boyuan 李伯元
Li Bozheng 李伯正
Li Chongji 李崇基
Li Gongpu 李公朴
Li Hongzhang 李鸿章
Li Huanzhang 李焕章
Li Jinxi 黎锦熙
Li Mubai 李慕白
Li Pan 李蟠
liquan 利权
Li Quanshi 李权时
Li Shiqun 李世群
Lixin 立信
Li Ze 李泽
lianhe 联合
lianyi 联谊
Liang Dingming 梁鼎铭
Liang Qichao 梁启超
Liang Shuming 梁漱溟
Liang Xueqing 梁雪清
Liangyou 良友
Liang Youming 梁又铭
Liang Zhongming 梁中铭
Lin Kanghou 林康侯
Lin Lifu 林立夫
lin yuan xian yu 临渊羡鱼
Liu Bannong 刘半农
Liu Changsheng 刘长胜
Liu Liangmo 刘良模
Liu Ti 柳提
Liu Zhan'en 刘湛恩
Lu Genrong 陆根荣
Lujiabang 陆家浜
Lu Shengzu 卢绳祖
Luwan 卢湾
Lu Xichao 卢希超

Lu Xun 鲁迅
Luo Gengmo 骆耕漠
Ma Xiangbo 马相伯
mai (chap. 2, in new terms; chap. 5, sale of bride) 卖
Manchukuo 满洲国
Mao Dun 矛盾
Mao Hongbin 毛鸿宾
meiren 美人
min (people) 民
Minguo 民国
Minsheng zhuyi 民生主义
minzhong 民众
Minzhu tongmeng (Democratic Alliance) 民主同盟
minzu jiefang 民族解放
Ming (dynasty) 明
mo (end) 末
mu (land measurement) 亩
Mu Ouchu 穆藕初
Nanchang 南昌
Nanchang xinwen ribao 南昌新闻日报
Nanjing 南京
Nanjing Minguo fazheng daxue 南京民国法政大学
Nanshi 南市
Nanting biji 南亭笔记
nian shang 年赏
Nie Yuntai 聂云台
Ningbo 宁波
nong (tiller) 农
nongzhan 农战
Pan Hannian 潘汉年
Pan Jie'an 潘洁庵
Pan Mingduo 潘明铎
Pan Xulun 潘序伦
Pan Yangyao 潘仰尧
peiqian huo 赔钱货
piaohao 票号
pochan de zhongdeng zichan jieji jiating 破产的中等资产阶级家庭
Pudong 浦东
qipao 旗袍
Qixin zhiye xuexiao 啓新职业学校
Qian Dajun 钱大钧

Qian Junrui 钱俊睿
Qianlong 乾隆
Qiantang River 钱塘江
Qian Xinzhi 钱新之
Qian Yishi 钱亦石
qianzhuang 钱庄
qiaokeli 巧克力
Qiao Ying 乔英
Qin Shihuang 秦始皇
Qing (dynasty) 清
qingxiang 清乡
Qiu Jin 秋瑾
Qiu Jinhai 丘金海
Qu Yingguang 屈映光
Quanyong guohuo hui 劝用国货会
Quanzhou 泉州
Renji shantang 仁济善堂
Ren Xiong 任雄
Richu 日出
Sanmin zhuyi 三民主义
Sanyu 三育
Shaanxi 陕西
Shandong 山东
shang (commerce/merchant) 商
shang ban (privately owned merchant industry) 商办
shangban (merchant management) 商办
shangban zaochuan chang zhuce guize 商办造船厂注册规则
shangbao 商报
shangbiao 商标
shangbiao fa 商标法
shangbiao fa shixing xize 商标法实行细则
shangbiao ju 商标局
shangbiao maimai 商标买卖
shangbiao zhuce 商标注册
shangbiao zhuce fei 商标注册费
shangbu 商埠
shangchuan hangxian 商船航线
shangchuan xuexiao 商船学校
shangdian (shop) 商店
shangdian (telegram) 商电
shangdian rizhi 商店日志
shangfa 商法
shanggang 商港

shanggang tiaoli 商港条例

Shanghai 上海

Shanghai cishan tuanti lianhe jiuzai hui 上海慈善团体联合救灾会

Shanghai shangwu zonghui 上海商务总会

Shanghai shangye gongyi huisuo 上海商业公议会所

Shanghai shangye huiyi gongsuo 上海商业会议公所

Shanghai shi yinqian ye yeyu lianyi hui 上海市银钱业业余联谊会

Shanghai Toa dobun shoyin 上海东亚同文书院

Shanghai zhiye jie jiuguo hui 上海职业界救国会

Shanghai zhuanke daxue 上海专科大学

Shanghai zong shanghui 上海总商会

shanghao 商号

shanghao zhuce 商号注册

shanghao zhuce fei 商号注册费

shanghao zhuanyong quan 商号专用权

shanghui 商会

shanghui fa 商会法

shanghui lianhe hui 商会联合会

shangke (business programs) 商科

shangke daxue 商科大学

shangkuang baogao 商况报告

shanglü 商旅

shanglü 商律

shanglüe 商略

shangmin xiehui 商民协会

shangpin 商品

shangpin baozhuang fa 商品包装法

shangpin chenlie chu 商品陈列处

shangpin chenlie chuang 商品陈列窗

shangpin chenlie shi 商品陈列室

shangpin chenlie suo 商品陈列所

shangpin daibiao zhengjuan 商品代表证卷

shangpin diaohuan juan 商品调换卷

shangpin jianding fa 商品检定法

shangpin jianyan fa 商品检验法

shangpin jianyan ju 商品检验局

shangpin jiaoyi suo 商品交易所

shangpin mulu 商品目录

shangqing baogao 商情报告

shangqing yuce tongji 商情预测统计

shangren 商人

Shangren baojian 商人宝鉴

shangren nengli 商人能力

shangren tongli 商人通例

shangren tongli shixing xize 商人通例施行细则

shangshi 商事

shangshi caipan chu 商事裁判处

shangshi gongduan chu 商事公断处

shangshi xintuo 商事信托

shangtie 商帖

shangtuan 商团

Shangwu guanbao 商务官报

Shangwu kaocha bao 商务考察报

shangwu xuetang 商务学堂

shangxi 商习

shang xiguan 商习惯

shang xiguan fa 商习惯法

shang xingwei 商行为

shang xingwei fa 商行为法

shangxue 商学

shangxue hui 商学会

Shangxue tuan 商学团

Shang Yang (Gongsun Yang) 商鞅 (公孙鞅)

shangye 商业

shangye baohu zuhe 商业保护组合

shangye buji 商业簿记

shangye buxi xuexiao 商业补习学校

shangye buzhu jiguan 商业补助机关

shangye chenzhi 商业沉滞

shangye chengzhao piaoju 商业承招票据

shangye chidu 商业尺度

shangye dili 商业地理

shangye diaocha chu 商业调查处

shangye huipiao 商业汇票

shangye jiaoyu 商业教育

shangye jinrong 商业金融

shangye jingzheng 商业竞争

shangye konghuang 商业恐慌

shangye piaoju 商业票据

shangye piaoju baoxian 商业票据
  保险

shangye piaoju suo 商业票据所

shangye shi 商业史

Shangye shiyong cidian 商业实
  用辞典

shangye shiyong ren 商业使用人

shangye si 商业司

shangye shuxin 商业书信

shangye suanshu 商业算术

shangye tongji 商业统计

shangye tongxin 商业通信

shangye xiguan 商业习惯

shangye xinyong 商业信用

shangye xinyong gongju 商业信用
  工具

shangye xue 商业学

shangye xunhuan 商业循环

shangye yinhang 商业银行

shangye yinhang chuxubu 商业银行
  储蓄部

shangye zhengce 商业政策

shangye zhengjuan 商业证卷

shangye zhiye xuexiao 商业职业
  学校

shangye zhuanmen xuexiao 商业专
  门学校

shangye zhuce 商业注册

shangye ziben 商业资本

shangyong baoshui duizhan 商用报
  税堆栈

shangyong lüeyu 商用略育

shangyong shujian 商用书简

shangyong xinjian 商用信件

shangyue 商约

shangyue dachen 商约大臣

shangzhan 商战

shangzheng 商政

Shangzi 商子

Shaoxing 绍兴

Sha Qianli 沙千里

shen 绅

Shenbao 申报

Sheng de yizhi 生的意志

shenghuo douzheng 生活斗争

Shenghuo zhoukan 生活周刊

Sheng shi wei yan 盛世危言

Sheng Xuanhuai 盛宣怀

Shen Junru 沈钧儒

Shenmei shuguan 审美书馆

Shenzhen 深圳

shi 士

shi 师

shidai 时代

shifu 士夫

shihu 失怙

shikumen 石库门

Shi Liangcai 史量才

shi shang yi shu er tong dao 士商异
  术而同道

Shisheng 市声

shixue 失学

shiye 失业

Shu jing 书经

Shu Yueqiao 舒月乔

si 私

Sichuan 四川

Sili Minsheng xiaoxue 私立民生
  小学

Sili Shaoxing lü Hu xiaoxue 私立绍
  兴旅沪小学

Song Hanzhang 宋汉章

Songjiang 松江

Song Meiling 宋美龄

Subei 苏北

Sui'an 遂安

Sun Jianqiu 孙剑秋

Sun Ruihuang 孙瑞璜

Sun Shuzhi 孙述之

Sun Xiafeng 孙夏峰

Sun Yatsen 孙逸仙

Sun Yefang 孙冶方

Su Qing 苏青

Suzhou 苏州

taiji 太极

Taiping 太平

tanci 弹词

Tan Fuyao 谭扶尧

Tang Jingxing (Tong King-sing)
  唐景星

Tang Qingzeng 唐庆曾

Tang Tingshu (Tong King-sing)
  唐廷枢

Tang Wenzhi 唐文治
Tang Yi'e 汤一鄂
Tang Zhigao 汤志高
Tao Guilin 陶桂林
Taohuawu 桃花邬
Tao Yuanming 陶渊明
Tianjin 天津
Tian xiao de 天晓得
tie 铁
tingzhong 听众
tongxunyuan 通讯员
tudi zhangcheng 土地章程
Tushanwan 土山湾
tuoli 脱离
wanhui 晚会
Wang Anyi 王安忆
Wang Guoying 王国英
Wang Jishen 王季深
Wang Jingwei 汪精卫
wang min 王民
Wang Ming 王明
Wang Ping 王平
Wang Xiaotong 王晓通
Wang Yangming 王阳明
Wang Zhixin 王志莘
wenwei 文委
Wuchang 武昌
Wuhan 武汉
Wu Jinglian 吴敬琏
Wu Limen 吴礼门
Wusong 吴淞
Wu Tiecheng 吴铁城
Wu Tingfang 伍廷芳
Wuxi 吴锡
Wu Youru 吴友如
Wu Yunzhai 吴蕴斋
Xishi 西施
xian qi liang mu 贤妻良母
Xiang Kangyuan 项康元
xiao jiating 小家庭
xiao shimin 小市民
Xia Yan 夏衍
Xia Zimei (Xia Zhengnong) 夏子美 (夏征农)
Xiedaxiang 协大祥
Xie Zhiguang 谢之光
xin 信

Xindaxiang 信大祥
Xindu 新都
Xinjiang 新疆
xin Shanghai ren 新上海人
Xinwen bao 新闻报
xiucai 秀才
xiuyang 修养
Xuan Tiewu 宣铁吾
Xue Fucheng 薛福成
Xu Guanqun 许冠群
Xu Jiqing 徐寄清
Xujiahui 徐家汇
Xu Run 徐润
Xu Shiying 许士英
Xu Yongqing 徐永青
Xu Yongzuo 徐永祚
Yadong shangxue she 亚东商学社
yamen 衙门
Yan'an 延安
Yancheng 盐城
Yan Fu 严复
Yan Laigen 严来根
Yan Xinhou 严信侯
Yanye Yinhang 盐业银行
yang 洋
Yang Ailan 杨爱兰
Yang Aimei 杨爱梅
Yang Fang (Takee) 杨芳
Yang Mingde 杨明德
Yang Shantong 杨善同
Yang Yinhang 杨荫航
Yangzhou 扬州
Ye Jianying 叶剑英
Yen Huiqing 颜惠庆
yi 义
Yi bei niunai 一杯牛奶
Yichang 宜昌
yi hang wei jia 以行为家
Yishe 蚁社
yishi guize 议事规则
yixing shili 异姓事例
yi ye er tong dao 异业而同道
Yiyou she 益友社
Yiyuan 医院
yi zhouye 一昼夜
yin 银
ying 营

Yinghuan zazhi 瀛環杂志
Yinghua shuyuan 英华书院
Yingqianbao 银钱报
Yingqian shixi tongxun she 银钱实
　习通讯社
yong zu 永租
You Huaigao 尤怀皋
yuren 愚人
Yu Rizhang 余日章
Yuan 元
Yuandong renmin fanri da
　tongmeng 远东人民反日大
　同盟
Yuan Guanlan 袁观澜
Yuan Shikai 袁世凯
yuefenpai 月份牌
Yue ji 粤籍
Yue Lin 岳霖
zai shang yan shang 在商言商
Zeng Guofan 曾国藩
Zhabei 闸北
Zhang Ailing 张爱玲
Zhang Chunqiao 张春桥
Zhang Gongquan (Zhang Jia'ao)
　张公权 (张嘉璈)
Zhang Jiasen 张嘉森
Zhang Jian 张建
Zhang Shijie 张士杰
Zhang Shizhao 章士钊
Zhang Xiaolin 张啸林
Zhang Xueliang 张学良
Zhang Youyu 张友渔
Zhang Yuguang 张裕光
Zhangyuan 张园
Zhang Yuanji 张元济
Zhang Zhidong 张之洞
Zhang Zhongli 张仲礼
Zhao Nianguo 赵念国
Zhao Zuyou 赵祖佑
Zhejiang 浙江
Zhenjiang 镇江
Zheng Guanying 郑观应
Zheng Mantuo 郑曼陀
Zheng Zhenduo 郑振铎

zhijiao pai (zhiye jiaoyu pai) 职教派
　(职业教育派)
Zhili 直隶
zhiye 职业
zhiye qingnian 职业青年
zhiye shenghuo 职业生活
Zhongchujuan 中储卷
"Zhongguo diyi shanghui" 中国第
　一商会
Zhongguo tongshang yinhang 中国
　通商银行
Zhonghua minzu wuzhuang ziwei
　weiyuanhui 中华民族武装自卫委
　员会
Zhonghua wenhua jiaoyu jijin hui
　中华文化教育基金会
Zhonghua yinhang 中华银行
Zhonghua zhiye jiaoyu she 中华
　职业教育社
Zhonghua zhiye jiaoyu xuexiao
　中华职业教育学校
Zhoubao 周报
Zhou Bosheng 周柏生
Zhou Daxin 周大昕
Zhou Fang 周方
Zhou Muqiao 周慕桥
Zhou Xuexi 周学熙
Zhou Yang 周杨
Zhou Zhuang 周庄
Zhu Jingchen 祝景辰
Zhu Jingnong 朱经农
Zhu Rongji 朱溶基
Zhuang Zexuan 庄泽宣
Ziye 子夜
Zizhi 自治
Zongdong 总董
zonghui 总会
zongli 总理
Zongli yamen 总理衙门
Zou Jiahua 邹家华
Zou Jinbao 邹金宝
Zouping 邹平
Zou Taofen 邹韬奋
Zuo Zongtang 左宗棠
Zunyi 遵义

Index

Text:	10/13 Sabon
Display:	Sabon
Compositor:	Integrated Composition Systems
Indexer:	Susan Stone
Printer and binder:	Maple-Vail